Collège Louis-Riel
585 rue St-Jean-Baptiste
Saint-Boniface (MB) R2H 2Y2

D1466115

The Writer's Workshop

The Writer's Workshop

Second Edition

John F. Parker

Addison-Wesley Publishers Limited

Don Mills, Ontario • Reading, Massachusetts
Menlo Park, California • New York
Wokingham, England • Amsterdam • Bonn
Sydney • Singapore • Tokyo
Madrid • San Juan

Senior Editor: Dianne Horton
Editors: Harriet Law, Kim S. G. Koh, Joanne Close, Susan Gosling, Debbie Brewer,
   Valerie Adams
Index: Peter Lewis
Design: Pamela Kinney
Illustration: Lynda Cooper
Handwriting: Wendy Thornycroft
Cover Photograph: Paul Till
Cover Model: Mark Hlady
Typesetting: Golda D. Wiseman

The author wishes to thank his wife, Mary, for her assistance throughout the writing
process; Barbara-Anne Eddy for help in research; Dianne Horton of Addison-Wesley
for pushing me in new directions; and the many students who allowed their work to
be in the company of other writers.

Text and photograph acknowledgments begin on page 456.

Canadian Cataloguing in Publication Data

Parker, John F. (John Frederick), 1933–
   The writer's workshop

Rev. ed
ISBN 0-201-19746-4

1. English language – Composition and exercises.
2. English language – Grammar – 1950–
I. Title

PE1408.P37 1990   808'.042   C90-093926-5

ISBN 0-201-19746-4

Printed and bound in Canada
   B C D E F – ALG – 94 93 92 91

For Bobbi

Contents

Preface

Are these statements true or false?
- All writers follow exactly the same procedures when they sit down to write.
- Writers need a special talent for writing that ordinary people do not have.
- Writers always know what they are going to say before they sit down to write.
- Good writers are able to turn out perfect products in a single sitting.

Most writers would say that all of these statements are false. First, the major difference between writers and other people is that writers write – a great deal! Second, writers do not usually sit down and turn out perfect products in one sitting. For most writers, writing is a process that sometimes happens quickly but that usually takes time. During their writing process, they experiment and make false starts. They often experience "writer's block." They frequently discuss their work with other people. Above all, they revise their material over and over until they are satisfied that it works.

The Writer's Workshop will help you to discover *your own* writing process in several ways:

a) by showing you how everything you do – talking, listening, reading, viewing, reflecting, acting – contributes to productive writing

b) by showing you how to find writing topics so that you can become an independent, confident writer

c) by encouraging you to write for your own purpose to a specific audience

d) by providing you with writing strategies to assist you – exploring, prewriting, drafting, revising and editing, conferencing, and publishing

e) by providing workshop sections that will help you build your writing skill and increase the variety of ways you express yourself

f) by showing you the effectiveness of revising and editing your own writing, and that of your classmates

g) by showing you how you can enjoy your writing process

The Writer's Workshop assumes that you learn to write by writing. The more you write, the better you'll be at it. And you get better at the craft of writing by making suggestions for revising and editing your own writing and that of your peers.

In this second edition, you'll find numerous, varied opportunities to draw on your own experiences as you write and to help you find your own voice. You'll be encouraged to connect your reading and writing, and a literature appendix – as well as literature included in each writing project – may help you do that.

Within the Drafting Suggestions for each writing project, you'll find guidelines to help you revise your work.

When you've taken a piece of writing as far as you can, you may want to ask for the help of a peer-editor. Within the Revising and Editing Suggestions for each writing project are questions for you to ask your peer-editor, so that you can make the most of your peer-editing sessions.

Throughout each writing project are questions labelled "Writer's Choice." These will help you to focus on where you are in a project – and what you might do next.

You'll also find suggestions for integrating computer use with your writing.

The Workshop sections will support you at every stage of your writing. Working with a writing partner, use these chapters – or parts of them – as you feel that your writing reveals a need.

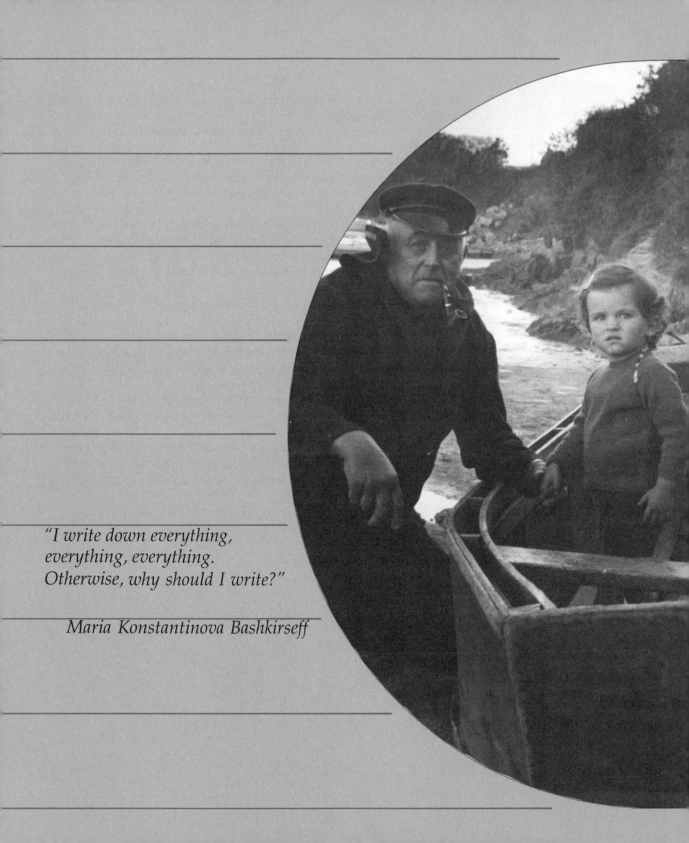

"I write down everything,
everything, everything.
Otherwise, why should I write?"

Maria Konstantinova Bashkirseff

Your Writing Process

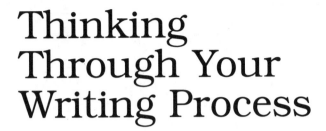

Thinking Through Your Writing Process

There is no single writing process. You might jot down a shopping list. End of your writing process. You might get a flash of inspiration, dash off a letter to a local newspaper, and drop your letter into the mail. End of your writing process. Or you might even struggle to come up with an idea, talk to friends for help, apprehensively start to write, rip up your work, start again, get more help, start again, finish, show your work to an editor who rejects it, start again, and, finally, get your writing to a point where you're happy with it. End of your writing process.

The Writer's Workshop points out steps in the writing process that you might wish to follow. But most writers do not go straight from step one to step two to step three and end up with a perfect product. They often backtrack, go forward, and backtrack again. Familiarity with the steps will help you to develop your *personal* writing process.

You can store materials for your writing in a number of ways: in your writing folder (page 9), on a word processor (page 9), in a journal (Chapter 21), in your notebook, on file cards, or on loose pieces of paper.

Exploring and Prewriting

Your writing process usually begins with exploring and prewriting, when you think about topics, ideas, and supporting details. For example, you might
a) brainstorm a topic by talking with other people
b) read a book or flip through a magazine until an idea comes to mind
c) look back through your journal and find a subject to explore in your writing
d) write about a film, game, or show that you've seen
e) listen to a piece of music and then write about it
f) jot down a few notes about something you have been thinking about
g) describe something you have been involved in

h) write (and write and write!) until an idea comes to mind

i) be given a general topic

You might also begin to think about your **writing variables**: audience, purpose, format, and voice (who you're writing to, why, how, when, and so on). You'll find out more about these writing variables on pages 14–19.

The Writer's Workshop provides specific exploring and prewriting suggestions for each writing project. And if you need them, three chapters can help you to open up your exploring and prewriting process: "Journal Writing and Instant Writing"; "Exploring Ideas"; and "Thesis Statements and Topic Sentences." Check the word processing section (page 9) as well. Word processors make exploring and prewriting freer and less worrisome.

Drafting

As you draft, you discover exactly what you want to say. You organize your thoughts and your information, work through an approach to your topic, and consider your sentence structure and word choice. And you actually sit down to write.

The Writer's Workshop offers a few specific suggestions for drafting each piece of writing, and three chapters provide special drafting help: "Beginnings and Endings"; "Unity"; and "Coherence." In addition, you can consult other chapters for particular writing techniques or a specific style. Again, check the word processing section; drafting on a word processor allows you to take chances and experiment with different sentence structures. A built-in thesaurus can point you toward the exact word you need.

A few self-editing suggestions will then help you to revise your draft.

Revising and Editing

Revising is an ongoing process for every writer. During revision, you focus your thoughts and shape your writing so that it communicates clearly what you want to say. Writers often change the focus of their work many times, both before and after they show it to others for comments and suggestions.

Even though you can revise your work by yourself, try to get into the habit of having a classmate – one of your peers – comment on everything you write. This might be hard to do at first, but you'll soon find that a peer-editor can help you to make your thinking and your writing clearer. Your peer-editor's questions will also help you to predict the kinds of questions your intended audience may ask about your writing. Before too long, you'll automatically ask yourself similar questions about your writing as you draft. When you edit something a classmate has written, ask two questions about the work: What did I really like about it (a word or words, the topic, the emphasis, and so on)? What one question do I have about it? (Is more information needed? How can the language be improved?) Thinking carefully about something a friend has written will also help you to think critically about your own writing.

After you have revised a piece of writing to your satisfaction, you edit it to give it a final polish for its intended audience. Each writing project in *The*

Writer's Workshop provides checklists of questions for you to ask yourself and your editor. Your editor can refer to these questions while reading your work and use them as a guide to making revising and editing suggestions for your writing. In addition, two chapters provide specific information to help you make revising and editing decisions: "Self-Editing, Peer-Editing, and Teacher-Editing" and "Summarizing – Paraphrase, Précis, and Outline."

If you are using a word processor to write, check out pages 9–12. Revising and editing on a word processor are a joy. You'll be able to move entire paragraphs, insert new material, delete unwanted words, and even check your spelling. If you have sophisticated software, it will flag possible problems with punctuation, subject-verb agreement, use of passive voice, weak verbs, and a number of other mechanical problems. Use your word processor, but don't substitute its capabilities for reading and thinking about your writing.

Publishing

When you are satisfied with a piece of writing, it is ready for publication. **Publication** can mean handing your piece of writing to its intended audience. It can also mean reading it aloud, performing it, submitting it to a school literary magazine, posting it on a bulletin board – or tucking it into your personal writing folder. If you have used a word processor for your writing, you will likely have a neat printout of your final product as well as a record of your preliminary or rough work. Be sure to keep all your drafts. By referring back to them, you will be able to see how your writing improves.

Using *The Writer's Workshop*

Besides this introductory section, *The Writer's Workshop* has a Writing Projects section, two Workshop sections, and an appendix. You'll need the help of your teacher-editor and your peers for the writing projects and the help of a writing partner – a classmate, a friend, or a relative at home – for the workshops.

Writing Projects. This section involves you in many writing projects, all with suggestions and strategies to help you shape your work at different stages of your writing process. You can work on the writing projects in any sequence. Each project will encourage you to keep your purpose and your reader or audience in mind as you write. Most contain selections that put you in the company of other writers. You can read these pieces for enjoyment, compare your work with that of the other writers, or use one of the pieces as a starting point for your writing.

Before you complete any of the writing projects, you might want to look at the Introductory Writing Project that begins on page 13. You'll be able to see one student's writing process and familiarize yourself with the writing variables.

First Workshop: Content and Organization. This section deals with all the steps of the writing process. If you're having difficulty, consult the appropriate chapter and work through the relevant sections with your writing partner.

While working through the chapters, you are invited to do special writing projects for or with your partner.

Second Workshop: Style. Most of this section provides suggestions to help you improve your writing style. You can use entire chapters or just parts of them, and you can use them in any order. While working through the chapters, you are invited to do special writing projects for or with your partner.

Appendix. The appendix provides a selection of literature for you to browse through for inspiration and pleasure. It also offers a useful dictionary of proof-readers' symbols and a glossary.

Your Writing Folder

Your writing folder is a resource for your writing. It should contain three major parts: one for the ideas, brainstorming notes, and exploratory materials you have to help you compose; a second for drafts of your work in progress; and a third for copies of your finished work.

If you find yourself in need of a new writing idea, the material you have collected in your writing folder might provide just the inspiration you need. A piece of writing that you have decided not to use for one audience at one time might be shaped into something you can use for another audience at another time.

Besides your own work, collect the work of other writers. Books, magazines, newspapers, and other materials are full of ideas; jot down anything that intrigues you. Try to record your sources for future reference. You might photocopy a letter to which you want to respond, or use an article as a starting point for research. Save examples of writing that you admire, and make a note of writing with which you would like to experiment. You might, for example, compose a new beginning or ending for a short story – or adapt it as a play.

Keeping all your drafts together will help you when you are preparing for an editing session. You'll have at your fingertips the appropriate notes and your earlier drafts for reference.

And if you find that you want to publish some of your finished work in another form, such as in a class magazine, you can easily sort through your pieces and choose the one that best suits your purpose and audience.

Word Processors and Your Writing Process

Nothing in recent times has made writing easier and faster than the invention of word-processing systems. Many writers even go so far as to say that word processing is the most important discovery of the twentieth century. It literally frees the writer from the time-consuming task of retyping drafts.

If you wonder what difference a word processor can make to your writing, then think about how you revise. After exploring your topic and completing a draft, revising your work and having it edited, you find that you have worked with, say, an essay, so much that you never want to see it again. Now you are ready to submit your work for a final editing session, but just before you do so, you notice that you have left out a word in the second line. What do you do? Insert the word and mess up the page, or ignore it and hope that your editor will not detect the omission?

With a word processor, you simply insert the disk on which you have stored your essay, call up the page on the screen, insert the word in an instant, and push a print key. Within seconds, you will have a new, correct copy. Even if your editor suggests that you make some structural changes to one of your paragraphs and then move it to another position in your work, you will be able to do so in a matter of a few seconds on a word processor. Word processing is revolutionizing writing.

If you have access to a word-processing system, use *The Writer's Workshop* in conjunction with it. Look around your school or in your local public library. You may find a word-processing system available for student use.

Because there are many texts, manuals, and classes available to teach you how to use a word processor, the following suggestions focus on how you can get the most out of a word processor in your writing, no matter what experience you have had with computers. If you own a word processor or have access to one, you might incorporate any of the suggestions as you write. If you have no experience whatsoever with word-processing equipment, begin by reading over the following with your writing partner. As you become more familiar with word processing, gradually introduce some of these suggestions.

Exploring and Prewriting Process. In general, nothing gets lost in the computer's memory; everything stays on the disk. Depending on the system you are using, a single disk can hold up to two hundred pages of information. It also can provide a printout of the contents of the disk. Think of the possibilities of storing all your exploring and prewriting ideas.

By storing a skeletal outline of all your exploration techniques in the word processor's memory, you will be able to recall the ones you want in order to explore a topic. At the touch of a button, for example, you can call Aristotle's Topics to the screen. Because you will have already stored all the leading questions in your computer's memory, you have to consider answering only the ones that appear on the screen; thus, you have saved yourself the time of typing the same brainstorming questions every time you explore an idea.

If, after you answer all the questions, you do not have enough material for your topic, you can call another brainstorming technique to the screen – for example, Newspaper Reporter's Questions. In addition, you might bring particular graphics to the screen (such as ladders or clusters) so that you can list your supporting evidence directly in the graphic.

You can continue to come up with a workable limited topic and a thesis statement. Then you can call up on the screen your list of writing variables, record pertinent details next to each of them, and print out your exploring and prewriting notes so that you have them available as you draft. Knowing that you can return to any aspect of your exploration to make necessary additions, changes, or deletions will give you additional security as you draft.

Drafting Process. Drafting on a word processor means that you can draft as many times as you like without losing any of your early drafts. You can start in the middle of a piece of writing – with a part that you feel sure of or comfortable with – and then go back to fill in the rest when you are ready. For example, when you want to write your introduction, all you need to do is take your cursor to the beginning and start to type. The introduction will appear on the screen before the middle section. Later, you can move your cursor to the end to write your conclusion.

Also, you can write without worrying about making errors. As you read over your draft on the screen, you can make corrections, add details, delete unnecessary details, change wording, and move entire sentences and paragraphs. At the same time, you can work through any of the chapters of the text in order to sharpen the style and organization, sentence structure, and mechanics of your work. For example, if you used the AAA/BBB method of comparison/contrast to develop an essay (Chapter 25), you can duplicate your entire essay and then move sentences and paragraphs within the duplicated copy to see the effect of using the ABABAB method. If you do not like the effect, you can delete the entire copy and return to your original.

You can also use your word processor to record and file your research material (Chapter 35) to help you write your research papers. You can call to the screen any of the quotations that you stored on the disk. Later, you will be able to recall all of the sources in alphabetical order so that you can list your cited references in the correct order. Some word-processing programs can help you to make the headings in an essay a consistent size and level of importance.

Just before you print a hard copy of your essay, you can check its **mechanics**. Depending on the capabilities of your word-processing program, you can do a spelling check (some systems have a built-in 50,000-word memory and will highlight words that are not spelled according to the memory bank); a punctuation and capitalization check (some systems will highlight irregularities); a synonym check (some systems have a built-in thesaurus that provides five or six alternative words for you to use in place of your original word choices); and a consistency check (some systems will highlight when your subject and verb do not agree or when you shift point of view in tense, voice, and person). Who knows what new capabilities will be available in the next few years?

As you can see, a word processor will help you become an independent writer. You still need to self-edit and to have someone else look at your work, because word processors cannot check your thought and logic or your organization, style, or sentence quality. Even though you and your word processor can come up with a neat and often accurate piece of writing, don't underestimate the benefit of having another eye look over your work before you present it to your intended audience.

Revising and Editing Process. Having the assistance of a word processor will make it easier to take your editor's advice when he or she suggests that you restructure your work to improve its clarity or style. After all, such reorganization will not mean hours of retyping. Each time that you go to an editor for advice, it will take you only minutes to prepare a clean copy for editing.

Furthermore, you can present to your peer-editor a list of specific questions about your writing. You can include some of the questions that accompany the writing project you are working on, as well as questions that occurred to you as you drafted. In addition, you can share your exploration ideas and your writing variables with your editor. In this way, your editor will be able to place himself or herself in the position of your intended audience. By providing plenty of material to help with editing, you will receive more helpful advice from your editor.

After your peer-editing session, you can call up your writing to the screen of your word processor and make the necessary changes, corrections, additions, or deletions. If you want your editor to see your paper again because you have changed it substantially, you can easily provide a fresh copy and repeat the process.

Once you are satisfied with your work, you can submit a clean, professional-looking copy to your intended audience (or to your teacher-editor for a final editing session).

Even if you have to rework your writing a number of times, you will appreciate the statement that "Writing is rewriting" – because it's more enjoyable to rewrite on your word processor.

Introductory
Writing Project

"There's no one way to write."

Peter Elbow

Often, the best way to learn something is to *do* it. If this is the way that you learn best, you can get to know your writing process by working through this project. As you work, remember:

1. You are working on this project to become familiar with your writing process.

2. Be sure to set aside sufficient time for revising and editing. Remember that rethinking and reorganizing your work are just as important as writing down your thoughts in the first place.

3. Be prepared to try new things.

4. Relax. As you learn more about your own writing process, you'll find that writing becomes easier and more interesting – and you'll be on your way to becoming a more confident and independent writer.

In most cases, the following suggestions assume you will be using pen and paper; if you are using the computer, adapt the suggestions accordingly.

WRITING PROJECT

> In about 125 words, write about an activity in which you have taken part.

Exploring and Prewriting Suggestions

1. There are many ways to explore writing topics.

a) To discover a topic quickly, focus your attention on activities that you like and dislike. To help you think more systematically, draw two columns on a sheet of paper, and label them, "Like" and "Dislike." In the appropriate column, jot down specific activities in which you have participated, including as many activities as you can.

Here is what Ben, a student, jotted down:

Like	Dislike
going to movies	seeing a play
playing racquetball	eating breakfast
debating	visiting a dentist
dancing	watching a demolition derby
jogging	boxing
fishing	hunting
people-watching	writing an essay

b) Get into a small group and share with other group members an activity that you enjoy. Your sharing can take any form you choose; for example, you might perform for your classmates or simply tell them about your activity.

c) Do some freewriting in your journal (see Chapter 21) on an activity that you do not enjoy.

d) Write invisibly (see Chapter 21) on an activity that you know a lot about. If you work on a computer, write with the screen turned off.

e) Many word processing packages include brainstorming activities; if yours does, refer to your word processing manual.

f) Refer to your "like" and "dislike" chart; choose an activity from each column, and write nonstop for ten minutes about each.

2. From your exploration, decide which activity you would most like to develop in this project. This can be your **broad topic**.

3. On a fresh piece of paper, write your broad topic. Ben wrote:

Broad topic: playing racquetball

Once you have decided on a broad topic, you may be ready to draft; or, like some writers, you may want to think about your writing variables – audience, purpose, format, and voice – at this point. You may find that the writing variables can help you to limit or narrow your topic and control the development of your piece of writing. Or, like other writers, you may prefer to consider your writing variables much later in your writing process – even after you have drafted your piece.

Writer's Choice

Do you want to consider all of your writing variables – audience, purpose, format, and voice – before you draft, or do you want to start your draft now?

4. If you decide to consider your writing variables before you draft, your next choice may be to consider your intended audience (who will read, listen to, or accept your work). To whom are you writing? Weak writing often occurs when writers have no sense of their audience – when they write to no one in particular or to everyone in general. Will your audience be real or imaginary? If you have no real person or persons to whom you want to write, you might want to choose an imaginary audience. (Think of your teacher as one of your editors, not as your final audience. Assume you are writing to someone who is not giving you a grade.)

For his intended audience, Ben considered the following: his girlfriend, his favorite racquetball opponent, his twelve-year-old brother, an imaginary world champion racquetball player, and classmates who have never played racquetball. (Can you see why Ben would have to change his writing style to satisfy each intended audience?) Finally he wrote:

Audience: Classmates who have never played racquetball. Real. I intend to let them read it.

If you have chosen your audience, jot down whatever you can about their age, knowledge of your topic, and so on, and whether your audience is real or imagined. (Remember that you can choose to change your audience at any time.)

5. By thinking about your reason for writing about a particular activity, you will discover your **purpose**. (Writing a paper simply to earn a grade will often produce a weak piece of work.)

Ben considered the following reasons for writing to classmates who have never played racquetball: to describe a racquetball game; to explain how to play racquetball; to persuade his readers to learn to play racquetball; to argue that racquetball is the best court game. (Can you see how each purpose would result in a different piece of writing?) Finally he wrote:

Purpose: to persuade my audience to learn to play racquetball

If you're ready, jot down your purpose for writing.

6. Next, you might consider your **format**. Because the purpose of this project is to help you familiarize yourself with your writing process, choose a format

that is comfortable for you – perhaps a paragraph, a letter, a TV advertisement, a radio talk, or a poem.

Ben thought about writing a self-contained paragraph, a set of instructions, or an advertisement. Finally he wrote:

Format: self-contained paragraph

If you've decided on your format, write it down.

7. Finally, you might consider the **voice** you intend to adopt. Voice can be impersonal or personal. For example, writing in newspapers or magazines often has an impersonal voice; you don't get a sense of the article or story having a "teller." In many cases writers write in their own voice, as themselves. Often, writers use another voice by adopting a **persona** – that is, by imagining they are someone else, such as a four-year-old, a creature from another planet, or an empty bowl.

Ben thought about using an impersonal voice, his own voice, and both the persona of someone who has never played racquetball and of an experienced racquetball teacher. (Can you see why each persona would result in a different piece of writing?) Finally he decided to use his own voice.

Voice: my own

You may have already decided on the voice you want to use. If so, jot it down. If you have decided to use a persona, provide as many details as possible – for example:

Voice: persona of an extraterrestrial; has extremely keen vision and has never seen a racquetball game before

8. Considering these writing variables (audience, purpose, format, and voice) may help you if you find that your broad topic is too broad and you want to try to **limit** or narrow it.

Ben reviewed his prewriting notes and then considered the following possibilities for his limited topic: how to play a racquetball game; the history of racquetball; where to go to play racquetball; benefits of playing racquetball. Finally he settled on:

Limited topic: benefits of playing racquetball

Write down your limited topic, if you have one.

What you have been doing in the previous steps is an important part of exploring and prewriting and is often called **brainstorming**. Throughout this book, you'll find suggestions to help you explore topics and ideas and find supporting details. You can brainstorm by yourself, with the assistance of a brainstorming program on your computer, or with other people. When you brainstorm alone or with the computer, you probe your own mind for ideas and details to support them. When you do it with others, you probe the minds of those in your "think tank." Although all ways of exploring are valuable, two or more people working together will usually build on each other's ideas and produce a larger number of ideas to consider. If there are any flaws in your thinking, you may realize they are present and be able to work on them.

Chapter 22 suggests different ways to explore a topic. If you work through the techniques, you'll soon have them at your command. Skim Aristotle's *Topics* (page 274) to see how Ben used this technique to explore his topic.

Now, if you're ready, record your own brainstorming notes about your limited topic.

Writer's Choice

Do you want to talk over your writing variables with one or two of your classmates, or are you ready to begin your draft?

Drafting Suggestions

1. You will often receive a great deal of help as you explore and prewrite, and again as you revise and edit, and you might even confer with your classmates as you draft. Usually, though, you will draft alone. The more you write, the easier drafting will be, and this book can help you to improve your organization and style and to reflect exactly what you want to say in the words and sentences you choose. If you are using a word processor, you'll find that composing several drafts is both possible and easy.

Writer's Choice

Do you want to get your text down quickly and go back to revise and edit later, or do you want to work through your draft slowly, testing each thought, sentence, and word to make sure that each is exactly right?

2. As you draft, think about your audience and your purpose for writing. As well, keep an open mind about your format and voice; for example: Would your piece of writing be more effective as a letter or advertisement? Would it have more impact written in the third person (*he, she*) than in the first person (*I*)? As you draft, you might want to change your format and voice. You might check your word processing manual for ways to set up your document so that you can keep your writing variables on part of your screen as you compose. Just remember to remain open to new possibilities as you draft – and always try to find ways to make your draft even better.

3. If you are writing a paragraph, you might like to present your main idea near the beginning of your work and develop it as fully as you can within the suggested 125-word limit.

4. When you finish your draft, consider the following guidelines.

Guidelines for Revising

☐ What is your main idea? Have you stated it clearly?

☐ Who is your audience? Will your audience know your purpose for writing? Why will your audience want to read what you have written? (Are you satisfied with that reason?)

☐ Are the words and sentences you have chosen appropriate to your audience?

☐ Will your title and opening "grab" the attention of your audience?

☐ Are you satisfied with the mechanics of your draft (spelling, punctuation, and grammar), or is there something you'd like to check before you let an editor see your work?

☐ Is there anything in your draft that you would like your editor to help you with?

Writer's Choice

Are you confident of your audience, purpose, format, and voice, or do you need to talk about them with your peer-editor? Do you want to revise your writing, or is your work ready for a classmate to edit?

If necessary, prepare a clean double-spaced copy of your draft for your editor.

Ben's first draft is on page 20. Be his peer-editor. As you read Ben's draft, think about two suggestions you would make to help him revise his paragraph.

Ben's Variables
Broad topic: playing racquetball
Audience: Classmates who have never played racquetball. Real. I intend to let them read it.
Purpose: to persuade my audience to learn to play racquetball
Format: self-contained paragraph
Voice: my own
Limited topic: benefits of playing racquetball

Ben's First Draft and His Peer-Editor's Comments

This could use a stronger title. Let's brainstorm some.

The beginning didn't really catch my interest. Perhaps begin with "We should all..."

Play Racquetball

Everyone should exercise, and if you can have fun at the same time, it would give you an extra bonus. Racquetball is an easily learned game that provides exercise and fun. It is also a relatively new court game. So if you feel out of sorts or depressed, play a game of racquetball every three or four days. Do you know

I don't get a sense of what you think is important here. Perhaps focus on exercise?

I find these choppy. Would joining them help?

how to play squash or handball? Racquetball is slower than squash, but faster then handball. But racquetball is easier to learn to play then either squash or handball. Most beginning players of racquetball need no more than one lesson to learn how to play. From then on, you'll be able to play, exercise, and have fun learning how to perfect your technique.

check

Will your audience understand these terms?

Then you'll be able to kill a shot in the corners, take a ball off the back wall, slam one from the back wall to the front, in fact, theirs nothing you won't try. Racquetball fanatics say "Racquetball takes minutes to learn, but a lifetime to perfect."

check

I like the direct quote — but feel you need a concluding sentence. What did you want me to get from reading this?

Revising and Editing Suggestions

Most professional writers depend on their editors to help them revise. Your peers and your teacher can help you to rethink and reorganize your writing. Later on, they can help you with the **mechanics** of language – spelling, punctuation, sentence structure, and so on.

If you've never been involved in a peer-editing session, this introductory writing project will help you to get the most out of it.

1. Find a classmate to edit your work. Give your draft to your peer-editor, and share your writing variables with him or her. Be sure to leave lots of space on your draft for your editor's suggestions.

2. Ask your editor for as much specific advice as possible, using the questions that follow in "Ask Your Peer-Editor" and any other questions that came to mind as you drafted or revised your work. Your editor's responses will help you determine the response of your intended audience, and you will be able to make any necessary revisions. Encourage your editor to use the proofreaders' symbols on page 453 and to write (a great deal) on your paper, consulting the "Guidelines for Revising" on page 19 and the checklists in Chapter 27 as necessary.

3. Plan to spend at least half an hour with your editor so that you can talk about the draft thoroughly.

Ask Your Peer-Editor

- □ What did you think of this piece of writing? What was your first impression of it? Why? Do you think my intended audience will find it interesting? Why?
- □ What did you like most about my piece? Least? Why? How might I improve my draft?
- □ Is it clear to you why I chose to write about this activity? Would my audience agree with you? What makes you think so?
- □ Have I expressed my main idea clearly? If not, can you suggest how I can make it clearer?
- □ Is there sufficient detail about the activity? Is there too much? Should I further narrow my topic to fit the suggested 125-word limit?
- □ Did the beginning grab your attention? Did the title? What changes or improvements would you suggest?
- □ Did you find the ending satisfying? If not, why not? How could I improve my ending?
- □ Do my thoughts flow logically and smoothly from one to the next? Can you suggest any transitional devices (Chapter 26)?
- □ Are there any problems with spelling, punctuation, capitalization, or sentence structure?
- □ Is there anything that you do not understand?

Have a look at what Ben's peer-editor wrote about his paragraph (see page 20). Do you agree or disagree with the comments? Why? What would you have said?

Writer's Choice

Is your draft ready to be published, or should you give it to your teacher-editor? Perhaps it needs another revision first. If it does, which of your peer-editor's comments will you consider as you revise? Do you want to rethink any of your writing variables? If you do a revision, do you want your peer-editor to edit the revised draft?

Now read Ben's revision and his teacher-editor's comments. Glance back to his earlier version. Find one change he has made that you think improves the paragraph. Then select one suggestion from his teacher that you consider important for further improvement.

Ben's Second Draft and His Teacher-Editor's Comments

Now that I've read this, I'd like to take up racquetball.

Your point of view shifts.

(check)

In your first draft, this worked well as a direct quotation.

Racquetball Mania

Racquetball is an easily learned game that provides exercise and fun. A game of racquetball maybe exactly what the doctor ordered for (those) who feel out of sorts or depressed. Racquetball <u>is</u> faster than handball and slower than squash, but <u>it is</u> easier than both to learn. If (you) have never played, no more (then) one lesson <u>will be</u> necessary. From then on (players) will be able to play, ex-(c)ercise, and have fun perfecting their technique. After only a few games, most players find themselves starting to play the corners, take a ball off the back-wall, and slam one from the back wall to the front; in fact, there's nothing they won't try. Enthusiasts say that racquet-ball takes minutes to learn but a life-time to perfect. <u>Why not try it?</u>

Your title really caught my attention.

Beginning this sentence with "Faster" would avoid overuse of "is."

I'd try to use active voice.

Strong ending. Why not begin the paragraph with a question, too?

You will probably have an editing session with your teacher. Consider inviting your peer-editor to sit in on this conference, because your teacher's comments may be useful to your editor as well. Keep in mind that writing means rewriting, and don't be discouraged or frustrated if your teacher suggests that you revise your work again.

Publishing Suggestions

Now prepare your final draft, making it a polished product. If you have been working on a computer, you may be able to add different typefaces, type sizes, or graphics to your work. You might also want to add illustrations. After you have completed your work, check to see that you have numbered and dated all your drafts, and tuck them into your writing folder.

> ### Writer's Choice
> Will you present your work in some form to someone else? Even if it was written to an imaginary audience, you might want to share it with others. Or is your work "for your eyes only"? Even if you wrote to a real audience, you may decide to keep your work in a personal writing folder.

Ben posted his final draft on a classroom bulletin board entitled "In the Company of Writers."

In the Company of Writers

Racquetball Mania
Ben Cohen, student

Who says exercise can't be fun? Racquetball is an easily learned game that provides exercise and fun. A game of racquetball every three or four days may be exactly what you need if you feel out of sorts or depressed. Faster than handball, slower than squash, racquetball is easier to learn than both. As a beginning player, you may need only one lesson. From then on, you'll be able to play, exercise, and have fun perfecting your technique. After only a few games, you will find yourself hitting the ball into the corners, taking a ricocheting ball off the back wall, and slamming one from the back wall to the front. In fact, there's nothing you will not try. Enthusiasts say, "Racquetball takes minutes to learn, but a lifetime to perfect." Why not try it?

Your Writing

1. How did your writing turn out? Was it better or worse than you expected? Why?

2. What single comment by your editors – peer and teacher – helped you to make a revision that satisfied you?

3. Now that you have completed this project, what have you learned about your writing? Make a short list of your strengths. What new confidence-builders have you discovered for future writing projects? What things do you still have to work on? Make a note of these as well. In your writing journal keep a running commentary on your ever-changing, ever-improving writing process.

"Writing leads only to writing."

Colette

Writing Projects

About the Writing Projects Section

The writing projects in this section are designed to meet a number of your needs. With your teacher-editor, select the ones that can help you.

Each writing project contains suggestions and strategies to help you develop your writing – exploring and prewriting, drafting, and revising and editing. Each writing project also contains selections by students, teachers, and professional writers – to put you *in* the company of other writers. Study these pieces before, as, and after you do your own writing. If you can, try to make use of a word-processing program and manual. You'll save time and discover new ways to improve your writing process.

Each writing project
- stresses exploration, drafting, and revision;
- promotes peer-editor and teacher-editor feedback;
- suggests that you think about your writing variables as you write;
- encourages you to write honestly, thoroughly, and emphatically;
- invites you to experiment in your writing.

1   Short Narration

"We dream in narrative, daydream in narrative, remember, anticipate, hope, despair, believe, doubt, plan, revise, criticize, construct, gossip, learn, hate, love by narrative."

Barbara Hardy, **The Appropriate Form, an Essay on the Novel**

WRITING PROJECT

Write a narrative that is approximately 250 words in length.

Exploring and Prewriting Suggestions

1. To help you explore topics for this project, do any of the following activities.

a) Get into small groups and (taking turns) tell a good story about yourself, your family, or your friends, or one that you've heard.

b) Do a ten- to fifteen-minute freewriting session in which you write a "tall" tale. You can exaggerate, even invent.

c) Within a small group, take something out of your pocket, wallet, or purse, and tell a story in which the object becomes the most important thing.

d) Interview the oldest person you know, asking that person to tell you a good, true story.

e) If you are reading a story that you are enjoying, choose its main character and make up a story that "could have happened" either *before* the story started or *after* it concludes. Write it invisibly (Chapter 21). If you're using a word processor, write with the screen turned off.

f) Read "The Nervous Man" by Jennifer Bauld (at the end of this chapter). She wrote the poem from the point of view of the television audience. Experiment with writing the poem from the point of view of the star.

g) Choose a historical personality and construct a cluster (Chapter 22) of an exciting event in that person's life.

h) Draw a time line, beginning with the first important story about yourself that you recall and ending at the present. Jot down a few positive incidents above the time line and a few negative incidents below the time line. You might include such things as your proudest, happiest, or saddest moments; a triumph or failure; your most embarrassing mistake; a "first," such as your first date, first dance, or first job interview; a "last," such as your last date with someone, a final farewell, or the last day of school; a disaster, such as a fire, an accident, a flood, or a storm; an argument with someone; or a difficult decision. For example:

	started Little League	visited Cairo			first date	started high school	
Age	Age	Age	Age	Age		Age	Age
4	6	8	10	12		14	16
	first day of school	Grandma died		lost Little League final game			

Writer's Choice

Have you discovered a topic for your narrative? Or do you want to explore some more?

---

i) If you feel that you need to explore further in order to generate ideas, approaches, and appropriate supporting details, consult Chapter 22. The following techniques are particularly useful for narratives: Experience/Write; Senses Cluster; Positive Cluster; Negative Cluster; and possibly the Cause-and-Effect Flowchart.

2. When choosing a topic to write about from among the incidents that you have explored, you may want to consider one that involves **conflict**, a struggle against something or someone. Conflict can be a physical struggle, a battle of wits with another person, a struggle with nature or society, or even a struggle within yourself. It is possible for a narrative to have more than one conflict. For example, your narrative might involve an argument with a relative (conflict with another person), may take place during a snowstorm (conflict with nature), and may also involve your attempt to control feelings of anger (conflict within yourself).

3. If you need help in narrowing your topic, you may want to consider your writing variables: audience, purpose, format, and voice. (See pages 14–17 if

you need more information about these.) If your narrative is to be part of a larger work, such as a letter, be sure to keep the larger format in mind as you draft.

You can begin to draft your narrative as soon as you feel ready.

Drafting Suggestions

1. Sometimes, writers find that "stretching the truth" improves their stories. Even if your narrative is based on an incident from your own life, feel free to invent and imagine, instead of sticking to what really happened, if your narrative is improved as a result, but make what you say "sound" true.

2. The beginning of your narrative should capture your reader's interest. Which of the following opening sentences would encourage you to continue reading the narrative? Why?
- I was sure the customs officer could hear my heart pounding in my chest as she opened my suitcase.
- The band started to play, and then I saw him coming toward me from across the room.
- "He's dead!" she kept screaming. "Your pet frog is dead!"

3. Narratives are often organized in **chronological** or time order, but you do not necessarily have to start your narrative with the part of your story that occurred first in time. You might begin *in medias res* (in the middle) and introduce past details as needed. (For other ways to organize your narrative, see Chapter 25.)

4. Most narratives contain a **climax**, a decisive moment and turning point. You can create suspense by using description and dialogue (the words spoken by the characters) to delay the climax.

5. Your ending should bring your narrative to a satisfying conclusion. Do you find any of the following endings unsatisfactory? Why?
- I counted my cash. I had enough.
- Cautiously I placed one foot in front of the other. A stone fell, plummeting to the base of the canyon far below. My foot slipped. I fell. Down, down I plunged. Suddenly I awoke, safe and sound in my bed.
- I waited impatiently for my mother's answer. Finally it came: "Yes."

6. Action, reaction, and dialogue can help your audience experience your story. Think about verbs you can use to describe your characters and their situations and to stimulate your audience's interest. Think about what the characters are doing and then consider how they are reacting to what occurs. How can you describe what they do and how they feel? You might also experiment with describing facial expressions to capture emotional reactions. If you base your narrative on a real-life incident, you might use some of the actual words that were spoken during the incident.

7. Showing what happened – by keeping in mind action, reaction, and dialogue – is usually more effective than simply telling. Notice the difference between telling and showing in the following two versions of the same incident.

Telling

Miss Flegg pushed me onto the stage where, clumsily and unhappily, I danced.

Showing

At the right moment Miss Flegg gave me a shove and I lurched onto the stage, trying to look, as she had instructed me, as much like a mothball as possible. Then I danced. There were no steps to my dance, as I hadn't been taught any, so I made it up as I went along. I swung my arms, I bumped into the butterflies, I spun in circles and stamped my feet as hard as I could on the boards of the flimsy stage, until it shook. I threw myself into the part, it was a dance of rage and destruction, tears rolled down my cheeks behind the fur, the butterflies would die; my feet hurt for days afterwards. "This isn't me," I kept saying to myself, "they're making me do it"; yet even though I was concealed in the teddy-bear suit, which flopped about me and made me sweat, I felt naked and exposed, as if this ridiculous dance was the truth about me and everyone could see it.

Margaret Atwood, **Lady Oracle**

Writer's Choice

How can you bring your narrative to life for your audience? Would dialogue help? Are there descriptive details that you should include to put your audience "in the scene"?

When you finish your draft, consider the following guidelines.

Guidelines for Revising Narration

☐ Why have you written this narrative? Is your purpose for writing clear?

☐ What have you done to make the characters in your narrative seem realistic? Will your audience care about your characters?

☐ How have you begun your narrative? Will your opening "grab" the attention of your audience, or should you experiment with another beginning?

☐ Have you told your story effectively within the suggested 250-word limit? Is there anything that you might save for another occasion?

☐ Look at how you have used description. Do your descriptions bring to life the people, places, and things in your narrative? In your description, do you appeal to all of your audience's senses?

☐ Have you used dialogue? Does the talk "sound real"? Would you like to ask a couple of your classmates to check your dialogue by reading it aloud? Would more dialogue make your narrative more effective? In what way?

☐ Why would your audience want to read (or listen to or perform) your narrative? Are your content, word choice, sentence structure, tone, and so on appropriate to your audience? Is there anything in your narrative that might confuse your audience? If so, how could you fix that?

☐ Does your ending bring your narrative to a satisfying conclusion?

☐ Is your title catchy?

☐ Is there anything in your draft that you would like your editor to help you with?

Writer's Choice

Is your draft ready for your intended audience? Or would you like an editor to make revising and editing suggestions?

If necessary, revise your work and prepare a clean double-spaced draft for your editor.

Revising and Editing Suggestions

Give your draft to your peer-editor, and share your writing variables. Encourage your editor to use the "Guidelines for Revising Narration" in this chapter and the checklists in Chapter 27. Your editor should also think about how he or she would answer the following questions.

Ask Your Peer-Editor

☐ What was your first impression of my narrative? How did it make you feel? Why?

☐ How do you think I feel about my story? How do you think my audience will feel about it? What makes you think so?

☐ What did you like most about my narrative? Least? Why? How can I build on the strengths of my piece and get rid of any weaknesses?

☐ Did you find my narrative interesting and believable? Is there sufficient conflict? Can you find the climax? Did the first sentence capture your interest? Did you find my ending satisfying? What changes would you suggest? Should I add more description or dialogue, for example?

☐ Is the sequence of events clear? Does everything that I have included contribute to the development of my narrative? Have I included all important details?

☐ Have I maintained a consistent point of view? (Have I consistently used *I* or *he* or *she*?)

☐ Have I kept my tenses clear and consistent? (Are all my verbs either in the present tense or in the past tense?) Do my verbs give a strong sense of action?

☐ Is my title a good one?

☐ Are there any problems with spelling, punctuation, capitalization, or sentence structure?

Writer's Choice

Should you revise and have your peer-editor edit your new draft, or should you ask your teacher-editor to have a look at your work? Or are you ready to publish?

Publishing Suggestions

Polish your narrative. Proofread it for spelling, grammar, word usage, and punctuation, and prepare it so it is clean and easy to read.

Think about how you might present your work to its final audience. For example, you might read your work aloud to students in another class, or you and your classmates might produce an illustrated anthology of your work.

Writer's Choice

If your classmates are your intended audience, how can you present your work to them?

When you are ready, present your work to its intended audience.

In the Company of Writers

from *And No Birds Sang*
Farley Mowat

At the end of the first day of the northward trek I was directing a column of supply trucks off the main road into a stone-walled farmyard. The entrance gap was narrow and one large truck, making too sharp a turn, threatened to pin me to the wall with its front fender. As my mouth opened to scream at the driver, a rear wheel ran over a Teller mine.

A savage force crushed me back against the wall then slammed me forward against the truck with such ferocity that I lost consciousness. When dim awareness began to return, I knew beyond doubt that I was dead. I seemed to hear the distant but mighty roaring of the sea in some vast cave, but could see nothing except a shimmering, translucent haze in which I appeared to float weightlessly. There was no pain, and in fact I felt euphoric – like a disembodied spirit drifting in some other worldly void. Intensely curious about this new state of being into which I had been so summarily dispatched, I allowed myself to drift toward the luminous edge of the haze …

… and staggered out of a pall of dust and smoke to fall full length over the body of a man whose head had been blown off.

Trapped
Bob Klettke, student

Completely dark. Can't move backward; can't see forward. Stuck. A rush of adrenalin into my pulsing arteries. My heart beats faster, stronger; my breath quickens, deepens; and my eyes widen, still blind. Yelling provides a safe, if temporary, escape from this tomb of darkness. Screaming uses up the adrenalin, allows a false calm to follow. A brief calm. Hard, harsh walls slowly move in, squeezing the air from my weakening body. My one free hand flails helplessly at walls somewhere in front of me. No freedom. My mind stalls. I pass out. Maybe seconds, minutes, hours. When I wake up nothing has changed. Stuck. Dark. Trapped.

from *The Accidental Tourist*

Anne Tyler

"I've brought my dog for boarding," Macon said. He had to raise his voice to be heard above Edward's moans.

Chewing her gum steadily, the girl handed him a printed form and a pencil. "Ever been here before?" she asked.

"Yes, often." "What's the last name?"

"Leary."

"Leary. Leary," she said, riffling through a box of index cards. Macon started filling out the form. Edward was standing upright now and clinging to Macon's knees, like a toddler scared of nursery school.

"Whoa," the girl said.

She frowned at the card she'd pulled.

"Edward?" she said. "On Rayford Road?"

"That's right."

"We can't accept him."

"What?"

"Says here he bit an attendant. Says, 'Bit Barry in the ankle, do not readmit.'"

"Nobody told me that."

"Well, they should have."

"Nobody said a word! I left him in June when we went to the beach; I came back and they handed him over."

The girl blinked at him, expressionless.

"Look," Macon said. "I'm on my way to the airport, right this minute. I've got a plane to catch."

"I'm only following orders," the girl said.

"And what set him off, anyhow?" Macon asked. "Did anyone think to wonder? Maybe Edward had a reason!"

The Nervous Man

Jennifer Bauld, student

The hot lights sear down,
Focusing on the man
Who nervously crosses his legs again.
He asks for water –
Gets his nose powdered instead.
We, the audience, buzz happily in anticipation.
The buzz increases as the director,
Resplendent in earphones and mechanical gadgets,
Asks us to practise applauding.
The brave ones do,
Amidst nervous giggles.
The lights above us shine white hot,
And sweaters are discarded.
The director starts a countdown –
The nervous man clears his throat –
Frantically, the "applause" sign flashes.
Astonished, we realize
That the nervous man has become
The Star.

Shopping

Shirley Friesen, student

Only five years old, I am fascinated by this place. The ceilings are as high as the sky, and the aisles are wider than the street near my house. I cling to Mommy's coattails so that she won't get lost as I walk along, admiring all the packages that line the shelves. When she stops for a moment, I let go of her to pick up a particularly intriguing cereal box. When I look up, to my horror, she is lost! I race up and down the aisles, screaming her name at the top of my lungs: "Mommy!" Out of breath, I stop running, and a smiling lady with snowy white shoes approaches me. Then gently taking my hand, she guides me to a room at the back of the store. The friendly lady sets me down, gives me some candy, and assures me that someone will find my mother in no time. After polishing off the last candy, I start thinking about Mommy again. It seems like hours now since we've been apart! No sooner have I finished that thought than the door swings open and there she is. I am so relieved I cry all the way home. You can be sure it will be a long time before I take my mother to the supermarket again!

The Land
Susan Perly

The land under this house
is weak, girl

you can't tell by looking
at it
but, see
it's all mined out
under here
and we're after sittin on
a bridge over caves

Now the other week
old Cameron down the road
dropped clean out of sight
into a hole

Drivin along now
mind, not out to harm a fly
dropped twenty foot
down
clean out of sight

Had to bring MacNeil
the fire chief
down in town
to come haul'em out

But nobody was surprised, eh?

Look, years ago
Dominion Coal
dried up these here wells
mining all under the town
minin
ya, and there we were with no water

What did they do?

Well I'll tell you what they did
brought a little truck around
every day

and every family
got two buckets of water
whether they needed it
or not.
Ha.
There's no support'all girl

Hell, no one was surprised
when old Cameron and his heap
went straight down
the company took it all,
see
whether they needed it or not.
Ha.

Your Writing

1. How does your writing stack up against the stories of the other writers? Is yours more suspenseful? Does it have a stronger conflict? Is the climax more satisfying for a reader? What makes you say so?

2. Does your piece of narration contain more or less dialogue and description than any of the others? For example, nearly all of Anne Tyler's piece is dialogue. Could you tell your story using only dialogue?

3. The author of "Shopping" has made use of the persona of a small child. Did you use a persona in your writing? If not, in another piece of writing, would you like to experiment with using a persona?

4. Bob Klettke and Farley Mowat both focus their narratives around the broad topic of entrapment. You might compare and contrast the beginning, middle,

and ending of the two narratives. Has either author used a technique that you tried (or would like to try out) in your writing?

5. In your journal, comment on your writing. What did you learn from writing your short narration? From editing a peer's work? In your next piece of narrative writing, is there anything that you might like to experiment with or follow up on?

2 Short Description

"An image may come through the eye as color, through the ear as sound, through the tongue as taste, or through one of the other senses as another kind of physical information. When we remember with any vividness, we remember in images."

John Frederick Nims, **Western Wind**

WRITING PROJECT

Create a word picture of a person, place, or thing in under 250 words.

Exploring and Prewriting Suggestions

1. Being able to describe something so well that your audience can *see*, *feel*, and *hear* it, and perhaps even have a sense of its *taste* and *smell*, takes a bit of practice. The following exploration activities should produce a number of possible, valid topics for this project.

a) Work in a group of any size. Volunteers can take turns describing something in their pocket, hand, or locker *without showing the object or naming it or its function* to the others in the group. Each volunteer should continue until all group members have figured out what is being described.

b) In groups of five or six, explore the following Senses Grid. Before reading the text that follows the grid, determine the relationships among the items in line 1, line 2, line 3, and so on.

1	a rooster crows	the laughter of children	groans of agony
2	the sun peeps over a barn	a kilometre of sandy beach	a room full of weight machines
3	the heavy fragrance of hay	marshmallows burning over an open fire	beads of sweat
4	the bitter flavor of morning coffee	drinking the last dregs of hot cocoa	a salty top lip
5	nippy frost in the air	balmy trade winds blow the palms	warm flesh on cold metal

If you're having trouble seeing the relationships among the items, then begin with the first line and discuss what the items have in common. (They are all sounds.) Repeat the procedure for the other lines.

Now read down each column, one by one, and create a setting for the combination of relationships. In your discussion, you might consider place, time, mood, atmosphere, and characters. For example, the setting for the images in the first column is a farmyard in the morning in late autumn.

Afterward, each group member individually might try to include the images and setting in a few lines of poetry or prose. Share your work in your group, and then your group might exchange your collected writings with the other groups.

c) Compose a similar Senses Grid by yourself or with a partner. Share your grid with your classmates, and invite them to interpret your entries. Ideas from this exploring activity might provide you with a topic for this writing project.

d) Close your eyes and listen to a piece of music. Then freewrite for ten minutes on whatever came to mind as you listened.

e) Write a haiku or other short descriptive poem of your choice. You might use your work as a starting point for a larger piece of descriptive writing or polish it for this project.

GARFIELD ®   **by Jim Davis**

© 1978 United Feature Syndicate, Inc.

2. Books that you are reading can provide starting points for your own writing. Or skim the selections at the end of this chapter and in the appendix.

a) Share with a partner a descriptive passage that you think works well, and discuss why the passage is effective. Work with your partner to expand the passsage by adding two or three sentences somewhere at the beginning, within, or at the end of the passage. Once you are both satisfied with your revised description, exchange your work with another pair of students and have them figure out which sentences are your work and which are the original. If you feel comfortable writing in the style of the author you have selected, you might experiment with creating a passage of your own in the same style.

b) Read the opening paragraph of "Naaholooyah" (in the appendix) to see how the storyteller describes the mother's hands. You might create a similar description of someone you admire.

c) Imagine that you are the best friend of a character in a book you are reading. Freewrite for fifteen minutes describing, in as much detail as you feel comfortable with, something about this person: appearance, clothing, home, or part-time job, for example.

d) Select an illustration or photograph in a book or magazine. With a few of your classmates, describe the picture. You can build on one another's descriptions and add imagined details.

Writer's Choice

How can you use descriptive writing in the other subjects you are studying?

3. Quickly list a few people, places, and things that are vivid in your mind. Your list might include everything from a single small object to a vast scene – for example:
- the face of a friend or relative;
- your family pet;
- your room at home;
- a classroom you hated or loved;
- the main street of your city or town;
- an orange;
- a crowd scene at a tied football game;
- a waterfall or other natural scene at night.

Choose one or two subjects to work with, and, in your journal, do one or more of the following.

a) Jot down some things that you associate with your subject. List words and phrases that describe what you see, hear, smell, touch, and taste.

b) Sketch or draw a picture of your subject. What features have you highlighted? Why? How can you highlight them in your writing?

c) Compare your subject with something else. Don't be afraid to make even a far-fetched comparison. For example, how is your subject like a watermelon, a sharp knife, or a cushion?

d) Determine where you are in relation to your subject. How would your subject look if you were on the same level? If you were above or below it? If you were moving through a scene as a television camera does? If you were viewing it through binoculars? Jot down some notes and then discuss them with a partner.

Writer's Choice

Is your picture firmly fixed in your mind? Are you ready to draft? Or do you need to explore some more? Have you thought about your writing variables, or do you want to think about them as you draft?

4. You might want to explore a subject further using one or more of the following techniques from Chapter 22: See/Write; Write/Write; Free Association Cluster; Absurd Analogies; or Senses Cluster.

Drafting Suggestions

1. Consider the **overall impression** you wish to create, and select your details accordingly. Do you want your reader to like the subject of your description? Dislike? Be frightened? Amused? Most writers select details to get a certain reaction from their readers. They also choose words with connotations, or associations, that create a single overall impression. The word *slender*, for example, creates a different impression than the word *scrawny* does, even though both words mean "thin."

2. To organize a description of your subject, start at one point and proceed in an orderly direction. You might experiment with moving from top to bottom or from near to far. Don't jump from one point to another unless you have a reason to do so. ("Spatial Order" in Chapter 25 may help you with your organization.)

3. As you draft, think about how you can make your subject as vivid for your audience as it is for you. Which words in the following sentences enable you to see, hear, or smell the subjects?
- The red-faced infant howled for attention.
- Perspiration and perfume mingled in the theatre.

(If you are using a word processor, you might be able to use a built-in thesaurus to help you find the exact words you are looking for.)

4. Experiment with similes or metaphors, which are stated or implied comparisons of unlike things. These can breathe new life into even the stalest subject. What comparisons do the following sentences make?
- The cherry blossom petals, caught by the wind, swirled in a miniature blizzard.
- Like a hawk, the salesperson swooped down upon the little man who had just come into the store.

Writer's Choice

What do you want your audience to feel after reading or listening to your description? Will your description stand on its own or be part of a longer piece of writing, such as a biology report, a friendly letter, or an autobiography?

When you finish your draft, consider the following guidelines.

Guidelines for Revising Description

□ Why have you written this description? Is your purpose for writing clear?

□ What have you done to bring your subject to life for your audience? Have you appealed to all of the senses?

□ Will your audience want to read (or listen to) your description? Are your content, word choice, sentence structure, tone, and so on, appropriate to your audience? Is there anything in your description that might confuse your audience? Is there anything in your description that really isn't needed?

□ Does your description work within the suggested 250-word limit? If it is to be part of a longer work, will it work within that larger format?

□ How have you organized your description? Do you describe your subject in an orderly fashion?

□ Does your ending bring your description to a satisfying conclusion?

□ Is your title catchy?

□ Is there anything in your draft that you would like your editor to help you with?

Writer's Choice

Is your draft ready for your intended audience? Or would you like an editor to make revising and editing suggestions?

If necessary, revise your work and prepare a clean double-spaced draft for your editor.

Revising and Editing Suggestions

Give your draft to your peer-editor, and share your writing variables. Encourage your editor to use the "Guidelines for Revising Description" in this chapter and the checklists in Chapter 27. Your editor should also think about how he or she would answer the following questions.

Ask Your Peer-Editor

- ☐ What was your first impression of my description? How did it make you feel? Why?
- ☐ What overall mood or impression have I created? Did my subject "come to life" for you? Can you suggest possible changes that might make my description more vivid?
- ☐ To how many of your senses have I appealed? To which ones does my description appeal most effectively? To which other senses could the description appeal?
- ☐ Does my choice of words add to the total effect? Should I add, delete, or substitute any words? Should I make any of my language more precise? (For example, have I used words such as *actually, very, really,* or *quite* that do not contribute to the overall effect of my writing?)
- ☐ Do my sentences have variety and emphasis? Do they reinforce the mood I am trying to create?
- ☐ Test my use of figurative comparisons. (See Chapter 32.) Have I used them effectively? Where could I add one or two?
- ☐ Are there any problems with my spelling, punctuation, capitalization, or sentence structure?

Writer's Choice

Are you satisfied with your description after using your peer-editor's suggestions? Are you ready to publish? Or would you like your teacher-editor to edit your work?

Publishing Suggestions

After you have finished revising, reread your description and then close your eyes. Do the words paint the exact picture you want your audience to see? Do they also bring to mind the sounds, smells, tastes, and tactile sensations you want your audience to imagine? If they do not, your work may need a final revision.

Descriptive writing lends itself to publishing in many ways. For example, you might invite a classmate to illustrate your work and then post the illustrated description on a classroom bulletin board or in a corridor display. You might set your description to music as you read it to your audience. Or you might use your description as part of a promotional or advertising brochure for your subject.

In the Company of Writers

The Flamingo
Tamara Neufeld, student

Pretty in Pink,
Poised in
    elegance.
Crinoline Petticoats,
A pageantry
    of ruffled
    feathers.
Striding gracefully.
Neck searching.
Straining for
    the sky.
Parading about
    in mute
Flamboyancy.
Living for
    Flattery.

from *Obasan*
Joy Kogawa

In the picture I am clinging to my mother's leg on a street corner in Vancouver. A small boy is standing hugging a lamp post and is staring at us. His thumb is in his mouth. I am mortified by the attention. I turn my face away from everyone. My mother places her cool hand on my cheek, its scent light and flowery. She whispers that the boy will laugh at me if I hide. Laugh? There is no worse horror. Laughter is a cold spray that chills the back of my neck, that makes the tears rush to my eyes. My mother's whisper flushes me out of my hiding-place behind the softness of her silk dress. Only the sidewalk is safe to look at. It does not have eyes.

A Memory of Grandmother
Laura Moorhead, student

A leaf scuttled across the floor, sent by a gust from the broken window. Time had changed this place. Grandma, with her soft afghans and shawls, was gone. The shelves that once had held pitchers held only dust and lacy cobwebs. I stared at the creaking for-sale sign through the front window. Then I whispered goodbye to my ghosts, and turned to leave. The door cried softly behind me.

The Locker Room
David Brand, student

The locker room is unique. Bodies are everywhere. Dirty bodies. Aching bodies. Stinking bodies. Filthy clothes are strewn on the floor like rags. Sweat saturates the air. Curses, boasts, and threats fly across the room. Injuries are bandaged and massaged to the grunts and groans of the wounded. Emotions drown in the showers.

The Construction Worker
Ross Eckroth, student

Hard hat, masculine, and mean,
and bolts for eyes, this guy's made
for work.
He grabs the sledge hammer,
crawls along the beam,
and wipes his brow clean
of sweat.
Looks at the spike, and gives
one last snort.
Colourless, and painless, the beam
awaits his connection.
Standing up, his vision increases.
Over the shoulder goes the hammer
and with no care in the world he
lets her fly...

Just Like You
Chrystos

I get a lot of junk mail   I read all mine because I don't have a TV
Today the American Eagle Outfitters catalogue arrived
for spring
Now I have many complex bitter feelings about the words American
& Eagle in conjunction but I opened to the first page anyway where
in romantic Patagonia
4 spray-starched Ken & Barbie dolls are leaning & sitting
on a stone balcony against a mountain backdrop
The women are looking sophisticatedly hostile in another direction
One blond boy smiles into nothingness
while the brunette one has his head tilted
toward the brunette woman in an attitude of tender indulgence
which you never see in life
Brunette's feet are bare despite snow in the background
she has matching rosy pink polish with no chips on all her nails
These icons are so clean
wear bright blue, red & yellow
are ready to go sailing on someone's rosewood & brass yacht
any minute
To the left of this beach ball collage
are four brown-skinned women
Their hair is uncombed
They are touching one another
huddled
3 have bare dusty feet
Their clothes are brown, black & white & appear to be from K Mart
The buttons are crooked
The oldest woman, perhaps 20, has a baby bundled on her back
These are the only brown people in the whole catalogue
I'm sure they were unpaid
& the only
person looking straight at the camera
is a small girl, perhaps 8 or 9
who is sitting on the stone like a buddha
She's wearing a large tan felt man's hat with a straight brim
that comes down almost over her eyes
Her shoes are old & split   you can see her toes
peeping out
In her hands is a slingshot with the strap drawn back
She looks as though she'd like to put a rock
right through the camera lens
just like me

Saturday Afternoon at Kensington Market
Raymond Souster
for Bill Brooks

Commerce, by which I don't mean
the Canadian Imperial Bank of,
but hand-to-hand transactions,
smiles on the faces of buyers and sellers,
a laugh here, a shouted joke there,
live fowls in splattered cages,
a counter with a hundred pairs
of fish eyes not so glassily staring,
dresses of rainbowed colourings, an old face
withdrawn behind a shawl staring out
from a store's dark cavern, oranges
Mr. Sunkist couldn't dream of,
beautiful chesterfields carried
from endless Portuguese furniture stores,
more overpowering fruit-of-the-sea smells
with DANGER EXCEPT FOR FISH LOVERS
more apt than its store owner dreams of,
birthday cakes four wine-glassed tiers high,
a woman hefting sacks of potatoes
and setting each down as easily as a shrug of the shoulders:

sun's glare streaming down on all of it
with a shine of spring, with the warm magic breath of living.

Your Writing

1. Which of the pieces is most similar to yours? In what ways? You might compare how you use concrete words – words that tell about shape, texture, color, taste, and sound – with how the other writers use them. You might also examine the different formats; perhaps you might experiment with a different format for this piece or when you draft your next piece of descriptive writing.
2. In "A Memory of Grandmother," the person being described is not present. The paragraph is a reflective recollection. On the other hand, "The Flamingo" presents a brightly focused description of a vivid object that seems alive and immediate. Is your piece reflective or focused? In a future writing project, you might think of an object, a person, or an event and try writing both a reflection of it and a description focused directly on it, as though it were right in front of you. When you're through, think about which works better, and why.
3. Chrystos, Raymond Souster, and David Brand all use lists in their work. Have you used a list in yours? Can you think of other events – perhaps a basketball game or an argument at a laundromat – that could provide you

with a catalogue or list? You might experiment with the idea. The look of such a list on the page also has possibilities. You might use a word processor to make and rearrange such a list.

4. Have a look at some of the figurative comparisons in the work of these other writers. Are there any that you particularly admire? Have you used figurative comparisons in your description?

5. In your journal, comment on your writing. What did you learn from writing your description? When you write your next description, is there anything you would like to experiment with?

3 Short Exposition

"Put an argumentative edge on your subject – and you will have found your thesis."

Sheridan Baker, **The Practical Stylist**

Writers use exposition to present information, ideas, and opinions. For example, you might have to explain a chemistry experiment, point out the causes of a historical event, analyse a short story or poem, or give your opinion on an issue that concerns you. You would use expository writing to do so.

The following examples illustrate differences in the major forms of writing on the subject of snow.

Narration: Last night I got lost in the snow.
Description: Under a microscope, a snowflake looks like a glittering gem.
Exposition: When the temperature is lower than zero degrees Celsius, water vapor in the air turns to snow (explains or informs).
Exposition: Snowball fights on school grounds can lead to injuries and should be banned (persuades, convinces, or argues).

You will often use narration and description within expository writing.

WRITING PROJECT

> In an exposition of not more than 250 words, either explain something you know well or convince someone that your opinion on an issue is important.

Exploring and Prewriting Suggestions

1. Use the following suggestions to help you explore your opinions on particular issues.

a) On two separate pieces of paper, write "Agree" and "Disagree." Under the appropriate heading, write these statements.

- An untidy room indicates an untidy mind.
- Amateur sports teams should include both males and females.
- Environmental pollution is the most serious issue facing us today.
- Censorship is a necessary evil.
- Legal penalties for teenage offenders should be the same as for adults.
- Car insurance should cost the same for both males and females.
- There should be university entrance exams.
- Smoking should be banned from all public places.
- Canada should introduce two-year compulsory service in the armed forces.

When you've finished, find a classmate who disagrees with you on a point, and try to convince that person to change his or her opinion. Try to do the same thing with another classmate or two. You might experiment with different arguments and perhaps different topics.

b) Freewrite for fifteen minutes on a topic that you feel strongly about. If you have already debated with a classmate on a particular topic, you might reconstruct your best arguments, including the ways that you countered your classmate's points.

c) Read recent letters to the editor in the daily newspaper. Find one that you disagree with, and freewrite for ten minutes in response.

d) In a small group, discuss movies you have recently seen. Take turns convincing others in your group to see or not to see a movie.

e) Choose a historical figure, and write a quick note trying to convince the person to change his or her plans. Give your reasons for wanting the change. For example, you might try to persuade Napoleon not to go to Waterloo or Sir John A. Macdonald to forget about Confederation.

f) Using the persona of one of the characters in a story or play you have enjoyed, convince another character to change his or her ways. (You might, for instance, compose a hasty-note.)

2. Use the following suggestions to help you explore some of the things that you know a great deal about.

a) Using invisible writing (Chapter 21), write for ten minutes about one of your hobbies.

b) Explain to a partner how to perform an activity such as tie a shoe, peel a banana, or bathe a pet.

c) The pieces at the end of this chapter might provide a prompt for your writing. Would you, for example, like to respond to the argument put forward by Tracey Rockwell? Develop a humorous explanation in the style of "Why Levi's Changed the 501"? Or answer the questions posed by Sparling Mills in her poem?

d) Go to the library and research a topic – for example, European history, natural disasters, sports, travel, or communication – that has always interested you. Try to record at least three interesting pieces of information about your topic, and make a note of your sources (Chapter 35).

e) Of all the places you've travelled to or lived in, which would you most like to go back to? Why? You might use Pro/Con Ladders (Chapter 22) to explore the advantages and disadvantages of your moving.

f) Which character in all the stories, films, and plays you've enjoyed do you identify with most? In a one-minute talk, explain why you empathize with this character. You can present your talk to one other person, within a small group, or to the whole class.

Writer's Choice

In this project, do you want to argue (persuade) or explain (inform)? Do you want to use one of the suggested exploration topics for this project, or do you want to continue brainstorming for another topic? If you do have a topic, are you ready to begin to draft, or do you want to try to focus your topic a bit more?

3. If you've settled on a broad topic for your exposition, you might want to jot down several possible approaches to your topic. You can state these approaches in the form of **thesis statements**. The following are three thesis statements derived from the broad topic of education. Can you think of others?

- Participating in school activities is as important as going to classes.
- Everyone should learn a second language.
- A high school diploma increases your opportunities after you leave school.

4. If you need further help before or as you draft, use one or more of the exploration techniques in Chapter 22. The following are especially useful for exposition that presents information: Classification/Division Flowcharts; Aristotle's Topics; and Newspaper Reporter's Questions. If your topic involves an argument, you will find the following techniques useful: Positive Cluster; Negative Cluster; Pro/Con Ladders; and Newspaper Reporter's Questions.

5. Think about your writing variables – your audience, your purpose for writing, the format of your exposition, and the voice you will adopt – both before and as you draft. Writing for a real purpose to a real audience will help you to focus your thoughts and to select appropriate information for your exposition. For instance, you might try to persuade the members of your school photography club to clean up the darkroom when they're through with it. Or you might inform the readers of a local newspaper about the history of a local landmark. Similarly, knowing your format will help you to decide how much

information you should gather. Will your exposition stand on its own? Or is it to be part of a larger piece of writing, such as a letter or an essay?

6. Be sure to save any ideas that you don't use.

> ## Writer's Choice
> Are you ready to begin your draft? Or would you like to consider the following drafting suggestions first?

Drafting Suggestions

1. If your exposition needs a thesis statement, then draft several, and choose one to work with. Be sure to keep an open mind about your approach to your topic, because your draft may take a different direction as you work on it. You may also discover that your subject is too broad to deal with within the suggested 250-word limit. If this is the case, think about how you can narrow or **limit** your topic. The following is an example of how to limit one broad topic.

education
↓
high school
↓
graduation
↓
Every high school student should graduate.

2. Consider the following as you draft.

a) Is your limited topic suitable for your exposition? Keep the suggested 250-word limit in mind. Which of the following would be most suitable for an exposition of this length? Why?

- Through the ages, actors have been both highly respected and regarded as the lowest form of humanity.
- Acting on stage is quite different from acting before a camera.
- There are many fine actors performing on stage and in films.

b) Can you write about your subject accurately? Do you either know something about your subject or want to research it? Which of the following sounds as if it came from a personal experience? Why?

- Wild animals are hostile to human intruders.
- You should not camp in a secluded part of a national park where grizzlies roam freely.
- Grizzly bears are quite different from polar bears.

c) Is your limited topic important to you? If you care about your limited topic, you will have a much better chance of arousing your reader's interest – and you will likely find that you have a great deal to say. In fact, your problem may be what to leave out, not what to include, which is an ideal situation for a writer. Which of the following thesis statements will probably lead to specific writing? Why?

• Students should have a voice in determining the content of a course.
• Schools today are very different from schools fifty years ago.
• All students should read every day.

3. Expository paragraphs often use the following structure: **introduction, development, conclusion.**

Introduction. In your introduction, you capture your audience's attention, state your topic, and show your attitude toward it. You might take one or two sentences to do so.

Development. As you develop your exposition, you provide supporting facts, examples, and reasons. You can organize your information in several different ways. (See Chapter 25 if you need help.)

Conclusion. In your conclusion, you can summarize your evidence, restate your thesis, and encourage your audience to link your work to their own knowledge and experience and the wider world. You might conclude your work with a question to encourage your audience to think about what you have written.

4. As you draft your exposition, you may find yourself substituting a word, phrase, or sentence for another and perhaps even changing the order of your sentences. You may decide to revise your writing one or more times before giving it to your peer-editor. Keep in mind that revising is a continuous process that goes on even as you draft. If you use a computer, you know that this kind of self-editing and revising can be one of the most exciting parts of your writing process. Seeing your words and sentences on the screen – moving, expanding, even disappearing – should give you a sense of power and ownership over what you write.

When you have finished your draft, consider the following guidelines.

Guidelines for Revising Exposition

☐ Why are you writing this exposition? Is your purpose to persuade or to inform your audience? Do you think you've succeeded? What makes you think so?

☐ Have you experimented with your format? Would your exposition work better as a poem or as an advertisement, for example?

☐ What is your main idea? Have you stated it clearly? Is your topic appropriate for the suggested 250-word limit? Is there anything that you should save for another piece of writing?

☐ Does your evidence solidly support your thesis statement? Have you included anything that does not move your exposition forward? Are there any important gaps in your information or your thinking?

☐ Does your introduction capture your audience's attention, set out your topic, and let your audience know how you feel about your subject?

☐ Do you thoughtfully and carefully develop the body of your exposition? (In other words, do you know how you have organized your writing? For more about organization, see Chapter 25.)

☐ Does your ending effectively conclude your exposition? Will it take your audience exactly where you want them to be?

☐ Are you satisfied with the mechanics of your draft (spelling, punctuation, and grammar), or is there something you'd like to check before you let an editor see your work?

☐ Do you have time to put your exposition aside for a few days? If so, you might come back to it with a new eye and spot any possible gaps, inconsistencies, or contradictions.

☐ Is there anything in your draft that you would like your editor to help you with?

Writer's Choice

Is your draft ready for your intended audience? Or would you like an editor to make revising and editing suggestions?

If necessary, revise your work and prepare a clean double-spaced draft for your editor.

Revising and Editing Suggestions

Give your draft to your peer-editor, and share your writing variables. Encourage your editor to use the "Guidelines for Revising Exposition" in this chapter and the checklists in Chapter 27. Your editor should also think about how he or she would answer the following questions.

Ask Your Peer-Editor

☐ What was your first impression of my work? Did my exposition make you think in a new way about my subject? About the world in general? Do you think it will convince or inform my audience? Why?

☐ Is my purpose for writing clear? Have I expressed my main idea clearly? If not, how could I improve these?

☐ Have I provided sufficient information to support my main idea? Have I provided too much?

☐ How have I organized my information? Is the organization appropriate to my subject?

☐ Is any part of my exposition unclear? Is there anything that you don't understand? Could you suggest ways to clear up fuzzy writing?

☐ Do the thoughts flow smoothly and logically? Can you suggest any transitional devices (Chapter 26)? Have I shifted my point of view?

☐ Did my title and beginning grab your attention? Was my conclusion appropriate? If not, how could I improve them?

☐ Do you see any errors in spelling, grammar, punctuation, and sentence structure?

Publishing Suggestions

Polish your piece, and proofread it for spelling, grammar, word usage, and punctuation.

Think about how you might present your writing to its final audience. Pieces of informative writing might be illustrated and gathered into a collaborative class magazine. (Think about using *OWL* magazine as a model and presenting your magazine to students in a younger grade.) Your persuasive writing might be shared in a classroom speaker's corner. Find a classmate who has taken an opposing position on your topic. Set a time limit (say, two or three minutes) and take turns trying to convince the rest of your classmates to come to your opinion.

**In the
Company
of Writers**

Smokers Beware
Tracey Rockwell, student

June 10, 1990

To the Editor:

I want to let my fellow students know how bad a habit smoking is.

Possibly the most disgusting habit a person could engage in, smoking not only endangers smokers' health, but also affects nonsmokers. According to some scientists, the second-hand smoke that enters the air from the burning end of a cigarette is more damaging than the smoke being inhaled. Often a smoker will ignore the fact that he or she pollutes the air with this deadly substance simply because smoking is accepted as normal behavior. Rather, the inconsiderate smoker invades the right of everyone to breathe air without fear of being damaged. Fortunately, the population of smokers is gradually decreasing. Some day, with any luck, smokers will be of such a minority as to do no damage to nonsmokers.

I would like to suggest that students work to have smoking banned in all public places.

Sincerely,

Tracey Rockwell
Tracey Rockwell

The Ozone War
Patricia Kmet, student

Many people may not be aware of this, but every time you throw away a foam egg carton or dispense spray-on oven cleaner, you are inadvertently destroying the ozone layer. This layer is vital to life on earth as we know it, since it is responsible for absorbing harmful ultraviolet radiation from the sun. When foam is crushed, ozone-eating molecules called chlorofluorocarbons (CFCs) are released by the hundreds and slowly float up to the stratosphere. It takes 50 to 75 years for these hazardous molecules to reach the ozone layer, so basically all the CFCs ever released still exist in the atmosphere.

Ironically, CFCs were first produced to dispense and manufacture certain substances without mixing with the product or posing any threats to human health. It was not until several years later that scientists discovered that this "miracle molecule" was indirectly harming all life forms. Just the increases in the cases of skin cancer is proof enough of the damage occurring as a result.

When CFCs reach the stratosphere, they create havoc in the skies. Since their appetite is not satisfied in simply destroying one ozone molecule, they continue to deplete thousands before they are "burned out." A dramatic cut in the production of CFCs will be required in order to protect the ozone layer. We will have to replace CFCs used in air conditioners and refrigerators, as blowing agents to form foam products, as solvents used for cleaning computer parts, as well as all aerosol products that use CFCs as propellants. Not only must all the people on earth salvage the ozone layer, but each individual must recognize and react to any ozone-threatening chemicals. Make your contribution by looking for products packaged in cardboard instead of foam, insulate your home with fibreglass rather than polyurethane foam, and check that your automobile air conditioning unit is well sealed. Making an effort is half the fight.

Poem After Months
Sparling Mills

How do others live
without poetry?
Action is fine,
Until strength collapses for the day.
We all come to the thought-times,
The aloneness of an empty house,
The fear that nothing we do
Really matters.

How do others fill emptiness,
If not with the tantalizing bubble
Of possible creation?

I have lived months without the stirrings
Of line rhythms;
Months I would not re-live for
Anything material.

Now, I am impressed
With the courage of men and women
Who find fulfillment in everyday affairs.
But I am one of the weak ones.
I must have the intoxicating goal
Of possible perfection;
I must live life in expectation of a poem,
The poem,
Which is always the next.

Why Levi's Changed the 501
from Everybody's Business: An Almanac
edited by Milton Moskowitz, Michael Katz, and Robert Levering

Picture a scene from the Old West, sometime in the 1870s. Weary cowboys in dusty Levi's gather around a blazing campfire, resting after a day of riding and roping on the open range. The lonely howl of a distant coyote counterpoints the notes of a guitar as the moon floats serenely overhead in an unpolluted sky afire with stars.

Suddenly a bellow of pain shatters the night, as a cowpoke leaps away from the fire, dancing in agony. Hot Rivet Syndrome has claimed another victim.

In those days Levi's were made, as they had been from the first days of Levi

Strauss, with copper rivets at stress points to provide extra strength. On these original Levi's – model 501 – there were rivets on the pockets, and there was a lone rivet at the crotch. The crotch rivet was the critical one: when cowboys crouched too long beside the campfire, the rivet grew uncomfortably hot.

For years the brave men of the West suffered from this curious occupational hazard. But nothing was done about it until 1933, when Walter Haas, Sr., president of Levi Strauss, chanced to go camping in his Levi's 501s. Haas was crouched contentedly by a crackling campfire in the high Sierras, drinking in the pure mountain air, when he fell prey to Hot Rivet Syndrome. He consulted with professional wranglers in his party. Had they ever suffered the same mishap? An impassioned yes was the reply. Haas vowed that the offending rivet must go, and the board of directors voted it into extinction at their next meeting.

Except for eliminating the crotch rivet, the company has made only one other stylistic change in its 501s since they were first marketed in 1873. Responding to schools' complaints that Levi's pocket rivets scratched school furniture, the company moved the rivets to the front pockets. Otherwise the Levi's 501 shrink-to-fit jeans on the market today are identical to the pants that won the West.

Your Writing

1. Which of these published pieces is most like yours in organization? On another occasion, you might experiment with organizing your material in a different way or using a different format – a poem or an advertisement, for example.

2. Which of the authors have used narrative in their exposition? Which have used description? How have you used narrative or descriptive illustrations in your own writing? How might you add such illustrations to your next piece of expository writing?

3. Writers often delay the introduction of their topic, especially for a comic effect. Have a look at the delayed introduction in "Why Levi's Changed the 501." How does the writer use the last sentence to return the reader to the opening description? Have you delayed the introduction of your topic? Does it (or would it) work? Why?

4. In your journal, comment on your writing. What did you learn from writing your short exposition? In your next piece of expository writing, is there anything that you might like to experiment with or follow up on?

4 Informative Essay

"If you hope to hold ... the attention of your reader, say something that is true, specific, and reasonably original."

Alan Dawe, **Four Approaches to Prose**

It is important to be able to inform clearly and at the same time hold the interest of an audience.

WRITING PROJECT

Write an informative essay that is at least 400 words long. You might write an essay for both this course and another, on either an assigned topic or one you select yourself. If you have a choice, select a topic that interests you.

Exploring and Prewriting Suggestions

1. You might refer to the exploring and prewriting suggestions in Chapter 3 to help you to find a suitable topic for your informative essay.

2. Have a look at some of your short expository pieces, especially those you feel strongly about. You may find that you have already arrived at a suitable topic for this project. In this project, you can modify and expand the topic, flesh it out, give it sharper focus, and structure it as a longer essay.

3. Consult Chapter 22 for suggestions to help you further explore your topic.
a) You might apply the Newspaper Reporter's Questions. Make as extensive a list as you can under each of the main headings: Who? What? When? Where? Why? and How?

b) You might develop a Classification Flowchart or a Division Flowchart to separate your topic into classes or categories.

c) If applicable, you might use Comparison/Contrast Ladders (to list similarities and differences within your topic) or a Cause-and-Effect Flowchart (to explore sequence within your topic).

4. You may need to take some time to research your topic. Be sure to acknowledge your sources. (Refer to Chapter 35 for researching tips.) If you are using a word processor, you can store all your quotations in its memory and recall them when you draft your essay.

Writer's Choice

Do you want to start drafting now, or do you want to focus your writing further? Do you want to consider your writing variables now or later? Do you want to make an outline? Do you want to compose several thesis statements?

5. If your writing project is a paper in social studies, science, or another subject, combine the suggestions in this chapter with those your teachers may make.

Drafting Suggestions

1. Consider how you will organize your essay. You might, for example, show cause and effect; compare and contrast your information; move from material that is familiar to most people to material that is unfamiliar; or present information in chronological order. (See Chapter 25 for more about organization.)

2. Follow **basic essay structure** – introduction, development, conclusion. A basic essay contains an introductory paragraph, several paragraphs that present supporting evidence, and a conclusion that summarizes the main ideas and encourages the reader to think about the essay. For your first informative essay, basic essay structure is easiest to follow. As you write other informative essays, you can experiment with other structures; for example, you might set out your thesis at the end of your essay rather than at the beginning.

3. Decide on your approach to your topic. For example, will you use a straightforward style? Or will you use irony, poking fun at your subject by saying the opposite of what you mean? (To discover the range of styles you might use, see the Second Workshop section, especially Chapters 29 and 34.)

4. Consider using description. In certain kinds of papers – for example, in a paper for a science class about a particular organism – description can help your reader understand your topic. "Bacterium," at the end of this chapter, contains some effective descriptions.

5. Consider using narrative illustrations. A narrative illustration is a brief story that provides an example of a point that you are trying to make. Sometimes it is the most effective kind of supporting evidence. (You'll find examples of narrative illustrations in "The Burrowing Owl," at the end of this chapter.)

6. Structure your paragraphs as carefully as you structure your essay. Try to include a topic sentence in each of your paragraphs (see Chapter 23), and develop each paragraph in an orderly fashion.

7. Leave plenty of time to revise and edit your essay before submitting it to your intended audience.

When you finish your draft, consider the following guidelines.

Guidelines for Revising an Informative Essay

☐ Why are you writing this informative essay? Is your purpose clear? Do you care about your topic? Will your audience be able to see that?

☐ What do you like best about your essay? Least? How can you build on your essay's strengths and get rid of its weaknesses?

☐ What is your main idea? Have you stated it clearly? Is your topic appropriate for an informative essay? Are you sure that you are informing rather than persuading?

☐ Does your introduction capture your audience's attention, set out your topic, and let your audience know how you feel about your subject?

☐ Do you logically and consistently support your main idea with appropriate details, examples, or narrative or descriptive illustrations? Have you included anything that does not move your essay forward? Are there any important gaps in your information or your thinking?

☐ Do you logically develop the body of your essay? How have you organized it? Is there anything that might confuse a reader? For example, have you taken for granted anything that your audience might not know?

☐ Does your ending effectively conclude your essay? Does it encourage your audience to reflect on your ideas and to relate your information to their own knowledge and experience?

☐ Are you satisfied with the mechanics of your draft (spelling, punctuation, and grammar), or is there something you'd like to check before you let an editor see your work?

☐ Have you left sufficient time to rethink and revise your draft?

☐ Is there anything in your draft that you would like your editor to help you with?

Writer's Choice

Is your draft ready for your intended audience? Or would you like an editor to make revising and editing suggestions?

If necessary, revise your work and prepare a clean double-spaced draft for your editor.

Revising and Editing Suggestions

Give your draft to your peer-editor, and share your writing variables. Encourage your editor to use the "Guidelines for Revising an Informative Essay" in this chapter and the checklists in Chapter 27. Your editor should also think about how he or she would answer the following questions.

Ask Your Peer-Editor

☐ What was your first impression of my work? Did my essay tell you anything you didn't know about my subject? Did it present information you did know in a new and interesting way? Do you think my essay will interest and inform my audience? In what ways?

☐ Is my purpose for writing clear? Have I expressed my main idea clearly in a thesis statement? Have I included a topic sentence in each paragraph?

☐ What part of my essay is clearest? Most effective? In what way? Is anything unclear? Why? What can I do to make it clearer?

☐ Have I properly emphasized my important points? If not, what needs more emphasis?

☐ Have I overemphasized or stated anything at too great a length? If so, what should I shorten or omit?

☐ Can you easily tell how I have organized my information? Is the organization easy to follow?

☐ Did you spot any obvious errors in the information I've presented? Are there any facts that I should double-check?

☐ Do you like my word choice and sentence structure? Are my spelling, punctuation, and grammar all right? Is there anything I should still work on?

Writer's Choice

How can you make your essay distinctly yours? Can you test each sentence, each word – as your audience will – to be sure it does precisely what you want it to do?

Try to find the time to put your essay away for a few days. Then take it out to read again with a fresh, open mind, and give it a final polish. If it's on your computer, you won't have to hesitate to make a few final changes.

Publishing Suggestions

You might prepare a cover for your essay and offer it to a local doctor or dentist as waiting room reading material. You might check into submitting your essay to an appropriate journal or magazine. Your school librarian might welcome a carefully researched paper as a resource. Of course, if you've prepared your essay for another of your classes, you can submit it to your teacher.

In the Company of Writers

Bacterium
Dora Anyfantis, student

Allow me to introduce myself; I am a microscopic bacterium, one of the thousand bacteria that surround you in your everyday life. You try to avoid me; however, no matter where you go, you will not get away from me. I will always be near you, inside you, everywhere.

I may be microscopic in size, but I can do more damage than all wars and natural disasters put together. I can start from anywhere, entering your organism from the air you breathe, the food you eat, and the water you drink. My favorite victim is a weak organism; I can conquer these easily. When I enter a weak organism, I multiply extremely rapidly. I become two bacteria, which become four, the four eight, and in only a few hours we become millions. Then, unfortunately for the organism, it is doomed. On the other hand, I find a lot of resistance in a strong organism. These things are not so great for me because when I enter it, a deadly battle starts. Both I, with my toxin, and the organism, with its antitoxin, try to win the battle. Unfortunately, the strong organism always wins. Every time I fail to conquer a body, it brings disaster; I die, you see.

In spite of the damage that I cause, do not think that your life would have been as great without my presence. Fermentation is one of the effects of my work. Without me, you would have to do without foods like bread and yogurt.

Even though the damages that I bring are many, I also offer you some vital services. Therefore, I am indispensable in your life. This is my story, a story full of death but also full of life.

Before the Audition
Rita Ringle, student

You might think it easy and a lot of fun to perform in a musical play production. You are right, but before you can perform in any production, you must do one thing: audition.

To be in a musical production you must possess many talents. You must have some knowledge of music reading, a good singing voice, good dancing skills, the ability to memorize quickly, and finally, the ability to perform in front of a large group of people without falling apart. During an audition you must demonstrate all these talents in only a few minutes.

You must prepare yourself for the audition in the same way you would prepare for a job interview. First, you should have a résumé. Your résumé should contain relevant information about yourself; for example, your personal data (height, weight, age, etc.), and information about all technical experience on and off stage, such as music lessons, voice lessons, dance experience, and prior play performances. You should also include the names of your instructors, years studied, and locations where you learned or performed in each field.

Next, you must sell yourself. In order to do this, you should familiarize yourself with the musical for which you are planning to audition. You should choose a good song and a monologue from the actual production and memorize it until it becomes second nature to you. Purchasing a record from the musical can acquaint you with the material so that you can introduce your own personality and showcase your talents.

Your monologue should be no shorter than one minute. Memorizing the monologue is easy, but how well can you make your character come alive? You should take into consideration the personality of the character you are portraying and his or her situation. Become your character and know everything about him or her.

Now you are almost ready. Before you go to your audition you should do a few things at home. First, eat a good meal. You should never perform on an empty stomach. Eating will prevent your having hunger pangs and losing your concentration. Next, you should exercise your voice so you will not strain your vocal cords during your song. If you smoke, wait until after the audition is over. Smoking will only serve to tighten your vocal cords. You should do a few stretching exercises so you don't pull any muscles when you are asked to dance. Finally, you should make sure you have a very neat appearance. Wear something nice but very loose fitting. Tight clothes only prevent you from doing your best when asked to dance. Remember, looks can tell a person much about you.

You are now ready for the audition. Don't be discouraged by the number of people auditioning for the same role. Do your very best and don't let others change the way you do things. Never make any last minute changes in your character; they will only serve to confuse you.

In conclusion, be patient. The director knows exactly what he or she is looking for. Even if you don't get the part you wanted or don't get a part at all, don't be discouraged. There is always next time!

The Burrowing Owl
Dale Hjertaas

Burrowing owls are small, sandy coloured birds about nine inches high, with long legs and a characteristic habit of bobbing up and down when approached. A grassland bird, burrowing owls are found across the prairies of the United States and Canada, with their range also extending into the Okanagan Valley of B.C.

These owls usually nest in old badger or gopher holes, laying from eight to eleven eggs. They prefer to nest in pasture land or along roadside ditches, where they can often be seen sitting on mounds of dirt next to their burrows.

The female incubates the eggs alone. During this period the male maintains an almost constant watch near the burrow entrance. This probably provides essential protection for the female who might otherwise be trapped in the nest chamber by a predator, such as a badger, which can dig or crawl into the burrow. During the course of the summer, the male's feathers are bleached by the sun. As early as the end of June the two adults are usually easily identified by this colour difference.

Burrowing owl nests are usually out in the open, and for the male owl, sitting outside the burrow entrance throughout a prairie summer day can be a very hot experience. To maintain his cool throughout the heat, the male uses one of two strategies. First, if there is something available that is elevated, he will sit on it. Fence posts, rocks, dirt mounds, machinery, and occasionally stakes placed by biologists to mark nests are all used as perches. One owl nesting beside the Western Development Museum in Moose Jaw, Saskatchewan, usually perches on the steering wheel of an old steam tractor. All of these perches have two things in common: they raise the owl off the hot ground to where the air is significantly cooler, and they provide more exposure to breezes.

If there is no perch, or the wind makes perching unpleasant, the burrowing owl will take the second approach – sitting in his burrow entrance barely peeking over the lip. Here he is relatively shaded from the sun and sheltered from the wind, but he can still watch for danger.

Burrowing owls use other strategies to avoid predators, even placing cow manure beside the nest hole! Gregory Green, who has studied burrowing owls in Oregon, suggests the smell of the manure confuses predators, especially badgers, which cannot detect the scent of the burrowing owl over that of cattle manure. He has noted cases where badgers have approached but not excavated burrowing owl nests lined with cattle manure. His observations indicated that out of 24 nests without manure, 13 were preyed upon by badgers, while only two out of 25 with manure were.

Unfortunately all is not well with this interesting little owl. In 1978, naturalist Jim Wedgewood reviewed the burrowing owl's status for the Committee on the Status of Endangered Wildlife in Canada (COSEWIC). Wedgewood estimated a total Canadian population in the order of 2,000 pairs. As well, the population appeared to be declining. COSEWIC accordingly designated the burrowing owl a threatened species in Canada.

Cultivation of the land where burrowing owls nest, accidental poisonings from insecticides, collisions with cars, and deliberate shootings are some of the problems that have contributed to the continuing decline in burrowing owl numbers. Fortunately, some recent developments suggest hope for this owl's future.

PHOTO COURTESY OF WORLD WILDLIFE FUND

One thing in the burrowing owl's favour is that almost everyone likes it. The owls bob and bow towards intruders, a behaviour which is intended to express alarm, concern or a warning by the owl, but which appears friendly or comical to most people. The owls also adapt to the presence of humans and actually nest in the city of Moose Jaw, as well as in several towns and in many farmyards. Near Avonlea, Saskatchewan, for example, eight pairs nest around Walter Bedford's large farmyard. An owl perched on a tractor or a cultivator watching Bedford as he works nearby is a common sight. Those prairie farmers who have burrowing owls on their land enjoy watching them, and the fact that the owl is a predator of grasshoppers and mice makes the birds doubly welcome.

In spite of the owl's popularity, a 1986 survey showed that most Saskatchewan farmers did not know the owls were a threatened species. The survey also showed that the grassland areas which burrowing owls use for nesting were disappearing at an alarming rate. Between 1979 and 1986, approximately 21 percent of potential nesting areas underwent cultivation. At a November

1986 steering committee meeting of the World Wildlife Fund's Wild West Program, the author raised this problem and suggested that because of the owl's popularity with farmers, perhaps the farmers would help protect it if they knew it was in trouble.

Operation Burrowing Owl, a cooperative project of the World Wildlife Fund (WWF), Wildlife Habitat Canada, the Saskatchewan Natural History Society, the Saskatchewan Wildlife Federation, Saskatchewan Parks, Recreation and Culture, and participating Saskatchewan landowners was born from that concept. The program has four principal objectives: to protect habitat through landowner recognition; to increase awareness of the burrowing owl as a threatened species; to make an inventory of the burrowing owl population and establish a method of annual population monitoring; and to collect information on habitat selection and use.

In 1987, a questionnaire mailed to 30,000 Saskatchewan farmers produced hundreds of burrowing owl observations. During the summers of 1987 and 1988, Operation Burrowing Owl staff members Wendy Lyon, Craig Palmer and John Pollock visited each reported owl site to inventory it and to explain Operation Burrowing Owl to the landowner. Each landowner is asked to retain the burrowing owl nesting habitat for five years and to report the number of owls using it each year. In return, sponsors provide an attractive gate sign and an annual newsletter on burrowing owl conservation which contains important information about the species.

In June 1987, His Royal Highness Prince Philip, president of WWF International, initiated the Landowner Recognition Program by presenting gate signs to five Saskatchewan landowners. Since then, Saskatchewan landowners have continued to enroll in the program, with 342 agreements involving a total of 26,000 acres of burrowing owl nesting habitat procured to date. This habitat was occupied by 724 pairs of owls in 1988.

Perhaps the most rewarding aspect of the Operation Burrowing Owl program has been the clear demonstration that Saskatchewan farmers care about wildlife conservation and are willing to give something extra to help protect a threatened species.

A second important discovery has been an increased understanding of the impact of pesticides on burrowing owls. The owls occupy the area of Canada prone to grasshopper outbreaks and feed primarily on these insects during years of high concentrations. Paul James of the Saskatchewan Museum of Natural History and Glen Fox of the Canadian Wildlife Service have shown that some pesticides used for grasshopper control have a serious impact on burrowing owls while others do not. This information has been forwarded to all the landowners involved with Operation Burrowing Owl and will hopefully lead to a reduction in the inadvertent poisoning of the birds.

A third positive note for the burrowing owl program comes from Manitoba where the provincial wildlife branch is reintroducing the burrowing owl, as well as protecting the 20 remaining pairs. During the past summer, five families of wild burrowing owls from Saskatchewan and 10 owls reared at the Owl Rehabilitation and Research Foundation in Vineland, Ontario, have been released. Similar releases of owls have successfully reestablished a small breeding population in the Okanagan Valley of British Columbia.

Bird houses are also helping the burrowing owl. A bit different from the standard wren house, burrowing owl nest boxes are dug into the ground and connected to the surface by a gently sloping six-foot tunnel made out of plywood or weeping tiles. The boxes serve a number of functions: they provide additional nest sites where natural gopher or badger holes may not be available for new pairs; they offer extra protection from digging predators; they provide instant homes for transplanted owls; and they facilitate study of the owl. As the lid of these boxes is only four to six inches below the surface, a biologist can open a nest box and band the young in a few minutes, whereas it may take hours to capture all the young from a natural burrow. Banding programs aided by nest-box use should eventually answer some important questions about the burrowing owl, including where it winters and annual survival rates. Nest boxes can even be used to move the owls to where people want them. The first use of nest boxes in Saskatchewan was on a Moose Jaw golf course. The use of nest boxes successfully moved nesting owls off the fairways and onto the rough, where they are more acceptable to the golfers!

A final note is that the three Prairie provinces and WWF cooperated to prepare a National Recovery Plan for the burrowing owl. The plan, which was put in place in 1989, will guide and stimulate further recovery work for this species.

The burrowing owl remains a threatened species. However, with the continued interest of government and conservation organizations and, most importantly, with the continued commitment of private landowners, the burrowing owl's future in Canada is beginning to look brighter.

Your Writing

1. How did your essay turn out? How do you think your essay stacks up against those of the other writers? What makes you say so?

2. If you included a lot of researched material in your essay, have you properly acknowledged your sources? (See Chapter 35.)

3. The author of "Bacterium" has used a persona to present scientific information. Did you use a persona? If not, you might experiment with redrafting your essay in a more unconventional style and use a persona.

4. In your journal, comment on your writing. What did you learn from writing your informative essay? Is there any part of your process that you would modify when you write your next informative essay? Why?

5 Argumentative Essay

"True [arguers] are like true sportsmen; their whole delight is in the pursuit."

Alexander Pope, ***Thoughts on Various Subjects***

You spend much of your life absorbing and giving out information. You read and listen to become informed, and you talk and write to inform others. Many times your purpose changes. You begin by trying to inform and then find yourself trying to persuade. In such cases, the need to persuade grows out of the need to inform. You want your audience to understand your information as you understand it. To persuade your audience to your way of thinking, you argue.

When you argue in writing, remember that your audience cannot argue back. You have to try to anticipate objections to your argument, and then answer them. To win your audience to your side, you must argue thoroughly, logically, and convincingly. An effective argument is perhaps the most difficult kind of writing to do, but sometimes it is the most useful.

WRITING PROJECT

> Write an argumentative essay of at least 400 words on a topic about which you feel strongly. Try to make your reader adopt, or at least appreciate, your opinion.

Exploring and Prewriting Suggestions

1. You might refer to the exploring and prewriting suggestions in Chapter 3 to help you to find a suitable topic for your argumentative essay.

2. Have a look at some of your short expository pieces, especially those you feel strongly about. A short exposition can often be turned into an argumentative essay with the use of more supporting details, such as facts, examples,

ON THE OTHER HAND, MOOSE, I CAN QUOTE NO SCIENTIFIC PRECEDENT THAT PROVES DAISIES AREN'T PRETTY!

and reasons. You may wish to look over some of your shorter expositions to see whether any of them contains the basis for a good argumentative essay.

3. Examine the argumentative essays at the end of this chapter. Is there anything that you would like to write a rebuttal to – or argue from a different perspective?

4. a) You might use invisible writing (Chapter 21), or a computer with the screen turned off, to write for ten minutes on something that troubles you or that you care strongly about (or any of the following).
- Should I get a part-time job?
- Should I lend money to my best friend?
- Should I work with the poor in Central America?
- Should I try out for a team?
- Should I join a political party?
- Should I continue my schooling?
- Should I take up a musical instrument?

b) Try freewriting for ten minutes on the following subject: Of everything in the world, I would change _____ .

Provide as many reasons as you can. If you run out of ideas, just keep writing the name of what you want to change until another reason occurs to you. Don't just sit staring at the paper.

c) You might explore a topic by completing a Cause-and-Effect Flowchart (Chapter 22). If you've already done some invisible writing or brainstorming, include those ideas, as well as the new thoughts that you have.

When you finish, talk over your flowchart with a classmate. As you discuss the flowchart, you may think of more causes and effects that you might include.

d) Write a comparison/contrast piece of freewriting using the following pictures as inspiration.

e) You might work with a partner to play Pro/Con. Give your partner a general topic (for instance, cats, holidays, shopping, computers, and so on). Your partner must speak *for* the subject until you clap; then, *against* the subject until you clap. Carry on for five or six claps, and then reverse speakers on a new topic.

For a literature variation of Pro/Con, you might give a character's name, a poem, an author, and so on, instead of a general topic.

For a social studies variation, you might give the name of a historical personality, a current world figure, a country, or a city, instead of a general topic.

Writer's Choice

Do you want to start drafting now? Have you thought through the details and techniques you will include to persuade your audience? Have you decided how you will develop your argument? Or do you want to continue to focus your writing: Perhaps consider your writing variables? Make an outline? Compose several possible thesis statements?

5. If your writing project is a paper in social studies, science, or another subject, combine the suggestions in this chapter with those your teacher may make.

Drafting Suggestions

1. Respect your audience. If your audience disagree with your view, they may be as convinced of their opinion as you are of yours. Stay away from name-calling, insults, or other underhanded tactics that weaken your argument. Argue fairly.

2. Use **basic essay structure** – introduction, development, conclusion. For your first argumentative essay, basic essay structure is easiest to follow. Your introduction should arouse interest and let your audience know how you feel about your topic. As you develop your argument, you present your supporting evidence and rebut any opposing points. In your conclusion, you effectively clinch your argument. Examine "The High Price of Soft Sell" and the comments that accompany it at the end of this chapter to see how one writer has used basic essay structure.

As you write other argumentative essays, you can experiment with other structures; for example, you might set out your thesis at the end of your essay rather than at the beginning.

3. Provide solid evidence to back up your opinion. The more supporting evidence you produce, the more convincing your argument will be. Again, do not overlook the opposing side. Although you do not need to build a good opposing argument, one may exist. Weigh both sides of the argument carefully when you decide what to include. Don't use unsupported generalizations such as, "Few teenagers are emotionally mature before the age of eighteen." Such statements can be entirely false or only partly true, and they can seriously weaken your argument.

4. Decide on your approach to your topic. For example, will you use a straightforward style? Or will you use irony, poking fun at your subject by saying the opposite of what you mean? (To discover the range of styles you might use, see the Second Workshop section, especially Chapters 29 and 34.)

5. Consider how you will organize your essay. Climactic order is often useful when you are presenting an argument.

6. Structure your paragraphs as carefully as you structure your essay. Try to include a topic sentence in each of your paragraphs (Chapter 23), and develop each paragraph in an orderly fashion.

7. Leave plenty of time to revise and edit your essay before submitting it to your intended audience.

8. Consult the chapter on slant (Chapter 33) to ensure that each of your words says exactly what you intend it to say.

> ## Writer's Choice
> Have you already made your case? Do you want to have your essay edited, or is it ready for its intended audience?

When you finish your draft, consider the following guidelines.

Guidelines for Revising an Argumentative Essay

- ☐ Why are you writing this essay? Will your audience know your opinion on your topic?
- ☐ What do you like best about your essay? Least? What is your strongest argument? Your weakest? How can you build on your essay's strengths and get rid of its weaknesses?
- ☐ Does your introduction capture your audience's attention, set out your topic, and let your audience know what you are arguing for or against?
- ☐ Do you logically and consistently support your main idea with appropriate details, facts, examples, and reasons? Have you effectively rebutted possible opposing arguments? Have you included anything that does not move your argument forward? Are there any important gaps in your information or your thinking? Have you saved your best argument to the last?
- ☐ Do you logically develop the body of your essay? Or should you experiment with rearranging your arguments?
- ☐ Does your conclusion clinch your argument?
- ☐ Are you satisfied with the mechanics of your draft (spelling, punctuation, and grammar), or is there something you'd like to check before you let an editor see your work?
- ☐ Have you left sufficient time to rethink and revise your draft?
- ☐ Is there anything in your draft that you would like your editor to help you with?

Writer's Choice

Is your draft ready for its intended audience? Or would you like an editor to make revising and editing suggestions?

If necessary, revise your work and prepare a clean double-spaced draft for your editor.

Revising and Editing Suggestions

Give your draft to your peer-editor, and share your writing variables. Encourage your editor to use the "Guidelines for Revising an Argumentative Essay" in this chapter and the checklists in Chapter 27. Your editor should also think about how he or she would answer the following questions.

Ask Your Peer-Editor

- ☐ What was your first impression of my work? Did it convince you? Will it convince my intended audience? In what ways?
- ☐ Is my purpose for writing clear? Have I expressed my thesis clearly? Have I supported my thesis with appropriate facts, incidents, reasons, examples, or other specific evidence? Have I used any unsupported generalizations? Have I treated opposing arguments (and my audience) with respect?
- ☐ What part of my essay is clearest? Most effective? In what way? Is anything unclear? Why? What can I do to make it clearer?
- ☐ What is my best argument? My weakest? What makes you say so?
- ☐ Have I properly emphasized my important points? If not, what needs more emphasis?
- ☐ Have I overemphasized or stated anything at too great a length? If so, what should I shorten or omit?
- ☐ Can you easily tell how I have organized my information – that I have used climactic organization or another form of organization? (See Chapter 25.) Is the organization logical and easy to follow? Are the topic sentences for paragraphs easy to find and understand? Does one paragraph lead smoothly and logically to another? Is the overall organization of the essay clear?
- ☐ Did you spot any obvious errors in the argument I've presented? Should I rework anything?
- ☐ Do you like my word choice and sentence structure? Are my spelling, punctuation, and grammar all right, or is there something I should still work on?

Writer's Choice

How can you make your essay distinctly yours? Can you test each sentence, each word – as your audience will – to be sure it does precisely what you want it to do?

When you are satisfied with the content and organization of your essay, proofread it for spelling, grammar, usage, and punctuation. Read it again to make sure it is an honest statement of the opinion you are expressing.

Publishing Suggestions

Polish your essay. If your argument is part of a letter, for example, to a local or federal politician, send it off. When the reply comes, check it against your original to see whether your audience has responded to all your points.

If some of your peers have presented an argument on your subject, you might post your work on a classroom bulletin board – or have an in-class debate – and invite the rest of your classmates to decide which argument is most effective, and why.

Or, you might set your argumentative essay into a letter to the editor and send it off to your local newspaper. (See Chapter 19.)

In the Company of Writers

The essay follows Basic Essay Structure. The introduction captures the reader's attention immediately because everyone has an opinion about TV advertising. The final question provides the writer's thesis statement and intrigues the reader as well.

The development portion contains three paragraphs. In the first paragraph, the writer hooks the reader with a question, then provides three detailed examples. The paragraph's final sentence suitably sums up the paragraph.

The High Price of Soft Sell
Ken MacMillan

We've all been told many times that television advertising is bad, that it is mindless and repetitive, that it appeals to the materialism in our nature, and that it uses half-truths and clever distortions to sell us products and services we don't need. Each of us, moreover, has personally been irritated and offended by commercials of the mindless "ring around the collar" variety, which grate on our nerves and offend our intelligence. Everyone joins in condemning the "word from our sponsor." But how do we reconcile this general attitude with the fact that we see commercials every day that are witty and entertaining?

Isn't it true that there are commercials that far surpass in quality the programs they interrupt? Think, for instance, of the Bell Telephone commercials with their superbly photographed scenes of people enjoying simple pleasures together while the sound track carries a nostalgic song like "Heart of my Heart" or "You'll Never Know." The actual message, that we should use long distance more to get in touch with old friends far away, is very quietly stated at the end. Or again, remember the aftershave commercial that makes fun of the old movie cliché, "Thanks, I needed that," to suggest how fresh and awake we will feel after using the product. In both these cases, the commercial message is largely implied rather than stated. A different type is the "Coke adds life" commercial with its lively scenes of people working and playing hard and quenching their thirst with icy bottles of Coke. Sentiment, humor, excitement are used effectively in these three examples of advertising at its most attractive.

The first sentence of the third paragraph not only links to the previous paragraph, but also hooks the reader again by pointing out the "danger to us all." After presenting examples of bad commercials (in a series of questions), the writer ends with an effective rhetorical fragment which points out the idea of this paragraph: all commercials are dangerous.

Commercials like this, however, present a particular kind of danger to us all. It is easy to dismiss a commercial with some local car dealer reading strained witticisms from the aptly named idiot cards. They affront our intelligence so flagrantly that we are in no danger of being persuaded by their pleadings. But how do we react when the commercial message is presented with such wit that it is entertaining? Do we even think of the implications behind the messages? Do we think that in these inflationary days Bell perhaps should not be encouraging us to spend even more money on useless long distance calls? Do we really believe that a slap in the face with a handful of scented alcohol makes us feel fresh? Or do we consider what a bottle of sugared soft drink does to our diets, not to mention our teeth? Probably not.

The first sentence of the fourth paragraph states the topic of the paragraph in a general way. The next sentence restates it in a way that applies to the writer's audience: "We have the tendency ..." The third sentence provides an example of the tendency, while the remainder of the paragraph relates the tendency to the writer's main concern, commercials that are witty and entertaining.

Advertising confronts us with the contemporary discrepancy between morality and proficiency. We have the tendency today to praise anything well done even if the thing is not worth doing. Our heroes are quarterbacks who have the ultimately useless skill of throwing a football further than anyone else. So our advertising agencies pay large sums of money to imaginative men and women to make art subservient to commerce. It is not surprising that commercials are skillful when more money is spent on creating a thirty-second commercial than on making the thirty-minute program it interrupts; we have to ask if we are not suffering from a confusion of values here. Perhaps we should ask if human virtues are any longer virtues when applied to a bad end. Is intelligence, in the mad scientist or the mad ad man, something to be praised when its effect is destructive or corrupting?

The conclusion sums up the main point of the essay: resist well-made commercials. Notice how the first sentence of this paragraph answers the question posed in the last sentence of the introductory paragraph.

What is disturbing about TV advertising, then, is not that it is so bad; rather, what should worry us is that it is so good. Its glossy, polished competence presents us with a meretricious beauty. We need to be able to make a clear distinction between what is said and how it is being said. We need to resist the lure of "good" advertising.

Smoking in Public Places

Meldon Ellis, student

The issue of smoking in public has become of increasing concern to nonsmokers. Living in a free country, we as citizens have individual rights. On this issue, the nonsmoker unequivocally deserves the right to be free from the annoyance of cigarette smoke in public places. The smoker, of course, has the right to decide whether or not he or she smokes. However, this right should definitely not extend to the point of causing irritation to others. When smoking in public infringes upon a nonsmoker's right to inhale clean air, when it causes the nonsmoker to cough or suffer adverse physiological effects, then we have reached a point when it must be regulated by law.

Generally, when we think of the potential health hazards surrounding smoking, we think in terms of dangers for the smoker as opposed to dangers for the nonsmoking public. Indeed, most of the information we receive on the topic tends to reinforce our thinking. Recently, however, the public health authorities have directed their concern towards the detrimental effects of tobacco smoke to nonsmokers. The Canadian Medical Association announced that at least thirteen percent of our population is sensitive to cigarette smoke. Though this figure includes persons with emphysema, asthma, bronchitis, hay fever, and heart disease, the average nonsmoker is also subject to reactions from cigarette smoke. These reactions range from eye irritation, coughing, and nasal symptoms, to headaches and even dizziness.

According to the Canadian Lung Association, sidestream smoke, the smoke that is exhaled, contains twice as much nicotine as the mainstream smoke inhaled by the smoker. Conclusive evidence to date suggests that sidestream smoke contains three times as much benzopyrene (a cancer-causing agent), and up to fifty times more ammonia than mainstream smoke.

Some would like to see more legislation to establish nonsmokers' rights. On one side of the argument we have the smokers, who champion that regulating this area of personal choice threatens the individual freedom this country was built upon. Unsurprisingly, this side receives support from the cigarette company executives, who maintain that in opening ourselves to this type of legislation, we are in effect leaving ourselves wide open to increased government restriction in every area of our lives. The nonsmokers, diametrically opposed to this view, simply feel that when in public places they should be afforded the right to inhale clean air without the hindrance of tobacco smoke.

If this issue could be resolved effectively through mutual respect and common courtesy, I could see no reason for government legislation. But, in concluding, I must state that an individual's right to smoke ends when the smoke of his cigarette reaches the nose of another person in a public place, who might suffer irritating or distressful consequences.

All Things Are Connected

Chief Seattle

The President in Washington sends word that he wishes to buy our land. But how can you buy or sell the sky? The land? The idea is strange to us. If we do not own the freshness of the air and the sparkle of the water, how can you buy them?

Every part of this earth is sacred to my people. Every shining pine needle, every sandy shore, every mist in the dark woods, every meadow, every humming insect. All are holy in the memory and experience of my people.

We know the sap which courses through the trees as we know that blood courses through our veins. We are part of the earth and it is part of us. The perfumed flowers are our sisters. The bear, the deer, the great eagle, these are our brothers. The rocky crests, the juices in the meadow, the body heat of the pony, and man, all belong to the same family.

The shining water that moves in the streams and rivers is not just water, but the blood of our ancestors. If we sell you our land, you must remember that it is sacred. Each ghostly reflection in the clear waters of the lakes tells of events and memories in the life of my people. The water's murmur is the voice of my father's father.

The rivers are our brothers. They quench our thirst. They carry our canoes and feed our children. So you must give to the rivers the kindness you would give any brother.

If we sell you our land, remember that the air is precious to us, that the air shares its spirit with all the life it supports. The wind that gave our grandfather his first breath also receives his last sigh. The wind also gives our children the spirit of life. So if we sell you our land, you must keep it apart and sacred, as a place where man can go to taste the wind that is sweetened by the meadow flowers.

Will you teach your children what we have taught our children? That the earth is our mother? What befalls the earth befalls all the sons of the earth.

This we know: the earth does not belong to man, man belongs to the earth. All things are connected like the blood that unites us all. Man did not weave the web of life, he is merely a strand in it. Whatever he does to the web, he does to himself.

One thing we know: our god is also your god. The earth is precious to him and to harm the earth is to heap contempt on its creator.

Your destiny is a mystery to us. What will happen when the buffalo are all slaughtered? The wild horses tamed? What will happen when the secret corners of the forest are heavy with the scent of many men and the view of the ripe hills is blotted by talking wires? Where will the thicket be? Gone! Where will the eagle be? Gone! And what is it to say goodbye to the swift pony and the hunt? The end of living and the beginning of survival.

When the last Red Man has vanished with his wilderness and his memory is only the shadow of a cloud moving across the prairie, will these shores and forests still be here? Will there be any of the spirit of my people left?

We love this earth as a newborn loves its mother's heartbeat. So, if we sell you our land, love it as we have loved it. Care for it as we have cared for it. Hold in your mind the memory of the land as it is when you receive it. Preserve the land for all children and love it, as God loves us all.

As we are part of the land, you too are part of the land. This earth is precious to us. It is also precious to you. One thing we know: there is only one God. No man, be he Red Man or White Man, can be apart. We are brothers after all.

Your Writing

1. Does the title of each essay in this chapter reveal the topic of the essay and the attitude of the author toward the topic? Does yours do so? Will your title make your audience want to read or listen to your essay? Why?

2. Have you followed the same basic essay structure as Ken MacMillan has followed? Would arranging your essay differently have made it more effective? Less effective? Why?

3. In your journal, comment on your writing. What did you learn from writing your argumentative essay? Is there any part of your process that you would modify when you write your next argumentative essay? Why?

6 Long Narration

"Story-telling, story-listening, and story-reading are among the oldest and most enduring of civilized, indeed human, pleasures."

Boyd Litzenger, **Story**

If you have already experimented with short narratives (Chapter 1), you know that a narrative tells a story. For this writing project you can tell a more involved story.

WRITING PROJECT

> Write a narrative that is at least 300 words long on a subject of your choice.

Exploring and Prewriting Suggestions

1. Try to explore several ideas for stories so that you hit on the best possible one for this project. Be sure to save all the ideas you don't use.

a) Have a look at the exploring suggestions in Chapter 1. Many are useful for this longer writing project.

b) Skim the writing at the end of this chapter and in the appendix. Is there a story that you would like to experiment with or add to? Perhaps tell from a different point of view? Or tell in a different place and time?

c) In a small group, tell a story based on something that happened either to you or to someone you know. Don't hesitate to stretch the truth or even lie, if it improves your story. Be sure to maintain eye contact with your audience so that you can gauge the effect of your story.

d) Form a group of four or five, and agree on a **genre** (such as adventure, mystery, romance, or science fiction) to write in. Each group member can begin to draft a story, and then, at a signal, pass his or her draft to the right. The next group member then reads the story and continues it in a logical way. At another signal, drafts are again passed to the right, and new writers work on them. Continue until the original authors get their stories back. They can then complete their drafts. Groups should end up with four or five different stories to share within the group. They might select one to share with the class.

e) Freewrite for fifteen minutes beginning with an opening of your choice, or start with, "As Bobbi sat down at her computer, it suddenly started to talk to her."

f) With a partner, choose two characters from two different films or pieces of literature. Imagine the characters in a conflicting situation and then create a dialogue, story, play, or rap session for them. Together, try to resolve the conflict.

g) Select a human interest story from the newspaper and develop a narrative based on it.

h) Imagine that you are a famous person from history, an entertainer, a world leader, or a famous scientist, and recall an incident in your life that contributed to your fame. Using the persona you have selected, try to write a page or more about the incident.

i) What stories do the following photographs bring to mind? Jot down a few possibilities and then explore one of them.

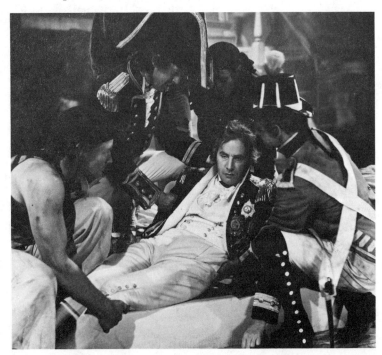

> ### Writer's Choice
> Have you discovered a topic for your narrative? Are you ready to begin your draft? Or do you want to brainstorm some more?

2. If you feel that you need to brainstorm in order to generate further ideas, approaches, and appropriate supporting details, consult Chapter 22. The following brainstorming techniques are particularly useful for narratives: Experience/Write; Senses Cluster; Positive Cluster; Negative Cluster; and possibly the Cause-and-Effect Flowchart.

3. Among the incidents that you explored, one may involve **conflict**, a struggle against something or someone. If you've already written a short narration, you probably already know that conflict can be a physical struggle, a battle of wits with another person, a struggle with nature or society, or even a struggle within yourself. Identify the conflicts in your story, and decide how you will approach them. Are they the most important thing in your narrative? Or, for example, is your character development more important?

> ### Writer's Choice
> Have you considered your writing variables – audience, purpose, format, and voice – or do you want to think about them as you draft?

Begin to draft your narrative as soon as you feel that you have sufficient material for it.

Drafting Suggestions

1. Feel free to invent or imagine. Sometimes, writers find that "stretching the truth" improves their stories. Even if your narrative is based on an incident from your own life, don't feel obliged to stick to the truth if your story is improved as a result – but keep your story believable.

2. Grab your reader's interest with your title and your opening. Experiment with different openings. Try dialogue, questions, a mood-setting description, or a single word such as "WHAM!"

3. Bring your narrative to life for your audience. Action, reaction, and dialogue can help your audience experience your story. If you're stuck, get your classmates to role-play your narrative. Encourage them to improvise actions and dialogue, and then use these in your writing.

4. Use vivid imagery, or word pictures, that appeal to the senses. Imagery will help your audience see, hear, feel, and even smell and taste, what happens in your narrative. Notice how the following sentences make the reader see and hear what happens through Steinbeck's use of a comparison, expressive verbs, and exact nouns.

> Pepe's wrist *flicked like the head of a snake*. The [knife] blade seemed to *fly open* in mid-air, and with a *thump* the point *dug* into the redwood post, and the black handle *quivered*.
>
> John Steinbeck, **Flight**

Writer's Choice

Do you want to include dialogue and description to help you to develop your characterization and plot? If so, how can you establish your characters and make their speech distinctive, so that you can present your dialogue without speech tags, such as "she cooed" or "he squealed"?

5. Experiment with the organization of your narrative. Although narratives are often organized in **chronological** or time order, you can organize yours as you wish. For example, beginning *in medias res* (in the middle of things) is one way to capture the attention of your audience. You can then introduce past details as needed. (See the use of this technique in "The Dirt Bike," at the end of this chapter.)

6. Use paragraphing as a writing tool. Short, punchy paragraphs can build tension or move a story along quickly. Long paragraphs can create a mood, call up a scene, or explore a thought in depth. There is no hard and fast rule to paragraphing narration. A single word, or even a few letters, might express a thought; on the other hand, a writer may write a story using only one long paragraph.

7. Build to the climax or turning point of your narrative. Longer narratives often build up to a climax. Using very short paragraphs just before the climax can create suspense; however, using several short sentences in a longer paragraph may work better. Experiment and see which works best for you. (Here's where a word processor becomes invaluable; you can rearrange long paragraphs into smaller ones within seconds, to see the effect.)

8. Work for sentence variety. (For more on sentence variety, see Chapter 30.) Try to create the same movement in your sentences as is in the action they are relating. For example, in telling about a runaway car on a canyon highway, one long, sweeping sentence is probably more effective than several jerky ones. How would you write about the final moments of a hockey game and the final winning goal? As one long sentence or several short ones? Why?

9. Make sure your point of view is consistent. If you begin telling your narrative in the first person (*I*), do not switch halfway through to the third person (*he* or *she*).

Writer's Choice
Would you like to tell your story in the first or the third person? Which do you think would be more effective for your story? Why?

10. Bring your narrative to a satisfying conclusion.

When you have completed your draft, consider the following guidelines.

Guidelines for Revising a Long Narration

☐ Why have you written this narrative? Is your purpose for writing clear?

☐ What is the strongest part of your narrative? The weakest? How can you build on the strengths and get rid of the weaknesses?

☐ What have you done to bring your characters to life? How have you shown your characters' thoughts and feelings? Will your audience care about your characters?

☐ How have you begun your narrative? Will your opening "grab" the attention of your audience, or should you experiment with another beginning?

☐ Does everything that you include – characters, plot, dialogue, description – advance your narrative? Is there anything that you should perhaps save for another occasion? Is your plot or story line believable?

☐ Look at how you have used description. Do your descriptions bring to life the people, places, and things in your narrative? In your description, do you appeal to all of your audience's senses?

☐ Have you used dialogue? Does the talk "sound real"? Would more dialogue make your narrative more effective? Why? Have you established your characters so that you don't always need to use speech tags?

☐ Why would your audience want to read (or listen to or perform) your narrative? Are your content, word choice, sentence structure, tone, and so on appropriate to your audience? Is there anything in your narrative that might confuse your audience? If so, how could you fix that?

☐ Does your ending bring your narrative to a satisfying conclusion?

☐ Is your title catchy?

☐ Is there anything in your draft that you would like your editor to help you with?

Writer's Choice

Is your narration ready for your intended audience? Or would you like an editor to see it first?

If necessary, revise your work and prepare a clean double-spaced draft for your editor.

Revising and Editing Suggestions

Give your draft to your peer-editor, and share your writing variables. Encourage your editor to use the "Guidelines for Revising a Long Narration" in this chapter and the checklists in Chapter 27. Your editor should also think about how he or she would answer the following questions.

Ask Your Peer-Editor

- ☐ What was your first impression of my narrative? How did it make you feel? Why?
- ☐ How do you think I feel about my story? How do you think my audience will feel about it? What makes you think so?
- ☐ What did you like most about my narrative? Least? Why? How can I build on the strengths of my piece and get rid of the weaknesses?
- ☐ Did you find my plot and characters interesting and believable? Is there sufficient conflict? Can you find the climax? Did my title and first sentence capture your interest? Did you find my ending satisfying? What changes would you suggest?
- ☐ Does the narrative encourage you to see, hear, and feel what happened? If not, how might I improve it?
- ☐ Is the sequence of events clear? Does everything that I have included contribute to the development of my narrative? Have I included all important details? Do I need to explain anything further? Does the narrative need more details to be clear and understandable?
- ☐ Is my dialogue realistic? Do my speech tags work well? If there is a problem with my speech tags, how do you think I could improve them?
- ☐ Have I maintained a consistent point of view? (Have I consistently used *I* or *he* or *she*?)
- ☐ Have I kept my tenses clear and consistent? (Are all my verbs either in the present tense or in the past tense?) Do my verbs give a strong sense of action?
- ☐ Are there any problems with spelling, punctuation, capitalization, or sentence structure?

Writer's Choice

Should you revise and have your peer-editor edit your new draft, or should you ask your teacher-editor to have a look at your work? Or are you ready to publish?

When you are satisfied with your draft, proofread it for spelling, grammar, usage, and punctuation. Reread it to make sure each word says exactly what you want it to say.

Publishing Suggestions

Polish your narrative, and then present your work to its final audience. If your classmates are your audience, you might gather in an authors' circle and take turns sharing your stories. Groups might work together to illustrate and publish their work in class anthologies. Consider giving your anthology to a senior citizens' home or to a local hospital. You might use your completed narrative as the basis for another piece of writing, such as a play or a video script.

In the Company of Writers

The Dirt Bike
Gina Garland, student

The ride down was quiet. Scarcely a car travelled the roads at this early hour. I stared into the distance. Out my side window, a cat's yellow eyes glistened in the fading moonlight.

"Are you sure about this?"

"Yes, I've got to try," I replied.

"You're not scared, are you?"

"Never," I stated matter-of-factly.

In truth though, I was shaking. My stomach growled and gurgled, both in fear and excitement. For a minute I was almost sick.

As the boys began unloading the trailer, I broke into a sweat. To avoid panic I turned my attention towards my surroundings. I was in a gravel pit, much like every other gravel pit I had seen. But this one had many grassy hills, with winding snakey paths for dirt bikers to use. The sun was just beginning to poke over the huge surrounding gravel mountains. As I scanned the horizon, a brown jackrabbit leapt into the shade of a big Manitoba pine, safe from the first rays of dawn.

V R O O O O M ! !

The noise couldn't have rung through my ears any more loudly had a cannon gone off. This time I knew there was no holding down breakfast.

"I really don't want you to go," mother had stressed repeatedly. "I'm going to worry about you all day," she added. But I was independent and besides, the boys had promised they wouldn't drive fast. Still, I found it hard to sleep the night before. As I tossed and turned, I recalled the first time I'd met Rob and Chris. They had been playing for a hockey team, The Boiler Makers. I was the manager. Afterwards, the three of us had become great friends and now they were about to introduce me to their favourite pastime – DIRT BIKE RIDING!

V R O O O O M ! !

The engine of the cold yellow machine screamed again. I was brought back to frightening reality. The boys were waiting. I swallowed hard and glanced over at Chris, dressed in bright green, large riding boots with the Cooper trademark on the side, gloves like those I'd seen worn by a goalie, and a helmet covering his blonde head. His bike coughed out huge clouds of grey smoke.

Chris tossed me a helmet which to my surprise, my trembling hands were able to fit over my head. It was too big and slipped right over my eyes. For a split second my tension was relieved and we all laughed. The helmet was soon adjusted and I could see the yellow beast once again.

The bike shook as my weary legs allowed me to mount it. I sat as close to Chris as I could.

"Now remember to keep your legs up and don't worry about falling, 'cause you won't," he said as soothingly as he could. I wrapped my fingers around the passenger strap and held on tight. Looking down I saw my knuckles had turned an off-white.

"Hold on!" someone yelled.

The bike leapt forward. The noise was deafening and my eyes were glued shut. I tried to pretend I was somewhere else, home maybe, but nothing helped. We hit a large bump and my eyes flung open! We travelled in a large cloud of dust and soon my eyes began to redden and ache. Ahead of us, Rob had his bike wide open. Chris was taking it easy, for my sake.

Blurs that were once trees raced past my eyes. Every corner brought a new obstacle which we conquered in turn. We were in rough terrain, yet nothing seemed to stop us. We rode up and down steep hills, and even over fallen trees. Then the bike turned, heading towards the forest. We crashed through the brush – as in a scene from the *Road Warriors*. (This wild and roaring machine had no limits.) Chris and I were aboard the "King of the Jungle" and as we raced and screamed, everything from the one jackrabbit to a small family of deer scattered as we neared.

My eyes were no longer closed. My butterflies had gone. I allowed the cool morning wind to whine and cry through my helmet, and my once pale face flushed with excitement. I was suddenly aware of everything around me. My head was clear of thought or worry. I was wild. I was crazy ... I WAS FREE ! ! !

from *Never Cry Wolf*
Farley Mowat

Quite by accident I had pitched my tent within ten yards of one of the major paths used by the wolves when they were going to, or coming from, their hunting grounds to the westward; and only a few hours after I had taken up residence one of the wolves came back from a trip and discovered me and my tent. He was at the end of a hard night's work and was clearly tired and anxious to go home to bed. He came over a small rise fifty yards from me with his head down, his eyes half-closed, and a preoccupied air about him. Far from being the preternaturally alert and suspicious beast of fiction, this wolf was so self-engrossed that he came straight on to within fifteen yards of me, and might have gone right past the tent without seeing it at all, had I not banged my elbow against the tea kettle, making a resounding clank. The wolf's head came up and his eyes opened wide, but he did not stop or falter in his pace. One brief, sidelong glance was all he vouchsafed to me as he continued on his way.

It was true that I wanted to be inconspicuous, but I felt uncomfortable at being so totally ignored. Nevertheless, during the two weeks which followed, one or more wolves used the track past my tent almost every night – and never, except on one memorable occasion, did they evince the slightest interest in me.

By the time this happened I had learned a good deal about my wolfish neighbors, and one of the facts which had emerged was that they were not nomadic roamers, as is almost universally believed, but were settled beasts and the possessors of a large permanent estate with very definite boundaries.

The territory owned by my wolf family comprised more than a hundred square miles, bounded on one side by a river but otherwise not delimited by geographical features. Nevertheless there *were* boundaries, clearly indicated in wolfish fashion.

Anyone who has observed a dog doing his neighborhood rounds and leaving his personal mark on each convenient post will have already guessed how the wolves marked out *their* property. Once a week, more or less, the clan made the rounds of the family lands and freshened up the boundary markers – a sort of lupine beating of the bounds. This careful attention to property rights was perhaps made necessary by the presence of two other wolf families whose lands abutted on ours, although I never discovered any evidence of bickering or disagreements between the owners of the various adjoining estates. I suspect, therefore, that it was more of a ritual activity.

In any event, once I had become aware of the strong feeling of property rights which existed amongst the wolves, I decided to use this knowledge to make them at least recognize my existence. One evening, after they had gone off for their regular nightly hunt, I staked out a property claim of my own, embracing perhaps three acres, with the tent at the middle, and *including a hundred-yard long section of the wolves' path.*

Staking the land turned out to be rather more difficult than I had antici-pated. In order to ensure that my claim would not be overlooked, I felt obliged to make a property mark on stones, clumps of moss, and patches of vegeta-tion at intervals of not more than fifteen feet around the circumference of my claim. This took most of the night and required frequent returns to the tent to consume copious quantities of tea; but before dawn brought the hunters home the task was done, and I retired, somewhat exhausted, to observe the results.

I had not long to wait. At 0814 hours, according to my wolf log, the leading male of the clan appeared over the ridge behind me, padding homeward with his usual air of preoccupation. As usual he did not deign to glance at the tent; but when he reached the point where my property line intersected the trail, he stopped as abruptly as if he had run into an invisible wall. He was only fifty yards from me and with my binoculars I could see his expression very clearly.

His attitude of fatigue vanished and was replaced by a look of bewilder-ment. Cautiously he extended his nose and sniffed at one of my marked bushes. He did not seem to know what to make of it or what to do about it. After a minute of complete indecision he backed away a few yards and sat down. And then, finally, he looked directly at the tent and at me. It was a long, thoughtful, considering sort of look.

Having achieved my object – that of forcing at least one of the wolves to take cognizance of my existence – I now began to wonder if, in my ignorance, I had transgressed some unknown wolf law of major importance and would have to pay for my temerity. I found myself regretting the absence of a weapon as the look I was getting became longer, yet more thoughtful, and still more intent.

I began to grow decidedly fidgety, for I dislike staring matches, and in this particular case I was up against a master, whose yellow glare seemed to become more baleful as I attempted to stare him down.

The situation was becoming intolerable. In an effort to break the impasse I loudly cleared my throat and turned my back on the wolf (for a tenth of a second) to indicate as clearly as possible that I found his continued scrutiny impolite, if not actually offensive.

He appeared to take the hint. Getting to his feet he had another sniff at my marker, and then he seemed to make up his mind. Briskly, and with an air of decision, he turned his attention away from me and began a systematic tour of the area I had staked out as my own. As he came to each boundary marker he sniffed it once or twice, then carefully placed *his* mark on the outside of each clump of grass or stone. As I watched I saw where I, in my ignorance, had erred. He made his mark with such economy that he was able to complete the entire circuit without having to reload once, or, to change the simile slightly, he did it all on one tank of fuel.

The task completed – and it had taken him no longer than fifteen min-utes – he rejoined the path at the point where it left my property and trotted off towards his home – leaving me with a good deal to occupy my thoughts.

David

Earle Birney

I

David and I that summer cut trails on the Survey,
All week in the valley for wages, in air that was steeped
In the wail of mosquitoes, but over the sunalive week-ends
We climbed, to get from the ruck of the camp, the surly

Poker, the wrangling, the snoring under the fetid
Tents, and because we had joy in our lengthening coltish
Muscles, and mountains for David were made to see over,
Stairs from the valleys and steps to the sun's retreats.

II

Our first was Mount Gleam. We hiked in the long afternoon
To a curling lake and lost the lure of the faceted
Cone in the swell of its sprawling shoulders. Past
The inlet we grilled our bacon, the strips festooned

On a poplar prong, in the hurrying slant of the sunset.
Then the two of us rolled in the blanket while round us the cold
Pines thrust at the stars. The dawn was a floating
Of mists till we reached to the slopes above timber, and won

To snow like fire in the sunlight. The peak was upthrust
Like a fist in a frozen ocean of rock that swirled
Into valleys the moon could be rolled in. Remotely unfurling
Eastward the alien prairie glittered. Down through the dusty

Skree on the west we descended, and David showed me
How to use the give of shale for giant incredible
Strides. I remember, before the larches' edge,
That I jumped a long green surf of juniper flowing

Away from the wind, and landed in gentian and saxifrage
Spilled on the moss. Then the darkening firs
And the sudden whirring of water that knifed down a fern-hidden
Cliff and splashed unseen into mist in the shadows.

III

One Sunday on Rampart's arête a rainsquall caught us,
And passed, and we clung by our blueing fingers and bootnails
An endless hour in the sun, not daring to move
Till the ice had steamed from the slate. And David taught me

How time on a knife-edge can pass with the guessing of fragments
Remembered from poets, the naming of strata beside one,
And matching of stories from schooldays.... We crawled astride
The peak to feast on the marching ranges flagged

By the fading shreds of the shattered stormcloud. Lingering
There it was David who spied to the south, remote,
And unmapped, a sunlit spire on Sawback, an overhang
Crooked like a talon. David named it the Finger.

That day we chanced on the skull and the splayed white ribs
Of a mountain goat underneath a cliff-face, caught
On a rock. Around were the silken feathers of hawks.
And that was the first I knew that a goat could slip.

IV

And then Inglismaldie. Now I remember only
The long ascent of the lonely valley, the live
Pine spirally scarred by lightning, the slicing pipe
Of invisible pika, and great prints, by the lowest

Snow, of a grizzly. There it was too that David
Taught me to read the scroll of coral in limestone
And the beetle-seal in the shale of ghostly trilobites,
Letters delivered to man from the Cambrian waves.

V

On Sundance we tried from the col and the going was hard.
The air howled from our feet to the smudged rocks
And the papery lake below. At an outthrust we baulked
Till David clung with his left to a dint in the scarp,

Lobbed the iceaxe over the rocky lip,
Slipped from his holds and hung by the quivering pick,
Twisted his long legs up into space and kicked
To the crest. Then grinning, he reached with his freckled wrist

And drew me up after. We set a new time for that climb.
That day returning we found a robin gyrating
In grass, wing-broken. I caught it to tame but David
Took and killed it, and said, "Could you teach it to fly?"

VI

In August, the second attempt, we ascended The Fortress,
By the forks of the Spray we caught five trout and fried them
Over a balsam fire. The woods were alive
With the vaulting of mule-deer and drenched with clouds all the morning,

Till we burst at noon to the flashing and floating round
Of the peaks. Coming down we picked in our hats the bright
And sunhot raspberries, eating them under a mighty
Spruce, while a marten moving like quicksilver scouted us.

VII

But always we talked of the Finger on Sawback, unknown
And hooked, till the first afternoon in September we slogged
Through the musky woods, past a swamp that quivered with frog-song,
And camped by a bottle-green lake. But under the cold

Breath of the glacier sleep would not come, the moon-light
Etching the Finger. We rose and trod past the feathery
Larch, while the stars went out, and the quiet heather
Flushed, and the skyline pulsed with the surging bloom

Of incredible dawn in the Rockies. David spotted
Bighorns across the moraine and sent them leaping
With yodels the ramparts redoubled and rolled to the peaks,
And the peaks to the sun. The ice in the morning thaw

Was a gurgling world of crystal and cold blue chasms,
And seracs that shone like frozen saltgreen waves.
At the base of the Finger we tried once and failed. Then David
Edged to the west and discovered the chimney; the last

Hundred feet we fought the rock and shouldered and kneed
Our way for an hour and made it. Unroping we formed
A cairn on the rotting tip. Then I turned to look north
At the glistening wedge of giant Assiniboine, heedless

Of handhold. And one foot gave. I swayed and shouted.
David turned sharp and reached out his arm and steadied me,
Turning again with a grin and his lips ready
To jest. But the strain crumbled his foothold. Without

A gasp he was gone. I froze to the sound of grating
Edge-nails and fingers, the slither of stones, the lone
Second of silence, the nightmare thud. Then only
The wind and the muted beat of unknowing cascades.

VIII

Somehow I worked down the fifty impossible feet
To the ledge, calling and getting no answer but echoes
Released in the cirque, and trying not to reflect
What an answer would mean. He lay still, with his lean

Young face upturned and strangely unmarred, but his legs
Splayed beneath him, beside the final drop,
Six hundred feet sheer to the ice. My throat stopped
When I reached him, for he was alive. He opened his gray

Straight eyes and brokenly murmured "over ... over."
And I, feeling beneath him a cruel fang
Of the ledge thrust in his back, but not understanding,
Mumbled stupidly, "Best not to move," and spoke

Of his pain. But he said, "I can't move.... If only I felt
Some pain." Then my shame stung the tears to my eyes
As I crouched, and I cursed myself, but he cried,
Louder, "No, Bobbie! Don't ever blame yourself.

I didn't test my foothold." He shut the lids
Of his eyes to the stare of the sky, while I moistened his lips
From our water flask and tearing my shirt into strips
I swabbed the shredded hands. But the blood slid

From his side and stained the stone and the thirsting lichens,
And yet I dared not lift him up from the gore
Of the rock. Then he whispered, "Bob, I want to go over!"
This time I knew what he meant and I grasped for a lie

And said, "I'll be back here by midnight with ropes
And men from the camp and we'll cradle you out." But I knew
That the day and the night must pass and the cold dews
Of another morning before such men unknowing

The ways of mountains could win to the chimney's top.
And then, how long? And he knew ... and the hell of hours
After that, if he lived till we came, roping him out.
But I curled beside him and whispered, "The bleeding will stop.

You can last." He said only, "Perhaps.... For what? A wheelchair,
Bob?" His eyes brightening with fever upbraided me.
I could not look at him more and said, "Then I'll stay
With you." But he did not speak, for the clouding fever.

I lay dazed and stared at the long valley,
The glistening hair of a creek on the rug stretched
By the firs, while the sun leaned round and flooded the ledge,
The moss, and David still as a broken doll.

I hunched to my knees to leave, but he called and his voice
Now was sharpened with fear. "For Christ's sake push me over!
If I could move.... Or die...." The sweat ran from his forehead,
But only his eyes moved. A hawk was buoying

Blackly its wings over the wrinkled ice.
The purr of a waterfall rose and sank with the wind.
Above us climbed the last joint of the Finger
Beckoning bleakly the wide indifferent sky.

Even then in the sun it grew cold lying there.... And I knew
He had tested his holds. It was I who had not.... I looked
At the blood on the ledge, and the far valley. I looked
At last in his eyes. He breathed, "I'd do it for you, Bob."

IX

I will not remember how nor why I could twist
Up the wind-devilled peak, and down through the chimney's empty
Horror, and over the traverse alone. I remember
Only the pounding fear I would stumble on It

When I came to the grave-cold maw of the bergschrund … reeling
Over the sun-cankered snowbridge, shying the caves
In the névé … the fear, and the need to make sure It was there
On the ice, the running and falling and running, leaping

Of gaping greenthroated crevasses, alone and pursued
By the Finger's lengthening shadow. At last through the fanged
And blinding seracs I slid to the milky wrangling
Falls at the glacier's snout, through the rocks piled huge

On the humped moraine, and into the spectral larches,
Alone. By the glooming lake I sank and chilled
My mouth but I could not rest and stumbled still
To the valley, losing my way in the ragged marsh.

I was glad of the mire that covered the stains, on my ripped
Boots, of his blood, but panic was on me, the reek
Of the bog, the purple glimmer of toadstools obscene
In the twilight. I staggered clear to a firewaste, tripped

And fell with a shriek on my shoulder. It somehow eased
My heart to know I was hurt, but I did not faint
And I could not stop while over me hung the range
Of the Sawback. In blackness I searched for the trail by the creek

And found it .... My feet squelched a slug and horror
Rose again in my nostrils. I hurled myself
Down the path. In the woods behind some animal yelped.
Then I saw the glimmer of tents and babbled my story.

I said that he fell straight to the ice where they found him,
And none but the sun and the incurious clouds have lingered
Around the marks of that day on the ledge of the Finger,
That day, the last of my youth, on the last of our mountains.

Your Writing

1. How have the other writers begun their stories? How have you begun yours? Which was most effective? Why? Would your story have been as effective if you had started *in medias res*, for example? Would you like to experiment with a different beginning on another occasion?

2. Examine the use of transitional devices in these selections. (You might also skim some of the short stories in the appendix.) Have you used similar devices? If not, you might experiment with them in your next long narration.

3. How do you develop the conflict in your narrative? How have the other authors done so? Which works best? Why?

4. In your journal, comment on your writing. What did you learn from writing your narration? Have you saved all of the ideas that you didn't use? Is there anything that you might like to experiment with in your next long narration?

7 Autobiography

"When writing about oneself, one must strive to be truthful. Truth is more important than modesty."

Roald Dahl, **Boy**

Entertainers, politicians, business leaders, and other celebrities usually write autobiographies because they are proud of themselves and the things they have done. In their writing, they can set out their own view of events and describe themselves in the best possible light. They may care deeply about a particular philosophy or issue and use an autobiography as a forum for their thoughts. And sales figures show that readers love to get an inside look at the worlds of entertainment, politics, and big business.

Here is your chance to write a brief autobiography. A few paragraphs, a letter, or a poem will be sufficient for this project.

WRITING PROJECT

> Write an autobiography to enable a reader to get acquainted with you.

Exploring and Prewriting Suggestions

1. Consider using one or more of the following suggestions to help you develop material for your autobiography.

a) Pair up with someone you do not know (or do not know very well). Facing your partner, and making eye contact, ask, "Who are you?" Your partner should respond in a word or two. After a five- or six-second pause for reflection, repeat your question: "Who are you?" Your partner should provide a *different* response. Pause again, and then repeat the procedure as many times as possible (at least a dozen times). Then switch roles so that your partner can ask you the same question.

This procedure will help you to uncover who you really are. After the first five or six responses, you will begin to search deeper and provide insightful answers to the question, "Who are you?"

b) Jot down some of the highlights of your life. A highlight is an event that – in some way – affected your life for better or worse. In other words, if the event had not occurred, you would be a different person. From your list, select the four stories or anecdotes that you feel would most interest your classmates. Then, in a group of four, share one of your highlights. Seat yourself comfortably or move around freely as you present. Begin by stating when and where your highlight occurred, and then tell your story. Limit yourself to about a minute. After each of the other members of your group has presented one anecdote, present your second one, and so on, until all group members have presented four anecdotes. You can present your four highlights in any order you want: randomly, chronologically, or climactically. (If time permits, present the highlights to the whole class instead of in a small group.)

When you're through, make a note in your journal of the details you included and whatever else comes to mind that might help you to draft your autobiography.

c) Bring to school a photograph of yourself that means a lot to you. Freewrite for ten minutes on everything that comes to mind as you look at your photo.

d) You might experiment with writing a twelve-line poem about yourself, beginning each line with "I am," as the ancient Celtic poet Amairgen did in the following:

I am the wind that blows o'er the sea;
I am the wave of the deep;
I am the bull of seven battles;
I am the eagle on the rock;
I am a tear of the sun;
I am the fairest of plants;
I am a boar for courage;
I am a salmon in the water;
I am a lake in the plain;
I am the word of knowledge;
I am the head of the battle-dealing spear;
I am the god who fashions fire [=thought] in the head.

You might find that your poem needs only polishing to become your final piece.

e) You might experiment with composing an **acrostic** using your name and adjectives that describe you. For example, read over this partial acrostic. You can already get a fair idea of the kind of person John Foster is.

Judgmental
Orderly
Honest
Nit-picky

Forthright
O
S
T
E
R

f) Create a fifty-word thumbnail sketch of yourself for your school yearbook. As a variation, you might write a fifty-word sketch of yourself ten years ago (or ten years in the future).

2. Adopt a persona, and freewrite for fifteen minutes in the role of your character.
a) You may want to tell about yourself using a persona, as Gino Nasato (page 110) has done.
b) You might prefer to draft a fictional autobiography. How might one of your favorite characters from a book or film – such as Little Red Riding Hood, Macbeth, or Batman – describe himself or herself?
c) Or you might assume that you are a historical personality, a scientist, actor, world leader, author, poet, playwright, and so on. (You may need to do some research before ghostwriting an autobiography as someone else.)

Writer's Choice

Will you use your own voice, or will you adopt a persona?

---

3. Try to think about your audience, purpose, format, and voice both before and as you draft. Although these may change as you write, being aware of them will help you to focus and structure your autobiography, and to select appropriate details for it.

4. You might like to try to find a thread to unify your autobiography. The thread might be a generalization about your life or a quality or characteristic you want to emphasize. Have a look at the following autobiographical excerpts, and find the thread that unifies each.

I was born in Fort Macleod, Alberta, in the foothills of the Canadian Rockies – an area of extreme temperatures and mirages…. When I was two feet off the ground, I collected broken glass and cats. When I was three feet off the ground, I made drawings of animals and forest fires. When I was four feet off the ground, I discovered boys and bicycles. When I was five feet, I began to dance to rock n' roll and sing the top ten … songs around campfires, and someone turned me on to Lambert, Hendrix, and Ross and Miles Davis and later Bob Dylan.

Joni Mitchell

In our house on North Congress Street in Jackson, Mississippi, where I was born, the oldest of three children, in 1909, we grew up to the striking of clocks. There was a mission-style oak grandfather clock standing in the hall, which sent its gong-like strokes through the living room, dining room, kitchen, and pantry, and up the sounding board of the stairwell. Through the night, it could find its way into our ears; sometimes, even on the sleeping porch, midnight could wake us up. My parents' bedroom had a smaller striking clock that answered it. Though the kitchen clock did nothing but show the time, the dining room clock was a cuckoo clock with weights on long chains, on one of which my baby brother, after climbing on a chair to the top of the china closet, once succeeded in suspending the cat for a moment. I don't know whether or not my father's Ohio family, in having been Swiss back in the 1700s before the first three Welty brothers came to America, had anything to do with this; but all of us have been time-minded all our lives. This was good at least for a future fiction writer, being able to learn so penetratingly, and almost first of all, about chronology. It was one of a good many things I learned almost without knowing it; it would be there when I needed it.

Eudora Welty, from **One Writer's Beginnings**

Thinking about your life can help you to find your connecting thread. Make up a list of questions, such as the following, to help you discover a pattern, detail, or theme to unify your autobiography.
• What are my three best characteristics? My three worst?
• What people played a significant role in my life? Why?
• What events have been significant in my life? Why?
• Of what accomplishments am I proud? Of what actions am I ashamed?
• What are my goals?

You might then list events that illustrate the generalization or characteristic you want to emphasize. For example:

I am outspoken

gets me into trouble	*gets me out of trouble*
embarrassed Mom's guests sent to principal got a black eye	saved the family from fire chosen class president won a case in student court

---

Writer's Choice

Are you ready to draft your autobiography? Or do you want to explore a bit more?

---

5. If you need more information, try two or three of the exploration techniques in Chapter 22. The following might be especially useful: Pro/Con Ladders or Cause-and-Effect Flowchart.

6. Try developing a few Absurd Analogies. These can loosen up your thinking and uncover facts and ideas you didn't realize you knew. If you have trouble thinking of your own analogies, you might develop the following.

- I am like a leaky faucet.
- People think of me as a lion.
- I'm a stew.
- I'm a marble.
- I'm a stony canyon.

You can begin to draft as soon as you feel that you have sufficient material for your autobiography.

Drafting Suggestions

1. Consider how you will organize your autobiography. Autobiographies are often organized chronologically or climactically. See Chapter 25 for other possible forms of organization. Be prepared to experiment if you're not satisfied with the way your autobiography shapes up.

2. Show, don't tell, what you're like. Use description, quotations, examples, and narrative illustrations to show your personal qualities.

3. Maintain a consistent style in your writing. Experiment with styles until you find one that suits you and the events you have decided to include. The following are four different ways of saying the same thing. Can you think of others?

Straightforward style: I was born in Baddeck, Nova Scotia, on July 15, 1975.

Colloquial style: I showed up in Baddeck on July 15, 1975.

Ironic style: (saying the opposite of what you mean): From the hour of my birth on July 15, 1975, I was a model child; my behavior was screamingly perfect.

Humorous style: It was absolutely marvellous the way so many people turned out for my birth on July 15, 1975. Even my mother was there.

Writer's Choice

Which style would you like to experiment with in your autobiography?

Experiment with different styles by writing a few sentences with the same content but in different styles.

4. Use your format as a writing tool. Can you best capture yourself in a song? In a job application? In a personal letter? In a few paragraphs?

5. Skim the autobiographies at the end of this chapter. They may provide pointers for drafting your own story.

When you have completed your draft, consider the following guidelines.

Guidelines for Revising an Autobiography

□ Why are you writing this autobiography? Is your purpose clear? Will your audience be interested in what you have to say?

□ What do you like best about your draft? Least? How can you build on the strengths of your draft and get rid of any weaknesses?

□ Have you used a unifying thread? What is it? Have you explored other possible ways of unifying your autobiography?

□ Have you provided anecdotes, description, and quotations to make your story interesting and lively?

□ Do you effectively present yourself in your introduction and make your audience want to read on? Have you tried to tell your whole life story instead of a particularly interesting part of it?

□ Do you logically develop the content of your autobiography? Will everything that you include add to your audience's understanding of you? Is there anything else that you should include?

□ Does your ending bring your writing to an appropriate conclusion? Does it sum up your autobiography, leave your audience with a question, or do some other thing?

□ Are you satisfied with the mechanics of your draft (spelling, punctuation, and grammar), or is there something you'd like to check before you let an editor see your work?

□ Is there anything in your draft that you would like your editor to help you with?

If necessary, revise your work and prepare a clean double-spaced draft for your editor.

Revising and Editing Suggestions

Give your draft to your peer-editor, and share your writing variables. Encourage your editor to use the "Guidelines for Revising an Autobiography" in this chapter and the checklists in Chapter 27. Your editor should also think about how he or she would answer the following questions.

Ask Your Peer-Editor

- What was your first impression of my work? Did my autobiography interest you? Do you think it will interest my audience? In what ways?
- Is my purpose for writing clear? Have I chosen the best possible style for my purpose and audience?
- Which part of my autobiography reveals the most about me? What is the most important thing you learn (or should learn)? Have I presented it clearly? If not, how could I improve it?
- Does a thread run through my autobiography? What is the thread? Does it clearly unify the piece?
- Does my autobiography include everything you'd like to know about me? What would you add? Have I tried to tell you too much? If so, what would you leave out? Can you easily recognize my qualities and accomplishments?
- Does my autobiography include the strongest possible word, sentence, and paragraph choices? What would you change? Why?

Publishing Suggestions

Polish your autobiography and then present it to your final audience. You might, for example, submit it as a job application. Or, you might play a game of "Who Am I?" A volunteer might read several autobiographies aloud and invite the rest of the class to guess the subject of each.

In the Company of Writers

Tai-Po Market
(New Territories, Hong Kong)
Rebecca Lo, student

I used to live in the country
Where there were liquid fields of rice,
And Grandmas carried infants on their backs,
And Grandpas yoked home the daily water;
And when I moved from the country
That image was embedded in my mind,
So that I can remember,
Even enclosed in concrete,
What it felt like
To have to walk
137 steps up
To my home,
All the while terrified
That the dog next door
Will make me his noon meal.
How high up it seemed;
Surrounded by squares of land,
It stood like all the others
Aging in the humidity.

I returned to the country,
And suddenly
My image,
The one that was 10 years out of style,
Shattered like green glass.
They tore down my home
To build a better one;
I shall never hear the neighbour's dog
Growling at me as I creep by
Anymore;
Running water is now in existence;
Grandpas are not needed;
Baby carriages were invented;
Grandmas are not needed.

Oh, yes
And there's a new dam –
Tonnes of concrete
Where a river used to flow;
And even now,
I ask myself,
Where are the rice fields?
They are no more.

Foot Loose

Gino Nasato, student

I am a foot. I was pulled kicking from warm security one almost-forgotten August day. It was not so much the cold that startled me that fateful morning, as my realization that I was forever attached to a stumbling lout named Gino Nasato. Still, life was grand during the early months; Gino simply lay on his back and played baby. At the age of eight months, though, our peaceful co-existence was shattered when the lout started to walk. Oh, to describe the pain of those early years brings back horrid memories. I was kicked, I was bumped, I was stubbed, and I was stomped. Self-preservation in mind, I fought back with a vengeance. For the first ten years I tripped him as often as possible. The knees and the elbows hated me for the pain I inflicted, and his poor mother despised me for the clothes she was always mending. Through the high-school years I was continually abused. If I wasn't being butted painfully against a soccer ball, I was risking toes and heels with daring slides into second base. My only hope was that Gino would get a soft desk job after graduating. I hoped in vain.

First it was logging and those terrible spiked boots. Tired of logging, Gino went to sea, where hard, slippery, cold steel decks awaited me. I still remember the light-footed feeling of the floor disappearing under me whenever the ship rolled. In his twenty-first year Gino decided to go to Europe. The dreams I had – visions of French music and Gino sitting in cafés, resting me on stools. Oh, the naïveté of a foot! That beggar shuffled me through Paris subways, blistered me in Athens midday heat, and hobbled me on cobbled streets in Amsterdam. My only respite came when we hit the beaches of Greece. For two glorious months I was in Dr. Scholl's heaven: cool wet sand to leave my autograph in and sparkling surf to soak my calluses. But, alas, it wasn't to last; chasing a pretty face who had cold feet, Gino wound up in Vancouver.

It was about this time that I felt my toes had been stepped on long enough. I formulated a plan with the ankle, and during one of Gino's efforts to kick up his heels, we twisted severely. I was tickled pink when the doctor prescribed one month of total rest, with me kept in an elevated position. Finally, after twenty-three years, I was put on the pedestal I rightfully deserved. With some guidance from me, Gino has finally recognized the prominent role I play in his life. He's now back studying at school, which gives me plenty of time to relax. In fact, things have been going so well lately, I'm thinking of passing on my secrets to other downtrodden feet. I might even start a revolution. After all, just think of all the foot soldiers I could recruit!

from *Lady Oracle*
Margaret Atwood

I loved dancing school. I was even quite good at the actual dancing, although Miss Flegg sometimes rapped her classroom pointer sharply on the floor and said, "Joan dear, I wish you would stop thumping." Like most little girls of that time I idealized ballet dancers, it was something girls could do, and I used to press my short piggy nose up against jewelry store windows and goggle at the china music-box figurines of shiny ladies in brittle pink skirts, with roses on their hard ceramic heads, and imagine myself leaping through the air, lifted by a thin man in black tights, light as a kite and wearing a modified doily, my hair full of rhinestones and glittering like hope. I worked hard at the classes, I concentrated, and I even used to practice at home, wrapping myself in a discarded lace bathroom curtain I had begged from my mother as she was about to stuff it into the garbage can. She washed it first though; she didn't like dirt. I longed for a pair of satin toe shoes, but we were too young, Miss Flegg explained, the bones in our feet had not hardened. So I had to settle for black slippers with an unromantic elastic over the instep.

Miss Flegg was an inventive woman; I suppose these days she would be called creative. She didn't have much scope for her inventiveness in the teaching of elementary steps to young children, which was largely a matter of drill, but she let herself go on the annual spring recital. The recital was mostly to impress the parents, but it was also to impress the little girls themselves so they would ask to be allowed to take lessons the next year.

Miss Flegg choreographed the entire program. She also constructed the sets and props, and she designed the costumes and handed out patterns and instructions to the mothers, who were supposed to sew them. My mother disliked sewing but for this event she buckled down and cut and pinned just like all the other mothers. Maybe she hadn't given up on me after all, maybe she was still making an effort.

Miss Flegg organized the recital into age groups, which corresponded to her dancing classes. There were five of them: Teenies, Tallers, Tensies, Tweeners and Teeners. Underneath her spiny exterior, the long bony hands, the hair wrenched into a bun, and the spidery eyebrows, done, I realized later, with a pencil, she had a layer of sentimentality, which set the tone for her inventions.

I was a Teenie, which was in itself a contradiction in terms, for as well as being heavier than everyone else in the class I had begun to be taller. But I didn't mind, I didn't even notice, for I was becoming more wildly excited about the recital every day. I practiced for hours in the basement, the only place I was allowed to do it after I had accidentally knocked over and broken my mother's white-and-gold living-room lamp in the shape of a pineapple, one of a set. I twirled beside the washing machine, humming the dance music in my head, I curtseyed to the furnace (which in those days still burned coal), I swayed in and out between the sheets drying double-folded on the line, and when I was exhausted I climbed the cellar stairs, out of breath and covered with coal dust, to be confronted by my mother with her mouth full of pins. After I'd been scrubbed I would be stood on a chair and told to turn around slowly. I could barely hold still even to have my costumes tried on.

My mother's impatience was almost equal to my own, though it was of another sort. She may have started to regret sending me to dancing school. For one thing, I wasn't getting any slimmer; for another, I now made twice as much noise as I had at first, especially when I rehearsed my tap number in my patent leather shoes with metal tips toe and heel, on the hardwood of the hall floor, which I had been ordered not to do; and for another, she was having trouble with the costumes. She'd followed the instructions, but she couldn't get them to look right.

There were three of them, for the Teenies were doing three numbers: "Tulip Time," a Dutch ballet routine for which we had to line up with partners and move our arms up and down to simulate windmills; "Anchors Aweigh," a tap dance with quick turns and salutes (this was soon after the end of the war and military motifs were still in vogue); and "The Butterfly Frolic," a graceful number whose delicate flittings were more like my idea of what dancing should be. It was my favorite, and it had my favorite costume too. This featured a gauzy skirt, short, like a real ballerina's, a tight bodice with shoulder straps, a headpiece with spangled insect antennae, and a pair of colored cellophane wings with coathanger frames, supplied by Miss Flegg.

The wings were what I really longed for but we weren't allowed to put them on until the day itself, for fear of breakage.

But it was this costume that was bothering my mother. The others were easier: the Dutch outfit was a long full skirt with a black bodice and white sleeves, and I was the rear partner anyway. The "Anchors Aweigh" number had middy dresses with naval braid trim, and this was all right too since they were high-necked, long-sleeved and loose around the waist. I was in the back row because of my height; I hadn't been picked as one of the three stars, all with Shirley Temple curls, who were doing solos on drums made out of cheese crates. But I didn't mind that much: I had my eye on the chief butterfly spot. There was a duet with the only boy in class; his name was Roger. I was slightly in love with him. I hoped the girl who was supposed to do it would get sick and they would have to call me in. I'd memorized her part as well as my own, more or less.

I stood on the chair and my mother stuck pins into me and sighed; then she told me to turn around slowly, and she frowned and stuck in more pins. The problem was fairly simple: in the short pink skirt, with my waist, arms and legs exposed, I was grotesque. I am reconstructing this from the point of view of an adult, an anxious, prudish adult like my mother or Miss Flegg; but with my jiggly thighs and the bulges of fat where breasts would later be and my plump upper arms and floppy waist, I must have looked obscene, senile almost, indecent; it must have been like watching a decaying stripper. I was the kind of child, they would have thought back then in the early months of 1949, who should not be seen in public with so little clothing on. No wonder I fell in love with the nineteenth century: back then, according to the dirty postcards of the time, flesh was a virtue.

My mother struggled with the costume, lengthening it, adding another layer of gauze to conceal the outlines, padding the bodice; but it was no use. Even I was a little taken aback when she finally allowed me to inspect myself in the three-sided mirror over her vanity table. Although I was too young to be much bothered by my size, it wasn't quite the effect I wanted. I did not look like a butterfly. But I knew the addition of the wings would make all the difference. I was hoping for magic transformations, even then.

The dress rehearsal was in the afternoon, the recital the same evening. They were so close together because the recital was to be held, not in the room over the butcher shop, which would have been too cramped, but in a public school auditorium, rented for a single Saturday. My mother went with me, carrying my costumes in a cardboard dress box. The stage was cramped and hollow-sounding but was redeemed by velvet curtains, soft purple ones; I felt them at the first opportunity. The space behind it was vibrating with excitement. A lot of the mothers were there. Some of them had volunteered to do makeup and were painting the faces of theirs and other people's daughters, the mouths with dark-red lipstick, the eyelashes with black mascara which stiffened them into spikes. The finished and costumed girls were standing against the wall so as not to damage themselves, inert as temple sacrifices. The bigger pupils were strolling about and chatting; it wasn't as important to them, they had done it before, and their numbers were to be rehearsed later.

"Tulip Time" and "Anchors Aweigh" went off without a hitch. We changed costumes backstage, in a tangle of arms and legs, giggling nervously and doing up each other's hooks and zippers. There was a crowd around the single mirror. The Tallers, who were alternating with us, did their number, "Kitty Kat Kapers," while Miss Flegg stood in the wings, evaluating, waving time with her pointer, and occasionally shouting. She was wrought up. As I was putting on my butterfly costume, I saw my mother standing beside her.

She was supposed to be out in the front row where I'd left her, sitting on a folding chair, her gloves in her lap, smoking and jiggling one of her feet in its high-heeled open-toed shoe, but now she was talking with Miss Flegg. Miss Flegg looked over at me; then she walked over, followed by my mother. She stood gazing down at me, her lips pressed together.

"I see what you mean," she said to my mother. When resenting this scene later on, I always felt that if my mother hadn't interfered Miss Flegg would have noticed nothing, but this is probably not true. What she was seeing, what they were both seeing, was her gay, her artistic, her *spiritual* "Butterfly Frolic" being reduced to something laughable and unseemly by the presence of a fat little girl who was more like a giant caterpillar than a butterfly, more like a white grub if you were really going to be accurate.

Miss Flegg could not have stood this. For her, the final effect was everything. She wished to be complimented on it, and wholeheartedly, not with pity or suppressed smiles. I sympathize with her now, although I couldn't then. Anyway, her inventiveness didn't desert her. She leaned down, placed her hand on my round bare shoulder, and drew me over to a corner. There she knelt down and gazed with her forceful black eyes into mine. Her blurred eyebrows rose and fell.

"Joan, dear," she said, "how would you like to be something special?"

I smiled at her uncertainly.

"Would you do something for me, dear?" she said, warmly.

I nodded. I liked to help.

"I've decided to change the dance a little," she said. "I've decided to add a new part to it: and because you're the brightest girl in the class, I've chosen you to be the special, new person. Do you think you can do that, dear?"

I had seen enough of her to know that this kindness was suspect, but I fell for it anyway. I nodded emphatically, thrilled to have been selected. Maybe I'd been picked to do the butterfly duet with Roger, maybe I would get bigger, more important wings. I was eager.

"Good," said Miss Flegg, clamping her hand on my arm. "Now come and hop into your new costume."

"What am I going to be?" I asked as she led me away.

"A mothball, dear," she answered serenely, as if this were the most natural thing in the world.

Her inventive mind, and possibly earlier experiences, had given her a fundamental rule for dealing with situations like this: if you're going to be made to look ridiculous and there's no way out of it, you may as well pretend you meant to. I didn't learn this rule till much later, not consciously. I was wounded, desolated in fact, when it turned out that Miss Flegg wanted me to remove my cloudy skirt and spangles and put on one of the white teddy-bear costumes the Teensies were using for their number, "Teddy Bears' Picnic." She also wanted me to hang around my neck a large sign that said MOTHBALL, "So they'll all understand, dear, what you're supposed to be." She herself would make the sign for me, in the interval between the rehearsal and the performance.

"Can I wear my wings?" I asked. It was beginning to seep through to me, the monstrousness of the renunciation she was asking me to make.

"Now, who ever heard of a mothball with wings?" she said in what was supposed to be a jocular but practical manner.

Her idea was that once the butterflies had finished their cavorting, I would lumber in among them in the white suit and the sign, and the butterflies would be coached to scatter. It would be so cute, she told me.

"I liked the dance the way it was," I said tentatively. "I want it to be the way it was." I was on the verge of crying; probably I had already begun.

Miss Flegg's manner changed. She put her face down close to mine so I could see the wrinkles around her eyes up close and smell the sour toothpaste smell of her mouth, and said, slowly and distinctly, "You'll do as I say or you won't be in the dance at all. Do you understand?"

Being left out altogether was too much for me. I capitulated, but I paid for it. I had to stand in the mothball suit with Miss Flegg's hand on my shoulder while she explained to the other Teenies, sylphlike in their wispy skirts and shining wings, about the change in plans and my new, starring role. They looked at me, scorn on their painted lips; they were not taken in.

I went home with my mother, refusing to speak to her because she had betrayed me. It was snowing lightly, though it was April, and I was glad because she had on her white open-toed shoes and her feet would get wet. I went into the bathroom and locked the door so she couldn't get at me; then I wept uncontrollably, lying on the floor with my face against the fluffy pink bath mat. Afterwards I pulled the laundry hamper over so I could stand on it and look into the bathroom mirror. My made-up face had run, there were black streaks down my cheeks like sooty tears and my purple mouth was smudged and swollen. What was the matter with me? It wasn't that I couldn't dance.

My mother pleaded briefly with me through the locked bathroom door, then she threatened. I came out, but I wouldn't eat any dinner: someone else besides me would have to suffer. My mother wiped the makeup off my face with Pond's Cold Cream, scolding me because it would have to be done over, and we set out again for the auditorium. (Where was my father? He wasn't there.)

I had to stand enviously in the wings, red-faced and steaming in the hated suit, listening to the preliminary coughs and the scraping of folding chairs, then watching while the butterflies tinkled through the movements I myself had memorized, I was sure, better than any of them. The worst thing was that I still didn't understand quite why this was being done to me, this humiliation disguised as a privilege.

At the right moment Miss Flegg gave me a shove and I lurched onto the stage, trying to look, as she had instructed me, as much like a mothball as possible. Then I danced. There were no steps to my dance, as I hadn't been taught any, so I made it up as I went along. I swung my arms, I bumped into the butterflies, I spun in circles and stamped my feet as hard as I could on the boards of the flimsy stage, until it shook. I threw myself into the part, it was a dance of rage and destruction, tears rolled down my cheeks behind the fur, the butterflies would die; my feet hurt for days afterwards. "This isn't me," I kept saying to myself, "they're making me do it"; yet even though I was concealed in the teddy-bear suit, which flopped about me and made me sweat, I felt naked and exposed, as if this ridiculous dance was the truth about me and everyone could see it.

The butterflies scampered away on cue and much to my surprise I was left in the centre of the stage, facing an audience that was not only laughing but applauding vigorously. Even when the beauties, the thin tiny ones, trooped back for their curtsey, the laughter and clapping went on, and several people, who must have been fathers rather than mothers, shouted "Bravo mothball!" It puzzled me that some of them seemed to like my ugly, bulky suit better than the pretty ones of the others.

After the recital Miss Flegg was congratulated on her priceless touch with the mothball. Even my mother appeared pleased. "You did fine," she said, but I still cried that night over my thwarted wings. I would never get a chance to use them now, since I had decided already that much as I loved dancing school I was not going back to it in the fall. It's true I had received more individual attention than the others, but I wasn't sure it was a kind I liked. Besides, who would think of marrying a mothball? A question my mother put to me often, later, in other forms.

Your Writing

1. In what style have you written your autobiography? Which of the examples is it most like? In what ways? Which is it least like?

2. What unifying thread has each author used? Have you used a thread to pull your autobiography together? Does your unifying thread capture you accurately? How would a different unifying thread change your autobiography? (On another occasion, you might experiment with using a different unifying theme.)

3. Is the format of your autobiography like one used by one of the other writers: a poem, an essay using a persona, or a novel excerpt? Or have you used another format? On another occasion would you like to experiment with writing your autobiography in a different format?

4. In your journal, comment on your writing. What did you learn from writing your autobiography? Is there any part of your process that you would modify if you were to write another autobiography? Why?

8　Biography

"The history of the world is but biography of great men [and women]."

*Thomas Carlyle, **Hero and Hero Worship***

For some people, writing a biography is easier than writing an autobiography. It often takes less effort to write about others than to reveal ourselves.

WRITING PROJECT

> Write a biography of someone you know well or about whom you can find out a great deal.

Exploring and Prewriting Suggestions

1. Jot down the names of a few people about whom you might like to write a biography. Then use one or more of the following suggestions to help you develop material for your biography.

a) Select a character from one of the stories you are studying, one of the authors, a poet, a character from a play, a film director, a historical character, a film or television actor, a rock singer, or a world leader, and present four highlights from that person's life. (See 1(b) in Chapter 7.) You can role-play the person of your choice.

> ## Writer's Choice
> Will you have to research before presenting your four highlights? Do you want to use props and costumes in your presentation?

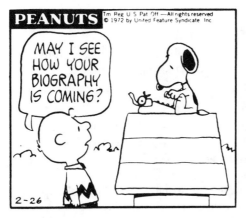

After presenting your four highlights, make a note in your writing journal about your subject. What parts of your presentation most interested your audience? How can you build on that interest as you draft your biography?

b) Do an acrostic of the name of one or more of the people on your list. (See 1(e) in Chapter 7 for more information about acrostics.)

c) Compose a "You are …" poem about one or more of the people on your list. (See the "I am …" poem on page 103, and adapt it for your subject.)

d) Freewrite for fifteen minutes about your pet.

e) Who is your most interesting relative or friend? Make a journal entry about some of the highlights in his or her life.

f) Draft a fifty-word Who's Who entry for one of your peer-editors. (If everyone in the class does this, you might post your completed biographies so that everyone can see "Who's Who" in your class.)

g) Draft an epitaph or eulogy for one of your subjects.

> ### Writer's Choice
> Have you chosen a subject for your biography? Are you ready to draft? Or do you want to explore a bit more?

2. Think about why your subject is important to you and why you want to write about him or her. You might try drafting several statements that set out why you are writing (your purpose) and who you are writing to (your audience). For example:
- I intend to write an article for our school paper to introduce a friend who is running for the student council.
- I must introduce a speaker at a school assembly so that students and teachers will know a little about her before she speaks.
- I have been invited to a "roast" for a friend of mine. I have to deliver a speech giving a humorous account of his life.

> ### Writer's Choice
> Will your audience be more interested in factual details or in finding out what kind of person your subject is?

3. If you know your subject personally, you might want to interview him or her. Use the Newspaper Reporter's Questions (Chapter 22) to help you get started.

4. Try to find a thread to unify your biography. (See Chapter 7 for more information about unifying threads.)

> ### Writer's Choice
> What theme can you use to unify your biography? Is your subject, for instance, a gifted storyteller? Does he or she have a special interest (such as motor racing) or a particular hobby or talent (such as playing lacrosse)?

Drafting Suggestions

1. Consider how you will organize your biography. Most biographies are arranged in chronological order, but you may wish to use another method discussed in Chapter 25; one possibility is Comparison/Contrast. You might also look at Cause-and-Effect in Chapter 22. If you're not wholly satisfied with one form of organization, experiment with another. Your statement of purpose and your unifying thread may help you to organize your biography.

2. Decide on your approach to your subject. For example, will you use a straightforward style? Or will you use irony, poking fun at your subject by saying the opposite of what you mean? (To discover the range of styles you might use, see the Second Workshop section, especially Chapters 29 and 33.)

3. Show, don't tell, what your subject is like. If your unifying thread is your subject's unfailing honesty, provide an anecdote that illustrates this. Relate things your subject has said and done, and allow your reader to infer his or her personal qualities. You can also quote what others have said about your subject. Or you might combine these methods.

4. Use your format as a writing tool. Can you best capture your subject in an informative essay? A humorous ballad? A dialogue? A free-verse poem?

5. Skim the biographies at the end of this chapter. They may provide pointers for drafting your biography.

When you have completed your draft, consider the following guidelines.

Guidelines for Revising a Biography

- ☐ Why are you writing this biography? Is your purpose clear? Do you care about your subject? Will your audience be able to see that?
- ☐ What do you like best about your draft? Least? How can you build on the strengths of your draft and get rid of its weaknesses?
- ☐ Have you used a unifying thread? What is it? Have you explored other possible ways of unifying your biography?
- ☐ Have you provided anecdotes, description, and quotations to bring your subject to life for your audience?
- ☐ Do you logically develop the content of your biography? Will everything you have included add to your audience's understanding of your subject? Is there anything else that you should include?
- ☐ Does your ending bring your writing to a satisfying conclusion? Does it sum up your biography, leave your audience with a question, or do some other thing?
- ☐ Are you satisfied with the mechanics of your draft (spelling, punctuation, and grammar), or is there something you'd like to check before you let an editor see your work?
- ☐ Is there anything in your draft that you would like your editor to help you with?

Writer's Choice

Is your biography ready for your intended audience? Or would you like to revise it and have an editor look at it?

If necessary, revise your work and prepare a clean double-spaced draft for your editor.

Revising and Editing Suggestions

Give your draft to your peer-editor, and share your writing variables. Encourage your editor to use the "Guidelines for Revising a Biography" in this chapter and the checklists in Chapter 27. Your editor should also think about how he or she would answer the following questions.

Ask Your Peer-Editor

☐ What was your first impression of my work? What did my biography tell you about my subject that you didn't already know? Did it present information you did know in a new and interesting way? Do you think my biography will interest my audience? Why?

☐ Is my purpose for writing clear? Is my use of a unifying thread clear and effective?

☐ What part of my biography is clearest? Most effective? In what ways? Is anything unclear? Why? What can I do to make it clearer?

☐ Have I presented my subject as a real, living, breathing person? If not, what is needed?

☐ Can you easily recognize my subject's qualities? My subject's accomplishments?

☐ Have I chosen the best possible style and format for my subject and intended audience? If you don't think so, what would you suggest?

☐ Have I chosen words, sentences (or stanzas), and paragraphs effectively? Is there anything you would change? Why?

Writer's Choice

Is your biography ready for its intended audience? Or would you like your teacher-editor to see it first?

Publishing Suggestions

When you have revised your biography to your satisfaction, give it a final polish, and then present it to your final audience. Give your speech; gather eulogies, epitaphs, or obituaries in an appropriate class anthology; mail your biography as a valentine; submit your biography to the school yearbook; or choose a different creative way to present your work.

In the Company of Writers

Cry of the Athlete
Carol McIntyre, student

As the roar dies,
Your job is done,
You've brought fame to your school,
    But who are you?
    What is your name?
  Oh yeah,
    You're the athlete.

The record broken,
Your leg in pain,
Yet you won a trophy for your school,
But who are you?
    What is your name?
  Oh yeah,
    You're the athlete.

Your social life non-existent,
Your free time always filled,
You have to represent your school,
But who are you?
    What is your name?
  Oh yeah,
    You're the athlete.

Your game was lost,
Your name's been cursed,
Oh, how you let down your school,
    But who are you?
– though I know your name
  Oh yeah.

The game days die as the years go by,
The legs unable to function,
I call out from my chair,
    "I represented your school, won trophies,
      Don't you remember me?
      I was the athlete.

Yes, I was
    the athlete."

No one remembers.

The Joy of Live Theatre
from *The Vancouver Sun*, July 29, 1987
Jamie Portman

Canadian actor Robert Joy is enjoying a soft drink in his dressing room at the Helen Hayes Theatre. It's essential relaxation time before he dons a garish green monster suit and makes his first entrance in a hysterically funny new Broadway play called *The Nerd*.

And why must he take it easy? Because he knows that by the end of the performance he'll be exhausted.

"When I finish each act, I feel as though I've been playing a non-stop game of basketball," he explains. "But I have to admit it's fun!"

The Newfoundland-born Joy is the nerd of the title in the late Larry Shue's comedy, portraying a crass and awful houseguest who turns the life of his hapless host, played by Mark Hamill of *Star Wars* fame, into comic chaos.

It's his latest triumph in a decade-long career that has seen Joy work in film with such top directors as Woody Allen (*Radio Days*), Milos Forman (*Ragtime*) and Louis Malle (*Atlantic City*) and on stage doing everything from Shakespeare to Noel Coward.

Although film and TV pay better, Joy admits he can't stand it if he's away from live theatre too long.

"As far as I'm concerned, doing those films was a killer. I can't stand all the waiting you have to do on a film set between shooting of scenes. I was desperate to get back on stage."

Even so, after the experience of his cameo role in *Radio Days*, he'll work for Woody Allen any time.

"It was only two days' work, and it was the calmest set I've ever been on. In a film you're normally aware of all the pressures – of everything threatening to fall apart. With Woody, his self-assurance was so evident that it was like spending a pleasant Sunday afternoon at home."

Joy has lived and worked in New York since 1978, yet there's a part of him that still yearns for Newfoundland and wonders at the course his professional career has taken.

For one thing, he's a Rhodes Scholar who followed his sojourn at Memorial University in St. John's with three years at Oxford University's Corpus Christi College studying English language and literature.

But a longtime interest in theatre led to an involvement with Newfoundland's irreverent CODCO company when he returned home from England.

"CODCO is committed to being funny," is the company motto as set down in the current guidebook to the Canadian stage published by the Professional Association of Canadian Theatres.

That same guidebook continues to list Joy as one of the seven zany Newfoundlanders who make up the collective artistic leadership of CODCO.

This organization, with its emphasis on collective creation and improvisation, taught him a type of stage discipline unobtainable elsewhere.

"The core of my theatrical education was with CODCO. Looking back, it was like a dive into enchanted waters. Its big strength was that it made us take responsibility for creating our own work ourselves. It taught us what responsibility really means."

The Magic of Karen Kain
from *Maclean's*, November 28, 1988

Kain's rise to stardom was meteoric. In 1970, at 19, she became the National Ballet of Canada's youngest principal dancer. Three years later, she and company colleague Frank Augustyn won the prize for best *pas de deux* – and she won the silver medal as best ballerina – at the Moscow International Ballet Festival. By that time, she was already a favorite partner of Soviet-born superstar Rudolf Nureyev. Since then, she has continued to dazzle audiences around the world with her flawless technique, sensitivity to music and dramatic intensity. But, despite many offers to join other companies, she has stayed in Canada.

Kain's associates offer various explanations for her immense talent. According to Nureyev, she has "the capacity to throw herself completely into her roles, as well as that special radiance which lights up a whole stage." Veronica Tennant, the National's most famous principal dancer apart from Kain, stresses the importance of Kain's innate understanding of music. "From the very beginning," she said, "Karen has been able to make music visible – it just emanates from her." For her part, National Ballet founder Celia Franca says that Kain's success stems partly from her mental and emotional makeup. "She was clever enough to remain vulnerable," Franca declared. "She remained sensitive instead of getting hardened, cut and dried, and ultimately less artistic. But at the same time, she has had enough common sense to learn from her life." Toronto writer Urjo Kareda wrote that Kain is "distinguished by the boldness of her dreaming onstage."

Ballet requires an almost maniacal commitment to perfection. Even an artist with the rare genius and physical gifts of Kain has to engage in a daily battle of wills with her body to give a single inspired – and seemingly effortless – performance. Like most of the greatest dancers, Kain forms a vision of how she should move in a performance and then strains and drills until she gets as close as possible to that ideal. As New York City choreographer Eliot Feld, who created *Echo* for Kain in 1985, put it: "She'll denigrate her entire ability as a dancer simply because she's 18 inches away from where she's supposed to be. I say to her, 'Karen, nobody in the world notices if a dancer is 18 inches off her mark.' But any imperfection will depress her."

Recently, she experienced a debilitating setback: two months after announcing that she was pregnant with her first child last March, she suffered a miscarriage. But with characteristic self-discipline, she quickly resumed her career – and enthralled the New York critics during the company's performances there last summer. Tennant, who recently announced that she would end her own 25-year career in February [1989], said, "I would like to see Karen dance her heart out because she is dancing more beautifully than she's ever danced before."

Kain is clearly savoring the magic period in a dancer's life when undiminished physical prowess and inner maturity add up to the best performances of a lifetime. "I think you develop a better understanding of what carries across the footlights," she said in a recent interview. "And now, I am more able to control what I want to do rather than just going on adrenaline, which I did when I was young." From a technical standpoint, she was able to handle such demanding parts as the dual role of The Swan Queen/Black Swan at 19 – but being able to act the evil Black Swan convincingly was another matter. Said Kain: "I always looked like I couldn't tell a lie. There's nothing that will substitute for growing up and being more of a person to be a better actress."

An Interview with John Milton (1608–1674)
Chantal Phillips, student

John Milton was one of the most exceptional men of the seventeenth century. His academic excellence, which arose from the diligence of his scholarly days and from his European travels, as well as from his lively career as author of many pamphlets, poems, books, and letters, attests to his intelligence and greatness of mind. The fact that he is still studied by high-school students three hundred years after his death is, unfortunately, more a deterrent to discovering his wit and humour than a help. Studying for this interview, however, has led me to an understanding that Milton was an exceptional man as well as an enjoyable one.

ME: Thank you for coming, Mr. Milton. I have conjured up this image of you to answer some questions on your works and your life. Are you willing to allow my readers to know about you?

MILTON: Certainly. I always enjoy talking about myself, as it is the subject I know most about.

ME: You were always a lively youth, used to your own tutors and a freedom of study that let you become learned in many subjects by the age of fifteen. When you were sixteen you entered Christ's College, Cambridge. How did you react to the situation there?

MILTON: Before Cambridge I had gone to St. Paul's school from the age of twelve until I was fifteen. I always preferred having the freedom of a private tutor, but the resources at the school and my studies in Sallust, Horace, Virgil, and the New Testament (Patrick 423) kept me very busy. I enjoyed the atmosphere of the school and all my schoolmates.

When I got to Cambridge, however, composing all those trivial declamations became more of a bore. I felt I was being dragged from my studies. I disagreed with my tutor so much that I was rusticated. But I have to admit that my university career wasn't only study. I also filled my time with walks, plays, girls, and, most of all, my friends, especially Charles Diodati. I wrote some lovely poems in those days. Nothing that was a test of my true intellect, though.

ME: From what I've read, your life in the country when you returned to your family home for five years was a complete renunciation of your more carefree days at university …

MILTON: To a certain extent it was in reaction to a belief that I have held all my life, a belief that I was appointed for some great work which could only come to me as the outgrowth of a life of austerity (Amiel xi). The renunciation of my carefree days, as you call it, gave me time to study …

ME: I believe most of your biographers refer to this as your "Horton Period."

MILTON: Yes, that's correct. I left university for Horton and spent my time studying and enjoying the pastoral scenery around me. God has instilled into me, if into anyone, a vehement love of the beautiful. I used the natural setting often to express moods I felt in my poetry.

But, it's not quite true to say I completely gave up my social life to study. I lived at Horton but I continued to be involved in the cultural life of London. I wrote "Comus" and my poem "On Shakespeare" while at Horton.

ME: In 1634 "Comus" was performed at Ludlow Castle. It marks the beginning of your concentration on temptation themes (Patrick 424). The villain in this musical comedy makes a very good argument in favour of seduction. In "Lycidas" you even suggest the idea that if God allows the young to die, why not give in to temptation, "sport with Amaryllis in the shade" while you have time?

MILTON: Yes, but I end that particular poem by stating that "laborious days are wasted": eternal life lies ahead, does it not? As for being concerned with temptation themes, I'm not sure. I never looked at it like that. The times forced many people to re-evaluate their ideas on temptation; certainly I myself tried to convince many that what I said in "Lycidas" holds true.

ME: That reminds me of your involvement in the Puritan movement. Somehow your love life, music, women, society – none of these reconciles with the bleak Puritan outlook on the world as it should be.

MILTON: I suggest to you that the Puritans were not trying to enslave people by shackling them with rules and regulations and social codes of austerity; quite the contrary. We were trying to free the people of England from the tyranny of royalty. All men have the right to break contracts they make with rulers …

ME: I agree with the Puritan cause, but what I was trying to illustrate was that you have two definite sides to your personality. Your social side seems to have been overshadowed in your later years by that of the dedicated scholar who continually read and produced great works.

MILTON: Thank you for the compliment. Certainly my blindness, my deteriorating health, and the return of the monarchy all led me to a more reclusive life. They also gave me the opportunity to write my greatest and most challenging work, *Paradise Lost*.

ME: *Paradise Lost* certainly is a masterpiece, and I'll end with a question on it. When I studied this work in school, we related it to the politics of the age, and I noticed a few jabs at Roman Catholicism in it as well. Did you mean *Paradise Lost* to be a satire of the political situation of the times?

MILTON: No, I did not. That is the most interesting part of watching people criticize your works. *Paradise Lost* was mainly derived from my imagination, and of course I was inspired by the Bible. It was not, however, meant to be taken as satire. I must admit I did insert those pokes at the Roman Catholics but that is all. I felt it to be my life's work, and an effort to convey God's wisdom and providence to my fellowman (Patrick 425).

ME: Thank you very much, Mr. Milton.

Works Cited

Amiel, Leon, ed. The Complete Poetical Works of John Milton. New York: Universal Classics, 1968.

Patrick, J. Max. "Milton" in Encyclopedia of World Biography. 1973.

Your Writing

1. What methods – similar to those used in the biographies in this chapter – did you employ in your biography? For example, did you interview and quote your subject or anyone who knows your subject? Should you have? Why?

2. What unifying thread has each writer used? Have you used a thread to pull your biography together? How would your biography have been different if you'd used a different thread or theme? You might want to experiment with this on another occasion.

3. On another occasion, you might experiment with casting the information you gathered for this biography in a different format. For instance, you might rewrite it as a job application, as an interview, or as a news story. How would a different format or style change your biography?

4. In your journal, comment on your writing. What did you learn from writing your biography? Is there any part of your process that you would modify if you were to write another biography? Why?

9 Review

"I must tell you what I think. I must also tell you why I think it. I do not tell you what someone else says I should think. I do not tell you what you are to think. It's as simple as that."

Wayne Edmonstone

Areview is a kind of argumentative essay about a particular work of art in which a writer presents an opinion with reasons to back it up. But a good review includes more than a well-presented opinion, because review writers cannot assume that their readers know anything about the work under review. They must present information as well as an opinion about the work. Therefore, a good review usually combines information and opinion.

WRITING PROJECT

> Write a review of a book, a film, a play, a television program, a recording, or other work of art.

Exploring and Prewriting Suggestions

1. If you have not already selected a work of art to review, the following suggestions may help you to choose one.

a) In a small group, talk about the best (or worst) movies you have ever seen. Be sure to explain why you thought they were the best or worst, giving examples to back up your opinion.

b) What is your favorite television show? Freewrite for fifteen minutes in your journal about the show, giving as many reasons as you can to support your opinion. If you find yourself running out of ideas, write the name of the program over and over again until something else comes to mind.

c) Who is your favorite performer? Novelist? Poet? Persuade a classmate that your favorite is the best in his or her field.

d) Of everything you have read in your literature class this year, which piece did you like best? Do a Positive Cluster (Chapter 22).

e) Choose a textbook that you use in one of your classes. List all the things you like and dislike about the book.

© 1975 United Feature Syndicate, Inc.

2. The following suggestions provide a general introduction to reviewing particular art forms.

a) If you are reviewing a film, play, or television program, try to watch it at least twice. The first time, you can get a sense of how the story goes and a general feel for the plot and the acting. The second time through, you can view the work more critically. You can look for strengths, the quality of the acting, any inconsistencies, and so on.

b) If you are reviewing a recording, listen to it uncritically once or twice to get a sense of how it makes you feel and your overall reaction to it. Then listen to the lyric and melody of the recording. What do you think the artist was trying to say to you? Was he or she successful or unsuccessful? In what ways? Finally, try to assess the technical merit of the recording (whether it has been competently produced, whether tracks have been skilfully laid down, and so on).

c) When you review a painting, sculpture, example of architecture, or other work of art, focus first of all on how the work makes you feel, and why. Then try to understand what the artist wants to communicate to the audience, and decide whether he or she is successful. Further review of such a work often requires some specialized knowledge. For example, if you can, try to look at the work in the context of the artist's own development and in the context of the current state of the art (stream or school, as appropriate). If you can, assess the technical ability shown in the work.

d) A book review may be the most difficult kind of review to do, because so much of a book's impact is in the reader's imagination. A response to a book is, therefore, highly personal. When you review a book, talk about how it made you feel, and why. Set down its strong and weak points as you see them. Back up your opinions with examples. And don't be surprised if someone in your audience disagrees with you.

Writer's Choice

Have you given some thought to the work of art that you want to review and the special things you should consider as you review the work? Are you ready to draft, or do you want to explore further?

3. Before drafting your review, you might like to do one or more of the following.

a) Look up reviews of books, plays, movies, and other works of art in back copies of newspapers and magazines. (You'll also find reviews at the end of this chapter and one by Michael Darling in Chapter 34.) Jot down some notes about the kinds of information contained in the reviews: plot summary, critiques of acting, scenes or setting, and quality of the direction, inventiveness of the work, and so on. Try separating examples of genuine criticism from statements that simply promote controversy and readership, such as the following:

- This play is the worst thing to have happened to our country since World War II.
- The emotions of the actress ran the gamut from A to B.
- This is Mr. Smith's first novel. Let us hope it is his last.

Many critics thrive on the controversy that often follows unfavorable reviews, so be sure to read critically, and keep in mind that reviewing a work of art does not mean being unfair or destructive. Avoid making such statements unless they truly express your opinion of the work you are reviewing and you are prepared to back them up.

b) As many times as you can, read or watch or look at the work of art under review. After each viewing freewrite for ten minutes on everything that came to mind.

c) You might list the things that you liked and didn't like about the work of art you are reviewing, as one book reviewer did:

Liked	*Disliked*
interesting major characters (you care what happens to them)	poor minor characters (you never really get to know them)
convincing dialogue	long descriptions hold up the action
exciting scenes	confusing plot
well written	poor ending (nothing resolved)

Then jot down facts, examples, and quotations to support each item on your list.

d) You might use one of the exploration techniques in Chapter 22, such as a Positive Cluster (if you liked the work) or a Negative Cluster (if you didn't like it).

Writer's Choice

What work or subject have you chosen to review? Did it succeed in entertaining you, informing you, or convincing you of something?

4. Think about your audience. Is it likely that your audience already knows something about your subject? Does your audience consist mostly of people your own age who share your interest in films, television, mystery novels, or whatever? Where might you publish your review?

Writer's Choice

Have you settled on your writing variables – your purpose, audience, format, and voice – or do you want to think about them as you draft?

Drafting Suggestions

1. Identify what you are reviewing. (What is the title? Is it a book, a play, a film, a television show?) Give other information appropriate to the kind of work; for example, author and publisher (if a book); theatre (if a play); director (if a play or film); network, date, and time (if a television show); musicians and recording label (if a recording).

2. Decide on your approach to your topic. For example, will you use a straightforward style? Or will you use irony, poking fun at your subject by saying the opposite of what you mean? (To discover the range of styles you might use, see the Second Workshop section, especially Chapters 29 and 34.)

3. Let your audience know where you stand. Be opinionated. (But back up your opinions!) Be emphatic. Indeed, try to include something memorable – a pun, perhaps, or a witty quotation – so that your audience will remember your opinion.

4. Reveal some of the plot. If you review a novel, film, play, or television program, give enough of the plot to let your audience decide whether they wish to read or see the work. Tell enough to whet the interest of your audience, but do not tell the whole story; a review is not a summary. In fact, identifying the murderer in a mystery is, to a mystery fan, almost as bad as committing the murder yourself. (If you are reviewing a nonfiction book, you should give some idea of the information it contains.)

Writer's Choice

How will you support the opinion you express? Will you use examples and quotations or some other means?

5. Illustrate the specific points you are making. Fit your examples, quotations, and so on, into your own prose so that your review flows smoothly. (See Chapter 25.)

6. Use basic essay structure – introduction, development, conclusion. For your first review, this structure is easiest to follow. In your introduction, present your subject, arouse interest, and let your audience know how you feel about your subject. As you develop your review, offer evidence to support your opinion. To conclude, leave your audience with something to think about.

7. Check the punctuation of your titles. Titles of novels, nonfiction books, plays, recordings, and paintings and sculptures need to be underlined or italicized. Titles of radio or television shows, poems, short stories, essays, or single songs need quotation marks.

Writer's Choice

Have you shown your opinion of the work? Have you provided evidence to support your opinion? Is your review ready to be seen by an editor?

When you finish your draft, consider the following guidelines.

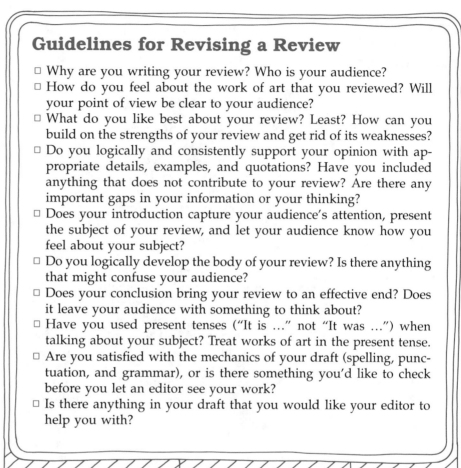

Guidelines for Revising a Review

□ Why are you writing your review? Who is your audience?

□ How do you feel about the work of art that you reviewed? Will your point of view be clear to your audience?

□ What do you like best about your review? Least? How can you build on the strengths of your review and get rid of its weaknesses?

□ Do you logically and consistently support your opinion with appropriate details, examples, and quotations? Have you included anything that does not contribute to your review? Are there any important gaps in your information or your thinking?

□ Does your introduction capture your audience's attention, present the subject of your review, and let your audience know how you feel about your subject?

□ Do you logically develop the body of your review? Is there anything that might confuse your audience?

□ Does your conclusion bring your review to an effective end? Does it leave your audience with something to think about?

□ Have you used present tenses ("It is ..." not "It was ...") when talking about your subject? Treat works of art in the present tense.

□ Are you satisfied with the mechanics of your draft (spelling, punctuation, and grammar), or is there something you'd like to check before you let an editor see your work?

□ Is there anything in your draft that you would like your editor to help you with?

If necessary, revise your work and prepare a clean double-spaced draft for your editor.

Writer's Choice

Why is it better not to edit your peer-editor's writing?

Revising and Editing Suggestions

Give your draft to your peer-editor, and share your writing variables. Encourage your editor to use the "Guidelines for Revising a Review" in this chapter and the checklists in Chapter 27. Your editor should also think about how he or she would answer the following questions.

Ask Your Peer-Editor

☐ What was your first impression of my review? Have I given you sufficient information to let you know what I think of my subject?

☐ Is my purpose for writing clear? Have I clearly expressed my opinion of the work? Have I properly supported my opinion with facts, reasons, examples, quotations, or other specific evidence? Have I used any unsupported generalizations?

☐ What part of my review is clearest? Most effective? In what ways? Is anything unclear? Why? What can I do to make it clearer?

☐ Have I overemphasized or stated anything at too great a length? Have I related too much of the plot? Is any of my criticism cruel and destructive instead of thoughtful? If so, what should I change?

☐ Can you easily tell how I have organized my information? Is my organization logical and easy to follow? Are my topic sentences for paragraphs easy to find and understand? Does each of my paragraphs lead smoothly and logically to the next? Is the overall organization of my review clear?

☐ Is my review convincing? That is, do you think my audience will feel as I do and either read or not read or see or not see the work I am reviewing?

☐ Do you like my word choice and sentence structure? Are my spelling, punctuation, and grammar all right? Is there anything I should still work on?

☐ Are my titles correctly punctuated?

When you are satisfied with your draft, proofread it for spelling, grammar, usage, and punctuation problems. Reread it to make sure that it honestly states your opinion.

Writer's Choice

Is your review ready for its intended audience? Or would you like your teacher-editor to have a look at it?

Publishing Suggestions

Polish your review. If other students are your intended audience, how can you best reach them? Through a class or school newspaper? Perhaps in a Reader's Circle in which you present your review? This might lead to a literature (or novel, play, or film) "Election." After everyone has presented a review, you can vote on what you'd most like to read or see.

In the Company of Writers

Review of *Watership Down*
Alexander Targ, student

The movie *Watership Down*, set in the English countryside sometime during the early 1900s, has an exciting plot as well as a number of other features that make it a most enjoyable film. The movie, directed by Martin Rosen, is an animated version of Richard Adams's book of the same title. *Watership Down* follows the adventures of a small group of rabbits, who learn from a clairvoyant member of the group that their warren is doomed to destruction and that they must migrate to a new location to save themselves. In their migration, the rabbits have many hair-raising adventures.

Watership Down creates a world of fantasy which is believable enough to permit viewers to lose themselves in it. The fairy-tale-like setting of *Watership Down* is made believable partly because the rabbits never do anything, aside from using language to communicate among themselves, that is outside the realm of a normal rabbit's capabilities. The viewers' easy identification with the rabbit characters helps them to immerse themselves in the world created by the movie. A factor strengthening the identification is the similarity between the rabbits' motivations and those of ourselves. They are leaving a doomed yet deceptively friendly home on a hazardous trip, not only to escape the menace at home but also to better their social positions. Similarly, most people have had to face temporary insecurity to bring about a change for the better.

The animation of *Watership Down* is extremely beautiful and changes with the moods of the film. Part of the animation is done with watercolor paints, which achieve a remarkable effect. The background abounds with a wealth of detail, all contributing to the believability of the settings. The film opens with a mythological interpretation of rabbit history, which is animated in the style of prehistoric art. Later, during a death sequence involving bounding symbolic red and blue rabbits, the style of drawing becomes reminiscent of Egyptian tomb paintings. The animation and watercolors are skilfully combined to produce a unique and versatile filmmaking style, which is the highlight of the film.

Through its stunning artwork and skilful portrayal of the characters, *Watership Down* presents a strong ecological message to its viewers. The rabbits must find a new home because of the destruction of their original warren by humans in preparation for a housing development. What the movie emphasizes through its characterizations of the rabbits is the humanity and degree of civilization and compassion of the rabbit way of life, as opposed to the seeming selfishness of people. By forcing one to realize that undeveloped land can be beautiful and valuable as a place where wild animals can live, the film makes one want to preserve the unspoiled lands remaining in the country.

Because of its animation, its unreal yet believable world, and its important social message, *Watership Down* is a potentially inspiring movie. The film definitely is entertaining, but the mark of a truly fine film is its ability to change the opinion of viewers or to move them lastingly in some way after they have left the theatre. Though many emotions are called forth during *Watership Down*, it fails to change this viewer's outlook on life in any way. It is a charming film, but it lacks ultimate seriousness. When the beautiful watercolor prints are gone and the rabbits stop flitting across the screen, the spell is broken and this viewer is left with little to take home. While the movie is definitely beautiful and engaging, it left me feeling merely entertained.

Stephen King's Best Friend

Maria Mangiola, student

A man's best friend is his dog, right? Not in the novel *Christine* by Stephen King. Arnie Cunningham, a scrawny kid who is excellent at auto mechanics, decides to purchase a beat-up car from the very strange Roland LeBay. While driving with his best friend, Dennis, Arnie sees Christine sitting in LeBay's corner lot. It's love at first sight! Once Arnie owns Christine, the frightening trouble starts.

The car Christine seems to have a mind of her own, and when she decides that she doesn't like a certain person because he knows her secret, she … (you honestly thought I'd tell you?) All I can tell you is that Christine slowly but surely becomes the most important character in the book. She speaks enticingly to Arnie: "Let's go for a ride, big guy. Let's cruise!"

The novel, in many parts, made me so scared that I didn't want to turn the pages. "Afraid of what?" you ask. Well, beginning in Chapter Seven, one of the scariest parts deals with Dennis. He reports, "And before I can answer … there is the terrible scream of rubber kissing off concrete and Christine lunges out at me, her grills snarling like an open mouthful of chrome teeth, her headlights glaring…." Well, that's about all I want to reveal.

After reading *Christine*, you'll probably never want to turn your back on a car again, especially if it happens to be a '58 Plymouth Fury. So, if you love a bit of gore, being scared out of your wits, and don't plan to walk in front of cars for a while, I suggest you read *Christine* (with as much courage as you can muster, of course).

Christine – **King's Downfall**

Anna Silva, student

A lame substitute for a suspense novel, Stephen King's *Christine* can only be called an overdrawn epic of predictability. Lengthy and tiresome, the story moves along at a snail's pace. In an attempt to present the story from all angles, King has taken what could have been a good horror story and turned it into one big yawn of a novel.

The disappointing part of the novel is that underneath the excessive fore-shadowing that renders *Christine* a boring read are the makings of a truly "quirky" horror story. After all, what teenager reaches driving age without first seeing a car for which he (or she) would do anything?

Christine tells the story of Arnie Cunningham, a pock-marked, scrawny teenager who is described by his best friend as being "a loser, you know. Every high school has to have at least two." Christine, the car, is an old '58 Plymouth Fury which Arnie cannot live without once he sees it on the drive home from work with his friend Dennis. Christine's original owner is a loud, obnoxious man named Roland D. LeBay. Once Arnie buys the car, sudden changes begin to take place. He begins to have "visions." While King's attention to detail can set the stage for the most frightening of episodes, *Christine* suffers from premature "whisperings" of that which will come to pass. Early in the novel, Arnie experiences a flashback in which he envisions Christine as she would have been in her prime: "for a moment the torn upholstery seemed to be gone. The seat covers were whole and smelling pleasantly of vinyl ... or maybe that smell was real leather." Then Arnie "hears" Christine "speak" to him: "Let's go for a ride big guy ... let's cruise." When Arnie returns home later that evening, still feeling that something "wasn't straight," it comes as little surprise when he dreams of Christine later that night. Everything in his dream happens "suddenly." "[S]uddenly the engine begins to rev and fall off." This happens after "the wipers suddenly start up, and that'd be strange because there's no one behind the wheel, the car is empty." While the details of Christine's ferocious visage are indeed vivid, the dream itself is not surprising, or even the least bit scary.

Later, Roland D. LeBay dies, and once again there is the early sense of what will be discovered. In fact, the repetition of the word "suddenly" takes away from the impact of the episode surrounding the news of LeBay's death and subsequent funeral. "LeBay had died suddenly on Saturday afternoon.... Suddenly. Suddenly can mean anything from a brain embolism to electrocuting yourself in the bathtub.... Coming out suddenly... Saturday afternoon.... Suddenly." We can only guess that Arnie will remember something oh so suddenly, which will no doubt confirm in his mind that there is something not quite right about Christine. Unfortunately, those of us who have figured out by now that there is a connection between Roland D. LeBay and the history of Christine the car already know that there is a dark secret lurking in LeBay's past even before Arnie learns what it is. The only thing we are left debating is what kind of dark secret. The only one who is surprised is Arnie. How did we know it would be "like a dash of cold water" in his face?

In his effort to acquaint his reader with the history of Roland D. LeBay and his peculiar history with Christine, King merely ends up hinting a little melodramatically, "I was seventeen years old, bound for college in another year, and I didn't believe in such things as curses and emotions that linger and … the spilled milk of dreams. I would not have allowed you the power of the past to reach out horrid dead hands towards the living…. But I'm a little older now." We are not given a chance to think of Christine's past and "her" relation to Arnie and his future; King tells us the whole history instead of allowing us to muse about the connection on our own.

These many subtle hints throughout the novel take away much that *Christine* has to offer. We end up knowing too much for the "scary" events to have much impact on our senses. Early in the novel Dennis notices a change in Arnie; his complexion appears to be clearing up. Later when other changes occur in Arnie's personality, as well as his appearance, it comes as no surprise that it is only since owning Christine that Arnie has changed. Later Arnie fights the school bully and his henchmen. Suddenly – there is that word again – one of the bullies is killed in a hit-and-run accident. During the autopsy of what is left of the body, red paint – the color of Christine's body – is found ingrained in the bully's skin. During all of this strangeness, Arnie continues to claim that "there is nothing going on." But only a brainless reader would not see that Christine is responsible for all the shedding of blood and gore.

Throughout the novel we view the events from many different points: Dennis, Arnie, as well as many others who are affected by Christine tell us bit by bit everything that happens. However, the telling takes much too long and is too drawn out to truly do *Christine* justice. There is none of the "edge of your seat" suspense so often felt in King's novels. And because of that missing ingredient, *Christine* is for the most part a disappointment. To tell any more would be to give what is left of the story away, and I wouldn't want to do that! The name Stephen King has been synonymous with the word horror, or it was until *Christine*. I can only hope that King's next novel will do more justice to his knack for storytelling and once again captivate his readers with spine-chilling suspense.

Your Writing

1. Which words or phrases or comparisons in your review give your opinion of the work? For example, Targ uses "exciting plot," "most enjoyable film," and other positive descriptions to show that he is basically recommending *Watership Down*. Likewise, Mangiola uses "made me so scared that I didn't want to turn the pages" to entice readers to read *Christine*, while Silva uses "lame substitute," and "moves along at a snail's pace," and "one big yawn of a novel" to show how she feels about the novel.

2. In your journal, comment on your writing. What did you learn from writing your review? What tips have you learned? Is there any part of your process that you would modify if you were to write another review? Why?

10 Informal Response to Literature (Personal Essay)

"The reader, not the text, holds the key to the meaning of any literary work."

Jane Ann Zaharias

WRITING PROJECT

Write a personal response to a piece of literature.

Exploring and Prewriting Suggestions

1. To help you experiment with giving a personal response to a piece of literature, you might try one of the following.

a) Select one of the poems or a short story in this book (or one of your own choice). Quickly read through the work once to get an overview and impression of it. Jot down your first response – whatever most struck you about the work, whether that was, for example, its content, its language, or something in your own life that you recalled as you read. Share your response in a small group. Then read the work a second time for details and subtleties. Again share your response.

b) In a small group, share with your classmates your favorite song, and explain why it is your favorite. (Is it because of the words, the images, the sounds, the rhythm, or the meaning? Does the music make the lyrics into a special kind of poem? If so, in what way?)

c) Choose a piece of literature that you had a strong reaction to – that you either liked a lot or disliked intensely. Working alone or with one or two of your peers, use creative movement, drama, dance, or mime to express your feelings about the work. Afterward, freewrite for ten minutes about what you did; why you chose the form of expression that you did; your audience's response (did they understand how you feel about the work?); or any new

142

insights into the work that you discovered as you expressed your response to it.

Writer's Choice

Are you ready to write a personal response to one of the pieces of literature you selected? Or do you need more time to explore before you begin to draft?

2. Select a piece of literature of your choice or the short story "Charles" (in the appendix).

a) Read the work once. Then freewrite for about five minutes on your first impressions of the story: the plot, the characters, the suspense, the setting, the problem, the episodes, the feelings, the humor, the resolution, an idea that stands out, or thoughts that came to mind as you read. Just jot down your impressions as they come to you while you write.

b) Choose one or more sentences or phrases that struck you as you read. Freewrite for five minutes about the language and what you liked or disliked about it (and why).

c) For five minutes, jot down as many questions about the story as you can think of. What confused you? What was unfamiliar? Why did the author write something in a particular way?

3. Form a group with three or four other students who have read the same piece of literature. Reread your freewriting, and underline a few things to share in your group. After each person has given his or her impression of the story, add to your freewriting notes anything you feel is important.

4. Read aloud to your group a part of the story that you particularly enjoyed. Explain why the excerpt is your favorite.

5. Look over the questions you wrote down. Have you found answers for all of them? Discuss any unanswered questions within your group. If any questions remain unanswered, reread the portion of the story that deals with the problem, consult a dictionary or other reference, or ask another group for suggestions.

6. Look over all the notes you have now collected about your piece of literature. Has the group helped you to appreciate the story better? What more have you learned through hearing the impressions and ideas of others in your group? In your journal, write for ten minutes about your expanded understanding of the work. Write as much and as quickly as you can. Try to use examples and reasons and, of course, refer to the notes you made.

> ### Writer's Choice
> Are you ready to prepare an informal response, or would you like to consider the following drafting suggestions? Have you thought about your writing variables, or do you want to think about them as you draft?

Drafting Suggestions

1. Whether you are preparing storyboards or drafting a feature article, an advertisement, an essay, or some other personal response, be sure to mention the author and title early in your response. And let your audience know where you stand on your subject.

2. Read through the notes and questions you've drafted and the interesting quotes you've jotted down. Select two or three ideas that you find particularly striking or interesting and that you could develop in your response.

> ### Writer's Choice
> Has your audience read the work or not? How will this knowledge affect your writing?

3. If it's unlikely that your audience knows the work, provide whatever information you need before setting out your response, but don't give the story away. If your audience is familiar with the work, then concentrate on explaining and expanding on your personal response. Your audience wants to know what you think of the selection, how it affected you, how it compares with other selections, and what struck you or particularly impressed you.

> ### Writer's Choice
> How can you enliven your response? Would quotes work best? Examples? Could you perhaps experiment with your tone or format? Do you want to express your response through art, drama, or music?

4. For more information about the range of styles, you might consult the Second Workshop section, especially Chapters 29 and 33. Keep an open mind on your format.

When you finish your draft, read it over to see whether it honestly reflects your feelings. Then use the following guidelines to help you revise it.

Guidelines for Revising an Informal Response to Literature

☐ Why have you prepared this response? Have you presented your response in the best possible format ? Does your response accurately reflect how you feel about the work?

☐ Will your audience know exactly what you think of the piece of literature?

☐ What is the strongest part of your response? The weakest? How can you build on the strengths and get rid of the weaknesses?

☐ Have you provided appropriate details, facts, examples, and quotations to support your response? Have you successfully integrated these with your own words? Is everything that you have included important to your response? If not, what should you change or omit?

☐ Are you satisfied with the mechanics of your draft (spelling, punctuation, and grammar), or is there something you'd like to check before you let an editor see your work?

☐ Is your title imaginative? Does it capture your view of the work?

☐ Is there anything in your draft that you would like your editor to help you with?

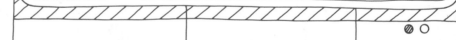

Writer's Choice

Do you want an editor to look over your work? Or is your personal response ready for its intended audience?

If necessary, revise your work and prepare a clean double-spaced draft for your editor.

Revising and Editing Suggestions

Give your draft to your peer-editor, and share your writing variables. Encourage your editor to use the "Guidelines for Revising an Informal Response to Literature" in this chapter and the checklists in Chapter 27. Your editor should also think about how he or she would answer the following questions.

Ask Your Peer-Editor

☐ What was your first impression of my work? Was my opinion clear? Do you feel as I do about the work? Will my audience?

☐ Have I expressed my main idea clearly? Have I supported it with convincing quotations, examples, or other specific evidence? Have I smoothly blended my supporting information with my own words? If not, what transitions (Chapter 26) would you suggest? Is there anything that I should add, delete, or change? What makes you say so?

☐ What part of my response is clearest? Most effective? In what way? Is anything unclear? Why? What can I do to make it clearer?

☐ Have I properly emphasized my important points? If not, what needs more emphasis? Is my organization clear? Should I rearrange any of my points?

☐ Have I overemphasized or stated anything at too great a length? If I've included a summary, did I need to? Is there anything that I should shorten or omit?

☐ Were you familiar with the work before you read my response? If so, did you gain a fresh or deeper understanding of the work as a result of reading my response? If you were not familiar with the work, will you now read it? Why?

☐ Is my title interesting and informative?

☐ Do you like my word choice and sentence structure? Are my spelling, punctuation, and grammar all right, or is there something I should still work on?

Writer's Choice

Is your response ready for its intended audience, or would you like your teacher-editor to see it first?

When you are satisfied with the content of your personal response, proofread it a final time for spelling, grammar, usage, and punctuation. Read it again to make sure it is an honest statement of the opinion you are expressing.

Publishing Suggestions

Personal responses to literature might be shared in a class magazine, in a class literature database, or on a class bulletin board. If you will be preparing a formal response to literature, you might prefer for the moment to save your personal response in your writing folder and use it as the basis for your formal response to the same work. Don't restrict yourself to a written response, though. You can express a personal response through art, drama, or music. Try to make your response truly personal.

<table>
<tr><td>

In the Company of Writers

</td><td>

In the following, three writers respond to "Charles." (See the appendix.)

I Like "Charles"
Nina Haley, student

I found the short story "Charles" by Shirley Jackson humorous and interesting. The opening paragraph immediately caught my atttention with its clear, descriptive phrases and its end-of-babyhood mood: "My sweet-voiced nursery school tot replaced by a long-trousered, swaggering character who forgot to stop at the corner and wave goodbye to me."

As the story's plot progresses, the relationship between the parents and the child becomes more interesting and specific. Laurie captures his parents' attention with outrageous stories about the "bad boy" at school: Charles. Through Charles, Laurie is able to keep his parents always interested and "on the edge of their seats" *without* invoking in them any negative reactions towards himself.

Much of the story is written in dialogue which helps make the characters more real for me. The characters and their individual needs and reactions become more personal through the dialogue. Many hints are given in the story that suggest to us its ironic outcome. That Charles has to stay after school, therefore, Laurie is late as well (because Laurie is watching Charles), is one clue which helps us to predict the story's conclusion. Recognizing these clues, I guessed early on in the story that Laurie and Charles were one and the same person. I was, however, curious to find out how the plot and character relationships were resolved. I enjoyed the story immensely.

</td></tr>
</table>

Down with "Charles"
Shauna Ulrich, student

In the story "Charles," by Shirley Jackson, I found myself getting quite bored with the plot. It was painfully obvious to me how the story was going to end. Suspenseless, the story left me bored, and I therefore found it didn't keep my attention.

The only thing I like about the story is the reality in the characters. Laurie's parents are real because I can well imagine how "blind" they are to their little boy's plea for attention. After all, no parents want to believe their child can be as bad as "Charles."

Despite the well-drawn characters, when Laurie's mother says, "this Charles boy sounds like such a bad influence," and his father says, "Bound to be people like Charles in the world. Might as well meet them now as later," I just knew how the story was going to end. Another line that gives away the ending is the one when Laurie's mother says to the teacher, "I suppose this time it's Charles's influence." Then the teacher responds with the answer I knew all along: "We don't have any Charles in kindergarten." For me, the story is absolutely without suspense.

Laurie's Imaginary Friend
Ivy Hadley, student

Reading "Charles" by Shirley Jackson made me think of when I was young. I liked the story because I figured out early that Charles was really Laurie. The author gave hints through the story that Laurie wanted to tell his parents of this. For example, "'The teacher spanked a boy, though' Laurie [says], addressing his bread and butter. 'For being fresh,' he [adds] with his mouth full."

Laurie makes me think of myself when I did not want to own up to something. I would blame it on someone else, like Laurie does with Charles.

The one thing that confuses me with this story is that Shirley Jackson does not give any information on how Laurie acts before the first day of school. She gives hints that he has changed but not enough for me to confirm that fact.

I like the end of the story where the author leaves me in suspense, not knowing what the mother is going to do when she gets home. I think she might ground Laurie for fibbing to her about Charles, but I also think she will try and understand her son's calls for attention. At least I hope she will!

In the following, two writers respond to the excerpt from **Lady Oracle** *(page 111).*

The Disguise of Humiliation
Marita Gustavsson, student

Reading the excerpt from *Lady Oracle* by Margaret Atwood made me realize how ageless memories of humiliation can be. Many unwanted, suppressed, and almost forgotten memories surfaced. Some memories stood out more than others.

One incident standing out clearly in my mind occurred when I was seven years old. Taken to a hairdresser for the first time by my mother, I asked to have only the split ends cut off from my already sparse head of hair. My mother watched as I was being prepared for my first adult haircut. The hairdresser and my mother exchanged looks and my mother winked as she left the hair parlor. I smiled broadly, thinking her wink was meant for me, unaware of the conspiracy against me. The busy scissors, maneuvered by the "monster" behind me, scalped me completely. Completing my haircut, the hairdresser, her face smiling as she spun me around to face the mirror, had a look of accomplishment in her eyes. My eyes full of tears, I did not want to believe what I saw: I looked just like a boy. My mother returned and excitedly told me how nice I looked. Told to thank the monster who scalped me, I refused, not wanting to play their game. The worst part of this experience was my not understanding the reason behind my unfortunate haircut, "this humiliation disguised as privilege." My mother, telling me I should be grateful for having enough money to afford a professional haircut, told me to stop crying. Like Joan, "I went home with my mother, refusing to speak to her because she had betrayed me."

Misplaced Childhoods
Steven Bartlett, student

Reading the excerpt from Margaret Atwood's novel *Lady Oracle* brought up many misplaced memories of my experiences at school as a child. Although never overweight, I resembled Joan in that I felt different from other children: less worthy.

One of the childhood experiences setting me apart from my peers took place in my grade three P.E. class. I sat on the stage of the gym, my bare feet swinging freely beneath me, when a classmate, noticing my feet, let out a scream I'm sure the entire school could hear. I felt hideous. Like Joan, I believed "I was grotesque," that I was someone "who should not be seen in public with little clothing on." To this day I'm not sure why my feet made an eight-year-old girl scream, but I must admit, I seldom walk around barefoot.

I grew older, and as opposed to Margaret Atwood's character, who got heavier and taller, I got skinnier and taller – or, as my mother would say, "lanky" (a term I learned to despise). I outgrew all my male classmates, who saw fit to rename me "giraffe-neck." The girls my age, who were also growing faster than the boys, found me an irresistible date for the school dances: they didn't have to look down at me when we slow-danced. Besides the name-calling and occasional dance with a girl who thought of me as "safe," I didn't really mind my size. In fact, like Joan, "I didn't even notice" my unusually tall stature; I saw everyone else as being ten feet taller. Inside my ten-year-old 5'10" body, I was ten inches tall!

Like Joan, who thought she "was ... good at dancing, although Miss Flegg sometimes ... said, 'Joan, dear, I wish you would stop thumping,'" I lived in my own private world where everyone acknowledged my "outstanding talents": in art class, I was Rembrandt; in music, Mozart; and in P.E., I was ... well, I wasn't exactly an Olympic contender.

Perhaps the strongest similarity between Joan and me is our "hoping for magic transformations." I may not have turned myself into the Greek god Adonis, but I have turned a negative self-image into a positive one. I only hope Joan managed as well.

Your Writing

1. How does your personal response stack up against those of the other writers? Why?

2. Do you notice that in the published responses, the writers refer to the characters using the present tense? Even when they use a quotation, they change past tense verbs to present. In your writing, do you use present tenses when you refer to the actions of literary characters?

3. In your journal, comment on your writing. What did you learn from preparing your personal response? Is there any part of your process that you would modify if you were to prepare another personal response? Or if you were to prepare a *formal* response to a piece of literature?

11 Formal Response to Literature (Literary Essay)

"To read a book for the first time is to make the acquaintance of a new friend; to read it a second time is to meet an old one."

S. G. Champion

A formal response to literature or a **literary essay** is essentially an argumentative essay in which a writer presents a point of view on a literary work or some aspect of it. It differs from the personal response (see Chapter 10) in several important ways.

- The writer usually writes in the third person (*the reader, he,* or *she*) instead of the first person (*I*) and uses literary terminology.
- The writer interprets the work keeping in mind what has been said and noticed by other critics.
- The writer includes analysis; that is, he or she examines the work to discover how its parts fit together.

Often, for a formal response, you are assigned a specific literary work to analyse as well as a specific topic. At other times you can choose both a work and a topic.

WRITING PROJECT

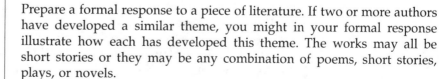

Prepare a formal response to a piece of literature. If two or more authors have developed a similar theme, you might in your formal response illustrate how each has developed this theme. The works may all be short stories or they may be any combination of poems, short stories, plays, or novels.

Exploring and Prewriting Suggestions

1. If you are confused about how to discuss the characters, setting, and conflict in a literary work, you might try one or more of the following before you begin to work on your formal response. Share and discuss your completed work in a small group.

a) Write a short character sketch of a member of your family or a friend. If that person were to walk into the room to pay a visit, your peers should be able to recognize the person by his or her appearance or personality.

b) Write a short description of one of your favorite places so that your peers will be able to visualize the setting.

c) Write a short account of a conflict in which you were involved so that your peers can know exactly with whom or what you were in conflict. You might also reveal how the conflict was resolved and any of its long-term effects.

You will find there is little difference between the way you discuss characters, setting, and conflict in real life and the way you discuss them in literature.

2. If you can choose your own literary work and topic, then select a work that influenced or affected you in some way. (You might develop a formal response to "Charles" or one of the other short stories in this book. Consult the Table of Contents.) If something is important to you, it is likely important to others. Your own contribution will help you and your audience reach a better understanding of what it means to be human.

> ## Writer's Choice
> Why is the selection important to you? Why might it be important to other people?

3. To write a formal response to a piece of literature, you should read the work closely – that is, respond to many levels, or issues, in the work and figure out how all its parts fit together. The following should help you to improve your **close reading** ability.

a) When you read, open yourself to the possibility of experiencing something new or of being reminded of something you had forgotten. Good writing can engage your emotions as well as your mind, so allow yourself to feel sad, happy, angry, contented, afraid, or whatever emotion the work awakens in you. Allow yourself to recall similar works.

b) The first time you read the work, do so without stopping to analyse it; just let it sweep you along. After you have explored your personal response to it (see Chapter 10), think about the work as a whole and what it means to you. Ask yourself what you have learned or what you have experienced in a new way. For example, you may have gained a deeper understanding of some aspect of the human condition, such as trust, honesty, people's inhumanity to others, aging, or death.

c) Reread the work. If it is a story or a play, go beyond the plot this time. Reading for the plot alone limits you. Reading for deeper meanings allows you to think about the **theme**, or underlying idea, that the writer wants to convey. Writers often provide clues to help you understand their work. As you reread, focus particularly on sections or aspects that moved you, intrigued you, or even confused you during your first reading. How and why did these parts affect you?

d) We all put something of ourselves into what we read; a personal response makes interpretation possible. Do not let your feelings or biases mislead you. For a formal response, concentrate on the subtext by reading between the lines, but use **textual evidence**, or what is actually on the printed page, to support your interpretation.

4. As you read a piece of literature, consider unity – what it adds up to as a unified work of art. Imagine that you are working on a jigsaw puzzle, with the pieces ready to be assembled. Your analysis of the work should be like the completed puzzle, in which all the pieces fit together and are recognizable as a picture. In your formal response, you should present a well-supported interpretation of a work (or part of a work) that demonstrates a close reading and careful analysis of the whole work of literature.

5. Thinking about the following literary elements can help you as you interpret what the author is saying.

Fiction

Tone. What is the author's tone or attitude toward the plot, setting, and characters as revealed in the language of the work? Is the author being direct or ironic? (Should you take the words at their face value or understand that the author means the opposite of what he or she seems to be saying?)

Narrator and Point of View. The narrator of a short story or novel may be one of the characters telling the story from a first-person point of view (*I*). Instead of telling the "whole" story, the character has a limited point of view and tells only that part of the story that he or she is involved in or knows about. First-person stories are open to a great deal of interpretation. If the story is told in the first person, ask yourself: Who is the narrator? Is he or she to be trusted? (Not all narrators in stories are trustworthy. Some may be biased, and others may be dishonest. Why might a writer choose a dishonest narrator to tell the story?)

An author can also tell a story from a third-person point of view (*he* or *she*). Sometimes the narrator is an all-knowing observer, who tells not only what the characters say and do but also what they think and feel. Some all-knowing narrators even speak directly to the reader, commenting on the characters and what they do. An author can also tell a story in the third person but reveal only what one character – usually the main protagonist, whether male or female – thinks and feels. In such a case, the work is essentially told from the character's point of view.

Experience and Conflict. You may think that no one else has experienced the joy or pain you have experienced, but as you read fine literature, you come to realize that the great majority of human beings have similar experiences. These are often called **archetypal experiences** because they are universal (they occur to human beings in all times and places). For example, a character may experience a loss of innocence, go on a journey or quest, become disillusioned, or escape from someone or something. These are archetypal experiences. Can you think of others?

Many types of conflicts are archetypal. Several examples of archetypal conflicts are the conflict between generations, the battle of the sexes, the "lovers' steeplechase" (boy meets girl, boy loses girl, boy gets girl), and the internal struggle to become a better person. Conflicts can be external – with other people, with nature – or they can be internal – within the opposing sides or desires of one character. As you read, focus on the fictional conflict to see how the central character deals with it. Afterward, reflect on how you would deal with a similar conflict. You might also compare the conflict with conflict in another similar work you have read.

When you read a work of fiction closely, make a mental note of the general experience and the specific conflict (or conflicts) and then think of them in archetypal terms.

Character. You can understand fictional characters by thinking about what they say or do, how other characters react to them, and (in some cases) what the author says about them. Just as there may be archetypal experiences and conflicts in fiction, so also an author can introduce **archetypal characters** – that is, characters representing general, universal types. Think about the characters you have encountered in fiction (as well as people you know). How many of them resemble or represent the following archetypal characters: the struggling student, the whiz kid, the frustrated lover, the artist, the trickster, the wise old man, Cinderella, the apprentice, the innocent, the victim, Mother Earth, the magician, the healer, the leader, the follower? (Characters do not have to be the same age or sex as the archetypal character to resemble that character. The boy Piggy in William Golding's novel *Lord of the Flies* is an archetypal wise old man. The hero of Charles Dickens's *Oliver Twist* is an archetypal Cinderella.)

Symbols. A symbol stands for something else, usually a quality or idea. For example, a rose usually symbolizes beauty, and a skull can symbolize death. A symbol often suggests several related ideas; thus a rose can stand for beauty and a dying rose for the fragility of beauty. Such related ideas can provide a clue to the work's underlying meaning, its theme.

Theme. To arrive at the theme of a work you need to recall each of the plot details – the "why" of character behavior or events. For example, we might say that "the grandfather dies and then the grandmother dies" is a story. When we add that the grandmother dies because of grief over the grandfather's death, we have a plot ("why"). To generalize by saying "True love needs its source to survive" is to suggest a possible theme. Other themes you may know could be "Beauty is skin deep" or "War is horror."

Poetry

Poems are often meant to be heard as well as read. To appreciate a poem fully, try reading it aloud. Many poems have been set to music – and many songs are simply musical poems.

In your first response to a poem, concentrate on how it affects you. Allow the sounds and the meaning to work within you so that you will be left with an overall impression, a combination of emotion and idea. After you have responded in a personal way, reread the poem to see how its elements work together to produce the emotion and idea. As you reread, think about the following.

☐ What is your immediate response to the poem? Does it make you feel happy, sad, confused, concerned, or hopeful, or do you feel some other emotion?

☐ How has the poet achieved this effect? Is it through *language* (the specific use of words), through *sound*, through *imagery* (word pictures), through *rhythm*, through *rhyme*, through *symbols*, or through the statement that the poem makes about the human condition?

Many poems use figurative language (Chapter 32) to suggest ideas and to arouse emotion. Think about the figurative language that the poem contains. How does the language affect you?

☐ Some poems rely as much on their look on the printed page as on their sound to create an effect. When you reread a poem, consider how it looks: its shape, its division into lines and stanzas (parts of a poem set off by extra space), and (in the case of "concrete" poems) its visual resemblance to its subject. Why does the poem have the shape it does?

☐ You will find in poetry many of the literary elements contained in fiction. Many poems deal with conflict. All poems have at least one character, the speaker of the poem. Consider what the poem's words tell you about that character. Also, consider the poem's theme and whether it is stated directly or implied.

Drama

Most plays are written to be performed rather than simply read. As you read a play, imagine it being performed. Even better (if the copyright allows you to do so), you and your classmates can choose parts and read the play aloud. Oral reading can help you to arrive at a better understanding of why a playwright has written something in a particular way. After you have given the play a first reading, reread it, keeping in mind the elements presented in the discussion of fiction in this chapter. Most of these elements apply to drama as well as to novels and short stories. In addition, the following strategies will help to make the play come alive for you.

☐ As you read the play and talk about it with others, imagine yourself having to act in it or direct it.

☐ Playwrights have specific reasons for including each event, character, and action in a play. To help you arrive at a deeper understanding of the play, think about what these reasons might be.

☐ Analysing the characters in a play is usually more difficult than analysing the characters in a short story or novel. A play often gives only the characters' dialogue with little indication of what the characters are thinking (although the stage directions may help; for example, "Orestes: [mockingly]" or "Ann: [perplexed]").

Pay attention to what the playwright says about the characters. You may find clues to character in a preface to the play, in a comment included within the play, or in a stage direction.

Study what the characters say, but be careful not to take everything they say at face value. A character could be deliberately misleading another character.

Note particularly what a character does (according to the stage directions). Actions are usually the best clue to character. In other words, a character may say one thing but do something different.

Note what the characters say to one another. Often, playwrights put significant information in the mouths of other characters.

Imagine the various ways in which an actor portraying the character might perform that character's lines with reference to the context or situation. Decide which way works best.

Find a line in the play that is difficult for you to interpret. Think about why and how the playwright might want the character to say that line in the context of what has gone on before.

☐ Make up a list of questions like the following about each principal character in a play, and try to answer the questions with reference to the play: How old is the character? Is he or she honest? Is he or she considerate of others or self-centred? Is he or she ambitious or lazy? A bully? Cruel or kind? Unhappy or unstable?

☐ Imagine you are a producer and you want to stage or film the play. Visualize an ideal full-scale production. (Imagine that money is no object and you can afford the best.) Consider your choice of actors, set, lighting, and costume design. Think about your reasons for your choices.

Writer's Choice

Do you want to think about your writing variables before or as you draft? For example, will your audience be an informed reader who has read the same piece of literature? Or will your audience be uninformed?

Drafting Suggestions

1. Early in your formal response, give the title and author of the work you are discussing. State the thesis of your formal response clearly and early. (For more about thesis statements, see Chapter 23.)

2. Consider your audience. How well do they know the work you are responding to? (Generally, you can assume your audience has read the selection and will read your work to gain some new understanding of it.)

3. Support each statement you make with textual evidence, but be selective in the evidence you provide, whether quotations, details of the plot, character descriptions, or symbols. Use only those that work to support your response. If you are writing about fiction or drama, never retell the entire plot. (You can use a brief summary, especially one giving those details that support your argument, to lead to your interpretation.)

4. When you quote from the work, use quotation marks. If the work is a long one, such as a novel or full-length play, you may want (or be asked) to give page references or act and scene references in parentheses after the quotations. Try to integrate any quotations with your own writing, so that your work reads smoothly, without any abrupt jumps or shifts. When you use a quotation that may be in the past tense, you should for consistency change it to the present tense. Set brackets around any changes you make to the original quotation. For example:

Original Quotation: "...he renounced corduroy overalls with bibs and began wearing blue jeans with a belt."

Quotation included within essay: After Laurie starts kindergarten, "he [renounces] corduroy overalls with bibs and [begins] wearing blue jeans with a belt."

If you want to use only a part or parts of a quotation, use ellipsis points to indicate missing words. For example:

Original Quotation: "The day my son Laurie started kindergarten he renounced corduroy overalls with bibs and began wearing blue jeans with a belt. I watched him go off the first morning with the older girl next door, seeing clearly that an era of my life was ended."

Quotation included within an essay: The narrator thinks about "the day... Laurie started kindergarten" and now sees "clearly that an era of [her] life... ended."

A computer can make it easier to draft your response. You can arrange quotations and examples within your own prose to achieve the most effective blend.

5. As you give evidence to support your thesis, ask yourself: Does this evidence prove what I want it to prove? If you decide it does not, you may want to look for stronger evidence or work out a new thesis statement. Each sentence in your response should, in some way, support your thesis. If it doesn't, leave the sentence out.

6. As a rule, you should use the third person (*he* or *she*), and the present tense rather than the past. Using the third person helps give your work a ring of authority, and using the present tense helps keep the literature alive. But before you write, find out which tense and person your intended audience prefers, especially if you are writing about an assigned work and topic and your intended audience is a teacher. Whatever person and tense you use, make sure you are consistent.

When you finish your draft, consider the following guidelines.

Guidelines for Revising a Formal Response to Literature

☐ Will your audience know why you have writtten this formal response? Does your introduction capture your audience's attention and set out the title and author of the work you are responding to? Will your audience know your thesis or claim?

☐ What is the strongest part of your response? The weakest? How can you build on the strengths and get rid of the weaknesses?

☐ Have you provided appropriate textual evidence – details, facts, examples, and quotations – to support your thesis statement? Have you smoothly integrated these with your own words? Is everything that you have included important to your response? If not, what should you change, move, or leave out?

☐ Do you logically develop your formal response? Is your organization climactic? Sequential? Should you experiment with the organization of your ideas? (See Chapter 25.)

☐ Is your title imaginative? Does it capture your view of the work?

☐ Are you satisfied with the mechanics of your draft (spelling, punctuation, and grammar)? Have you consistently used one tense and person? Is there anything you'd like to check before you let an editor see your work?

☐ Have you left sufficient time to rethink and revise your draft? If you are writing on an assigned topic or selection, have you addressed all the points you were asked to address?

☐ Is there anything in your draft that you would like your editor to help you with?

Writer's Choice

Do you want an editor to look over your work? (Make sure that your editor knows the piece of literature well.) Or is your formal response ready for its intended audience?

If necessary, revise your work and prepare a clean double-spaced draft for your editor.

Revising and Editing Suggestions

Give your draft to your peer-editor, and share your writing variables. Encourage your editor to use the "Guidelines for Revising a Formal Response to Literature" in this chapter and the checklists in Chapter 27. Your editor should also think about how he or she would answer the following questions.

Ask Your Peer-Editor

☐ What was your first impression of my work? Was my opinion clear? Will it be clear to my intended audience? Do you have a new insight into the piece of literature? Will my audience? What makes you say so?

☐ Have I clearly and early set out the author and title of the work? Have I supported my main claim with convincing quotations, examples, or other specific evidence? Have I smoothly blended my supporting information with my own words? If this needs work, could you suggest alternative wording? Is there anything that I should add, delete, or change? What makes you say so?

☐ What part of my response is clearest? Most effective? In what way? Is anything unclear? Why? What can I do to make it clearer?

☐ Have I properly emphasized my important points? If not, what needs more emphasis?

☐ Have I overemphasized or stated anything at too great a length? If I've included a summary, did I need to? Is all the textual evidence I provided necessary? Is there anything that I should shorten or omit?

☐ If I've responded to an assigned topic, have I addressed everything I should have addressed?

☐ Is my title interesting and informative? Is it appropriate? If not, what would you suggest to improve it?

☐ Do you like my word choice and sentence structure? Are tenses and person consistent? Are my spelling, punctuation, and grammar all right, or is there something I should still work on?

☐ Will my audience arrive at a new or different understanding about the work and perhaps about the world or the human condition in general? What makes you say so?

Writer's Choice

Is your response ready for its intended audience, or would you like your teacher-editor to see it first?

Publishing Suggestions

Submit your formal response to your intended audience. It might also be filed as part of a class literature database, or you might like to duplicate it for a literature class or send it to your school newspaper or literary journal.

In the Company of Writers

The following three essays refer to the short story "Charles." (See the appendix.)

Attention, Please
Ming Choo, student

In "Charles," Shirley Jackson shows the reader how a child like Laurie, the protagonist, loses innocence while constantly searching for recognition and attention. His parents, on the other hand, ironically misinterpret Laurie's unusual behaviour and his enthusiasm for school (or Charles).

After Laurie starts kindergarten, "he [renounces] corduroy overalls with bibs and [begins] wearing blue jeans with a belt." This action by Laurie gives the reader a clear hint that he is growing up and is losing his innocence.

The first time Laurie talks about Charles, he shyly addresses "his bread and butter" instead of his parents. The expression of shyness by Laurie indicates that he is in the process of telling a lie, talking about himself indirectly through "Charles."

All Laurie actually wants is recognition and attention from his teacher, from his classmates, and from his parents. He gains attention from his teacher by "being fresh," by hitting the teacher, and by kicking the teacher's friend. He gets attention from his classmates by bouncing "a see-saw on the head of a little girl and [making] her bleed," as well as yelling and throwing chalk. Finally, at home, he receives the attention that he most desires, his parents', by boasting about Charles. His parents, who all this time give Charles the attention, do not realize that they are unconsciously and unknowingly giving Laurie the attention he wants.

As part of his growing-up process, Laurie tries to discover the best way to gain his parents' attention. He knows that if he behaves badly in school he will receive negative attention from his teacher and his parents, but Charles will not, so he acts a bit and talks excitedly about Charles in front of his parents, gaining exactly the attention he wants.

The story ends with an ironic note, when the narrator, Laurie's mother, goes to the PTA meeting, hoping to meet Charles's mother, and in fact she meets herself. The truth is revealed and Laurie's mother, ironically, loses her innocence about her son and "Charles."

The Other Laurie

Cathy McNeill, student

"Charles," written by Shirley Jackson, shows how children can manipulate their parents in order to receive attention. Because Laurie behaves badly in kindergarten, he creates Charles. Charles takes all the blame for Laurie's actions while also bringing attention to Laurie.

When Laurie leaves for his first day at school, his change in clothing and forgetting to wave goodbye to his mother immediately gets her attention. Slamming the front door, leaving "his hat on the floor" and shouting, Laurie is immediately noticed by his parents upon his return from school. These scenes enable Laurie to test his parents for their reactions, as well as showing how Laurie learns to manipulate his parents.

When he feels he may get into trouble for the things he has done at school, Laurie creates Charles. Charles will take the blame and be frowned upon, and Laurie will be praised. Talking about Charles will be a way for Laurie to get attention without punishment.

Speaking "insolently to his father" and "spilling his baby sister's milk," Laurie misbehaves to gain attention from his parents. However, since these actions are far less dramatic than Charles's actions, Laurie is not scolded. Instead, Laurie's parents become more curious about Charles's influence on Laurie, and Laurie receives more attention when he brings home stories of Charles's latest adventure.

The rebellious character Laurie creates enables him to receive attention from his parents without implicating himself. Charles is the ultimate scapegoat. Charles takes the blame for everything Laurie does at school. Charles is every child's dream and every mother's nightmare – the child named "I-didn't-do-it."

Mom Wakes Up

Marta Miranda, student

In "Charles," Shirley Jackson demonstrates the archetypal experience of coming of age through the narrator as well as through Laurie.

The narrator first notices a change when she "[watches her son] go off the first morning with the older girl next door, seeing clearly that an era of [her] life [has] ended." She sees the changes in her son; however, she does not change to the parent of a "raucous shouting," "insolently" speaking and "swaggering" son, but continues to deal with her son as a "sweet-voiced nursery school tot." In other words, she refuses to come of age or be disillusioned.

The careful reader quickly senses a strong connection between Charles and Laurie, but the narrator does not connect her son to the naughty Charles. Indeed, she remarks that "kindergarten may be too unsettling for Laurie … [with] … toughness and bad grammar, and … [Charles's] … bad influence."

The narrator finally becomes disillusioned at the end of the story. She attends a PTA meeting (after missing the first one and becoming disillusioned earlier) and discovers that Laurie "had a little trouble adjusting, the first week or so ... with occasional lapses." The narrator then finds out that no Charles in the kindergarten exists, but rather that her "nursery school tot" is the "bad influence" in the classroom.

By having Laurie's mother tell the story, Jackson allows the reader not only to see the changes in Laurie through his mother's eyes but also – and at the same time – to see the narrator come of age and see her son as he really is.

The following essay makes reference to three selections: the excerpt from **Lady Oracle** *(Chapter 7), and "The Late Man" and "Naaholooyah," which are in the appendix.*

Dangerous Gaps
Agathe Polach, student

The generation gap plays the role of an inexhaustible theme in literature. Margaret Atwood, Andreas Schroeder, and Mary TallMountain show that the generation gap between young and old breaks down communication in *Lady Oracle*, "The Late Man," and "Naaholooyah."

In Atwood's story readers witness how Miss Flegg and Joan's mother do not try to understand the "fat little girl." By bridging the generation gap, both women could have spared Joan the sorrow and "the monstrousness of the renunciation." Because Miss Flegg and Joan's mother live in an adult world and do not step into the child's head and heart, Joan gives up her "favorite costume" and, later on, her dancing lessons. It is interesting to see how two grown women are so involved with their respective adult preoccupations that they do not see that their indifference is costing Joan her self-esteem. Miss Flegg's interest lies in "the final effect" and she is blind to Joan's "dance of rage and destruction": the destruction of Joan's confidence in herself. The mother fears that her daughter will look "grotesque" and, therefore, agrees with Miss Flegg to take away from Joan the butterfly costume. Ultimately, Joan's life is scarred because the two women do not leap the generation gap and she wonders, "Who would think of marrying a mothball?"

A generation gap can occur with people of the same generation as shown in Andreas Schroeder's "The Late Man." When "the late man" gets older by discovering "his detective activities ... into the nature of himself" and finding "that all this is beyond his control," he creates a kind of time-bomb that keeps on enlarging the gap between his mates and himself. As he consistently follows his "plan-like deceleration of pace in relation to the normal fishing schedule," the other fishermen and he widen the gap. They see "the desperate undertow in his eyes and [say] nothing." The fishermen "can't figure 'm out" as he grows "older." They even say nothing at his death and bury him "without looking at each other." Unlike Atwood's story where not one of the other characters tries to bridge the generation gap, Schroeder brings in the young fisherman who tries understand the "suddenly old" late man, and who finally "detects traces of the intoxication of discovery in his feelings." As he relates to the late man's generation, the young fisherman finds himself "fifteen minutes" late, and a generation older.

Readers are brought back to the archetypal parent/child generation gap in Mary TallMountain's "Naaholooyah." Although Mamma, Grandpa, and the adults of the council do not tell Lidwynne and Michael about their imminent adoption by a white couple, they care for and love the children. Unlike Miss Flegg and Joan's mother, they are not caught up in their selfish desires; they simply do not relate to children and underestimate Lidwynne's awareness of the events. The native parents talk "a lot, secretly" or so the children think, and they do not perceive how Lidwynne is "sleepy and lazy now because [she's] lain awake so long trying to hear what they [say]." It seems outrageous that Mamma, who loves Lidwynne, would hide something as important as her children's forthcoming adoption and her own death. Nevertheless, the generation gap blinds Mamma from seeing her daughter's worries over the "scary things" going on. In hiding from her daughter that terrible secret, Mamma has alienated herself from her daughter; only when she informs Lidwynne of the events can "she [be] back from wherever [she's] gone." As Lidwynne gets treated fairly and told of the future disappearance of her "naaholooyah," the generation gap is bridged and mother and daughter can laugh.

The three authors show how destructive the generation gap can be. In Atwood's story, Joan is stripped of her self-esteem through adults' "betrayal" of not trying to understand her. Schroeder demonstrates how the late man's self-discovery creates a gap that alienates his fellow fishermen and that ultimately kills him. Schroeder also creates a new gap between the young fisherman and his mates. Finally, TallMountain uses the archetypal generation gap to show how "scary" it is for Lidwynne not to be informed by the adults about what is going on around her. Loss of self-esteem, loss of life, and loss of parents and culture are only a few by-products of society's generation gaps.

Your Writing

1. How does your formal response compare with those of the other writers? Is yours similarly organized? Have you provided equally thoughtful insights into your piece of literature?

2. Do you find that your formal response reveals more about the story than a personal response would reveal? Why or why not?

3. If you first prepared a personal response, did it help you to draft your formal response? Would you prepare one again if you were asked to do another formal response to literature? Why?

4. In your journal, comment on your writing. What did you learn from preparing your formal response? Is there any part of your process that you would modify if you were to prepare another formal response to a piece of literature? Why?

12

Short Research Paper

"Knowledge is of two kinds: we know a subject ourselves, or we know where we can find information upon it."

Samuel Johnson

Finding information and then communicating what you have found in a research paper is one of the most common assignments you will get in school or in business. The research paper requires a careful and diligent search for facts, but the researcher then goes beyond the facts to create something new and personal from them. In many cases, it is useful to support a research paper with quotations from the source documents.

WRITING PROJECT

Write a short research paper (about 250 words) about a topic of your choice or a nursery rhyme, a holiday, the origin of an interesting or picturesque word, or an invention or discovery. Include at least two quotations from different sources in your paper.

Exploring and Prewriting Suggestions

1. You find out information in a variety of ways, including interviewing, listening to lectures, seeing documentaries, reading journals, or reading reference books. Try one or more of the following activities. Each will reveal information that you never knew before.

a) Form a group of three with classmates that you do not know too well. In ten minutes, find out things that you all have in common. Have one group member record your findings.

b) Form a group of three. Each person can role-play a character from one of the works you've been studying. Through questioning and discussing, identify each of the other two characters. You can ask questions involving character analysis or personal, psychological, or physical questions, but you can't ask a "yes" or "no" question, and you can't ask a question similar to "Are you in (*title of work*)?" As a variation, you might role-play a historical character, an author, or some contemporary person.

c) Conduct a treasure hunt in your classroom. On a piece of paper, write "A" to "P" on separate lines. Try to fill in as many blanks as you can – but don't use the same classmate more than once.

Find someone in the class who:

A. has travelled to a foreign country

B. was born in another country
    (which one?)

C. enjoys eating food from another
    country (what?)

D. has read at least two books by
    the same author (who?)

E. writes to a friend in a foreign
    country

F. enjoys a music group from
    another country (which group?)

G. has worked in a fast-food
    restaurant

H. has a favorite food (what?)

I. speaks a second language fluently

J. reads books by an author from
    another country (who?)

K. is wearing something made in Japan
    (what?)

L. recently saw a foreign film
    (what was it?)

M. has a parent born in another
    country

N. regularly reads the editorial page of
    the newspaper

O. has a hero
    (find out who the hero is)

P. has never moved

Freewrite on your findings. You might then use some of the information you've collected as the basis for a short research report.

2. You might use one or more of the following suggestions to explore your topic.

a) Freewrite for fifteen minutes to help you discover everything you already know about your topic.

b) Form a group of four or five. Name your topic, and have your classmates brainstorm a list of questions about it. Make a note of the questions they ask and then choose one or more to answer in this project.

3. Choose one of the topics below, and ask yourself what you and your intended audience might want to know about the topic. Then draw up a list of questions to help you focus on the information you want to find.

Nursery rhymes. Choose a nursery rhyme. When did people first begin to recite it, and why? To help you focus on a specific nursery rhyme, you might research such questions as: Who was "Little Jack Horner"? Why was "Mary, Mary quite contrary"? Why was it that "Jack Sprat could eat no fat"? Why was "Old King Cole" so merry?

Holidays. Choose a holiday. When and why did the holiday come into existence? (For example, did Parliament proclaim a particular day to be a national holiday?) Has the name of the holiday ever been changed? What are people expected to do on this holiday? Here are a few holidays to consider: Victoria Day, Canada Day, Labor Day, Remembrance Day, Saint-Jean Baptiste Day, Ramadan, Passover, or Christmas.

Interesting and picturesque words. Choose a word that intrigues you. In which language did the word originate? When did it come into use? (Consulting the *Oxford English Dictionary* will help you find information about a word's use.) What did it first mean? Has the meaning changed through the ages? If so, how? Here are some words to research, if you cannot think of one yourself: bluestocking, laconic, taciturn, sanguine, gerrymander, serendipity. You might try consulting the category *etymology* – the study of word origins – in your library's card catalogue for books about words and phrases.

Inventions and discoveries. Choose an invention or discovery. When, by whom, why, and how was it invented or discovered? Here are some topics to research if you cannot think of one yourself: gravity, quantum mechanics, eyeglasses, the thumbtack, the umbrella, the lightning rod, penicillin, the video cassette recorder, the compact disc, the computer chip.

4. Now, research your project. Learn where your library keeps fiction and nonfiction books, reference books, magazines, and newspapers. Get in the habit of using the card catalogue, a guide to the information found in your library's books. Learn to use the *Readers' Guide to Periodical Literature,* a guide to information in magazine articles. Find out which encyclopedias your library has and familiarize yourself with them. Do not hesitate to consult your library's most important and often most helpful resource, the librarian. (In Chapter 35 you will find pointers for using your local library and suggestions for recording the information you collect.)

5. Once you have located your sources of information, record the facts and quotations you need in the form of notes. You might write your notes, for example, on index cards, which are easy to use, carry, and organize, or on separate sheets of paper. (Be sure to include only one piece of information per sheet, so that, when you begin to draft, you can easily organize and reorganize your notes.) Familiarize yourself with the researching capabilities of your computer. For example, a school or library computer might be hooked up to an on-line research database. Check your word-processing manual for suggestions for storing and using your research notes.

For each piece of information you collect, list the topic, subtopic, and a fact relevant to that subtopic. You can also include quotations in your research notes. Double check your facts and your quotations to make sure that they are absolutely accurate. Include the source of each piece of information you collect. If the source is a book, list the author, title, publisher, year of publication, and page number. If your fact or quotation comes from a magazine or newspaper, list the author, title of the article, name of the magazine or newspaper, date of publication, and page number. Notice how one student writer has recorded facts on an index card.

> Lawrence Wright
> Clean and Decent
> New York: Viking Press, 1960, p. 245.
>
> Toothbrush commissioned by
> Queen Elizabeth I of England
> "whose teeth, once yellow, were
> in her old age, jet black."

Whatever method you use to collect your information, you have to be able to arrange (and rearrange) your information easily. (Any gaps in the organization may indicate a need for further research.) Once you have organized your notes into what seems to be a logical order, you can use them as the basis for a working outline. The outline can indicate the subtopics of your paper and the facts supporting each subtopic. The following working outline organized the information presented in "Under the Eaves." (You'll find the completed essay later in this chapter.)

Origin of Eavesdrop

I. First use
  A. Eaves: from Old English efes
  B. Overhanging edge of a roof
  C. Eavesdrop: place where water drips from eaves

II. Origin of verb
  A. 1606: first use of eavesdrop as verb
  B. To eavesdrop: to stand within eavesdrop of a house to overhear secrets
  C. Eaves: an excellent place for listening
  D. Snoopers called "eavesdroppers"

III. Today's meaning
  A. Similar to 1606 meaning
  B. Expanded to include other ways of listening in on a private conversation.

> ### ◢ Writer's Choice
>
> Do you want to think about your writing variables before or as you draft? Have you thought about the tone of your report? For example, would a humorous paper be appropriate for your topic? Take a few minutes to read the short research reports at the end of this chapter. Are you ready to begin to draft, or would you like to brainstorm further?

6. For more information about style, consult Chapter 29. You might also choose to explore your topic further by using one of the exploration techniques in Chapter 22. The following are particularly helpful for research reports: Free Association Cluster; Aristotle's Topics; or Newspaper Reporter's Questions.

Drafting Suggestions

1. Think about the structure of your report. For example, you might want to follow basic essay structure – introduction, development, conclusion. You include an introductory paragraph that sets out your topic, several paragraphs that present supporting evidence, and a conclusion that summarizes the main ideas and encourages the reader to think about your report.

2. Consider how you will organize your report. You might, for example, show cause and effect; compare and contrast your information; move from material that is familiar to most people to material that is unfamiliar; or present information in chronological order. (See Chapter 25 for more about organization.)

3. Decide on your approach to your topic. For example, will you use a straightforward style? Or will you use irony, poking fun at your subject by saying the opposite of what you mean? (To discover the range of styles you might use, see the Second Workshop section, especially Chapters 29 and 33.)

4. Don't settle for a dull beginning such as "This research paper is about...." (For more interesting beginnings and more interesting ways of stating a thesis, see the first paragraphs of the reports at the end of this chapter.)

> ### ◢ Writer's Choice
>
> Are you bringing a fresh insight into your topic? How are you doing that?

5. Use well-chosen quotations to add authority to your research report. Keep in mind that for this writing project, it is suggested that you include at least two quotations from two different sources; however, you might like to include several direct and indirect quotations, giving appropriate credit.

6. Indicate all the sources of the information in your paper. The traditional way of indicating sources is through footnotes; however, the papers at the end of this chapter and Chapter 35 use a method recommended in 1984 by the Modern Language Association. Indicate sources using **parenthetical citations**. After a fact or quotation, cite the last name of the source's author and the number of the page on which the fact or direct quotation appears. Enclose this information within parentheses. Then indicate the full source in the bibliography.

For example, suppose you were writing a research paper in which you quoted the first sentence of this suggestion. You would indicate the source of your quotation as follows:

"Indicate all the sources of the information in your paper" (Parker 172).

Notice that no mark of punctuation separates the author's name from the page reference, and that the period ending the sentence appears *after* the parenthetical citation. If the book or article has no author, or if you have taken your information from a well-known reference work, use a short form of the title as part of the parenthetical citation. For example, the *Shorter Oxford English Dictionary* can be cited as SOED.

If you are writing this paper as an assignment for a particular teacher, check how he or she wants references cited. If your teacher prefers that you document with footnotes rather than parenthetical citations, consult a handbook published *before* 1984 as a guide for proper forms. Otherwise, use parenthetical citations.

7. Parenthetical citations depend on a list of sources, or bibliography, to make clear what is being cited. Include such a list at the end of your research report with the heading "Works Cited." (For more about bibliographies, consult Chapter 35.)

8. Consult the research reports at the end of this chapter if you need help with the form of quotations, parenthetical citations, and bibliographies.

9. If your intended audience is a teacher, you may have to include a title page. Use whatever set-up he or she requests, or see the title page accompanying "Under the Eaves."

10. Leave plenty of time to revise and edit your report before submitting it to your intended audience.

When you finish your draft, consider the following guidelines.

Guidelines for Revising a Short Research Paper

☐ Why are you writing this paper? Have you expressed your purpose clearly? Do you care about your topic? Will your audience be able to see that?

☐ What do you like best about your draft? Least? How can you build on your paper's strengths and get rid of its weaknesses?

☐ What is the limited topic of your paper? Have you stated it clearly in a thesis statement? Do you effectively deal with your topic within the suggested 250-word limit?

☐ Do you logically and consistently support your main idea with appropriate details, examples, and quotations? Have you blended the quotations smoothly with your own prose? Have you included at least two quotations from two different sources?

☐ Have you included anything that does not move your paper forward? Are there any important gaps in your information or your thinking?

☐ Does your introduction capture the attention of your audience, set out your topic, and let your audience know how you feel about your subject?

☐ Do you logically develop the body of your paper? Is there anything that might confuse your audience? For example, have you taken for granted anything that your audience might not know about your topic?

☐ Does your ending conclude your paper effectively? Does it encourage your audience to reflect on your ideas and to relate your information to their own knowledge and experience?

☐ Are you satisfied with the mechanics of your draft (parenthetical citations, bibliography, spelling, punctuation, and grammar), or is there something you'd like to check before you let an editor see your work?

☐ Have you left sufficient time to rethink and revise your draft?

☐ Is there anything in your draft that you would like your editor to help you with?

> ## Writer's Choice
>
> Is your draft ready for your intended audience? Or would you like an editor to make revising and editing suggestions?

If necessary, revise your work and prepare a clean double-spaced draft for your editor.

Revising and Editing Suggestions

Give your draft to your peer-editor, and share your writing variables. Encourage your editor to use the "Guidelines for Revising a Short Research Paper" in this chapter and the checklists in Chapter 27. Your editor should also think about how he or she would answer the following questions.

Ask Your Peer-Editor

☐ What was your first impression of my work? Did my paper tell you anything you didn't know about my subject? Did it present information you did know in a new and interesting way? Do you think my paper will interest my audience? Why?

☐ Is my purpose for writing clear? Does the paper achieve its purpose? Did I introduce my thesis in an interesting way? If not, let's talk about possible changes.

☐ What part of my essay is clearest? Most effective? Why? Is anything unclear? Why? What should I do to make it clearer?

☐ Have I properly emphasized my important points? In not, what needs more emphasis?

☐ Is anything important missing? Is there anything else you would like to know about my subject?

☐ Have I overemphasized or stated anything at too great a length? If so, what should I shorten or omit?

☐ Can you easily tell how I have organized my information? Is the organization easy to follow? Is it consistent and logical?

☐ Have I perfectly blended my prose and supporting quotations? If not, what changes would you suggest? Do any of my transitions (Chapter 26) need work?

☐ Did you spot any obvious errors in the information I've presented? Are there any facts that I should double-check?

☐ Do you like my word choice and sentence structure? Are my spelling, punctuation, and grammar all right? Is there anything I should still work on?

☐ Are my quotations punctuated properly? Are my parenthetical citations properly done? Have I correctly listed my sources in my bibliography?

Try to find the time to put your paper away for a few days. Then take it out to read again with a fresh, open mind, and give it a final polish. If it's on your computer, you won't have to hesitate to make a few final changes.

Publishing Suggestions

With your classmates, you might develop a collaborative trivia book based on your short research papers. You might add technical illustrations or humorous cartoons to your work. Consider offering your book as a resource to the school library, a doctor's office, an airline, or other locations where people would have to wait and would enjoy reading a book to pass the time.

In the Company of Writers

Under the Eaves
Judy Chapelsky, student

In researching the origins of words, I came upon a particularly interesting account of the verb eavesdrop.

Derived from the Old English word efes, the noun eaves refers to the overhanging edge of a roof of a house ("Eaves," SOED). The noun eavesdrop (or eavesdrip) can refer to either "the dripping of water from the eaves" or "the space of ground on which such water falls" ("Eavesdrip," SOED).

But around 1606, eavesdrop began to be used as a verb, meaning to "stand within the 'eavesdrop' of a house in order to overhear secrets; hence, to listen secretly to private conversation" ("Eavesdrop," SOED). This meaning is based on the fact that there was about two feet of space between the edge of the eaves and the wall of the house, an area that turned out to be an excellent place for snoopers to crouch and listen to conversations. These snoopers were defined by law as "Such that listen under windows or the eaves of a house to hearken after discourse, and thereon to frame slanderous and mischievous tales" (Evans 137). The snoopers were called "eavesdroppers" and were said to be "eavesdropping."

Today's dictionary meaning of eavesdrop is strikingly similar to the 1606 use of the verb, but the everyday meaning has expanded to include more than just snooping by standing under the eaves of a house. We now speak of eavesdropping on the telephone and through closed doors, and use the verb casually to refer to the many other ways people can secretly overhear private conversations.

"Eaves." The Shorter Oxford English Dictionary. Third Edition.

"Eavesdrip, -drop." The Shorter Oxford English Dictionary. Third Edition.

"Eavesdrop." The Shorter Oxford English Dictionary. Third Edition.

Evans, Bergen. Comfortable Words. New York: Random House, 1959.

```
                    Under the Eaves




                    Judy Chapelsky
                    Writing 11A
                    Ms. D. Travell
                    March 25, 1990.
```

The Dynamic Duo
Steven Greenaway, student

Most of us use them, one on top of the other, at least twice a day. Some spend hours polishing with them while others just use the pair for a quick rinse. Yet have any of us ever bothered to look into the history of our beloved bathroom buddies – the faithful toothbrush and its underrated partner, toothpaste?

Toothbrushes are of uncertain origin. While the Romans are said to have used them in hopes of preserving their teeth, judging from the skeletal remains that have been found, the practice seems to have had little success.

Laurence Wright, a noted authority on the subject of toothbrushes, believes the first recorded toothbrush in England was one commissioned in 1561 by Queen Elizabeth I, "whose teeth, once yellow, were in her old age, jet black" (245).

Along with the toothbrush, the aristocracy of England often used tepid water to clean their pearly whites every morning. For a majority of the working class, however, soot was popular. Other formulas for homemade "tooth soap" included ashes mixed with honey, charcoal, areca nuts, and cuttlefish bone (Wright 246).

Perhaps the next time we squeeze a cylinder of breath-freshening Aim or Colgate (with MFP) onto our specially tapered Squibb or Reach, we should pay tribute to the wonders of modern technology!

Work Cited

Wright, Laurence. <u>Clean and Decent</u>. New York: Viking Press, 1960.

Where Does Blood Come From?
John Trottier, student

The title involves the readers immediately; they want to find the answer to the question.

The first sentence clearly states the thesis of the report. Readers will find out how the procedures for collecting blood differ between Canada and the U.S. The essay's development will clearly contrast the two procedures.

The development contains two paragraphs. In this paragraph, the writer discusses the procedures for giving blood in Canada by providing several examples.

The first sentence of the third paragraph sets up the contrast to reinforce the method of organization. The writer discusses the procedures for selling blood in the U.S. by providing examples and one long quotation from an interview.

Every day thousands of people enter hospitals and medical facilities all over North America for a life-saving dose of blood. Whether because of severe injury, during major surgery, or for treatment of diseases such as leukemia or hemophilia, blood or blood products will be crucial to the lives of many of these patients. Fortunately, these products are readily available in Canada and the United States, though the procedure for collecting blood differs in the two countries.

Blood has been collected from donors since 1947 by the Canadian Red Cross Society ("Red Cross"). So that no one who needs blood will go without it because of cost, the Red Cross maintains a voluntary blood donor system. "Anyone who is in good health between the ages of seventeen and up to their 66th birthday" (Canadian Red Cross) can give blood; many donors have given over 100 times! There are occasional problems with a voluntary system; during the summer, for example, when regular donors may be on vacation, blood supplies can run short, especially of rare types of blood. Generally, however, Red Cross blood banks can collect enough blood for the needs of local hospitals; in British Columbia, for example, the Red Cross processes 500–600 units of blood every day (Jones interview).

In contrast to the Canadian voluntary system, "only about seven percent of all donations in the United States are derived from voluntary donors" (Titmuss 111); and "paid donors contribute about one half of all blood and plasma donations" (Titmuss 112). "Maria," a worker in a private clinic, describes the procedure used to collect blood and pay donors:

The first time somebody comes in, they have to fill out a questionnaire about their medical history. Then they have to have their blood tested to make sure they aren't carrying AIDS or hepatitis or any other diseases; the tests take a couple of hours. If everything's okay, we accept the person as a donor. Some people come as often as once a week, but most only come once a month. A lot of our donors are on welfare, and so we get a lot of business just before the welfare cheques go out. We pay $8–10 a pint, depending on how rare the blood type is and what the blood's going to be used for, and the waiting room's full from 8 in the morning till 8 at night.

The conclusion sums up the main point of the report by restating the thesis. The report is strictly informative throughout.

The five sources of information that the writer has quoted from are listed alphabetically.

In summary, the blood-collection services in Canada and the United States have provided blood donors with different motivations for giving blood, but each system works satisfactorily to serve the needs of those who must have this life-saving fluid.

Works Cited

Canadian Red Cross Society, BC-Yukon Division. "Blood Programme Fact Sheet." September 9, 1986.

Jones, Ina. Personal interview. January 28, 1987.

"Maria." Personal interview. February 1, 1987.

"Red Cross." Encyclopedia Canadiana. 1977 ed.

Titmuss, Richard M. The Gift Relationship: From Human Blood to Social Policy. New York: Pantheon, 1971.

Dear Mom,

Recently, for an English assignment, I had the opportunity to research the expression "mind your p's and q's." Since you use this saying often, I thought you might be interested in what it means and where it comes from.

All sources I researched agree: the expression means "to be careful or particular as to one's words or behaviour" (OED 357). However, there are three different theories about the origin of the cliché.

Practical, logical, and boring, the first explanation probably comes closest to the truth. Some children learning the alphabet had difficulty distinguishing between p and q. Teachers or parents reminded them to "mind your p's and q's" (Partridge 145).

The second explanation, a little more imaginative, is my favourite: this expression originated in taverns some time during the nineteenth century. A running tab was kept for the amount of ale a customer consumed during the evening: "p" for pint and "q" for quart. Afraid the customer might consume too much of the numbing brew or be unable to pay the bill when it came due, the tavern master would remind him to "mind your p's and q's" (Evans 821).

The last theory is that the expression originated in France during the reign of Louis XIV, when huge wigs were fashionable. Dancing masters warned their pupils to " 'mind your p's (i.e., <u>pieds</u>, feet) and q's (i.e., <u>queues</u>, wigs)' lest the latter fall off when bending low to make a formal bow" (Evans 821).

So you see, Mom, you were using an international expression without realizing it. I hope you enjoyed reading this explanation of your favourite quote as much as I did researching it. And just think, Mom, I'm getting credit in my English class for this letter!

Love,

Robin

Works Cited

Evans, Ivor, ed. <u>Brewer's Dictionary of Phrase and Fable</u>. New York: Harper & Row, 1981.

<u>The Oxford English Dictionary</u>. London: Oxford University Press, Vol VII, 1978.

Partridge, Eric. <u>Dictionary of Clichés</u>. London: Routledge and Kegan Paul, 1962.

Your Writing

1. Have a look at the different ways these writers have presented their topics. Do you think that the style and tone of your paper present your topic in the best way? In looking back now at your paper, is there anything that you would have changed? Why?

2. What research techniques have you used? Which were most effective? Why? Is there anything you would do differently on another occasion? Why?

3. In your journal, comment on your writing. What did you learn from preparing your short research paper? Is there any part of your process that you would modify when you write your next research paper? Why?

13

Long Research Paper

"There is little point to traveling around the world and learning new things about fishes in far-off places, if you don't make your findings available for the possible use of others."

Eugenie Clark

Throughout your life, you will likely have to prepare research reports. This writing project will give you help in some of the more important aspects of such projects.

WRITING PROJECT

> Write a research paper at least 1,000 words long. It can be on an assigned topic or one of your choice. Use at least five sources of information, such as books, magazine or newspaper articles, or personal interviews.

Exploring and Prewriting Suggestions

1. If you've already done a short research paper (Chapter 12), you've already covered the basics of this project. Before you begin, have a look at the Exploring and Prewriting Suggestions in Chapter 12. Most apply to this project as well. Think about how you can integrate your computer's capabilities into your researching.

2. If you're having difficulty coming up with a topic for your research report, you might experiment with one or more of the following.
a) In a small group, share possible research topics. They can be personal (for example, provide a full family tree); social (for example, provide details

about a society with which you are familiar); or political (for example, provide background information on a political party that interests you).

b) Choose one of your favorite authors. In a ten-minute freewriting session write everything you know about the author. As well, jot down questions about the author that you might like to try to answer.

c) Which historical figure or living world personality intrigues you most? Apply the Newspaper Reporter's Questions (Chapter 22) to your subject. Questions without answers may often appear. That's all right. If you choose this subject as your topic, you will be able to find the answers.

Writer's Choice
Would you like to write your research paper collaboratively?

3. If you decide to write collaboratively, form a group of four. Together choose five or six topics that you would all like to research and write a paper on. At this point, you might choose a topic and begin your research; or you might exchange your list of topics with another group and have that group choose one from your list. Then you can collaboratively research and write your paper *for* that group.

4. If you have been assigned a research paper for another class, such as history, check with your teachers to see whether you can write this paper to fulfil both purposes. This way, you can get the benefit of your editors' comments before you write your final draft.

5. Consult Chapter 35 for researching suggestions and tips on note-making.

Keep in mind that you have to report your information accurately. Check and double-check your facts and quotations, and make sure that you correctly record the sources of your information. (Indicating, for example, that a quotation appears on page 128 of a book when it really appears on page 182 suggests you are a careless researcher and may raise doubts about all your research.)

Writer's Choice
Are you ready to draft your paper? Or do you need to brainstorm further?

6. To help you think about the kind of information you need, you might try one or more of the exploration techniques in Chapter 22.

7. There are a number of ways to organize the facts in a research paper – for example, chronological order, sequential order, order of importance, and comparison and contrast. (For more about organization, see Chapter 25.) Organizing your research notes will probably point you toward the organization of your paper. An outline of your topics, subtopics, and important information will also help.

8. Make sure that you record all the sources you consult and that you have all the information you need for your bibliography.

- For books, you need the following information: the author's name, the title of the book, the publisher, the place of publication, the date of publication, and page references for each quotation.
- For magazine and newspaper articles, you need the author's name, the title of the article, the name of the magazine or newspaper, the date of the issue, and the page or pages on which the article appears.

(Nothing is more frustrating than sitting down to compile your bibliography, only to find that you have not written down all the details and must return to the library to find a particular book.)

AHHH! THERE YOU ARE, SMEDLEY, BE A GOOD CHAP AND FETCH ME ANOTHER TEA, WHILE I FINISH THIS REPORT ON THE SASQUATCH MYTH!

> ## Writer's Choice
>
> Do you want to consider your writing variables before or as you draft? Are you ready to begin your draft, or do you want to consider the following drafting suggestions?

Drafting Suggestions

1. You might want to consult the suggestions in Chapter 12. You might also skim the research paper and outline at the end of this chapter. Notice particularly the paper's organization, its use of quotations and parenthetical citations, and its bibliography.

2. Long research papers can consist of several parts. Whether you should include some of these parts depends on the topic you choose and what your audience asks you to provide.

a) *Title page.* The information on the title page usually includes your name, the title of your paper, your class name, the name of your teacher, and whatever other information you may be asked to provide. (See the sample on page 187.) Find out whether your audience has a preferred form or set-up for the title page.

b) *Outline.* Many teachers require a formal outline to accompany a research paper. You can use the rough outline you prepared when organizing your facts as a basis for a more formal outline. For a discussion of outlines, see Chapter 28.

c) *Appendix.* If your paper includes charts, graphs, or long lists of items such as names or dates, you may decide to include these in an appendix at the end of your paper, just before your bibliography.

d) *Bibliography.* Include a bibliography listing the sources of your facts and quotations. The Modern Language Association recommends that the bibliography be labelled "Works Cited." (See Chapter 35 for guidelines on setting up a bibliography.)

3. Be sure to give the source of each fact and each quotation. (See Chapter 35 for more about sources.)

When you finish your draft, consider the following guidelines.

Guidelines for Revising a Long Research Paper

☐ Why are you writing this paper? Is your purpose clear? Will your audience be able to see that you care about your topic and really want to share your research?

☐ What is the strongest feature of your draft? Your weakest? How can you build on your paper's strengths and get rid of its weaknesses?

☐ What is the topic of your paper? Have you stated it clearly? Is it appropriate for a paper of this suggested length?

☐ Do you logically and consistently support your main idea with appropriate details, examples, and quotations? Have you smoothly blended your source material with your own prose? Have you included anything that does not move your paper forward? Are there any important gaps in your information or your thinking?

☐ Does your introduction capture the attention of your audience, set out your topic, and let your audience know how you are approaching your subject?

☐ Do you logically develop the body of your paper? You might try moving paragraphs around to find the best order for them. Is there anything that might confuse your audience? For example, have you taken for granted anything that your audience might not know about?

☐ Does your ending conclude your paper effectively? Does it encourage your audience to reflect on your ideas and to relate your information to their own knowledge and experience?

☐ Are you satisfied with the mechanics of your draft (parenthetical citations, bibliography, spelling, punctuation, and grammar), or is there something you'd like to check before you let an editor see your work?

☐ Have you left sufficient time to rethink and revise your draft?

☐ Is there anything in your draft that you would like your editor to help you with?

Writer's Choice

Is your draft ready for your intended audience? Or would you like an editor to make revising and editing suggestions?

If necessary, revise your work and prepare a clean double-spaced draft for your editor.

Revising and Editing Suggestions

Give your draft to your peer-editor, and share your writing variables. Encourage your editor to use the "Guidelines for Revising a Long Research Paper" in this chapter and the checklists in Chapter 27. Your editor should also think about how he or she would answer the following questions.

Ask Your Peer-Editor

- ☐ What was your first impression of my work? What did my paper tell you about my subject that you didn't already know? Did it present information you did know in a new and interesting way? Do you think my paper will interest my audience? Why?
- ☐ Is my purpose for writing clear? Does the paper achieve its purpose? Did I introduce my thesis in an interesting way?
- ☐ What part of my paper is clearest? Most effective? Why? Is anything unclear? Why? What should I do to make it clearer?
- ☐ Have I properly emphasized my important points? If not, what needs more emphasis?
- ☐ Is anything important missing? Is there anything else you would like to know about my subject?
- ☐ Have I overemphasized or stated anything at too great a length? If so, what should I shorten or omit?
- ☐ Can you easily tell how I have organized my information? Is the organization easy to follow? Is it consistent and logical?
- ☐ Have I perfectly blended my prose and supporting quotations? Do any of my transitions (Chapter 26) need work?
- ☐ Did you spot any obvious errors in the information I've presented? Are there any facts that I should double-check?
- ☐ Do you like my word choice and sentence structure? Are my spelling, punctuation, and grammar all right? Is there anything I should still work on?
- ☐ Are my quotations punctuated properly? Are my parenthetical citations properly done? Have I correctly listed my sources in my bibliography?

Try to find the time to put your paper away for a few days. Then take it out to read again with a fresh, open mind, and give it a final polish.

Publishing Suggestions

Completed research papers might become a classroom resource, either as a source of information or as a guide to appropriate forms for such papers. Papers on similar themes might be gathered into "research periodicals" and illustrated.

In the Company of Writers

Acupuncture
Lynn Stefonovich, student

I. Explanation of acupuncture
   A. Insertion of fine needles into skin
   B. Absence of pain and drawn blood

II. Chinese theory of acupuncture
   A. Meridians
      1. Relation to cause and cure of disease
      2. Basis of all theory and treatment
   B. Opposing forces: Yin and Yang
      1. Feminine and masculine principles
      2. Use of acupuncture to restore balance between forces

III. Western theory of acupuncture
   A. Relieves pain but does not cure
   B. Effect of needles' insertion
      1. Impulses sent to brain
      2. Natural chemicals secreted
      3. "Analgesia rather than anesthesia"

IV. Acupuncturists' procedures
   A. Complete examination before treatment
   B. Methods of diagnosis
      1. Acupuncture points
      2. Pulses
      3. Changes in body openings and in skin
      4. Body odors
      5. Changes in voice
   C. Use of needles to stimulate affected organs
      1. Slow insertion and rapid withdrawal of needles
      2. Hot needles for Yang treatment and cold needles for Yin
      3. Clockwise twist for Yang and counterclockwise for Yin
   D. Response to treatment

V. Status of acupuncture in the West
   A. Researchers' attitudes
   B. Possible acceptance by Western doctors as a valid technique

Acupuncture

Lynn Stefonovich
Writing 11A
Ms. D. Travell
March 25, 1990.

Acupuncture, the ancient Chinese art of healing, is the practice by which a needle is inserted a few millimetres into the skin, left for a predetermined amount of time, and then withdrawn. Fine, flexible, and sharp, the needles may be made of various substances, but silver and stainless steel needles seem to be the most popular. Insertion of the needles should not cause pain or draw blood ("Curious" 38). Though the Western scientific theory about acupuncture differs considerably from the Chinese theory, this art of healing is apparently effective.

According to traditional Chinese theory, as set forth by Ling Shu, the human body is divided into twelve passages or meridians. These relate to the causes and cures of diseases. The "twelve meridians are the basis of all theory and treatment" (Mann 35). Through these passages flow the vital forces of life. There are two life forces, Yin (the feminine force) and Yang (the masculine force). If a person is healthy, the life forces are considered to be in proper proportion. Acupuncturists will manipulate the forces by inserting needles at critical points until a proper balance is achieved (Hassett 86). They are concerned with the energy behind the invisible forces of Yin and Yang.

Western theory differs considerably from the Yin/Yang theory. Scientific research performed on rats proves that acupuncture relieves pain but does not cure disease. When the needles are inserted, impulses are sent to the brain by way of the central nervous system, which acts as a conductor. The brain causes the body to secrete natural chemicals that resemble painkilling drugs such as morphine (Hassett 82). Scientists believe that "acupuncture produces analgesia rather than anesthesia; that is the reduction of pain rather than the loss of sensation" (Hassett 89).

Before a diagnosis is made, the patient must have a complete examination from head to toe. Acupuncture points and the organs they are associated with are not usually close together. For example, the acupuncture points on the leg are associated with the liver, gall bladder, kidney, bladder, spleen, and stomach. Any points that are painful, even if no pressure is applied to them, are connected with a diseased organ. When the disease is cured, whether by acupuncture, Western medical methods, or the passage of time, there will be no pain at the acupuncture point (Mann 27–30).

Another way to reach a diagnosis requiring the application of acupuncture is by taking the patient's pulses. There are twelve different pulses, six on each wrist within a given area. Six are taken by acupuncturists applying a light pressure on the area, and the other six by a heavier pressure on the same area. Each pulse is associated with a certain organ. Acupuncturists compare the characteristics of each pulse with those of a healthy pulse to form a decision. They believe that by feeling the pulse, they "can detect illness long before it appears as a noticeable symptom" (Duke 150). The pulses and the tender acupuncture points are the two most important factors in a diagnosis, but many minor observations also affect acupuncturists' decisions.

Since all the organs have counterparts on the body's surface, well-trained acupuncturists observe changes in the patient's skin and body openings. They study the patient's eyes, tongue, and coloring because different colors relate to different organs. The senses of hearing and smell also assist acupuncturists. Body odors and changes in a patient's voice can mean a Yin/Yang disturbance (Duke 140). Combining all the necessary information from observing and touching, acupuncturists reach their diagnoses. Before treatment begins, they know precisely where the needles will go, how deep they will be placed, and how many times they will be used. The aim of acupuncturists is to "stimulate the affected organ through its meridian and restore the harmonious flow" (Moss 40). They will balance the Yin and Yang energy among the various organs, the nervous system, and the blood.

To stimulate the Yang, acupuncturists insert the needle slowly, withdraw it rapidly, and massage the spot after the needle is taken out. They stimulate the Yin in the same way. Hot needles are used for Yang treatment, cold ones for Yin. If the needle is twisted clockwise as it is inserted, the Yang will be influenced; a counterclockwise motion will produce a change in the Yin (Duke 162). Response to the treatment differs from patient to patient; some respond within a few seconds of the first needle's insertion, but some require as many as forty-two needles and several visits. A very small proportion of patients who do not improve while being treated may notice a cure some months later. Following each treatment, a patient may feel an increase in energy, due to the stimulating effect of the needles, or may feel a pleasant drowsiness due to the sudden release in tension (Mann 200–201).

Although acupuncture will continue to be a subject of controversy, physiologist David Meyer may have summed up the general feeling of researchers when he stated, "I don't think any researcher in this field now doubts that acupuncture can reduce experimental pain in the laboratory" (Hassett 85).

More people are turning to acupuncture as a last resort to alleviate pain and disease. Some are concluding that it should perhaps have been their first resort. In the future, Western medical science may use acupuncture as a technique to treat certain painful conditions.

Works Cited

"A Curious Cure That Works." Changing Times. Nov. 1980: 37–39.

Duke, Mark, Acupuncture. New York: Pyramid House, 1973.

Hassett, James. "Acupuncture Is Proving Its Points." Psychology Today. Dec. 1980: 37–39.

Mann, Felix, M.D. Acupuncture: The Ancient Chinese Art of Healing and How It Works Scientifically. New York: Random House, 1971.

Moss, Louis, M.D. Acupuncture and You. Secaucus: Citadel Press, 1964.

Your Writing

1. How does your paper stack up against "Acupuncture"? Do you state your thesis clearly and early in the essay? Does the paper move smoothly from your own prose to the quotations you use?

2. How would your paper be different if you wrote it for another audience, such as a grade six class?

3. In your journal, comment on your writing. What did you learn from writing your long research paper? Is there any part of your process that you would modify when you write your next research paper? Why?

14 Feature Article

"The new journalism demands flair and artistry rather than dull, "objective" coverage. Biases that can never be eliminated anyway are therefore exploited for their artistry rather than suppressed by a need to appear unbiased."

Ronald Primeau

Like a research paper, a feature article communicates information, but its approach and style are different. A research paper is often formal, like someone wearing dress clothes; a feature article can be informal, like someone in a sports jacket and blue jeans. Research papers rely mostly on printed matter – books, magazines, newspapers, pamphlets – for information. Feature articles use those sources, but they also draw from the writer's own experience and what can be learned from talking with others (often through interviews).

While a research paper is usually intended as a school or business project, many feature articles are written for magazine and newspaper readers. You have probably come across articles with titles such as "Canadian Native History: Voices from the Past Speak to the Present," "Hard Rock Makes a Comeback," "Women in Top Jobs," and "When Labor Talks, Government Listens." When you write your feature article, think of a title that will draw attention.

WRITING PROJECT

> Write a feature article about 1,000 words long on a topic that interests you and that you think will interest others.

Exploring and Prewriting Suggestions

1. If you haven't already selected a topic for your feature article, you might experiment with one or more of the following until you find one.

a) Imagine that you are a writer for a magazine or the editorial pages of a newspaper. Your editor-in-chief has told you to come up with a *current* story idea in ten minutes because she wants you to write a full feature article for the next edition. You've already written successful articles on recent developments in education, fashion trends, popular dances, local historic sites, and visiting personalities. Your editor-in-chief wants a fifty-word treatment, proposal, or abstract in ten minutes, so start writing quickly.

b) With a partner, explore possible topics for a feature article. Once you have chosen a topic, apply the following seven controlling questions to it and respond as fully as you can to each one. For example, if you were writing on *dyslexia*, you would substitute *dyslexia* for the X.

- What are the causes of X?
- What are the theories about X?
- What are the characteristics or symptoms of X?
- What are the capacities for and likelihood of change in X; and what are the effects of any change in X?
- What are the characteristics of the family or social group of X?
- What are the similarities or differences in X, depending on the environment?
- What is the history of X?

c) Choose a topic that you might use for a social studies or science magazine and brainstorm using one of the exploration techniques in Chapter 22. Particularly useful are Newspaper Reporter's Questions and Aristotle's Topics.

d) Gather as many issues of as many magazines as you can. In a small group, try to determine the audience and the interests of the audience of each. (For example, to whom does *Sports Illustrated* appeal? *Rolling Stone*? *Car and Driver*? *Maclean's*? *Seventeen*? What do the readers of each of these magazines want to know about?) Decide which magazine you would like to write for. Then choose a topic you think will appeal to the magazine's readers. Explore style and topic in fifty words or less.

e) Flip through a newspaper or magazine until you find an article that interests you. Imagine that you have been asked to do a related article, either a follow-up that expands on the existing article or an article on a related topic. Freewrite for ten minutes to discover what you already know about your topic. You might also jot down questions that you'd like to ask about your subject – and then answer them in your article.

Writer's Choice

Do you want to consider your writing variables now or as you draft? Are you ready to draft a thesis statement?

2. Because a feature article presents a lot of information, allow plenty of time to research your article. Some of your information may come from watching television and listening to the radio, but much of it will probably come from reading books, magazines, and newspapers. You might consult Chapter 35 for some researching pointers.

3. Part of your information may come from first-hand sources – your own experience and what you learn from other people. You may want to arrange interviews with people who are knowledgeable about your topic. If you do conduct interviews, think about what information you need, and prepare your questions in advance. (But be prepared to listen carefully to your source and to ask follow-up questions that clarify information you are given.) If you have a cassette recorder, use it to record the interview (with your source's permission). If you don't have a recording device, bring a notebook and pencil or pen, and take notes.

4. Think about how you want to record your information: on index cards, individual sheets of paper, or on a computer database. Be sure to keep your notes in a form that you can easily organize and reorganize.

Writer's Choice

Have you gathered all the information you need, or do you need to explore a bit more?

5. You may want to use one of the exploration techniques in Chapter 22, especially Newspaper Reporter's Questions.

Drafting Suggestions

1. Be selective in the information that you use. You've probably collected more information than you need for your feature article. Think about your thesis, and use only the information that directly relates to it.

2. To make your article lively and interesting, you might try to include quotations, personal observations, descriptions, anecdotes, and opinions (including your own).

3. Remember that a feature article is often informal in tone. Usually, you don't have to indicate sources of information in parenthetical citations or include a bibliography. Instead, try to include your source in the sentence or paragraph along with your information. To see how one writer moves smoothly from mentioning sources to presenting information, see "The Fascinating World of Dreams" at the end of this chapter (especially the sixth paragraph).

4. The tone of a feature article can move from the objective (presenting facts) to the subjective (expressing thoughts and feelings). It can switch from the third-person point of view to the first person and go back again. Notice how the author of "The Fascinating World of Dreams" blends third-person and first-person writing and subjective and objective tone.

Writer's Choice

Can you present some of your information in graphs, charts, illustrations, photographs, or cartoons?

5. Feature articles often include visuals. Think about how you might support (or replace some of) your text with visuals.

When you finish your draft, consider the following guidelines.

Guidelines for Revising a Feature Article

☐ Why are you writing this article? Do you set out your purpose clearly in a thesis statement or in your introductory paragraph? Or do you imply your purpose?

☐ What do you like best about your article? Least? If you are making an argument, which is your strongest point? Your weakest? How can you build on your article's strongest argument or points?

☐ Do you care about your topic? Will your audience be able to see that? Is your topic appropriate for a feature article – and for your intended audience?

☐ Does your introduction capture your audience's attention, set out your topic, and let your audience know how you feel about your subject?

☐ Do you logically and consistently present your material using appropriate details, examples, dialogue, observations, descriptions, anecdotes, visual illustrations, or quotations? Have you included anything that does not move your article forward? Are there any important gaps in your information or your thinking?

☐ Do you logically develop the body of your article? How have you organized your information? Is there anything that might confuse a reader? For example, have you taken for granted anything that your audience might not know?

☐ Does your ending effectively conclude your article? Does it encourage your audience to reflect on your ideas and to relate your information and opinions to their own knowledge and experience?

☐ If you've used visuals, do they effectively link with your text?

☐ Are you satisfied with the mechanics of your draft (spelling, punctuation, and grammar), or is there something you'd like to check before you let an editor see your work?

☐ Have you left sufficient time to rethink and revise your draft?

☐ Is there anything in your draft that you would like your editor to help you with?

> ### Writer's Choice
>
> Do you want an editor to look over your work? Or is your feature article ready to be published?

If necessary, revise your work and prepare a clean double-spaced draft for your editor.

Revising and Editing Suggestions

Give your draft to your peer-editor, and share your writing variables. Encourage your editor to use the "Guidelines for Revising a Feature Article" in this chapter and the checklists in Chapter 27. Your editor should also think about how he or she would answer the following questions.

Ask Your Peer-Editor

- □ What was your first impression of my feature article? What new information about my subject did you learn? Did I present information that you already knew in an interesting way?
- □ Do you think the article is appropriate for its intended audience? Do you think my information and opinions will interest and inform my audience? Why?
- □ What part of my article is clearest? Most effective? In what way? Is anything unclear? Why? What can I do to make it clearer?
- □ Have I properly emphasized my important points? Have I overemphasized or stated anything at too great a length? Is my information clearly organized and easy to follow? If not, what should I change?
- □ Do I grab the attention of my audience right at the beginning of the article, or does it take too long for my audience to know what I am trying to present? In other words, when you start reading this article, do you want to read it right to the end?
- □ Is my style informal, yet informative and opinionated, or do you think I tend to "talk down" to my audience? If so, what should I do?
- □ Do I use quotations, anecdotes, and dialogue accurately and effectively? Do my graphics complement my text, or do they seem out of place? If there are no graphic additions, can you suggest any that might make the article more interesting or entertaining?
- □ Does my article have an interesting title? Can you suggest one that's more "grabby"?
- □ Did you spot any obvious errors in the information I've presented? Are there any facts that I should double-check?
- □ Do you like my word choice and sentence structure? Are my spelling, punctuation, and grammar all right? Is there anything I should still work on?

Writer's Choice

Is your feature article eye-catching? Would it "jump off the page" at your audience?

Publishing Suggestions

You may want to submit your feature article to your school newspaper or yearbook, or, as a class, publish several feature articles yourselves. If you decide to publish your own newspaper or magazine, spend some time looking at the design of existing publications. Examine how they use space, position of advertisements, different kinds of type, and different graphic elements such as diamonds, triangles, and bands of color. Try to incorporate some of these in the design of your publication.

You may even want to send your article to a local or national magazine or newspaper. Don't be intimidated by the idea of writing to an "official" publication. Many journals publish articles by freelance writers all the time. But don't get disheartened if you get turned down initially. Magazines may prefer that you send a query letter, a sample of your writing (perhaps this article), and a proposal or two for another article. It sometimes takes a lot of time and effort to see your first piece published in a national magazine.

In the Company of Writers

The Fascinating World of Dreams
Mike Chan, student

In recent years the study of dreams has become increasingly popular. Theories and conjectures about dreams abound, as they have throughout history, yet only recently has dreaming been investigated seriously on a large scale. The modern scientific techniques of dream research now provide very reliable data. However, much of the mystery of dreaming still remains; many questions on the topic remain unanswered.

According to the magazine *Psychology*, the earliest Greeks believed dreams came from the gods: several passages in the *Iliad* refer to dreams sent by Zeus. During the Middle Ages, religious authorities held demons responsible for bad dreams. According to *Psychology Today*, not until Sigmund Freud's work in the late nineteenth century were psychological states recognized as the cause of dreams.

Although my aunt insists she never dreams, psychologists have confirmed that everybody dreams every night. The reason for forgetting dreams, however, is still not clear.

Many people have wondered whether or not animals dream. Studies performed at the University of Southern California were designed to answer their question. Dr. C. Y. Vaughn conducted various experiments with monkeys, concluding that "animals also perceive visual images during sleep." Unable to communicate verbally with his subjects, Dr. Vaughn was uncertain what his monkeys dreamt about. Nevertheless, the doctor reports, "Judging from their facial expressions, the dreams were most likely hostile in nature."

Eye movement is the predominant physical activity during the dreaming process. Authorities report that rapid eye movements nearly always accompany dreams.

Contrary to popular belief, dreaming of an activity takes approximately as long as carrying out the activity in waking life. According to *Psychology*, "Dreams do not occur in a split second, as many of us believe." A conversation I had with Dr. I. Olsen, my psychology teacher, confirmed this hypothesis. Dr. Olsen states, "People think dreams occur in a split second, but actually it takes equally as long to dream of an activity as it does to carry out the activity in the waking state. When we are asleep, our perception of time is lost."

Many people argue that dreams completely lack color. A constant dreamer myself, I tended to believe this claim. Yet, an investigation done by doctors Allen Kahn and Stuart Fisher at Texas State University provides evidence to prove all dreams are in color, but the color may be forgotten when the subject recalls the dream.

Interestingly enough, studies have shown that we dream an average of four times per night, each dream separated by a ninety-minute interval. The first dream usually occurs one hour after the onset of sleep; the last dream is nearly always the only one people remember.

A film entitled *Sleep*, shown to our class, claims that a major shift in body position indicates a dream has just ended. Dr. Joseph Collins, featured in the film, stresses the relationship between rapid eye movement and shifts in body position. According to Dr. Collins, "Rapid eye movement ceases after a major shift in body position, thus indicating the termination of a dream."

As reported in *Psychology*, dreams develop from four primary sources: day residue, past experience, external stimuli, and physiological states. Day residue and past experience are the dominant factors in determining our dreams, but the other two are equally important.

External stimuli incorporated into our dreams fascinate me the most. Upon hearing my alarm clock some mornings, I have incorporated the sound into my dream. Before awakening, I have dreamt the phone was ringing; subsequently in my dream, I have gone to answer it.

Dreaming has always been associated with the mysterious, supernatural world of precognition and mental telepathy. History is filled with tales of prophetic dreams, and yields many eerie, unexplained accounts of the supernatural. Abraham Lincoln, for example, dreamed he entered the East Room of the White House and saw a coffin. When he asked who had died, the reply was, "The President." Lincoln died three days later, the victim of an assassin's bullet. Lincoln's dream and its subsequent realization have been considered coincidental. According to Dr. William Levy, a prominent psychologist in Boston, "Lincoln was preoccupied with death. He often dreamt of being assassinated, and I see no correlation between his last dream and the fate that befell him."

Dr. Levy does point out, on the other hand, that telepathic messages can be transmitted through dreams. A team of scientists at Maimonides Hospital in New York conducted systematic studies of thought transmission to sleeping subjects. Their findings were astonishing. Dr. Peter Krippner, head of the investigation, stated, "Certain people are able to perceive thoughts while dreaming. Further studies will hopefully teach us how these messages are sent and received."

Although the study of dreams has become much more widespread over the years and although greater knowledge of the subject has been gained, dreaming is still one activity that continues to amaze us. Fascinating, mysterious, elusive, the world of dreams will undoubtedly continue to fascinate people for many years to come.

A Heavenly View of Hellish Volcanoes
from *The Globe and Mail*, March 25, 1989
Stephen Strauss

Scientists have moved their thoughts heavenward to satellites in order to better understand the belchings of hell, volcanic eruptions. In doing so, they are beginning to resolve fundamental questions that have evaded ground observers.

The first step is a surprisingly elemental one – determining just how many active and potentially active volcanoes there are in the world and when they erupt. "Most volcanic eruptions are not ever recorded," said William Rose, a geologist at Michigan Technical University. Indeed, one of the bonuses for vulcanologists during flights of the U.S. space shuttle is that astronauts see volcanic activity that nobody has previously reported.

The rough estimate is that there may be as many as 60 eruptions a year from the 800 to 1,000 active volcanoes, a number of which are under water. But no one knows for sure.

"They're too remote; the ground is too rough; you need too many people, and sometimes it is just too dangerous," said David Pieri, a vulcanology team leader at the U.S. National Aeronautics and Space Administration's Jet Propulsion Laboratory in California.

A good indication of the advance that satellites as volcanic survey instruments can make is illustrated by the work of Peter Francis and his associates at the NASA-backed Lunar and Planetary Institute in Houston. Using *Landsat* satellite images they have already located about 50 previously unreported live volcanoes in the barren and unpopulated central region of the Andes. This effort is the first step in a planned systematic mapping and monitoring of the world's volcanoes. The Earth Observing System, a number of platforms and sensors, would be set up in conjunction with the international space station in a massive scientific effort NASA is calling Missions to Planet Earth. It is scheduled to be launched in the mid-nineties.

A second area of interest has been in differentiating volcanic plumes from ordinary rainclouds. There are major air safety issues at stake, because jet engines have shut down when planes inadvertently blundered into volcanic clouds. Perhaps the best known example of this was two near-crashes of airplanes en route to Australia when their engines became fouled with the ash from the explosion of Mount Galunggung on the island of Java.

The problem for pilots is that their on-board radar does not differentiate between water-vapor clouds and volcanic plumes. Using data collected from weather satellites, Prof. Rose and Stephen Self of the University of Texas at Arlington have been able to separate volcanic material from normal clouds. This allows scientists to track volcanic emissions and their eventual deposition and to advise commercial airlines of their existence.

On a more fundamental scientific level, Lori Glaze, now at JPL, and Mr. Francis have recently published a paper in *Nature* that may foreshadow the prediction of volcanic eruptions. Using the *Landsat 4* and *5* satellite infra-red images, which are traditionally used for crop-forecasting and mineral exploration, they were able to follow the activity of a hot spot in the crater of the Lascar volcano in northern Chile.

What their study before and after an eruption suggests is that the hotspot decreased in size up to the explosion and increased afterwards. "It was kind of surprising that it occurs that way. I expected it to build up beforehand," Ms Glaze said. She and Mr. Francis are studying other volcanic hotspots to see if the signature of activity they identified in Chile is unique, or whether it represents a generalized pattern of volcanic reaction before an eruption.

Data teased out of satellite images are also obliging scientists to rethink their theories of volcanic formation. Prof. Self and Mr. Francis have analyzed data from the *Geos 9* satellite and seen what they believe is a new type of volcano. They have found in northern Chile three peculiar craters with low walls that look as if they were created by the impact of a meteor rather than by lava flow. "They look less like volcanoes and more like craters on the moon,"

Prof. Self said of the large formations. One is 6 kilometres across.

A visit to the site in 1987 verified that the craters are of volcanic origin but the mystery remains as to how they could have formed in an area dominated by traditional volcanic peaks, Prof. Self said. An upshot of the discovery is that the group is advising astronomers to be cautious in what they label as meteorite craters on planets and moons.

There is also much interest in what satellite images can tell about the course of an eruption. Where will the lava flow? How fast will it move? What are the dynamics of the hot and turbulent interior of molten rock that allow it to move uphill? Mr. Pieri has been using satellites and airplane observations to track the lava flows on Hawaii. What is clear already is that from the air they can differentiate among recent flows, those from 10 to 160 years ago, and thus track the eccentric courses the liquid rock took.

This means that scientists can start to build a base of data on old lava streams and compare them to the paths, thicknesses and heat of fresh eruptions. The goal again is prediction. "We want to look down during the course of an eruption and say, it looks like your property is going to be overrun, or no, your place looks okay," Mr. Pieri said.

While the new use of satellites has produced results and promised more, the technique is hindered by clouds and delayed responses. "We call up and say, we have an eruption, can you get us a picture? and they say, yeah, we can get you one in two months. But by that time the eruption is over," Mr. Pieri said.

Compounding the problem is that two of the satellites that have been very active in studying volcanoes, *Landsat 4* and *5*, may be shut down by the U.S. government in a budget-cutting move. Scientists hope many of these problems will be resolved by the EOS venture and by yet-to-be-approved plans to build satellites that will track an area of the planet all the time.

Your Writing

1. Who is the intended audience for your feature article? How would you change your article to suit a different audience – such as the residents of another country or the readers of different magazines?
2. Have you used photos, illustrations, tables, or other graphics in your article? If not, how might you have used these to replace some of your text? How could visuals have been used with the articles in this chapter?
3. If you saw these articles (and your own) in your favorite magazine, which would you read first? Would you read it through? Is there one you wouldn't read? Why?
4. In your journal, comment on your writing. What did you learn from writing your feature article? Have you saved all the information you didn't use? Is there anything that you might like to experiment with in your next feature article?

15   Set of Instructions

"The best direction is the least possible direction."

John Manley

Think about how much time you spend giving and receiving instructions. How often have you directed someone to your home or to an unfamiliar place? ("Turn right just beyond the shopping mall; then turn left at the STOP sign....") How often have you heard or read a step-by-step procedure for performing an experiment, assembling a model plane, making a dress, programming a VCR, filling out an application form, or cooking a new dish? Instructions are a part of everyday life.

WRITING PROJECT

> In 200 to 400 words, write a set of instructions.

Exploring and Prewriting Suggestions

1. To tell others how to do something, you have to know how to do it yourself. You may wish to try one or more of the following exploration ideas to help you think about the steps in a procedure.

a) With a classmate, brainstorm a list of things you could prepare instructions for. For example, you might post step-by-step instructions explaining to your co-workers how to clean a deep-fryer; prepare an enclosure card for a young relative setting out how to tie a necktie; write an outline for an informative essay on how to meditate (or participate in a specific sport); draft instructions for retrieving a deleted document on your computer; or include a recipe for cheesecake or brownies in a personal letter.

Choose one of the items on your list and freewrite for ten minutes on it, setting out everything you know about the procedure. Afterward, with your partner, organize the steps in the order they should be performed. Check with your partner whether he or she can follow your instructions or needs additional information.

b) You might imagine that you are an inventor and have just completed a fabulous invention. With your partner, discuss how you can make the invention "real" in your mind. Then prepare a set of instructions explaining how to use the invention. You might want to add illustrations to your work.

c) Think about something that you do every day. Freewrite for ten minutes, explaining your activity to someone from another culture or to someone who cannot see what you do.

d) Think about something that you do every day. Then develop the most outrageous set of instructions you can think of that would still allow your audience to carry out your activity – for example, set an alarm clock, open up a locker, or eat lunch.

e) Working in a small group, brainstorm possible activities and then choose one. Each group member in turn can give one instruction for how to carry out the activity. When the group has brainstormed all the steps in the procedure, the final speaker can provide a summary sentence.

f) As a class, you might work on a common topic, with each class member writing on a single aspect of the topic. You might choose one of the following topics: setting up your own business; starting up a school newspaper; hitchhiking around the world; cleaning up the environment. Freewrite for ten minutes on the topic and then use your freewriting notes to develop your set of instructions.

Writer's Choice

Do you have a good general sense of the steps you want to include? Are you ready to begin organizing and expanding them? Have you considered your writing variables, or will you settle on some of them as you draft?

2. Jot down, with as much detail as you care to include, the main steps of your procedure.

Drafting Suggestions

1. Think about how you want to present your instructions. Often, instructions are written in the second person, almost as commands: "Do this. Then do that." (The pronoun *you* is understood.) You might also write them in the first person: "After I ... then I ...."

2. If you decide to write your instructions as an informative essay, try to include an introduction and a conclusion. Your introduction, including your thesis sentence, can indicate how your set of instructions is useful or necessary. (Notice how the writers of "How to Throw a Frisbee," at the end of this chapter, indicate the usefulness of their instructions.)

3. If one of your steps seems complicated or otherwise difficult to explain, you may find it useful to divide the step into substeps or parts.

4. You may want to include one or more lists as part of your instructions – for example, a list of the tools you need to perform a certain operation.

Writer's Choice

Would you like to include any illustrations with your set of instructions? Would diagrams, flowcharts, or other graphics make your instructions easier to follow?

5. Add graphics, if they clarify your instructions.

6. Define any technical terms if you have to, but keep in mind that your audience does not want to learn terminology but to follow your instructions.

7. To help make your writing move smoothly, you may wish to use one or more of the transitional devices presented in Chapter 26.

8. Often, short paragraphs produce clearer instructions than do long ones that seem to jam a great deal of information together. Short paragraphs can make your instructions seem less complicated and easier to follow. Empty or "white" space can also make instructions easier to follow.

9. You may wish to number each step of the procedure you explain.

10. Check your draft to make sure that your audience will understand how to perform the procedure. Is each step clear? Are the steps complete and in the right order?

   You have just read a set of instructions. When you have completed your draft, consider the following guidelines.

Guidelines for Revising a Set of Instructions

☐ Why are you writing this set of instructions? Have you presented your instructions in an essay, letter, or poem? Which format would work best? Why?

☐ What is the clearest part of your instructions? Is anything unclear? How can you further clarify your instructions?

☐ Does your introduction capture your audience's attention and invite them to follow the procedure you set out?

☐ Will your audience be able to follow your instructions? Are the steps that you set out logical? Are there any important gaps in the steps you present? For example, have you taken for granted anything that your audience might not know?

☐ Have you included anything that might confuse your audience – or that your audience doesn't need to know? Have you bogged down in terminology or in defining what you mean?

☐ Do you effectively conclude your set of instructions?

☐ If you've used visuals, do they relate appropriately to your text?

☐ Are you satisfied with the mechanics of your draft (spelling, punctuation, and grammar), or is there something you'd like to check before you let an editor see your work?

☐ Does your set of instructions look inviting? That is, have you left plenty of white space around each instruction?

☐ Is there anything in your draft that you would like your editor to help you with?

Writer's Choice

Are your instructions ready for your intended audience? Or would you like an editor to look at them first?

If necessary, revise your work and prepare a clean double-spaced draft for your editor.

Revising and Editing Suggestions

Give your draft to your peer-editor, and share your writing variables. Encourage your editor to use the "Guidelines for Revising a Set of Instructions" in this chapter and the checklists in Chapter 27. Your editor should also think about how he or she would answer the following questions.

Ask Your Peer-Editor

☐ What was your first impression of my work? Did you find my instructions clear and easy to follow? Will my audience? If not, what can I do to make my instructions clearer? Should I add more details? Should I leave anything out?

☐ Do my illustrations or diagrams (if I've used them) do their job? That is, do they help make the explanations clear? Should I add illustrations or diagrams for greater clarity?

☐ Have I presented each step of the procedure in the order it should be performed? Is there anything you would change or express differently? Why?

☐ Have I used appropriate transitional words – such as *first, next, then*, and *finally* – to lead my audience from one step to the next? Should I add any transitional words?

☐ Have I done anything to make my instructions seem more complicated than they really are? (For example, have I jammed them together into long paragraphs?) Is there anything I should do to make my instructions easier to follow?

Writer's Choice

Do you want to test your instructions by giving them to another classmate to follow?

Publishing Suggestions

The true test of the clarity of your instructions lies with your intended audience. If that person can successfully complete the procedure you have explained, then both you and your audience have succeeded. You should, however, test your instructions *before* presenting them to your audience. As you go through the steps, ask yourself: Have I left out anything? Are the steps in a logical order?

You and your classmates might publish sets of instructions on related subjects in how-to manuals. If your set of instructions is a recipe, you may want to save it in a recipe file or binder for future reference.

In the Company of Writers

How to Throw a Frisbee
Murray Suid and Ron Harris

Frisbee tossers use dozens of different throws and catches. These range from the simple techniques to elaborate trick shots only an expert can do. Here are the basics of throwing a Frisbee. Once you have them down pat, you can work on fancier throws.

The basic Frisbee grip. Hold the Frisbee comfortably in the palm of your throwing hand. Your first finger should rest along the rim of the Frisbee. The other three fingers curl underneath. Your thumb is on top of the Frisbee.

The *backhand toss* is one of the most common Frisbee throws. Turn your shoulder toward the target. Extend your arm so that your index finger points where you want the Frisbee to go. Bring your throwing arm back, bending your elbow and cocking your wrist around. Then straighten your arm. At the moment your arm is fully extended, let the Frisbee go with a snap of the wrist. At the same time take a step forward with your right foot (if you're right-handed). At the end of the throw your finger should be pointing at the target.

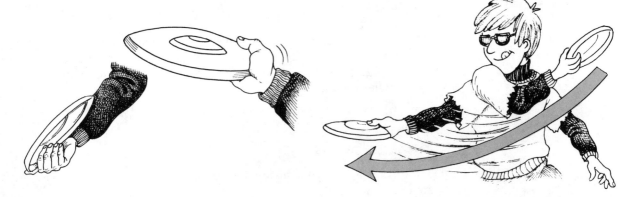

The key to accurate throws is to keep the Frisbee as flat as possible when you let it go. The flatter your throw, the straighter the Frisbee's path will be. When you start out, throw at a target that isn't too far away; nine or ten metres will do. Once you've perfected your short-range aim, begin moving the target back.

Another popular throw is the *underhand toss.* Face the target squarely, your arm pointing where you want the Frisbee to go. Use the same basic grip. But this time bring your arm behind you until it's nearly parallel to the ground. To toss the Frisbee, bring your arm forward, bending the elbow slightly as your hand comes under. Extend your arm, launching the Frisbee with a flip of the wrist. As you throw, take a step forward with the foot opposite your throwing arm (the left foot if you are right-handed). Once again, try to keep the Frisbee on a level, flat flight path.

Even if you are a beginning Frisbee thrower, you have probably learned how to throw *curves*. You simply tip the disc as it is released. To make the Frisbee flight path curve to the right, toss the disc with the left side up and the right down. For a left-hand curve, keep the left side of the Frisbee lower than the right.

Preparation Is the Key to Success

Terry Thilken, student

For you to succeed in a job interview, career advisers and interviewers suggest these steps:

1. Research the firm you are interested in joining. If possible, talk to people who already work there. Be prepared to show interest in and ask questions about the company.

2. Know specifically what you want to do. Be prepared to explain how your skills relate to a specific opening.

3. Make a list of positive points about yourself. If asked about your strengths, don't be afraid to say, "I'm good with numbers" or "My human-relations skills are good."

4. Practise your responses. Ask a friend to join you in role-playing and to alert you to potentially annoying characteristics such as distracting slang or speech patterns.

5. Be on time, or phone ahead if you are delayed.

6. Watch your appearance. You don't have to appear in your best "going out" clothes, but you should appear to be neat and professional. Some companies are more formal than others; if possible, note the attire of people doing the job that you are applying for.

7. Give the interviewer your full attention. An employer likes to know that you are interested in working for the company.

8. Don't initiate salary discussion in the first interview, but be prepared to discuss salary so that you don't sell yourself too cheaply.

9. Be prepared to answer questions such as the following in an interview:
- Why should I hire you?
- Why do you want to work here?
- What interests you about this position?
- What are your ambitions?
- What are your greatest accomplishments?
- Why do you want to change jobs?

10. Relax. Consider the interview as a conversation.

11. Be tenacious. Don't be afraid to ask when a decision will be made. If your interviewer says he or she will call you in four days, but fails to do so, call back and ask politely if a decision has been reached yet.

How to Eat a Poem

Eve Merriam

Don't be polite.
Bite in.
Pick it up with your fingers and lick the juice
    that may run down your chin.
It is ready and ripe now, whenever you are.

You do not need a knife or fork or spoon
or plate or napkin or tablecloth.

For there is no core
or stem
or rind
or pit
or seed
or skin
to throw away.

Your Writing

1. Who is the audience for each of these pieces of writing? Who is your audience? How would you alter your set of instructions if you were to write to a different audience? Would you include more information? Diagrams? Why?

2. Do you think that writing a set of instructions will make you more articulate in giving directions in the future? What makes you say so?

3. In your journal, comment on your writing. What did you learn from writing your set of instructions? Is there anything that you might like to experiment with in your next set of instructions?

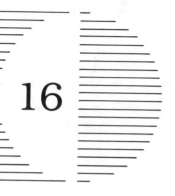

16

Demand Essay (Answering Questions on an Essay Test)

"I always get seventy-eight. No more, no less. It's nerve-wracking. I'd almost rather flunk once in a while."

Ruth Gordon

A demand essay is a piece of writing that you have to complete within a specific period of time. This essay is like both the informative essay in Chapter 4 and the argumentative essay in Chapter 5, but with two important differences. The topic is assigned to you, and you have only a limited amount of time to think and write. Writing to meet this kind of deadline can be alarming. This chapter will give you strategies for tackling this job and increase your confidence in undertaking it.

WRITING PROJECT

> Write a demand essay on an assigned topic, in class, within a certain period of time.

Exploring and Prewriting Suggestions

1. Being well prepared is the best prewriting strategy for writing a demand essay. There is nothing like the feeling of confidence that comes from knowing you can answer any question that may be asked about a subject.

 Writer's Choice

Of all the different ways to prepare for demand essays, which method do you regularly choose? Why? How does this method help you?

2. Begin by reviewing your material thoroughly. Try to compose summaries of your notes. (See Chapter 28.)

3. Identify key subject areas: What has your teacher stressed in class? What has your textbook stressed? What have you written down the most notes about? If essays were assigned through the term, what were the topics?

4. Predict questions that your teacher might ask about your subject, and write answers for them. This will give you experience in writing answers for the particular subject.

Writer's Choice

Because you have no choice in writing demand essays, how can you become more comfortable doing it?

5. To get into the habit of predicting and answering questions, you might try one or more of the following.
a) With a partner, pretend that you are a literary character from a story or play that you have studied. Ask a question as if you were the character, for example, "When I did such and such, how did you feel?" Encourage your partner to respond as one of the other characters.
b) With a partner, imagine that you are the author of one of your textbooks. As the author, pose a question about a portion of the text; let your partner respond; then switch roles.
c) After studying a unit in one of your classes, make up as many well-worded questions as you can, maybe fifteen to twenty. Put them in a box. Every time you have a few minutes, choose one and answer it as completely as you can. (For variety, you might like to have one or more of your classmates make up questions and add them to the box. They, too, could choose and answer questions.)

6. Try to practise answering questions that are assigned to you. The following are some suggestions on how to proceed.
a) Your teacher may provide a list of topics, ask you to choose one, and specify the deadline by which you must complete the demand essay.
b) You might ask one of your teachers to provide a test question in a sealed envelope. Open the envelope at the beginning of your writing class and, for ten minutes, plan your essay. Then, if you wish, write the whole essay.
c) Have a writing partner (who may share another class with you) assign a question for you to answer. You can do the same for your partner. Give yourself time to prepare. Then write a demand essay for your partner, within a specific time period.

d) With a partner or in a small group, brainstorm a list of questions for demand essays. Have one of your group members assign a question to you, and write a demand essay.

e) If no other topic is available, you might use one of the following.

- List the four major types of compounds found in living things. Describe the basic structure of each, and give examples.
- Write a critique of this book. Let the critique reflect your own experience in doing the writing projects.
- Compare and contrast a novel and the film based on it.
- Compare the first-person narrators (characters telling the stories) of two short stories. (You'll find examples of short stories throughout this book.)
- Summarize the breakdown of a molecule of glucose during cellular respiration.
- Apply Mackenzie King's personality to his deal with the C.C.F. under Woodsworth in the 1926 constitutional crisis.
- Analyse the rhythm, language, and use (if any) of figurative language in a poem in this book.

f) Occasionally, engage in an instant-writing session. (See Chapter 21.) For ten minutes, respond in your journal to a question posed by your teacher, another student, or yourself.

Writer's Choice

What should you look for in the language of a demand-essay question?

7. Try to familiarize yourself with the usual elements of demand essay questions.

a) Generally, a demand essay question has three parts: a key verb that tells you what you are supposed to do; an object that names what you are to perform your task on; and a limiting factor (or factors) that tells you how to go about your task. Here is an example to help you see the three parts in action.

Explain how Shirley Jackson, in the subtext of "Charles," shows that the narrator comes of age. (For the text of "Charles," see the appendix.)

Key verb: explain
Object: methods that Shirley Jackson uses to show how the narrator, Laurie's mother, comes of age
Limiting factor: refer to all the parts of the story where the narrator – not Laurie – comes of age

b) Notice how the question ties you down fairly specifically. Clearly, it would do you no good to refer to the more obvious coming of age of Laurie in the text of "Charles." (Be sure not to **pad** your answer by including such irrelevant information.) You must make inferences – or look into the **subtext** of the story – to answer this question.

8. Because the key verb is the most important part of an exam question, try to familiarize yourself with what is wanted when a particular verb is used. In the following list, you'll find some key verbs. Read each one with your partner; then provide an oral question that would be appropriate for a body of material you are studying.

> **Analyse** means to break down into parts and examine each part critically.
> **Apply** means to demonstrate your knowledge and understanding of material by using it extensively and confidently in various situations.
> **Compare** means to make an idea clear by calling attention to similarities (and sometimes differences). Use specific examples.
> **Contrast** means to make an idea clear by calling attention to differences. Use specific examples.
> **Define** means to explain the meaning of a particular expression. Illustrate a definition with at least one specific example.
> **Describe** means to write about an object or event using details.
> **Discuss** is an ambiguous term. (If you are ever asked to discuss, try to ask your examiner exactly what he or she wants. If you cannot ask, set out your understanding of the question and answer it as best you can.)
> **Evaluate** means to judge, critique, or give your opinion of something.
> **Explain** means to write an expository piece, including clear and concise details.
> **Illustrate** means to support a point using short, key quotations and specific references to the work in question.
> **List** means to jot down points about a subject at random, unless you are asked to do so in a particular order.
> **Outline** means to draft a brief plan for a fully developed essay, perhaps with headings and subheadings.
> **Point out** means to look specifically and precisely at some aspect of a topic.
> **State** means to be as clear and concise as possible in answering.
> **Summarize** means to take a larger work or concept and reduce it to its main ideas.
> **Synthesize** means to blend two or more things you know in order to produce something original.
> **Trace** means to arrange items in a meaningful sequence (chronological, climactic, cause/effect).

9. Form a small group. Together, on a body of material that you either choose yourself or that your teacher gives you, compose several questions. Evaluate your questions and then present one to the class for review and discussion. (Your teacher may assign one of your questions as a demand-essay writing project.)

Drafting Suggestions

1. If you are writing an exam, make sure you come into the examination room with the proper tools: pen, pencil, eraser, ruler (if needed), dictionary (if permitted), and any other tools you may need.

2. If you are writing one or more demand essays for a test, begin by reading over the entire test.

a) Notice all the significant words in the directions. (Don't miss the *or* in an instruction that tells you to answer part 1, 2, *or* 3!) If the test allows you to make a choice, choose the questions you feel most comfortable answering, and answer them first.

b) So that you do not run out of time, estimate how much time you will spend answering each question. Notice the point value of each question. Don't spend most of your time on a question worth twenty points if you also have to answer one worth fifty points. Plan before you write.

c) Carefully read and reread each question. Identify the parts of each. Do not write until you have a clear idea of what a question asks you to do. Then do neither more nor less than the question tells you to do.

Writer's Choice

After you have chosen a demand-essay question, what do you do first? Next?

3. If you do not understand a term, you may be able to ask your teacher to explain it before you begin to draft. If you cannot ask, set out your understanding of the question at the beginning of your essay. You can then answer it appropriately.

4. Since you'll have little time to revise your demand essay, invest a few minutes in planning.

a) Organize your ideas so that your essay will look as though you have sound reasons for the content in each paragraph. Use a brainstorming technique you are comfortable with (see Chapter 22), and take a few minutes to jot down your key points. Use an outline (Chapter 28), if you're familiar with the form.

b) Rephrasing a question into a thesis statement can often guide you in organizing your answer. It can also serve as a good beginning for your answer. For example:

Question: Explain what you would do to stop XYZ Corporation from dropping chemical wastes into the sea.

Thesis statement: There are five things I would do to stop the XYZ Corporation from dumping chemical wastes into the sea.

5. When you draft, try to use basic essay structure – introduction, development, and conclusion. In your introduction, set out your topic, and let your audience know your view on your topic. Present your supporting evidence in your development. Then clinch your essay in your conclusion.

6. Because there will be no opportunity to have another person edit your exam, leave some time to do it yourself. Be sure to double-space so that you can revise and edit easily and clearly.

Guidelines for Revising a Demand Essay

☐ Have you answered all the required questions?

☐ Have you thoughtfully and completely answered each question? To make sure that you have answered a question as best you can, reread the question, noting its language and subparts, if any. Then reread your answer. Have you done what the question asks you to do? Have you answered all parts? Does your thesis statement clearly indicate what you are answering?

☐ Have you included appropriate support, examples, details, reasons, or quotations? If you find that you have left something out, insert an asterisk (*) where you want the new material to go. At the end of your essay, key your new material to your asterisk.

☐ As you reread your essay, test its organization. If a transitional word or two will help keep your reader on track, add it. If you think that a paragraph is too long or that you have changed your focus in a paragraph, use the new paragraph symbol (¶) so that your reader knows what you want.

☐ Look at your ending. Does it capture the essence of your response? If not, try to sum up your answer in a memorable way.

☐ Correct any errors in spelling, punctuation, or grammar, and repair any parts that are hard to read. Don't scribble them out (it's too messy) or use opaquing fluid (it takes too long to apply). Instead, use proofreaders' symbols (page 443) and write the new parts on the space above the line or in the margin.

☐ Keep in mind that you're responsible for how your audience reads your demand essay, so take control of it.

Revising and Editing Suggestions

Polish your essay to the best of your ability within the time allowed.

Publishing Suggestions

Present your demand essay to its intended audience.

In the Company of Writers

Four Answers to an Exam Question

Read the four students' responses to this question:

> "Excluding the United States, which of the other three nations studied (Spain, Russia, Great Britain) had the best claim in the Pacific Northwest (area from Alaska to Oregon) because of exploration by sea? Develop a thesis paragraph, a body (using evidence), and a conclusion."

Use the "Guidelines for Revising a Demand Essay" in this chapter and the checklists in Chapter 27 to evaluate the content, organization, style, and usage and mechanics of these essays. (You might want to assign a grade to each as well before you read their teacher's comments.)

1. [Untitled]

In the 16th, 17th, and 18th centuries 3 countries lay claim on the Pacific Northwest. In this essay I will discuss the claims of England, Russia, and Spain and tell who had the best claim.

Spain had the first claim on the Pacific Northwest. They came in 1542 for three main reasons: (1) to take control of any Native American civilizations; (2) seeking mineral riches, especially gold and silver; (3) to find the Northwest Passage. Spain set up forts and settlements and mapped the coastline.

England had the second claim saying it was part of their Canadian territory. They thought of trapping furs and making settlements.

Russia had the third claim on the Pacific Northwest. Their claim was it was attached to Russia which it wasn't. (They wanted it to hunt seals.)

In my opinion Spain is the nation that had the best claim on the Pacific Northwest.

2. Essay Test

I feel that due to the reasons later presented, Britain had the best claim on the Pacific Northwest. Explorers, their discoveries, and the advantage of claiming the discoveries will be presented in the following paragraphs in an effort to prove that Britain had the best claim on the Pacific Northwest.

To begin with, James Cook explored the area from Alaska to Oregon. He realized that the Pacific Northwest was rich in furs, fish, and forests. Since Britain, after the defeat of the Spanish Armada, was rising in naval power, they would be sure to make an attempt to settle the area. James Cook also found that there was no Northwest Passage. This is but one set of factors which led me to believe that Britain had the best claim in the Pacific Northwest.

Next John Meares was another prominent factor in strengthening the British claims in the Pacific Northwest. He was credited for discovering Willapa Bay, Cape Disappointment, Cape Shoalwater, Tilklamook Bay, and the mouth of the Columbia River. Control of these areas could prove to be very important in claiming other parts of the Pacific Northwest. These capes and bays could develop into important ports for importing goods and military forts as defence against over-zealous explorers from other countries. John Meares' claims of the Pacific Northwest are a major reason that Britain had the best claim.

A final person who made Britain's claims the best is George Vancouver. He made an extensive exploration of the Puget Sound area. Also he circled around Vancouver Island. Captain Vancouver's numerous discoveries and explorative thoroughness greatly strengthened Great Britain's claims to the region. As you can see, Captain Vancouver's discoveries gave Britain the best claim on the Pacific Northwest.

All of the areas discovered by the previously named explorers had great potential of developing into settlements. This reason lead me to believe that Britain had the best claim on the Pacific Northwest.

3. Which of the Nations Studied Had the Best Claim on the Pacific Northwest?

Three countries, Spain, Great Britain, and Russia, disagreed on the rights of ownership of the Pacific Northwest. Great Britain, though, had the best European claim on the Pacific Northwest for several reasons. (Of course, the North American Indians, being there all along, had the very best claim.)

With the defeat of the Spanish Armada in 1588, Great Britain began its rise as the world's strongest sea power. This event also triggered the beginning of the search for the Northwest Passage.

In 1776, Captain James Cook explored south from Alaska and travelled along and claimed the Washington and Oregon coasts. Cook was the first to realize the value of the resources of the Pacific Northwest. These included fish, forest, and furs. While exploring thousands of miles of the Pacific Ocean he concluded that the Northwest Passage never existed.

Next in 1786, John Meares, a British opportunist and adventurer, travelled to the Pacific Northwest. It was there that he discovered Willapa Bay, Cape Disappointment, Cape Shoalwater, Tillamook Bay, and the mouth of the Columbia River. He also sailed into the Strait of Juan de Fuca and San Juan Islands. Meares established the first lumber mill and built the first ships in the Pacific Northwest. He also conducted the first fur trade with the Orient and

China. Returning from the Orient with laborers to Nootka Sound on Vancouver Island, he stirred up the so-called "Nootka Sound Controversy" because he was infringing on Spain's "exclusive rights." This nearly caused a major war between Great Britain and Spain.

Another explorer from Britain was George Vancouver, who sailed to the Pacific Northwest in 1792. He went near the mouth of the Columbia River, but instead of exploring it, he travelled north into the Strait of Juan de Fuca and Puget Sound. It was there that he met with Bodega y Quadra of Spain, to settle the Nootka Sound Controversy. Spain's exclusive rights were given up and John Meares was paid $210,000, thus weakening Spain's absolute claim on the Pacific Northwest.

Even though from 1542–1792 Spain and Great Britain both sent many explorers to the Pacific Northwest, none of them ever established any permanent settlements or developed the wealth of the area. However, the interest that Great Britain had in the Pacific Northwest is illustrated by the building of the first lumber mill, the building of ships, and the establishment of the fur trade with the Orient.

Because of Russia's lack of interest in the Pacific Northwest, it will not even be included in this essay.

With these verifiable facts from Dale Lambert's The Pacific Northwest: Past, Present, and Future and other sources, Great Britain would be the logical choice for the nation with the best claim on the Pacific Northwest.

4. Spain's Claim to the Pacific Northwest

During the sixteenth to nineteenth centuries, four countries vied for the rights to the Pacific Northwest. These four countries were Spain, Russia, Great Britain, and the United States. Of these countries Spain had the best claim to the Pacific Northwest based on discovery, exploration, colonization, and the Demarcation Treaty.

Dale A. Lambert, author of The Pacific Northwest: Past, Present, and Future, states that Spain was the first to discover the Pacific Northwest in 1542. Spain established a few colonies along the Pacific coast, with the most significant at Nootka Sound on Vancouver Island.

Strengthening Spain's claim was the fact that Great Britain did not appear until 1577. Lambert also writes that Russia arrived in 1728 and that it was more interested in the land north of the 51st parallel. The United States also had a slight claim to the Pacific Northwest but it made a major appearance much later, in 1792.

Lambert also demonstrated Spain's claim to the Pacific Northwest when he listed explorers of the four countries. From the discovery of the Pacific Northwest in 1542 until 1603, 61 years later, Spain sent four sea explorers to the area. They were Bartolome Ferrelo, Michael Lok, Sebastian Viscaino, and Martin Aguilar.

In 1578 Great Britain sent one sea explorer, Sir Francis Drake. Russia didn't have a single explorer in the area. The United States also didn't commission any explorers because it wasn't in existence at that time.

In the 1490s Pope Clement established the Demarcation Line. Lambert wrote that this line divided the world for exploration purposes. Portugal was given the lands east of the line, and Spain received the lands to the west, including all of North America with the Pacific Northwest. The Demarcation Line thus strengthened Spain's claim to the Pacific Northwest.

Considering dates of discovery, exploration and colonization, combined with the significance of the Line of Demarcation, Spain had the strongest claim to the Pacific Northwest.

What makes the essays different? (To help you answer, look at the introductions, thesis statements, development, and conclusions. Examine the sentence variety, transitions, and style. Are there any writing problems? Do the essays include anything that is irrelevant?) Assess the essays using the checklists in Chapter 27. Then read the teacher's assessments.

History Teacher's Comments

1. We have a long way to go this year; if you work with me, we will see much improvement by spring. Avoid using written numerals for short numbers in a formal essay. Stay away from first-person reference. Order of paragraphs is good, but none of them really contains the specific information needed. Please use specific names, places and events – spell them out and explain what each means. Finally, your conclusion doesn't restate anything other than your personal opinion. Be a trial lawyer in a courtroom. Lay out the evidence before your jury, explain it, then in your final arguments sum up all the pertinent facts. The jury must vote in your favor. LOW GRADE (D)

2. This paper has a proper focus and sticks to its task without wandering from the point. Try to avoid using first person; stay away from personal references. This paper is to be a factual argument using accumulated evidence from your study of all explorers. Your spelling is good, and you generally use strong, well-put-together sentences. Let's see you use some analysis now and then. Together we'll make much better and stronger written documents. MEDIUM GRADE (C)

3. Consider developing a stronger thesis paragraph. Perhaps name the explorers you are going to use as evidence to back up your thesis claim to Great Britain's "rights to ownership." The second paragraph should be developed with greater detail; it lacks necessary body. The evidence is presented in a logical chronological order and provides the necessary support. Your use of specific names, places, and events shows knowledge of your subject. Again, like your thesis, your conclusion needs more than the title of the book. Perhaps a summation of evidence? For the first essay this shows promise. I will

help you develop stronger written arguments during the year. HIGH GRADE (B)

4. Your work certainly shows promise. For a first essay this paper shows research and organization, and you have the ability to express yourself clearly. Your thesis paragraph is well done and gives the reader a statement of things to come. The body contains good information, all of it to the point. Perhaps you might reorder the paragraphs in chronological order (by dates). You certainly make use of a goodly number of names, places, and events. On the next paper, do a rough draft, proofread it for minor errors, then do a final copy. The mechanics are good, and your paper shows considerable effort. I'm looking forward to your next paper. HIGH GRADE (A)

Your Writing

1. The answers in the last two essays are very different. How do you explain the fact that both essays – with their opposing views – received high grades?
2. Were you able to organize your ideas in the time available? If not, what did you spend too much time doing?
3. How did you plan your answer before you started to write? Did you know the direction your essay was going to take before you started writing?
4. In your journal, comment on your writing. What did you learn about preparing to write a demand essay? About predicting demand-essay questions? About how to read demand-essay questions? About the steps in developing a demand essay? Is there any part of your process that you would change when you write your next demand essay? Why?

17 Personal Letter

"She had sat down and read the letter over again; but there were phrases that insisted on being read many times, they had a life of their own, separate from others."

Katherine Anne Porter

The invention of the telephone dealt a serious blow to the art of writing letters. Nowadays, people are more likely to pick up a phone and talk to a friend or relative than to write. Making a phone call is a quick and easy way to communicate. When you talk on the telephone, you are part of conversational turn-taking. You experience an immediate response. But writing a letter allows you time to think over your ideas, organize them, and find the best words to express them. And the personal computer may re-introduce letter-writing because of modems and electronic mail.

WRITING PROJECT

Write a personal letter to someone.

Exploring and Prewriting Suggestions

1. As you explore possible topics and audiences, you might experiment with one or more of the following.

a) Write to a friend you haven't seen for a while (or to whom you owe a letter). Or write to a pen pal.

b) Think about something that has happened to someone you know. Perhaps he or she has won an award – or lost a pet. Write to this person expressing how you feel about what's happened.

c) You and your classmates might all put your names in a box. Draw a name, and write a "Valentine" love letter to your classmate using the persona of a famous person. Here's your chance to be Michael J. Fox, Queen Elizabeth, Fred Flintstone, Barbara Frum, Big Bird, or your favorite athlete. When you're through, take turns sharing your celebrity "Valentines."

d) Using the persona of a teacher or principal, write a letter to the parents of a famous politician, explaining how their son or daughter is doing in school.

e) Using the persona of a character from a story or play you are studying, write a letter to Ann Landers or Dear Abby asking for advice.

f) Write to a character in a story or play you are studying. You might, for example, ask the character for a favor.

g) Assume that you are living in the year 2050. Write to Canadians living in the 1990s pointing out a problem in 2050 that could have been prevented.

h) Write a letter to Santa Claus using your own voice or that of a persona.

2. To help you get started on your letter, you might try one or more of the following.

a) In a small group, share something that's happened to you recently. Invite the other members of your group to ask you questions about what happened. When you draft, keep your group's questions in mind.

b) Try freewriting for ten minutes on something that is important to you. Is it a public issue? A memory you share with a friend? Or something else?

c) Bring to class a photograph that is important to you. Compose a brief narrative about the photo – when the photo was taken, the people in it, what is happening, and so on. Restrict yourself to about the amount of text that you could fit on the back of your photo. In your letter, elaborate on your brief narrative.

d) To help you begin to think like a persona you want to use, try generating several diary entries that he or she might have written. For example, you might write about what your character has accomplished or what has happened to your character and his or her friends or family.

e) Jot down a list of everything you love (or can't stand) about the neighborhood you live in. To whom do you want to write? When you write, focus on the two or three things on your list that are most important to you.

Writer's Choice

Have you decided who you're going to write to, and why? Will you use a persona or your own voice? Are you ready to draft your letter, or do you want to consider the following suggestions?

Drafting Suggestions

1. Personal letters are usually handwritten. Choose any size or color of paper that is suitable for your purpose, but be kind to your reader – write clearly and use margins to give your letter a feeling of space. Try to keep a 3 cm margin on all sides.

> ## Writer's Choice
> How can you show your personality through your letter?

2. If you are using a persona, be sure to consider your writing variables from the point of view of the persona.

3. Don't just dash off a confused letter because you think it looks casual – or because you know your audience well. Organize your thoughts to show the best side of your personality. Let your audience know that you care sufficiently to express yourself clearly and well.

4. Personal letters usually contain five standard parts:

- **Heading** (upper right-hand corner). It gives the writer's street address and the date on which the letter was written.
- **Salutation or greeting** (flush at the left margin). It's a way of saying hello to your reader. Most salutations begin "Dear _____," but feel free to write any salutation that is appropriate. Usually, you end the salutation of a personal letter with a comma.
- **Body of the letter**. Your message to your audience begins two spaces below the salutation. Don't forget the paragraph indents to separate your ideas.
- **Complimentary close.** It's your way of saying goodbye. Begin it just to the right of the centre of your sheet of paper. Use a capital letter and a comma (as in the letters at the end of this chapter).
- **Signature**. Sign your name under the complimentary close.

5. Address the envelope as shown later in the chapter using precise punctuation to help speed your letter to its destination. Try to use the following list of provincial and territorial symbols when you address your letter. The two-letter code is compatible with the Canadian Post Office's computer system. (The two-letter codes have also been chosen to avoid conflict with the USA codes; for example, Manitoba's code is MB rather than MN (Minnesota).)

Provincial and Territorial Codes

Newfoundland — NF
Labrador — LB
Nova Scotia — NS
New Brunswick — NB
Prince Edward Island — PEI
   (only three-letter code)
Province of Quebec — PQ

Ontario — ON
Manitoba — MB
Saskatchewan — SK
Alberta — AB
British Columbia — BC
Yukon — YT
Northwest Territories — NT

When you have completed your letter, use the following guidelines to help you revise it.

Guidelines for Revising a Personal Letter

□ Why are you writing this letter? Is your purpose clear? Will your audience be interested in and appreciate what you have to say?

□ If you've used a persona, have you kept your purpose and audience in mind as you wrote? Is your voice consistent?

□ Have you been able to keep your style informal? When you reread your letter, does it sound like you talking? If not, is there anything that you should change?

□ Do you include everything that you want to include? Is your writing interesting and lively? Have you included vivid descriptions and interesting anecdotes?

□ Have you included the five standard parts of a personal letter? Have you addressed the envelope correctly?

□ Are you satisfied with the mechanics of your draft (spelling, punctuation, and grammar), or is there something you'd like to check before you let an editor see your work?

□ Is there anything in your draft that you would like your editor to help you with?

Writer's Choice

Is your letter ready for your intended audience? Or would you like an editor to look at it first?

If necessary, revise your work and prepare a clean double-spaced draft for your editor.

Revising and Editing Suggestions

Give your draft to your peer-editor, and share your writing variables. Encourage your editor to use the "Guidelines for Revising a Personal Letter" in this chapter and the checklists in Chapter 27. Your editor should also think about how he or she would answer the following questions.

Ask Your Peer-Editor

☐ What was your first impression of my letter? Did it interest you? Do you think it will interest my audience? In what ways?

☐ Does my letter reflect my personality – or the personality of my persona? If not, what should I change?

☐ Are my stories or anecdotes interesting? Do I express my opinions clearly? If not, what should I change? Should I add more detail? Should I leave anything out?

☐ Do you like my word choice? Are my grammar and punctuation all right?

If necessary, revise your draft. Then submit your letter to its intended audience.

Writer's Choice

Do you want to save a copy of your letter and your envelope in your writing folder so that you can refer to their format when you write your next personal letter?

Publishing Suggestions

If you've written a letter to a personal friend, then mail it. If you and your classmates have written letters either to or from a persona, take time to share and enjoy one another's work. Volunteers might read their letters aloud; letters might become a resource for drama activities.

**In the
Company
of Writers**

13 Smith St.,
Edmonton, AB
T3N 1J0
March 6, 1990

Dear Antonio,

So much has happened to me since I came from Genoa to Edmonton that I haven't had time to sit down and tell you about everything. Today, I have time.

Our stopover in Paris was interesting. While we were there, the security guards blew up someone's suitcase. I would have been upset except the shopkeeper was killing herself laughing about it. Apparently it happens all the time. She told me they once exploded an unattended suitcase that was full of shrimps and artichokes. There were shrimps and artichokes everywhere! I can just imagine.

Then, our plane was three hours late arriving in Edmonton because of bad weather. In fact, we almost went back to Toronto, but the pilot decided to go on instead.

Then, the customs inspector opened all my suitcases and checked everything. I really felt like a newcomer.

When I finally arrived in the area where people were waiting for arriving passengers, I could not find Uncle Giovanni. I didn't want to start looking for him in case I got lost in the airport. Finally I went to one of the airline counters, and the lady phoned Uncle Giovanni for me and found out he was on his way. He arrived about half an hour later and took me home, where Aunt Rita had supper ready. I was so tired I fell asleep right after supper.

I love Edmonton – except it's so cold. (Not the people, though. Already, I have lots of friends. I'll tell you all about them and my ski trip to Banff in my next letter.) Right now, I have to get to my next class.

I miss you and Carlo and Mama very much. Write soon.

Love,

Lucia

Box 246
Halifax, NS
B2L 1N2
April 5, 1990

Dear Helena,

I was thrilled to hear about the new addition to your
trophy collection. The regional award for best pianist is
really hard to win, but I was not surprised to find out
you left the other contestants behind in a cloud of music
notes.

Where do you play next? Are you going to the Canada-Wide
Music Festival? Wherever you go, I am sure you will play
your best and win whatever prize is being offered.

I feel congratulations are in order and am sending them
along with my love and heartfelt wishes. May you succeed
at whatever you try.

Take care of yourself. Watch those fingers!

Best wishes always,

Roger.

Roger

Box 246
Halifax, NS
B2L 1N2

Ms. Helena Troy
Box 334
Kentville, NS
B4N 3W8

A Letter from Camp
Words by Allan Sherman

Hello Mudduh, hello Fadduh,
Here I am at Camp Granada;
Camp is very entertaining,
And they say we'll have some fun if it stops raining.

I went hiking with Joe Spivy,
He developed poison ivy;
You remember Leonard Skinner?
He got ptomaine pois'ning last night after dinner.

All the couns'lors hate the waiters
And the lake has alligators;
And the head coach wants no sissies,
So he reads to us from something called Ulysses.

Now I don't want this should scare ya,
But my bunkmate has malaria;
You remember Jeffrey Hardy?
They're about to organize a searching party.

Take me home, oh Mudduh, Fadduh
Take me home, I hate Granada;
Don't leave me out in the forest, where
I might get eaten by a bear.

Take me home, I promise I will not make noise,
Or mess the house with other boys.
Oh please don't make me stay,
I've been here one whole day.

Dearest Fadduh, darling Mudduh,
How's my precious little brudduh?
Let me come home if you miss me,
I would even let Aunt Bertha hug and kiss me.

Wait a minute, it stopped hailing,
Guys are swimming, guys are sailing!
Playing baseball, gee, that's better,
Mudduh, Fadduh, kindly disregard this letter.

Your Writing

1. Who was the audience for your letter? How would your letter be different if you were sending the same content to a different audience?

2. Did you use a persona in your writing as Allan Sherman has done? Do you think that using a persona is an effective way to write a letter? When would it be appropriate to use a persona when writing a personal letter?

3. In your journal, comment on your writing. What did you learn about writing personal letters? Is there any part of your process that you would change when you write your next personal letter? Why?

18 Business Letter

"Letters are above all useful as a means of expressing the ideal self; and no other method of communication is quite so good for this purpose."

Elizabeth Hardwick

While a friendly letter is like one part of a conversation with a friend, a business letter is often like part of a business transaction. Such a letter is written to get a definite result. For example, you may want to have damaged goods replaced, request information about a particular subject, or order something advertised in a magazine or newspaper. These situations are all occasions for business letters.

WRITING PROJECT

> Write a business letter. You might make a request, seek information, or write a letter of complaint – or write any business letter that fulfils a purpose of your choice.

Exploring and Prewriting Suggestions

1. Take advantage of this writing project to tidy up some item of business in your own life. Let your audience be a real person or company, and write your letter to accomplish a purpose you really want to accomplish. You might explore one or more of the following suggestions.
a) Ask a former employer to be your reference for a new job.
b) Ask your local newspaper to provide more detailed coverage of your school's sporting events.

c) Ask an elected official about a stand on an issue that concerns you – or write a letter to your Member of Parliament expressing your view on an issue and asking your MP's position on the matter.

d) Complain to a mail order company that has not filled your order but has cashed your cheque.

e) Request information about an organization's charitable activities.

f) Request a speaker for the next meeting of a club you belong to.

g) Write a business letter for a reason that is important to you.

2. You might assume a persona and write a business letter.

a) Imagine that you are a well-known scientist or inventor and have just invented something that you think will change the course of history. Write to someone with money and try to convince him or her to support your invention.

b) Assume the role of a head of state and write to another world leader concerning a situation that involves both of you.

c) Imagine that you are a character in a piece of literature you are reading, and write a business letter. You might, for example, apply for a job.

3. Think about *who* you want to write to, *what* you want your letter to accomplish, *why* you want to accomplish your purpose, and *how* you plan to accomplish it.

Writer's Choice

Are you ready to begin your draft, or do you want to explore a bit more?

4. To gather supporting details for your letter, you might use one of the exploration techniques in Chapter 22, especially Talk/Write, Free Association Cluster, or Pro/Con Ladders.

Drafting Suggestions

1. While writing a personal letter allows you a choice of stationery, plain white paper is best for a business letter.

2. If possible, type your letter, or use a word processor. Leave a 3 cm margin at the top and sides. If your letter is a long one, leave a 3 cm margin at the bottom, and continue on the second page. (A word processor will allow you to format your letter quickly and easily. And if you write a lot of business letters, you might set up a format that you can use every time. Check your word-processing manual.)

3. Be concise; get to the point quickly. Pleasant chitchat may be welcome in a friendly letter but is usually beside the point – and undesirable – in a business letter.

4. While business letters call for fairly formal writing, you should not write in a stilted, overly formal style. Avoid such phrases as *I am in receipt of* and *Please arrange to return*. Instead, write *I received* and *Please return*. Notice the difference between these two complaints.

> As of this date I am in receipt of your parcel. In regard to the aforementioned parcel, there is an error in size in filling catalogue item No. 332 534 567 B at $16.99 on Invoice No. 636.

> On the enclosed Order No. 636, you will see that I ordered a size forty-two. I received a size thirty-two.

Which complaint do you think is more likely to get results? Why?

5. Make sure your writing is clear and direct and gets your message across. As you write, keep asking yourself: What facts are involved? What message do I want to convey? Am I conveying it? Compare the following two requests.

> Have you anything good for a project on Spain and how to start a project on that country? Like travel brochures, maps, posters, etc. Hopefully free.

> I am doing a project on Spain for a social studies class. I have heard that your travel agency has been very helpful to other students with similar projects. Could you recommend some useful books and articles on Spain, as well as film strips and other audio-visual material? If you have any free posters or brochures about Spain, I would appreciate receiving them.

Which request is clearer? Confused or vague requests are more likely to be filed or thrown away than answered.

6. Make sure your letter follows one of the accepted forms for business letters. Two common forms, which are shown at the end of this chapter, have six parts.

- **Heading.** The heading appears either at the top near the right margin (semi-block style) or flush at the left margin (block style). It includes the sender's street address, city, province, and postal code, and the date on which the letter is written. Punctuation can either be open (no punctuation) or closed (commas at the end of each line, with a period after the last word). As in a personal letter, a comma separates the city and province, and the postal code appears on a line of its own below the name of the province without any punctuation.

- **Inside Address.** The inside address (not included in a friendly letter) appears about four spaces below the heading and flush at the left margin. It includes the receiver's complete name and title of address (such as Dr., Mr., or Ms.); the name of the business firm or other organization to which the letter is being sent; the firm's street address; the city, province, and postal code. Continue the same style of punctuation, either open or closed. If you do not know the exact person to whom you want to send the letter, you can address the letter to a person holding a particular position in the company. For example:

Open Punctuation	*or*	*Closed Punctuation*
Director		Director,
Ace Travel Service		Ace Travel Service,
200 Booth Way		200 Booth Way,
Montreal, PQ		Montreal, PQ.
H3G 1S4		H3G 1S4

Writer's Choice

Do you want to use block or semi-block style? Open or closed punctuation?

- **Salutation**. The salutation appears two spaces below the inside address. In a business letter, the salutation is always followed by a colon. For example:

    Dear Dr. Hsien:

    Notice that a business letter's salutation is more formal than the salutation in a friendly letter. A title of address – such as Mr., Mrs., Ms., or Dr. – is almost always used, and a first name is hardly ever used.

- **Body**. The body of a business letter contains your message and appears two spaces below the salutation. Business letters written in block style do not contain indented paragraphs; letters in semiblock style do indent. (See the end of this chapter for examples of both styles.) If you type the letter, skip a space between paragraphs, whichever style you follow. If you write the letter in longhand, use semiblock style.

- **Complimentary close**. The complimentary close aligns with the heading; if the heading is flush at the left margin, then so is the complimentary close. If the heading is at the right margin, then so is the complimentary close. The complimentary close appears two spaces below the body. In a business letter, the complimentary close is usually more formal than in a friendly letter. For example:

    Sincerely,
    Respectfully,
    Yours truly,
    Best wishes,

    Notice that only the first word of the close is capitalized and that a comma ends the close.

- **Signature**. The signature, appearing below the close, is always written in ink (not typed). If you type your business letter, type your name four spaces below the close and then put your signature above the typed name.

7. Keep a copy of one or all of these business letter formats in your writing file so that you can refer to them when you are formatting your next business letter. If you use a computer to write, you might set up a business letter format so that your letters are consistent.

8. Address an envelope for your business letter, with your name and address in the upper left corner and the sender's name and address in the centre of the envelope. (See Chapter 17 for abbreviations of provincial names.)

When you have completed your letter, use the following guidelines to help you revise it.

Guidelines for Revising a Business Letter

- □ Why are you writing this letter? Is your purpose clear? Will your audience understand what you are trying to say?
- □ Is your style formal but not stilted? If not, what should you change?
- □ Have you included all relevant documentation or references?
- □ Have you correctly set out the six standard parts of a business letter? What format have you used? Have you used it consistently? Have you addressed the envelope correctly?
- □ Are you satisfied with the mechanics of your draft (spelling, punctuation, and grammar), or is there something you'd like to check before you let an editor see your work?
- □ Is there anything in your draft that you would like your editor to help you with?

Writer's Choice

Is your letter ready for your intended audience? Or would you like an editor to look at it first?

If necessary, revise your work and prepare a clean double-spaced draft for your editor.

Revising and Editing Suggestions

Give your draft to your peer-editor, and share your writing variables. Encourage your editor to use the "Guidelines for Revising a Business Letter" in this chapter and the checklists in Chapter 27. Your editor should also think about how he or she would answer the following questions.

Ask Your Peer-Editor

☐ Is my purpose for writing clear? Will it be clear to my audience? Do I get my message across? If not, what should I change?

☐ Is my letter concise and to the point? Should I shorten or omit any part of it? If so, why?

☐ Is any part of my letter too brief? What information would you add? Why?

☐ Is my style formal but not stilted? Should I change any stilted or wordy phrases? If so, what words or phrases would you use instead?

☐ Do you think my letter will get results? What could I do to make it more effective?

☐ Does my letter contain all six parts of an accepted standard form for business letters? Have I punctuated and capitalized it correctly? Have I addressed the envelope correctly?

If necessary, revise your draft before sending it to your intended audience.

Publishing Suggestions

Polish your letter and send it to your intended audience. After a couple of weeks, you and your classmates might see which letters were answered most quickly. Try to decide why. Then, together, you might develop your own handbook on "How to Get Things Done."

In the Company of Writers

Semi-block style

Closed punctuation

Box 2120, Postal Stn A,
St. John, NB.
E2M 4X7
November 5, 1990

Mr. Lesley Swain,
Fashionaire Inc.,
Box 3000, Postal Stn B,
St. John, NB.
E2L 4K9

Dear Mr. Swain:

   Yesterday I bought a blouse in the Fine Fashions store at Wildford Shopping Centre. It was expensive. When I brought it home, I noticed that it was poorly made and in many places the seams were not caught under, leaving raw edges.

   I was very disappointed and have returned the blouse. Your merchandise is generally satisfactory, but I feel that you should be aware of this matter.

Yours truly,

Kimiko Karpoff

Kimiko Karpoff

Block style

Open punctuation

4782 Main St.
Winnipeg, MB
R2W 3N4
February 4, 1990

Ms. L. Gerard, President
Vanner School for Disabled Children
28 Douglas Drive
Winnipeg, MB
R3C 2G7

Dear Ms. Gerard:

I am writing to inform you of my desire to perform volunteer work for your organization.

Having received the list of services you need, I am requesting that I be considered for the following duties:

1. children's tutor
2. organizer of accommodations for out-of-town parents

I feel that I could be of help in these areas, having worked in my high-school library for two years, while tutoring other students in mathematics. I also have strong organizational abilities.

I will be available for work Monday through Thursday from 6:00 to 9:00 p.m., and on Fridays from 1:30 to 3:00 p.m.

I hope that my services will be of some benefit to your organization. Please contact me at home if you wish to interview me.

Sincerely,

John Leung

Your Writing

1. Does your letter achieve its purpose? Did you, for example, receive the information you asked for?

2. Check the format of any reply you receive. Does it conform to a standard business letter format?

3. In your journal, comment on your writing. What did you learn about writing business letters? Is there any part of your process that you would change when you write your next business letter? Why?

19 Letter to the Editor

"A blow with a word strikes deeper than a blow with a sword."

Robert Burton, **The Anatomy of Melancholy**

WRITING PROJECT

> Write a letter to the editor. Your letter can be narrative, persuasive, or informative.

Exploring and Prewriting Suggestions

1. If you do not already have a topic in mind for this writing project, you might do one or more of the following. To start, try to gather as many issues of as many current newspapers and magazines as you can, and spend some time looking at them.

a) Working in a small group, try to figure out the editorial policy of several newspapers and magazines, as expressed on the editorial page and in the selection, treatment, and placement of news stories, feature articles, and advertisements. Try to come to a conclusion about the target market of each. In your journal, freewrite for ten minutes about one of the publications you have discussed. Your freewriting might become the basis of a letter to the editor commenting on the publication's general editorial policy.

b) With some classmates, compare the treatment of a current news item in two or more publications over several days. You might look at how much of the story is "hard news," how much is attributed to unidentified sources, and how much is opinion. You might look at the slant (see Chapter 33) in each report: Is the slant negative or positive? Which facts are highlighted? Does anything seem exaggerated or sensationalized? Does a report seem to contain thoughtless generalizations? Is the tone subjective or objective? You might also track where a news item appears in a publication on Day 1, Day 2, and so on; whether a story is accompanied by photographs or other graphics and captions; and the tone and prominence of headings. Freewrite a letter to the editor. You might summarize your investigation; you might also critique or applaud the coverage.

c) You might locate several newspaper or magazine articles, editorials, or letters to the editor that express strong opinions. Decide which one you most agree or disagree with, and freewrite for ten minutes setting out your opinion on the subject. (Disagreeing with a piece will probably give you more to say than agreeing with it. If you choose a piece with which you agree, think about the ideas and evidence you can bring to it, so that you do not simply echo what it says.) Use your freewriting as the basis for your letter to the editor.

d) Think about something that bothers you; for example, transit costs in your home town; the gap between rich and poor in our society; people who let their pets run loose; the fact that your local newspaper frequently misspells certain words. Freewrite for ten minutes on everything that comes to mind when you think about your topic. You might also try exploring it using an Absurd Analogy. (See Chapter 22.)

e) You might want to write a letter to a peer-editor about how he or she is handling your writing.

2. If you plan to write a persuasive letter, you might want to debate your topic informally with someone who disagrees with you. A fifteen-minute debate can help you develop strong reasons in support of your position and alert you to the arguments against it.

Writer's Choice

Do you want to consider your writing variables now or as you draft? For example, who is your audience? Is it the editor? Or is it readers of the publication? Are you ready to begin your draft, or do you want to explore your topic a bit more?

3. If you decide that you want to explore your topic more fully, consult the suggestions in Chapter 22.

Drafting Suggestions

1. A letter to the editor is usually a type of essay: an informative essay (Chapter 4); an argumentative essay (Chapter 5); or a narrative essay (Chapter 6). You might wish to consult the drafting suggestions in those chapters.

2. Experiment with several thesis statements until you come up with one that captures the essence of what you want to say.

3. Write a strong opening to grab the attention of the editor – and your final audience. You'll also need a snappy conclusion to help your audience remember what you've said. (For more about beginnings and endings, see Chapter 24.)

4. If you are writing in response to something you have seen in the publication, identify that article, editorial, or advertisement. You may want to summarize an opposing argument very briefly before replying to it. For example:

> Your editorial of December 7 asserts that our province's high schools are doing a poor job of educating us. My own schooling at Mackenzie High School makes me laugh at such a silly generalization.

A concise summary and statement of your own position might provide the strong opening you need.

5. Present your story, information, or argument clearly and concisely. Try to supply only one or two brief quotations, examples, or narrative illustrations to support your thesis. Keep in mind that most newspapers do not provide a great deal of space for letters, and editors often cut sentences and paragraphs from readers' letters before printing them. If you keep your letter brief, it will more likely be published as you have written it.

6. To pack all the punch you can into a brief space, make every word count. You might use positive or negative slant for effect. (See Chapter 33.) Or you might use a rhetorical device such as climactic parallelism to increase your letter's effectiveness. (See Chapter 31.)

7. Use a standard business letter format. (See Chapter 18.)

When you have completed your letter, use the following guidelines to help you revise it.

Guidelines for Revising a Letter to the Editor

☐ Why are you writing this letter? Is your purpose clear? Have you set out your thesis clearly and concisely?

☐ If you are responding to something that was published in the publication, have you made clear what you are responding to?

☐ The publication may allow you to present only one fact – or make a single argument. Are you certain that you have selected your strongest point?

☐ Will your beginning capture your audience's attention? Is your conclusion memorable?

☐ Have you made every word count so that your letter is published as you've written it?

☐ Are you satisfied with the mechanics of your draft (spelling, punctuation, and grammar), or is there something you'd like to check before you let a peer-editor see your work? Have you used a standard business letter format?

☐ Is there anything in your draft that you'd like your editor to help you with – before you send off your letter to another editor?

Writer's Choice

Is your draft ready for its intended audience? Or would you like a peer-editor to make revising and editing suggestions?

Revising and Editing Suggestions

Give your draft to your peer-editor, and share your writing variables. Encourage your editor to use the "Guidelines for Revising a Letter to the Editor" in this chapter and the checklists in Chapter 27. Your editor should also think about how he or she would answer the following questions.

Ask Your Peer-Editor

- [ ] If I'm responding to something that has appeared in a publication, have I given you a copy of it to read? If not, have I clearly summarized it?
- [ ] Is my purpose for writing clear? Does my letter's opening capture your interest? Will my audience read it? Why do you say so?
- [ ] Does my letter present clear information or solid reasons and evidence to support my thesis? Have I clearly organized my information? Is there anything you would change? Why?
- [ ] If I'm presenting an argument, have I treated the opposing position fairly?
- [ ] Did you spot any errors in the information I am presenting? Any faulty logic? (Is there anything that doesn't make sense?)
- [ ] Have I effectively used rhetorical devices or slant? Could I?
- [ ] Did my conclusion really make you think about what I have to say?
- [ ] Think about the publication's space restrictions. Have I included anything that I don't need? Is there anything you would leave out? Why?
- [ ] Have I used a standard format for a business letter?
- [ ] Do you like my word choice and sentence structure? Have I made every word count? Are my spelling, punctuation, and grammar all right, or is there something I should still work on?

Publishing Suggestions

When you're ready, send off your letter to the newspaper or magazine of your choice. You might see your name and ideas "go national." You might also want to experiment with a class chain letter using the format of a letter to the editor. Each person in the chain can respond to a point or points made in previous letters (as in the letters that follow).

In the Company of Writers

A Draining Myth

September 26, 1981

Twice during the last week in your columns I have seen reference to, as fact, the hoary old myth that water running out of a plug-hole rotates in an opposite direction in the Northern and Southern hemispheres. The second occasion was Michael Valpy's report on his arrival in Australia ("Just Like Home").

As L.M. Milne-Thomson points out in his classical work, *Theoretical Hydrodynamics*, if you have separate hot and cold taps, you can change the direction of rotation merely by changing taps. As a then young and recent graduate in physics, I conducted an experiment during the war on a long and boring voyage by troopship from Brisbane, Australia, to San Francisco. I only had one tap, but the water swirled in the same direction throughout the voyage.

The myth is interesting because it has a foundation in scientific fact – the existence of the Coriolis force due to Earth's rotation, which is of major importance in world meteorology. The magnitude of the Coriolis effect in the bath-water case is however completely swamped by the local "viscous" or frictional forces. Several experts in fluid mechanics have conducted highly refined experiments to see if the (undoubtedly existing) Coriolis effect could be detected at all in the plug-hole context but, as far as I know, the results have been inconclusive.

J.H. Blackwell
London, Ontario

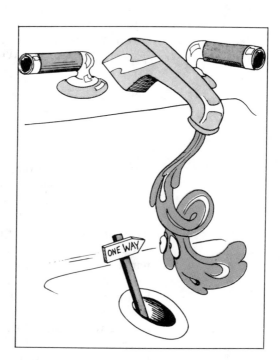

October 10, 1981

The mantle of accurate reporting needs to be restored to your two columnists who correctly reported the direction of rotation in water draining out of a plug-hole. The direction of rotation is different in the two hemispheres: clockwise in the northern.

This fact was challenged in this space, in an apparently learned opinion that reminds one of the similarly learned opinion that bumblebees are unable to fly. A novel one-tap, two-tap theory was advanced to explain the direction of rotation and this may be adequate as a first-blush observation. However, in the same terms I advance the "n" tap theory of rotation where "n" equals the number of taps filling the basin. The theory will state, "as 'n' approached infinity, the direction of rotation will become clockwise in the northern hemisphere and anti-clockwise in the southern."

But for more ordinary folk such as myself, I can suggest that the basin be filled by whatever means with the stopper firmly in place. Then, when the water has come to a rest, pull the stopper and observe. I too have done this experiment (as described) while travelling by ship from the antipodes to North America. The motion of the ship appears to affect the direction of rotation so that near the equator, one cannot be certain of the direction of rotation. Other than that, the case appears closed.

Just in case doubters are left, I am embarking soon on another voyage to the other hemisphere. I can repeat these experiments and report again in this space in the new year. What more can you want?

L.C. Allen
Ottawa

October 17, 1981

I find it regrettable that you published the letter from L.C. Allen since it is quite apparent that he doesn't know what he is talking about but is instead allowing his prejudices to perpetuate an old myth. Perhaps neither you nor Mr. Allen recognized that the writer, J. H. Blackwell of London, Ont., is (or was) a professor of both mathematics and physics at the University of Western Ontario and is supremely well qualified to comment on the matter. His remarks were comprehensive yet brief, and absolutely correct.

Questions about the same myth have turned up many times over the years in a number of books and periodicals. I would like to quote one which appeared in the periodical *The Physics Teacher* in the 1976 January issue. The answer was provided by Malcolm Correll of the University of Colorado and concludes as follows: "If a drain orifice is carefully opened at the bottom of a basin of undisturbed water, we might expect to see the existing water rotate counter clockwise in the northern hemisphere and clockwise in the southern. However, to produce the effect requires very elaborate controlled conditions. Vanes, roughnesses, or other deflecting elements and initial residual motion of the water, including any stirring as the plug is removed, will almost certainly mask the comparatively tiny Coriolis effect. Bowls of water have memories of the direction of initial rotation that may last for hours. Toilets usually introduce flushing water from the top rim and some have a jet that enters from below. These violent effects can easily mask the weak Coriolis force, and the true effect is never seen with household devices."

Robert E. Heath
Sault Ste. Marie, Ontario

October 17, 1981

The diverting arguments on the direction of rotation of water draining from a basin in the northern or southern hemispheres are all very well, but as I have a digital timekeeper, will someone please explain to me what "clockwise" means?

   Furthermore, if you are in outer space, the water will not rotate at all when you unplug the basin but will rise straight up and hit you in the face.

Austin Small
Oakville, Ontario

Your Writing

1. Each writer in the examples included with this chapter establishes a personal voice by the feelings he signals in the very first sentence. Can you identify the feeling – insulted, annoyed, "diverted," or amused – at the outset? Does your own piece convey a particular mood right from the beginning? Is the mood consistent or is it mixed?
2. Have you used effective transitions in your piece? Is it easy to locate the transition you make (a) from what you object to (b) to why you object (c) to your own position?
3. Have you made use of any rhetorical devices? If so, how do you think they help you support your argument?
4. In your journal, comment on your writing. What did you learn about writing a letter to the editor? Is there any part of your process that you would change the next time you do so? Why?

20

Résumé and Cover Letter

"A résumé, along with the application letter, is the first contact the reader will have with you."

W. Ross Winterowd

Sometimes you are able to get a job through personal contacts, but more often you will write a letter and enclose a résumé. A résumé is a summary of a job applicant's work experience, education, and other qualifications. The accompanying letter introduces you, highlights the contribution you feel you can make to a prospective employer, and may request an interview. Your chances of obtaining an interview usually depend on how well you present yourself on paper.

WRITING PROJECT

Prepare a résumé and write a cover letter to a prospective employer.

Exploring and Prewriting Suggestions

1. To familiarize yourself with preparing a résumé, you might try one or more of the following.

a) Think about a job that you would like to have some day, such as Prime Minister, or right wing for the Montreal Canadiens, or the presidency of a major company. Brainstorm a list of qualifications for the position; then "apply."

b) Develop a résumé and cover letter for one of the following. (Address your cover letter to the street address given, and use the name and postal code of your own city or town.) Applying for an imaginary job will give you the opportunity to take stock of your qualifications.

MACKENZIE'S HAMBURGER EMPORIUM

3400 E. First St.
Part-time counter-help applications are now being accepted. Apply in writing, please, to Dominique Tremblay, Manager.

ACCOMPANIST

Needed to assist in auditions for musical. Must be able to sight-read music. Apply to Hal Davis, Regency Theatre, 1101 Ziegfeld Boulevard.

ROCK BAND

Am forming a rock band. Looking for instrumentalists and singer. Apply in writing to Donna Turner, 5 Penny Lane.

PART-TIME

Trainee mechanic. Hours 4–6 p.m. Monday–Friday, all day Saturday. Looking for someone who likes to tinker with cars and wants to learn more about them. Apply to Andy Starkowski, Chief Mechanic, Bayshore Garage, 48611 W. Ford Street.

c) Applying for a real job could get you the job! Find several job listings to which you might want to reply. You can find such listings at employment offices, on school and community bulletin boards, and in the "Help Wanted" or "Employment Opportunities" section of a newspaper's classified ads.

2. Study the requirements of the position for which you are applying, and jot down your answers to the following.
• What are the job's requirements?
• In what ways do you qualify for the job?

- What direct experience do you have? Which of your jobs – paid or un-paid – are similar to or have something in common with the job you want?
- What indirect experience do you have? Have any of your interests and activities given you some preparation for the job? (For example, raising funds for a school club or activity might qualify as sales experience.)

3. List the information you want to present in your résumé, including:
- educational background, including the schools you have attended and the courses you have taken that relate to the job you are seeking
- previous jobs, including outstanding accomplishments and recognition
- activities and interests, especially those that relate to the job you seek
- references, both personal (people who can testify to your character and ability) and business (people who can tell about your performance on a job)

Writer's Choice

Do you want to think about your writing variables before or as you draft?

Drafting Suggestions for a Résumé

1. Have a look at the résumé at the end of this chapter before you write your own.

2. Keep your résumé brief and to the point – one page at the most. Busy employers do not have time to read long résumés. Think about your experience and interests, and include the information that directly relates to the job you are applying for. What is most important for your prospective employer to know?

3. Usually, you will organize the information in your résumé in categories – such as education, work experience, and hobbies and interests – and present it in reverse chronological order. That is, you begin with your most recent schooling and most recent experience and work back in time. This organization makes it easy for a prospective employer to check on your progress.

4. You may want to organize your résumé as follows.
a) Present your name, address, and telephone number at the top of your résumé so that your prospective employer can contact you easily.
b) Next, list your education, beginning with your most recent schooling. If you have taken any courses that have prepared you for the job you are applying for, then list them. Be sure to include any specialized training that relates to the job.
c) Present your employment history, specifying the dates of employment, the full names of the companies you worked for (your prospective employer may

want to contact them), and the positions you held. Give brief but specific descriptions of what your jobs required. A phrase such as "helped in the lunchroom" is too vague. Tell your prospective employer exactly how you helped.

d) List your interests and hobbies (if they relate to the job or help show the kind of person you are), and mention any awards you have received.

e) At the end of your résumé, present your personal and business references or simply state, "References available upon request." Talk to the people you plan to list as references to make sure it is all right to include them. Try to get your references from a variety of sources: work, school, church, team, club, and any other organization to which you belong.

5. Phrases, rather than complete sentences, often work well in a résumé.

6. If you have access to a computer, you can keep a copy of your résumé on disk and customize it for each job that you apply for.

Drafting Suggestions for a Cover Letter

1. You may want to look at the cover letter at the end of this chapter before you begin to write your own.

2. Because a cover letter is a business letter, read or review Chapter 18, which deals with the correct forms for business letters. Be sure that your cover letter contains the six parts of a business letter.

3. Your letter should do the following:
- establish contact with the employer by indicating what job you are applying for and how you know about the job (advertisement, employment agency, personal contact, or other source)
- arouse the interest of the employer by telling why you are interested in the position
- convince the employer to read your résumé by briefly mentioning your qualifications
- thank the prospective employer for considering your application (and perhaps politely request an interview)

4. If you do not have any work experience, or if your experience is not related to the job you seek, emphasize the personal qualities that would make you suitable for the position. For example:

Although I do not have any direct sales experience, my participation in many clubs shows that I have the ability to get along with others. I believe that this, coupled with my competitive spirit, would allow me to make a valuable contribution to your organization.

5. When you are deciding which qualities to mention, consider the requirements of the job. A sales position, for example, might require someone who has an attractive personality, speaks well, and is aggressive. A clerical position might require good organizational ability and attention to detail.

6. Address your envelope correctly. (See Chapter 17.)

When you have completed your résumé and cover letter, use the following guidelines to help you revise them.

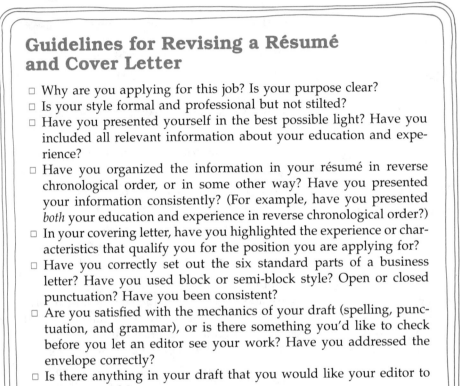

Guidelines for Revising a Résumé and Cover Letter

☐ Why are you applying for this job? Is your purpose clear?

☐ Is your style formal and professional but not stilted?

☐ Have you presented yourself in the best possible light? Have you included all relevant information about your education and experience?

☐ Have you organized the information in your résumé in reverse chronological order, or in some other way? Have you presented your information consistently? (For example, have you presented *both* your education and experience in reverse chronological order?)

☐ In your covering letter, have you highlighted the experience or characteristics that qualify you for the position you are applying for?

☐ Have you correctly set out the six standard parts of a business letter? Have you used block or semi-block style? Open or closed punctuation? Have you been consistent?

☐ Are you satisfied with the mechanics of your draft (spelling, punctuation, and grammar), or is there something you'd like to check before you let an editor see your work? Have you addressed the envelope correctly?

☐ Is there anything in your draft that you would like your editor to help you with?

Writer's Choice

Are your résumé and cover letter ready for your intended audience? Or would you like an editor to look at them first?

If necessary, revise your work and prepare a clean double-spaced draft for your editor.

Revising and Editing Suggestions

Give your drafts to your peer-editor, and share your writing variables. Encourage your editor to use the "Guidelines for Revising a Résumé and Cover Letter" in this chapter and the checklists in Chapter 27. Your editor should also think about how he or she would answer the following questions.

Ask Your Peer-Editor

☐ Do my résumé and cover letter provide the following information clearly?

what experience and education I have
where I gained my experience and education
when I gained my experience and education
why I want the job

☐ If I am replying to a job posting or advertisement, have I linked my education and experience to the requirements of the position?
☐ Does the cover letter have all six parts of a business letter? Are the parts punctuated and capitalized correctly?
☐ Is my style formal but not stilted? Is there anything that you would change? Why?
☐ Imagine that you are my prospective employer. Have I told you everything about myself that you need to know? If not, what would you add?
☐ If you were my prospective employer, would you hire me? Why or why not?

Publishing Suggestions

If you have written your résumé and cover letter for a real job, double-check to make sure that you have presented yourself as favorably and accurately as possible. If you are answering an employment advertisement or responding to a job posting, be sure that you have addressed all (or most) of the qualifications that are set out in the ad or job posting.

To gain experience in interviews, you and your classmates might have a class "Job Fair." You can take turns role-playing employers and job applicants, asking and answering questions.

Many employers now invite you to submit your application by FAX (facsimile machine). Before you do so, make sure that your résumé is attractively set up and that you have typed or word-processed it using a new ribbon so that it will transmit clearly.

**In the
Company
of Writers**

Cover Letter

1515 Award Avenue
Calgary, AB
T2A 5N5
May 3, 1990

Douglas Catering Inc.
3900 Hottens Road
Edmonton, AB
T6C 2B7

Dear Mr. Douglas:

I am responding to your recent newspaper advertisement for a short-order cook.

For the past few years, I have held jobs in the restaurant business in Calgary. I find it an interesting and challenging area and hope to pursue a career as a chef, following graduation from high school.

At present, I am attending McNair Career Academy in Calgary, majoring in food preparation. My family is planning to move to Edmonton at the end of June, and I am looking for evening and weekend work that will give me experience in the restaurant field.

I have enclosed a résumé outlining my experience and qualifications for the position you offer. If my qualifications interest you, I would be grateful if you would grant me an interview during the May 24th weekend, when I can easily get to Edmonton. During that weekend, I will endeavor to see you any time at your convenience.

Thank you for your consideration.

Yours truly,

John Brant.

John Brant

Résumé

John Brant
1515 Award Ave.
Calgary, AB
T2A 5N5
(403) 555-6767

EDUCATIONAL DATA
Sept. 1989-present   McNair Career Academy, Calgary
                          Specialized in food preparation
                          and catering with grades of A in
                          all related courses. General
                          grade average B+.

EMPLOYMENT DATA
Sept. 1989-present   Cafeteria helper, McNair Career
                          Academy
                          Serve lunches, prepare salads
Sept. 1988-present   Busperson, Dino's Place, 6420
                          Number Road, Calgary
May 1984-June 1988   Carrier, Star, 4310 Staves
                          Street, Calgary

AWARDS
Most Promising Cook Award, McNair Career Academy,
December 1989.

References available upon request.

Your Writing

1. Are your résumé and cover letter as effective as John Brant's? Are they better? What makes you say so?

2. How do you grab the attention of your prospective employer in your cover letter? Does your approach work?

3. In your journal, comment on your writing. What did you learn about applying for a job? Is there any part of your process that you would change the next time you do so? Why?

"It is not generally understood that most writing takes place away from the typewriter. When you finally approach the machine, it is really the beginning of the end. Nine-tenths of your work has already been done; it remains to put on paper what you have already created. It is this creative process that takes most of the time."

Pierre Berton

First Workshop: Content and Organization

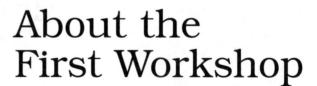

About the First Workshop

The chapters in this First Workshop section will support you at every stage of your writing. They will help you to come up with ideas for a writing project, draft and revise your work, and then polish your writing for your intended audience.

Use the chapters in the First Workshop as a resource. Dip into them to check a brainstorming technique, review how to summarize, help you find a good transitional word or phrase, and so on.

Find a writing partner – a classmate, friend, or relative at home – to work with as you sample the chapters in the First Workshop section. You'll need someone to brainstorm with, help you revise your work, and talk with about writing.

Each chapter contains one or more special writing projects that you can do for your partner. It is possible for you to do a special writing project for your teacher-editor as well.

21

Journal Writing and Instant Writing

"A journal is useful to the person who keeps it, dull to the contemporary who reads it, invaluable to the student, centuries afterwards, who treasures it!"

Ellen Terry, **The Story of My Life**

During the last years of her short life, Anne Frank, a young Jewish girl in Holland, kept a journal where she recorded her impressions of the small world in which she and her family hid while the Second World War ravaged the larger world. The result brought *The Diary of Anne Frank* into millions of homes in book form, and onto stages and screens throughout the world in play and film form.

Keeping a writing journal is one way to discover that you have many interesting, valuable thoughts and experiences to record. Try to write in your journal for at least ten minutes each day, in or out of class. Returning to your journal even a few weeks or months from now will provide enlightening, enjoyable reading.

Because journal writing is a private experience, it can become the writing you most enjoy doing. When you write in your journal, you do not have to worry about spelling, punctuation, grammar, or sentence structure. Just enjoy the experience of putting your thoughts on paper. One day you may write in your journal for fun, with no intention of reading or even thinking about what you have written; another day you may write more seriously, with plans to use what you have written as the start of a major writing project. Journal writing can become an important part of your exploration and prewriting, when you try out various ideas, jot down details to flesh out your thoughts, and experiment with various writing styles and techniques.

You might use your journal to make a daily commentary on what you are doing during your English class or any other class. You might extend a short story you have just read, compose a few lines of poetry, do a character sketch, annotate a formula, summarize a teacher's lecture, or comment on any number of other things that happen in your classes.

On some occasions you might like to write about your developing writing process. Choose a writing project and keep track of your thoughts and what you do as you explore and prewrite, draft, and revise and edit your work. By making regular, frequent (at least once a week) entries on different writing projects, you will become more aware of your development as a writer.

Often, you will want to use your journal to explore ideas. This chapter also offers you and your writing partner – a fellow classmate, a friend, or a relative at home – several suggestions for exploration through **instant writing**. Writing in your journal will help you to identify subjects that you want to write about. There may be times, however, when you need some help getting started, and the following suggestions may do just that.

Journal Entry Suggestions

Repeat any of the following suggestions as often as you like.

1. Write about a friend or a member of your family. Do not be concerned about how your piece will end – just let yourself write.

2. Daydreaming can provide you with many ideas. Choose one of the following beginnings, fill in the blanks, and write nonstop for five minutes. Use your imagination. Stretch your mind. Repeat this item often to stretch your imaginative powers.

- If I could be someone other than myself, I would be _____ because ...
- If I could be something other than myself, I would be a _____ because ...
- If I could live in another place and time than here and now, it would be _____ (*place*) in _____ (*time*) because ...
- If I won a million dollars, I'd ...
- If only I had _____, instead of _____, then ...
- If I were the principal of this school, I'd ...
- If what I suggested were to be followed by every human being in the world, I would tell everyone to ...
- If I were shipwrecked on a desert island, I would take _____ with me because ...

3. Everyone's life has been influenced by someone else. Who has changed your life in some way? In what ways? Write about this person and his or her influence on your life. How would you be different if you had never even heard of that person? Why?

4. We usually try to go through life following some kind of logical organization. However, we often do illogical things: buy things we do not need, make resolutions we never intend to keep, say things we do not believe. One day in your journal write about the most illogical thing you have ever done; the next day write about the most logical thing.

5. One day, write in your journal about your favorite subject in school, explaining why it is your favorite. The next day write about the subject you like least, explaining why you don't like it. On the following day respond to this question: What would have to happen to make this subject your favorite? Why?

6. You might keep a portion of your journal to record your thoughts on your writing process. Comment on any of the following:
- your attitude to writing throughout the term;
- your feelings about using the exploring and prewriting, drafting, and revising and editing stages in your writing projects;
- your improvement, as you see and feel it;
- your feelings about watching and listening to your editors;
- your feelings about being a peer-editor;
- your feelings about the reactions of your intended audience.

7. Your journal can be a place to draw as well as to write. You do not have to be an artist to make useful journal drawings. Brainstorming graphics and diagrams, such as clusters and ladders (Chapter 22), can be useful additions to, or substitutes for, written descriptions. A visual plan can sometimes help you to see an idea and its organization before you write words, sentences, and paragraphs. Words might then come more easily.

Freewriting

When you freewrite, you write and write and write (usually for a set period of time, such as ten or fifteen minutes) without worrying about your content, format, spelling, punctuation, or grammar. You can write in any format you choose, including poetry, a letter, or long or short paragraphs. Freewriting will help you get into the habit of writing. And it's a great brainstorming tool. Because you write so much when you freewrite, you get a lot of possible ideas down on paper.

You can freewrite on any topic. The following are some suggestions.

1. Begin by writing down one of the aspects of human life, such as love, fear, death, greed, loneliness, or birth. Or write the word of a broad or narrow topic that you are working on for a major writing assignment, such as socialism, volcanoes, Napoleon, Jamaica, the giant panda, or patriotism. Write the name of your topic over and over until something else comes into your mind; then continue writing about that thought. Don't censor yourself. Just free-associate with your word. If you get stuck, go back to writing the original word until something new comes into your mind. You may write messages to yourself about your topic, such as "I don't know enough about Napoleon and the battle of Waterloo, so I will have to do some research before I start drafting my essay. I do know a lot about Napoleon's retreat from Moscow, however."

2. Think of a number from one to thirty-five. Turn to that chapter number in this book and read the quotation that introduces the chapter. Using it for inspiration, freewrite for ten minutes.

Instant Writing

As an alternative to solitary journal writing and freewriting, try instant writing. Practising to write on demand at least once a week should not only prepare you to produce better short exam essays but also give you another opportunity to have a piece of writing edited.

Plan each instant writing session with your writing partner. Consider the following:
- the exact day and time the writing will take place;
- which of the instant writing suggestions you will follow;
- how much time to allot to each session – never more than ten minutes;
- how the piece of writing will be edited;
- whether you will have an opportunity to rewrite the piece.

Until you and your partner make up your own topics for your instant writing sessions, you could use the following suggestions.

1. *What's the Problem?*

Write out a question, and exchange questions with your partner. In a journal entry, answer, to the best of your ability, your partner's question. The questions can be as personal as you wish; for example: "My friend drinks a lot (I think he may be an alcoholic). What should I do?"

2. *What's the Answer?*

Answer the question you are given as though it were an exam question. Exchange questions with your partner, perhaps basing your questions on some that your partner should answer in another class; for example: "Point out two reasons that a railway was built from one end of this country to the other."

3. *If I were ...*

Using your partner's beginning, write either a serious or humorous piece. Use the following: "If I were _____, then I'd _____." Fill in the first blank only, and exchange beginnings with your partner. Use your imagination; for example, "If I were *a toad (the richest person in the world, a horseshoe, my mother),* then I'd...."

4. *A Word*

Use a given word and other words related to it in a piece of writing. Exchange topics and a single word with your partner; for example: "Write on the topic of mountain-climbing, using the word *serene* and other words with the same root."

You may use your dictionary if you are unfamiliar with a word or if you do not know all the related words. Two words associated with *serene* would be *serenity* and *serenely.*

5. *Almost Freewriting*

Although the choice of topic is not free, the procedure of this instant writing suggestion is similar to that of freewriting. Exchange a single word with your partner; for example, *money, sports, clothes.*

Then write about that word for a specified number of minutes. If you cannot think of anything to say, keep returning to the word and simply write it down until something comes into your mind.

6. *The Unknown*

With your partner, arrange to write a mystery story. Do not discuss the subject or the format either *before* or *during* the actual writing. Each of you should draft an opening sentence and then exchange your writing. Compose a second sentence for the opening you received. When you have both completed the second sentence, exchange your work again in order to add the third sentence. When one of you writes "The End," the project is over.

In your evaluation discuss whether the pieces are effective; how difficult they were to write; what problems, if any, they might have; and other ideas that will lead to a possible revision. Which of the two mysteries is a stronger piece of writing? Why?

7. *Poems and Stories*

Ask your partner to choose a short story you have both read or a play you have both watched on film or television, and extend the story. For example, you might write about what a character is doing a year after the story ends, or you might try your hand at a short poem that the story inspires, such as a haiku (5-7-5 syllabic pattern) or some other type of poem you are familiar with.

8. *Found Poetry*

Independently, you and your partner select a part of one of the pieces of writing in this book (especially a sentence or two that you may not fully understand or appreciate). Exchange and rewrite the excerpt as a found poem. Experiment by repositioning words until you find an arrangement that either makes the meaning clear or brings forth an appreciation of the setting. To clarify meaning, you can leave out parts of a sentence or combine sentences. You could also position words on a page so that the poem's appearance contributes to its meaning.

9. *Reacting to a Quotation*

Find a quotation – for example: "Injustice anywhere is a threat to justice everywhere" (Martin Luther King, Jr.). Exchange quotations with your partner. For several minutes, write about the quotation you receive. If you cannot think of anything to write, keep returning to the quotation and simply write it down until something comes into your mind.

Invisible Writing

Use invisible writing for any of the suggestions in this chapter. Using two pieces of paper with a sheet of carbon paper between them, write with a pen that has run out of ink. Or, if you make your journal entries on your computer, turn off the screen. Writing invisibly forces you to carry on to the end of your project instead of looking back, changing wording, or correcting errors. When you finish an invisible writing session, read your carbon copy, or turn on the screen and read what you've written. What do you think? Does your writing need much editing? Revise your work, if you choose to.

22 Exploring Ideas

"It is strange how much you can remember about places ... once you allow your mind to return into the grooves which lead back."

E. B. White, **Once More to the Lake**

Even professional writers are lucky when they have an inspired, full-blown, completely organized idea spring into their minds before they draft. After years of experiences and observations they often have only a rough idea of what they want to write about before they start to write. In order to find an idea and generate supporting details, they may think about their idea by themselves and explore many possible drafts, or they may talk about their idea with several people until their thoughts become clear enough for them to begin a draft.

When you explore ideas or **brainstorm**, let your creative juices flow. As you explore and prewrite, record everything that you are thinking about, no matter how obvious, ridiculous, or peculiar an idea may seem.

After several exploration sessions, you will often be able to link certain items, recognize forceful points, eliminate useless details, see the need for additions, and realize that you may need to explore your topic further, either before or as you write. Everything you say or think can provide the spark for more ideas and more supporting evidence.

Keep your exploration notes; they are often useful during later writing sessions (for a particular piece of writing – or to begin a new one). If you detect a weakness in one of your drafts, you may want to check your notes and then continue brainstorming for further ideas.

There are many ways to explore ideas. For your first few writing projects, use as many methods as possible in order to familiarize yourself with the mechanics of each one. Eventually, you might use a combination of techniques or even devise a new one to suit your needs. But keep in mind four points:

- There are no rules to follow.
- There is no special order to follow.
- Record everything about your topic that you can think of.
- Keep everything. After a thorough exploring and prewriting session, you will have a mass of material that is all related in some way to your writing project.

This chapter should help you to learn specific exploration techniques. These are organized into three types:
- those to help you clarify and limit your topic
- those to help you find supporting details
- those to help you organize your ideas and supporting details

If you have access to a computer, think about how you can adapt any of the following techniques to assist you as you write. In addition, many software packages contain brainstorming packages. Check whether yours does.

Exploration Techniques to Clarify and Limit Your Topic

1.   Think/Write

This first technique is especially useful when you are alone and know you will soon begin a writing project. Most writers do a lot of thinking before they put any words on paper. They may even compose whole sentences in their mind and then write the sentences from memory when they begin their draft. Other writers may carry a notepad to record their thoughts, experiences, and observations so that they can draw on these as they write. Take a few minutes with your writing partner to list some of the ideas or problems that have been concerning both of you. They might relate to society, the environment, politics, or something personal. Choose a topic from your list and explain to your partner why you might want to write about it and who your audience might be.

2.   Talk/Write

It is often useful to talk through your ideas rather than write them out. Sometimes you can explore a topic by talking with one or more people. By listening to other people voice their opinions, you are more able to clarify your own thoughts.

Where do you do your best brainstorming? In a classroom? Around your dinner table? On the street or in a park?

Choose a topic that you've thought about on another occasion – or select one from the list that follows – and explore it by talking about it with your partner. Try to pick a topic on which you have differing opinions, and explore it to the point where you could use it for a writing project. (Before you draft, however, you might like to brainstorm further by using one or two other techniques.)

- Should the driving age be raised to eighteen?
- Should a student have a personal credit card?
- Should all students be required to take a year of home economics or family studies?
- Should personnel in essential services (teachers, bus drivers, pilots, post office and telephone workers, for example) be allowed to strike?
- Should students with AIDS be allowed to attend school?

3.   See/Write

Tell your partner about something that you see on a regular basis; for example, a particular sports event or television show. Why do you watch the event or show? What events or shows would you not see on a regular basis? Why?

Share with your partner something you have seen recently that you would like to write about. To whom do you want to write? Why?

You may like to explore further to discover supporting evidence.

4.   Experience/Write

Tell your partner about some of the things that you enjoy doing. What do you particularly enjoy about these experiences? Why? What are some of the things that you do not enjoy? What do you particularly dislike about these experiences? Why?

Share with your partner something you have experienced that you would like to write about. It may be something that you enjoyed or disliked. To whom do you want to write? Why?

Afterward, you may like to explore further to find more supporting evidence for your ideas.

5.   Read/Write

Tell your partner about your reading habits. Which newspaper do you read? What parts of the paper do you read regularly? Do you have favorite columnists? Which magazines do you read? Other than your schoolbooks, name the last three books you read. Who are your favorite authors? Why are they your favorites? Is there a book, essay, or poem about which you would like to write? A character or plot line that you would like to develop? Why?

6.   Assign/Write

As a student, you can use this technique for most of your classes. If you have an assignment coming up in a class, ask your partner to predict a question you might have to answer. Explain how you would answer it. Perhaps you might then use one or two other exploration techniques to gather more supporting evidence. After a short discussion, spend half an hour writing your assigned short piece in your journal. Repeating this technique several times during the term will make it easier for you to write pieces assigned by your teachers, especially if you find that you have already written on a similar topic.

7.   Write/Write

Many writers do not know what they want to write about until they start to write. In fact, they write to *find* a topic. If you keep a writing journal, you perhaps know how it feels to sit down, without preparation, and write. As you write, you find that ideas do come.

   Choose a topic, even if you do not know whether you will fully develop it into a polished piece of writing. Record all your thoughts about that topic as they occur to you. Do not worry about getting your thoughts well organized.

8.   Free Association Cluster

A Free Association Cluster can be especially useful when you want to gather ideas to produce a limited topic to write about. Using free association is similar to playing a word association game. In word association you say the first word that comes into your mind when you hear another word. In free association, you continue generating words or phrases based on your own responses. For example, to *thunder* you might add *lightning*, to *lightning* you might add *bad storm*, to *bad storm* you might add *I am afraid to be in a bad storm*, and so on, until you have a great deal of material. If you get stuck along the way, go back to an earlier word and begin the process again. For example, to *lightning* you might add *streaks of electricity*, and then continue free-associating.

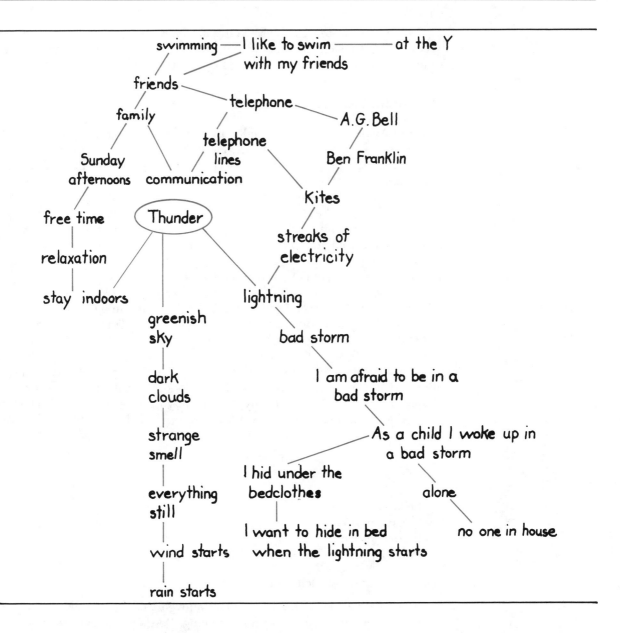

So that you do not lose any of your material, gather it by using a clustering method similar to the Free Association Cluster above. Note that the cluster begins with the word *thunder*. If you wish, you can add to this cluster.

When you complete a Free Association Cluster, connect various entries to see whether you can come up with a suitable limited topic for a writing project. When you have a limited topic, choose one or two other exploring techniques to gather supporting details.

When you free-associate with your partner, work together to develop a Free Association Cluster. Keep going until each of you comes across a topic that might become a good limited topic for a writing project.

9. Absurd Analogies

Absurd Analogies can be especially useful for creative writing projects, poetry, short stories, drama, narrations, reviews, and literary analyses. Sometimes in the course of a project, you may decide that you want to illustrate an idea, problem, or event. Consider using an analogy, in which you compare something unknown (or imprecisely known) to something known. To get at all aspects of your subject, explore Absurd Analogies in your journal. Compare your topic to anything; literally *anything*. Have some fun, stimulate your imagination – and come up with some provocative ideas. You can then transfer to your writing either your Absurd Analogy or the ideas that you generated while developing your Absurd Analogy.

When you create an Absurd Analogy, list an aspect of your topic (thing, activity, problem, event) and say that it "is like" another thing, activity, problem, or event that you know. For example, for her topic "Bag Ladies," a student tried comparing a bag lady to a chocolate chip cookie, to a theatre, and to a rose. "How absurd!" you may think. "There is nothing that a chocolate chip cookie, a theatre, and a rose have in common with bag ladies." Nonetheless, the student continued to think about and work on her Absurd Analogy. Eventually she wrote more specifically: "A bag lady is like a faded rose." Then, she started to make a list to describe a faded rose. The list included the following:

> once colorful
> beautiful smell has disappeared
> smells foul
> pale
> brown around the edges
> broken, twisted, bent
> thorns hardened
> fragile, a light breeze could blow petals off stem

Here is what the student drafted.

> A bag lady is like a faded rose. Once a lovely and sweet-smelling bud, she is now withered, pale, and foul-smelling. Resting in alleyways or feeding off refuse, a bag lady will often appear broken, twisted, and bent, ready to be uprooted and thrown on the trash heap. Indeed, she looks as though a light breeze would blow her apart, leaving only an old stem. But come too close or try to interfere with this lady and you will feel her thorns. She may be old, but a bag lady can draw blood if you don't approach with care.

Produce a few Absurd Analogies for a topic of your choice. Ask some of your peers to read over your Absurd Analogies so that you can get their reactions. If you cannot think of a topic and an Absurd Analogy, choose one topic from the first column and one analogy from the second.

Possible Topics	*Absurd Analogies*
writing an essay	eating
Disneyland	peeling an onion
a crisis in a foreign country	getting a vaccination
computers	a venetian blind
a problem you have	any musical instrument
a type of dancing	making a sand castle
a federal law	any toy
insomnia	a river

SPECIAL WRITING PROJECT

- ☐ Write a short persuasive piece to convince your writing partner to use exploration techniques when he or she is trying to find a suitable topic for a writing project. Then give the piece to your partner.
- ☐ Find out whether your argument convinces your partner that exploration is essential to his or her writing process.

Exploration Techniques to Find Supporting Details

10. Random Lists

You may already make lists – a shopping list, a packing list, or a list of things to take on a picnic – to remind yourself to do certain things. The order of the list is usually random, depending on what you thought of first, second, third, and so on.

You can make a random list to help you prepare for a piece of writing, too. For example, assume that you and your partner want to write a paragraph explaining how you prepare for an exam, host a barbecue, or pack for a trip. Independently, make random lists of about twenty items. Afterward, compare your lists to see whether you have thought of the same items. You might then discuss how you should re-order your items to include them in a paragraph.

If items on your list need to be in a particular order, you can number them in an appropriate order and recopy your list according to a plan that serves your needs – for instance, from particular to general, or in chronological, climactic, or sequential order. (These and other plans for organizing a piece of writing are discussed in Chapter 25).

11. Senses Cluster

By thinking creatively about your topic and its sound, sight, taste, smell, and feel, you can enliven a piece of writing. To help you gather words and phrases that link and extend your topic, jot them down in the form of a Senses Cluster. How detailed your Senses Cluster will be depends on how creatively you explore ideas. Before he wrote a description of his dog, a student produced the following Senses Cluster. Can you add to it?

After choosing a specific topic that you might use for a piece of writing, enrich it by using a Senses Cluster. If you cannot think of a topic, you might use one of the following: a dish of ice cream, a ballet dancer, a football player, the villain in a movie, or a particular location near your school or home. (Also, see the Senses Grid in Chapter 2.)

12. Positive Cluster

Positive Clusters can be especially useful for argumentative writing. To probe your limited topic deeply, you might select a single point of view and think only of your topic and its positive associations. Notice in the cluster that follows how one student decided to connect his topic "The Rewards of Going to School" with seven positive characteristics of the human condition. Can you add to this Positive Cluster?

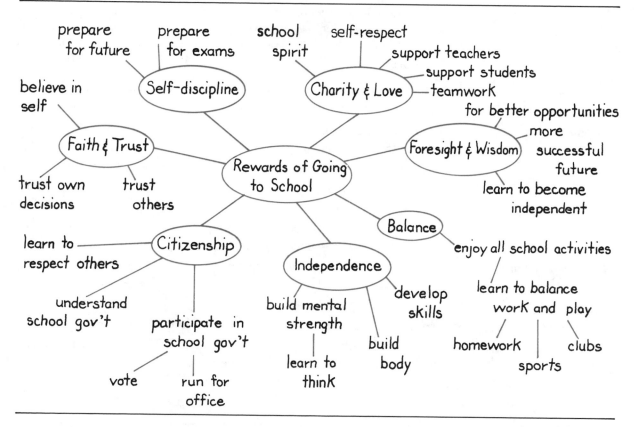

After choosing a limited topic that you might use for a piece of writing, enrich it by using a Positive Cluster. Use the seven aspects of the human condition set out in the sample cluster, or choose your own positive characteristics. If you cannot think of a topic, use one of these:

- a style of dancing;
- an incident that recently happened to you;
- a holiday outing;
- a family conflict;
- an event that you learned about from a friend.

13. Negative Cluster

Negative Clusters can also be useful for argumentative writing. By focusing only on the negative aspects of your limited topic and recording them in the form of a cluster, you will already be thinking about the organization of your writing. If you've already done a Positive Cluster for your topic, you probably have solid evidence for a piece of writing that involves contrast and comparison.

If, for example, you were writing about the benefits of buying a car, you would want to consider the negative aspects as well. By making a Negative Cluster, you will write a less biased piece. Notice how a student recorded the negative aspects of buying a car. Can you add to this Negative Cluster?

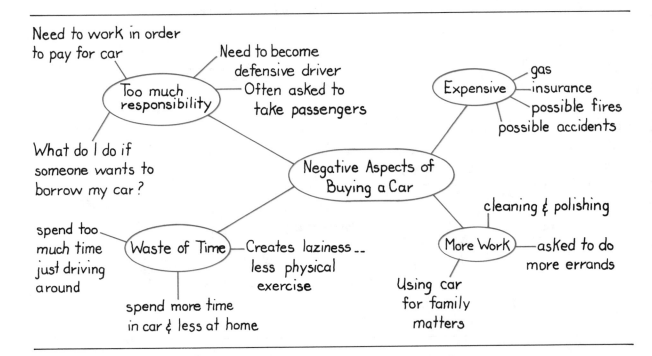

SPECIAL WRITING PROJECT

☐ Write a short piece for your partner pointing out the negative aspects of going to school or the positive aspects of buying a car – or choose another topic that interests you. Begin by making up either a Negative Cluster or a Positive Cluster.

☐ When you finish, discuss your cluster and your piece of writing with your partner.

Exploration Techniques to Organize Your Ideas and Supporting Details

Writing, like creative thought, rarely progresses in perfect steps. You may blend two steps, repeat one, or move from drafting back to exploring. The following exploring techniques will help you to generate ideas and information, but they also have a built-in bonus: if you do them thoroughly, they will practically organize your writing for you.

14.   Aristotle's Topics

In his *Rhetoric*, Aristotle provided instructions for public speakers in ancient Greece. Today, you can still use his suggestions to organize your ideas. Put simply, you should:
- *define* your limited topic;
- *compare and contrast* it;
- point out its *cause-and-effect* relationship;
- *provide evidence* to support your idea.

The following is an example of how one student used Aristotle's Topics to brainstorm his topic of racquetball. (See pages 14–24.) Have a look at the example, and then use Aristotle's Topics to explore a topic of your choice. If you cannot think of one, here are some possibilities:
- feeding birds in the winter;
- the force of gravity;
- cable television;
- professional wrestling.

Definition	Racquetball is a court game. Played with short racquets and a single ball. Object is to hit the ball to the end wall and make it bounce on the floor twice before your opponent can return the ball. It's a fast game.
Comparison and Contrast	It's like squash and handball. But it's faster than handball and slower than squash. It's easier to play than both. I think it's more fun than both. Keeping score is the same for all three games. You can play doubles in racquetball as you can in handball and squash.
Cause and Effect	Racquetball is such a fast game that you couldn't possibly be aware of any outside problems. There is no time to be aware of anything but the game. No time to feel depressed. Racquetball is a great way to have a good workout. I'm sweating after five minutes. Game is easy to learn but hard to play. Enthusiasts say that racquetball takes minutes to learn but a lifetime to perfect.
Supporting Evidence	Racquetball is popular. Most players play three or four times a week. Racquetball provides exercise, play, and fun. The more experienced players learn to kill a shot, zigzag serves, and play the back wall. They dive for the ball before it has a chance to bounce on the floor twice. It's a fast sport.

15.   Pro/Con Ladders

Pro/Con Ladders are especially useful in argumentative writing. If you want to produce a piece of writing in which you argue for or against a particular action or opinion, use Pro/Con Ladders. Draw two ladders, each with ten rungs. Label one ladder "Pro" to indicate support for your argument. Label the other "Con" to indicate support for the oppposite point of view. Under the ladders, draw a box showing your limited topic. By filling in as many rungs as you can on *both* ladders, you will see your argument from both your vantage point and that of an opponent. Thus, you will not be able to ignore your opponent's viewpoint.

Study the following partial Pro/Con Ladders. Can you complete them?

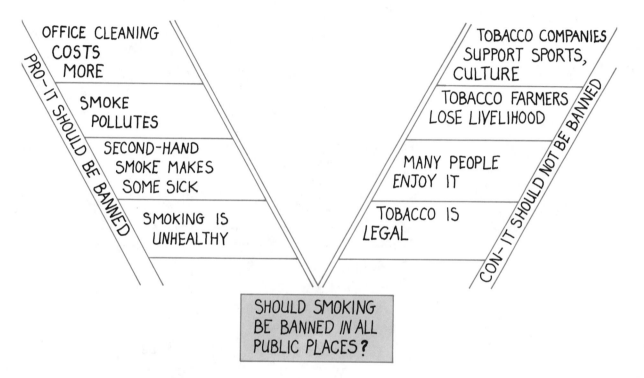

Use Pro/Con Ladders to develop a topic. If you cannot think of one, try one of the following. Talk over your results with your partner.
- My family should move.
- I should get a part-time job.
- Development of oil resources is important for the North.

16.   Comparison/Contrast Ladders

Similar to Pro/Con Ladders, Comparison/Contrast Ladders allow you to list similarities and differences in a useful way.

Assume that, in your writing, you want to compare and contrast yourself with your writing partner. Through discussion, attempt to find out all of your similarities and differences. Use two ladders to help you organize your facts, one for similarities and one for differences. When you hit upon a similarity or a difference, record the detail on the rung of the appropriate ladder, as shown below.

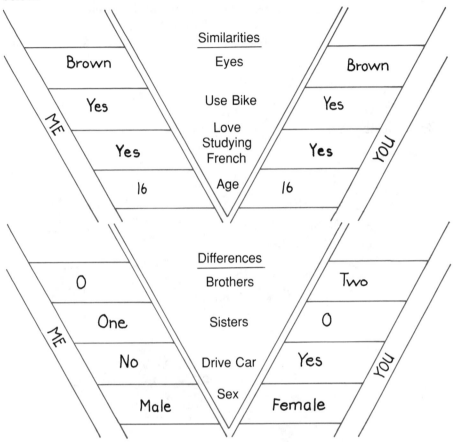

Choose a broad topic, narrow it, and explore it by completing Comparison/Contrast Ladders. Or choose one of the following topics to explore: two school teams; the Prime Minister and the Leader of the Opposition; two TV shows; two singers; or the benefits of writing with a pen and paper or with a computer.

17.   Newspaper Reporter's Questions

If you use the traditional newspaper reporter's investigative questions to explore a topic, you can locate broad and useful information. With your writing partner, brainstorm as many questions as you can. As you conduct your research, keep asking yourself questions.

For example, before one student started on her argumentative paper on the limited topic of providing homes for homeless teenagers, she and her writing partner produced the following extensive list by using the Newspaper Reporter's Questions. As you examine the Who? – What? – When? – Where? – Why? – How? list, note its details and its usefulness. Can you add to any of the six parts?

Homeless Teenagers

Who? poor/unemployed/"street kids"/school dropouts/runaways/the parasites who use them/and authorities who allow the situation to exist

What kinds of people are involved with the problem?
- teenagers
- their parents and families
- government officials (social workers)
- religious groups
- police
- criminals
-

How do these people affect the problem?
- home problems add to number of runaways
- social workers try to intervene to reunite families
- some religious groups offer shelter, while others recruit from street kids
- police often regard homeless kids as potential or actual criminals
- criminals use teenagers as customers or recruit them as couriers or accomplices
-

What is each person's relationship to the problem?
- the different parties involved with homeless teenagers have different and often incompatible solutions – for example:
- social workers and many parents strive to return runaways to their homes, while some kids want secure shelter away from their homes
- some criminals see teens as victims to be exploited
-

How do other societies deal with the problem?
- (more research needed) In Sweden, for example, there is compulsory military service beginning at age ?? (I absolutely don't know.) The problem in the United States is far worse than it is in Canada.
-

Are there more or fewer people involved now than in the past?
- more blended and single-parent families can make for more tension in families, therefore, more runaways
- involvement of criminals and religious cults with runaway teens has increased
- more social workers specialize in the problems of runaways
- media are more concerned
-

(NOTE: As long as they produce useful answers, you can keep asking other questions that focus on who you are writing about. Likewise, you can compose additional questions for the following categories.)

What? money/different crimes
- What are the details of the problem? Which are the most important? Which are less important?
- Do all those involved agree on what the details are?
-

When? past/present/future
- Does the problem have a general chronology?
- How does time affect the problem?
- When is a bad/good time for the problem?
-

Where? back alleys, cheap hotel rooms, flophouses, hostels, abandoned buildings, all-night restaurants and movie houses, the streets
- Does the problem reside mostly with you and/or others involved with it?
- Does it get better in some places? Worse in others?
- What and who determines where it occurs?
- Does the place of occurrence contribute anything to the problem?
-

Why?
- Why does the problem exist?
- Why does it qualify as a problem?
- Why will it eventually end? Why will it perhaps never end?
- Why don't we end it right now?
-

How?
- How does the problem occur? Who or what causes it?
- How could it be prevented? How could it be resolved?
- How are aspects of the problem (and/or the solution) linked?
-

Make up a similar list of questions on a narrow topic of your choice. (If you are using a computer, you can quickly and easily set up this brainstorming format.) You might use one of the following topics if you cannot think of one of your own.

* a current social problem in your community;
* a family conflict;
* one of your ambitions;
* a topic from one of your other classes.

SPECIAL WRITING PROJECT

☐ Using Aristotle's Topics, Comparison/Contrast Ladders, Pro/Con Ladders, or Newspaper Reporter's Questions, write a short piece on a topic of your choice for your partner.

☐ Discuss with your partner both the content of your piece and its organization. Be sure to have your exploration notes available for reference.

18.   Classification Flowchart

When you classify, you separate a topic into classes or categories. Then you can break down the class into divisions or subcategories.

As a student, you will often write an essay on a broad topic such as: "Write a 500-word essay on communication." You will have to explore this topic to discover a limited or more manageable one. For this communication topic, a student produced the following Classification Flowchart.

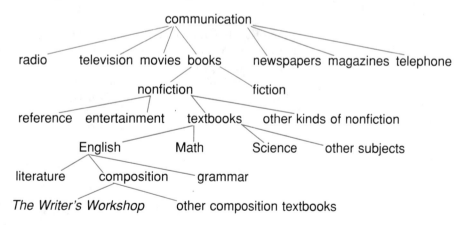

Do you see how this Classification Flowchart divides the topic into ever-narrower categories until it becomes difficult to classify any more? Do you also see that as you move down the flowchart, each category becomes more manageable? "Textbooks" is a much more limited (and therefore manageable) topic than "Communication."

Make a new Classification Flowchart on communication. Use one of the other main categories from the sample flowchart you have just skimmed. When you finish, make sure that your categories don't overlap.

Think of a problem that can serve as a topic for a paper, and create a Classification Flowchart to help you arrive at a solution. If you cannot think of a problem, choose one of the following:
• Which computer should I buy?
• What country is the most (least) ideal to visit?
• Which kind of books should I read?

The following illustrates how you might begin a Classification Flowchart in response to the first question.

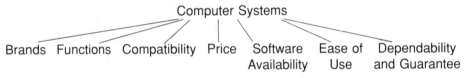

Notice that the headings do not overlap. If you then continue the Classification Flowchart to concentrate on manufacturers, your flowchart might resemble the following.

(NOTE: For the purposes of this flowchart, made-up names are used for manufacturers and computer models. If you develop your own flowchart, use your knowledge of real manufacturers and models.)

If you continue the Classification Flowchart to concentrate on the models of the first manufacturer, you might get:

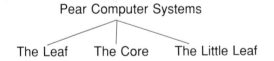

To add more details to the flowchart, you would need to use the division process presented next. How would a Division Flowchart help you decide which computer to buy?

19.   Division Flowchart

When you divide something, you break it down into its parts. It might be helpful for you to examine the following Division Flowchart to see the parts of this book.

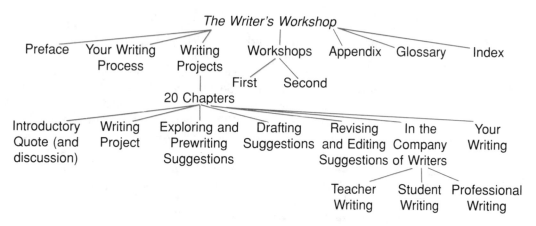

Do you see how the Division Flowchart limits the topic into narrower and narrower parts until it becomes difficult to divide any more? Do you also see that as you move down the flowchart, each part becomes more manageable as a possible topic?

Make a Division Flowchart for one of your other textbooks. When you finish, check to make sure that you cannot divide any of the parts into more specific parts. You might continue your exploration of which computer to buy by making a Division Flowchart.

20.   Cause-and-Effect Flowchart

For want of a nail, the shoe was lost;
For want of the shoe, the horse was lost;
For want of the horse, the rider was lost;
For want of the rider, the battle was lost;
For want of the battle, the kingdom was lost ...

(Anonymous)

Cause and effect form a continuum, stretching from the most distant past into the most distant future. In the lines from the famous proverb above, can you follow the cause-and-effect relationships that eventually resulted in the "fact" that an entire kingdom was lost because a nail was lacking?

You cannot exist without affecting people or things, and they in turn affect you. Even the air around you changes because of your presence. A cause produces an effect; an effect is produced by a cause and then itself becomes a cause. People and things are both causes and effects. In other words, literally everything about you and in you is a part of the continuous cause-and-effect process.

You can employ a Cause-and-Effect Flowchart not only to help you organize your writing, but also to reveal a more precise, limited topic. You can use cause and effect in reasoning, in solving problems, in determining the significance of facts and ideas, and in predicting possible outcomes.

To find causes, you work backward in time and ask the question "Why?" To find effects, you work forward and ask "So what happened?" To find possible future effects, you ask "So what will happen?" If, for example, you had to explain to a police officer why you were speeding, you might answer, "I am late getting to school." [Why?] "Because I slept late." [Why?] "Because I didn't hear the alarm." [Why?] "Because I went to bed at three o'clock this morning." [Why?] "Because I was studying." ...

Listening to you relate this later, a friend might ask what happened. "The police officer felt sorry for me." [So what happened?] "She gave me a police escort to school." [So what happened?] "With boosted self-confidence, I aced the exam." [So what will happen?] "I will get an A in marketing." ...

Take a few minutes to list two or three things in which you excel. If you are an extremely talented athlete, artist, or musician, you will have an easy time making up your list, but look beyond the obvious when you are doing so. You might like to include that you are an excellent listener, talker, walker, babysitter, sports fan, or friend.

Decide on one skill that you would like to analyse for past causes and present and future effects; for example, Gilles felt that he excels at watching television. Using the Cause-and-Effect Flowchart to analyse his viewing habits, he kept asking himself questions.

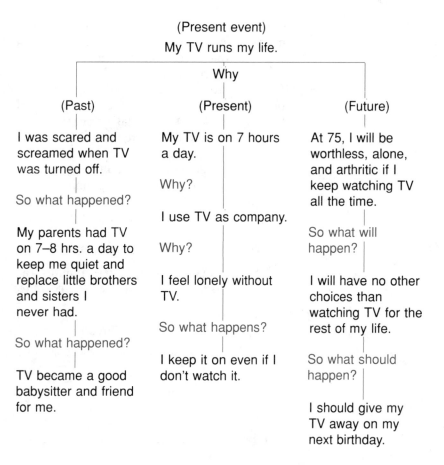

(Present event)
My TV runs my life.

Why

(Past)	(Present)	(Future)
I was scared and screamed when TV was turned off.	My TV is on 7 hours a day.	At 75, I will be worthless, alone, and arthritic if I keep watching TV all the time.
So what happened?	Why?	
My parents had TV on 7–8 hrs. a day to keep me quiet and replace little brothers and sisters I never had.	I use TV as company. Why?	So what will happen?
So what happened?	I feel lonely without TV.	I will have no other choices than watching TV for the rest of my life.
TV became a good babysitter and friend for me.	So what happens? I keep it on even if I don't watch it.	So what should happen? I should give my TV away on my next birthday.

Try to make a similar flowchart for your skill. Start with an event, a situation, a decision, a judgment, or a question, and write about the present. Then work back into the past and forward into the possible future. Your flowchart should be similar to the one that Gilles made.

When you brainstorm a cause-and-effect relationship, you should include in your flowchart every cause and effect that occurs to you. But not every point will contribute directly to the development of your limited topic. Other causes and effects that Gilles thought of included: "I don't have any older brothers and sisters," "I try to watch *The Young and the Restless* every day," "My parents gave me a VCR for Christmas," and "I'll probably have to have my eyeglass prescription changed soon." Why do you think he excluded each of these from his flowchart?

As he examined the causal relationships in his flowchart, Gilles came to the conclusion that his "skill" of watching TV might have undesirable effects. In addition, because he thought that many North Americans have become TV addicts for the same reasons he did, he decided to make the limited topic of an argumentative essay: "North Americans watch too much TV."

Choose one of the following questions or another question that is important to you. Then make up a flowchart, and compose a set of writing variables. If you are successful in brainstorming cause-and-effect relationships for your topic, you may want to use the flowchart to draft a piece of writing.

- If an election is soon to take place, what would be the possible effects if a particular candidate were to win? (Consider your school's elections as well as other elections.)
- What were some of the results of the Laporte and Cross kidnappings, the Meech Lake Accord, the invention of the computer, or the popularity of home videos?
- If a nuclear power plant were built near my home, what would be the effects?
- What would happen if I won a million dollars in a lottery?

Brainstorm your topic for a few minutes, and then draw a Cause-and-Effect Flowchart, using specific cause-and-effect questions. For example:

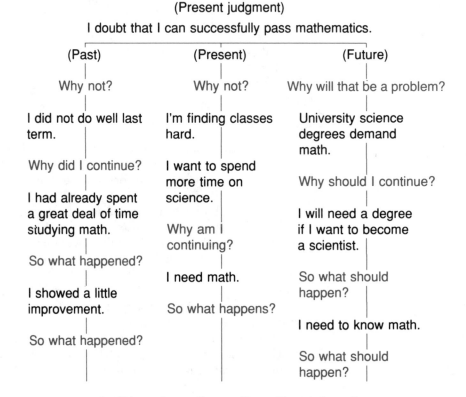

(Present judgment)
I doubt that I can successfully pass mathematics.

(Past)	(Present)	(Future)
Why not?	Why not?	Why will that be a problem?
I did not do well last term.	I'm finding classes hard.	University science degrees demand math.
Why did I continue?	I want to spend more time on science.	Why should I continue?
I had already spent a great deal of time studying math.	Why am I continuing?	I will need a degree if I want to become a scientist.
So what happened?	I need math.	So what should happen?
I showed a little improvement.	So what happens?	I need to know math.
So what happened?		So what should happen?

I will have to continue with math and do well.

When you make a flowchart, be sure to identify causes and effects precisely. Make sure you differentiate a cause or an effect. Establish whether the cause or effect is past, present, or future. Distinguish real causes and effects from possible and probable ones.

SPECIAL WRITING PROJECT

- ☐ For your partner, write up a short piece that uses the information you gathered and organized in a flowchart.
- ☐ Discuss the effectiveness of your flowchart and its influence on your draft.

21. Exploring Ideas Across the Curriculum

1. To illustrate how you would write on the same topic for several courses, spend a few minutes exploring one of the following broad topics: corn, teenagers, jewellery, sailboats, spaceships, hairstyles, running, or alcohol.

Assume that you are to write five papers *on the same topic* for five different classes. Choose one of the topics listed above and five of the following: art, geography, history, literature, computer science, consumer education, health, physical education, mathematics, religious studies, music, drama, home economics, or any other subject you may be studying.

Keep in mind the subject you are writing for, and narrow your topic. Because this is experimental, and because you will probably not complete any of these papers, stretch your imagination to create limited topics that are as dissimilar as possible. When you have narrowed your topic, invent a purpose, a suitable format, an appropriate audience, and "real" or "imagined" occasions for you to present your proposed pieces of writing. For example, note how one student narrowed the broad topic "corn."

Geography: a research paper that points out the best places in the world for growing corn.

History: a term paper to point out the attitudes of various peoples in the fifteenth and sixteenth centuries to eating corn.

Literature: a literary essay to point out the importance and significance of the Corn God in Thomas Tryon's *Harvest Home* and Stephen King's *Children of the Corn*.

Drama: a monologue to illustrate why it's all right to eat popcorn during a movie but not during a play.

Consumer Education: a report to contrast sales of various corn products: canned creamed corn, canned kernel corn, frozen kernel corn, frozen corn-on-the-cob, frozen corn-in-a-pouch, corn relish.

2. Once you have narrowed a single topic for use in five different classes, choose one and continue to limit the topic, give it direction, and focus it so that you could develop an original piece of writing with a strong point of view.

If you were going to write on all five topics, you would now brainstorm each topic until you could confidently begin to draft each one.

SPECIAL WRITING PROJECT

☐ Using the results of any one of your exploration sessions, compose a piece of writing for your partner.
☐ Discuss with your partner the effectiveness of your draft. Bring your exploring notes with you so that you can add to them, in case you want to revise your draft.

23 Thesis Statements and Topic Sentences

"The central idea, or thesis, is your essay's life and spirit."

Sheridan Baker, **The Practical Stylist**

When you write exposition, you choose a broad topic to write about and then limit the topic by narrowing it to a workable size. Considering your audience, purpose, format, and voice – your writing variables – helps you limit your topic and bring it into focus. Finally, you present your limited topic in a sentence called a **thesis statement**, which controls the development of your entire expository piece. In a longer work, your thesis statement will probably contain several points that you want to discuss. You usually treat each point in a separate paragraph and express that point in a statement called a **topic sentence**, which controls the content of a single supporting paragraph.

When you include a clear thesis statement and topic sentences in a piece of exposition, you use them not only to help you develop and structure your work, but also to guide your audience. Thesis statements and topic sentences are like road signs. When road signs are well posted, both driver and passengers enjoy the scenery and arrive at their destination without getting lost. In the same way, when thesis statements and topic sentences are clearly expressed, both writer and audience enjoy the details and arrive at a clear understanding of the writing without losing their way.

So that you begin this chapter with a clear understanding of the terms used, study and discuss the following flowcharts with your writing partner. They illustrate the development of a topic.

Broad Topic (a large subject that can be classified and divided)

|

Limited Topic (a specific, narrow subject)

|

Focus (the main aspect or part of the
limited topic that you want to write about)

|

Thesis Statement (a sentence that
controls the development of an entire work)

/ | \

Topic Sentence   Topic Sentence   Topic Sentence
(a sentence that controls the content
of each paragraph within a longer work)

Arachnids (Broad Topic)

Spiders (Limited Topic)

Poisonous Spiders in North America (Focus)

Two species of poisonous spiders in North America can cause
severe local or general damage to their victims. (Thesis Statement)

The black widow spider is   The bite of the brown recluse
notorious. (Topic Sentence   spider causes severe reactions.
for first supporting paragraph)   (Topic Sentence for second
                                            supporting paragraph)

1.   Purpose of Thesis Statements and Topic Sentences

Writers need a controlling idea in the form of a sentence both to limit the ideas discussed and to order the structure of an expository essay or paragraph. The following paragraph demonstrates an uncontrolled piece of writing. The ideas and details are fine, but the piece is aimless – neither the writer nor the reader really knows where the paragraph is going. Read the piece to yourself. Then either you or your partner should read it aloud. What evidence do you find that both writer and reader are hampered because the paragraph contains no controlling sentence? Can you figure out how this paragraph is organized?

The air is permeated with the smells of bubbling cauldrons of shellfish at Fisherman's Wharf, which is in San Francisco. You also notice rows of white-tiled counters neatly stacked with clean, red cooked crabs, lobsters, and prawns. If you stand near the edge of a pier and look down, you see all kinds of sea life – some quickly moving, some lying in wait for a bit of food, and others dead and floating. Sounds of the fiesta spirit of the tourists who crowd the streets under brightly colored awnings fill your ears. And your nostrils fill with the persistent tang of the sea: seaweed, fish, and spilled fuel from pleasure crafts. You can hear the creak of swaying fishing boats, the cries of sea gulls, and the persuasive cries of noisy barkers inveigling customers into the seafood restaurants. The crowds are always huge on Fisherman's Wharf. You can also see the parked automobiles with little trays of seafood cocktails hooked onto the open windows. People love to eat seafood when they visit this other world.

Now read the following aloud, noticing how the topic sentence limits the content of the paragraph by telling you exactly what to expect. In her prewriting, the writer of this paragraph has carefully considered which details to include, how to focus them, and how to bring her audience right into her paragraph.

At Fisherman's Wharf in San Francisco you enter another world, a world filled with inviting smells, sounds, and sights. It is a world pervaded with the aroma of bubbling cauldrons of shellfish, the fiesta spirit of the tourists who crowd the streets under brightly colored awnings, the persistent tang of the sea, the creak of swaying fishing boats, the cries of sea gulls, and the persuasive cries of noisy barkers inveigling customers into the seafood restaurants. The parked automobiles with little trays of seafood cocktails hooked onto the open windows and the rows of white-tiled counters neatly stacked with clean, red cooked crabs, lobsters, and prawns beckon you to eat.

The first paragraph contains more details than the second. Why do you think the writer omitted some of these details when she wrote the second paragraph? The opening sentence of the second paragraph reveals what the content will be. Find words in the rest of the paragraph that reinforce the topic "filled with inviting smells, sounds, and sights."

(NOTE: These paragraphs are modified versions of one taken from *Fifth Chinese Daughter* by Jade Snow Wong. Her original will appear later in this chapter.)

2. Placement of Topic Sentences

A topic sentence can be placed anywhere within a paragraph. It is up to the writer to decide on the most effective position of the topic sentence.

1. *At the beginning.* The most common place for a topic sentence is in the first sentence of the paragraph. After reading an opening statement, an audience will expect to see supporting details such as examples, reasons, or explanations. Consider the following example.

At Fisherman's Wharf in San Francisco, Jade Snow Wong and her brother en-tered another world, a world filled with inviting smells, sounds, and sights. This world was pervaded with the aroma of bubbling cauldrons of shellfish, the fiesta spirit of the tourists who crowded the streets under brightly colored awnings, the persistent tang of the sea, the creak of swaying fishing boats, the cries of sea gulls, and the persuasive cries of noisy barkers inveigling customers into the seafood restaurants. The parked automobiles with little trays of seafood cocktails hooked onto the open windows and the rows of white-tiled counters neatly stacked with clean, red cooked crabs, lobsters, and prawns beckoned them to eat.

2. *At the end.* The second most common position of the topic sentence is in the last sentence of the paragraph, using the supporting details to build up to the main idea. The following paragraph (on which the other paragraphs in this section are based) is from *Fifth Chinese Daughter* by Jade Snow Wong.

They entered another world, a world permeated with the aroma of bubbling cauldrons of shellfish, with the fiesta spirit of the tourists who crowded the streets under gay awnings, with the persistent tang of the sea, the creak of swaying fishing boats, the cries of sea gulls, and the persuasive cries of noisy barkers inveigling customers into the seafood restaurants. The parked automobiles with little trays of seafood cocktails hooked onto the open windows, the rows of white-tiled counters neatly stacked with clean, red cooked crabs, lobsters, and prawns – *where else would you find all these sights and sounds and smells but at Fisherman's Wharf in San Francisco?*

3. *At the beginning, with a clincher sentence at the end.* Sometimes you might use both the first and last sentences to show your complete topic. The last sentence can clinch (emphasize) a topic that you expressed in the first sentence, and can even extend that topic.

At Fisherman's Wharf in San Francisco Jade Snow Wong and her brother entered another world. This world was pervaded with the aroma of bubbling cauldrons of shellfish, the fiesta spirit of the tourists who crowded the streets under brightly colored awnings, the persistent tang of the sea, the creak of swaying fishing boats, the cries of sea gulls, and the persuasive cries of noisy barkers inveigling customers into the seafood restaurants. The parked automobiles with little trays of seafood cocktails hooked onto the open windows and the rows of white-tiled counters neatly stacked with clean, red cooked crabs, lobsters, and prawns beckoned them to eat. *Indeed, they were in a world filled with inviting smells, sounds, and sights.*

Experiment with where you position topic sentences in your paragraphs. If you are using a computer in your writing, you can shift sentences around quickly and easily to test their effectiveness. If you don't have a computer, you might ask your writing partner to read your paragraphs to you with your topic sentences in different positions. This procedure might be a bit less laborious than rewriting your paragraphs with topic sentences moved. You could also try cutting and pasting your sentences.

3. Limiting Your Topic and Coming Up with Your Focus

To come up with a suitable focus and ultimately a successful piece of writing, you have to choose a topic that interests you, limit it to a manageable size, and consider your narrow topic in the light of your writing variables: audience, purpose, format, and voice. You can use these writing variable to help you flesh out your limited topic, so that you arrive at the precise focus you want.

Assume, for example, that your broad topic is *dancing*.

1. Independently, you and your partner should both jot down possible writing variables, as in the examples below. In addition, record a specific aspect of the topic on which your writing might focus. Finally, write either a thesis statement (for a longer work) or a topic sentence (for a paragraph within a longer work).

Broad topic:	dancing
Audience:	my cousin Cliff. Real. I intend to send it to him.
Purpose:	to suggest that he enter a country-wide dance contest for teenagers
Format:	a letter
Voice:	my own
Limited topic:	how much fun it is to dance
Focus:	the thrill of entering a dance contest
Thesis statement:	I think you should enter the dance contest this Saturday night at the mall for several good reasons.

Broad topic:	dancing
Audience:	my biology teacher. Real. I will hand it to her.
Purpose:	to support her criticism that ballet can injure growing teens
Format:	scientific review paper
Voice:	my own
Limited topic:	the dangers of ballet
Focus:	I will stress that ballet dancers can hurt their feet and legs if they don't warm up properly before they dance.
Thesis statement:	Scientific research demonstrates that ballet can permanently damage the feet and legs of young teens.

If you have trouble writing your thesis statement, you might have to think more carefully about your writing variables. Who is your audience? What do you want to tell your audience about your topic? How do you want to present your information? In the alternative, you might begin drafting your exposition to get a sense of the flow and the language; later on, you can draft and position your thesis statement.

2. Compare and discuss the writing variables that you and your partner have developed. Which will lead to the most effective piece of writing? Why?

4.   Writing Thesis Statements and Topic Sentences

Both thesis statements and topic sentences should be clear, unified, precise, and limited. A thesis statement controls the development of an entire piece of exposition (and usually is placed at or near the beginning of the work), while a topic sentence focuses on the content of a single paragraph within a work (and can be placed anywhere within the paragraph).

1. With your partner, discuss the difference between the thesis statement and topic sentence in each of the following pairs.

Thesis statement: In most high schools throughout the nation, students are able to choose from a variety of extracurricular activities.

Topic sentence: The drama club consists of students with both on-stage and backstage interests.

Thesis statement: When I go out to dinner, I go to either an Italian or a Chinese restaurant.

Topic sentence: My favorite Italian dish is linguine with clam sauce.

2. Look over the following list of questions. Independently of your partner, answer each question "yes" or "no." Choose one that you both have strong

ideas about and, through discussion, narrow it to the point where you could use it as a limited topic with a specific focus for a writing project.

- Should teenagers work for spending money instead of receiving allowances?
- Should the voting age be lowered to sixteen?
- Should teenagers who break the law be tried in adult court?
- Should drunk drivers lose their licences?
- Should hitchhiking be illegal?
- Should Canada reinstate the death penalty?
- Should anabolic steroids be legal for professional and amateur athletes?
- Should school boards censor books and other media?
- Should Canada decrease spending for defence?
- Should beauty pageants be banned from national television?

Using the same limited topic as your partner, work separately for a few minutes. Jot down a possible set of writing variables and a thesis statement for a long piece of exposition. Finally, develop possible topic sentences for one or more of your supporting paragraphs.

3. Compare and discuss with your partner your thesis statement and topic sentences. Could they become road signs for your audience so that they will easily find their way through your work? Should you change anything to make the journey easier for your audience?

5. Recognizing and Evaluating Thesis Statements and Topic Sentences

1. Ask your partner to assign a piece of exposition for you to read. (For example, see Chapters 4 and 5.) Find and evaluate the thesis statement in the assigned work. Then comment on how well the writer developed the thesis statement. Finally, find and evaluate the topic sentences for each of the paragraphs in the piece.

2. Discuss your findings with your partner. If you felt that any of the thesis or topic sentences needed work, how would you revise them? Why?

6. Filling in the Blanks with Thesis Statements and Topic Sentences

1. Read the following example. Then, for the remaining topics, write a thesis statement and two topic sentences. Remember that each should be a complete sentence that controls what is discussed. For example:

Limited topic:	dining out
Focus:	joys and disasters of dining out
Thesis statement:	At times, dining out can be a joyous affair; other times, it can be disastrous.
1st topic sentence:	Three weeks ago, when my date and I went to O'Cookie's, I hoped the evening would never end.
2nd topic sentence:	Last night, in the same restaurant with the same date, I discovered that I had forgotten my wallet.

Limited topic:	vitamins and minerals
Focus:	benefits of taking vitamins and minerals
Thesis statement:	
1st topic sentence:	
2nd topic sentence:	

Limited topic:	swimming
Focus:	comparing recreational and competitive swimming
Thesis statement:	
1st topic sentence:	
2nd topic sentence:	

2. Have your partner present to you another limited topic and focus so that you can practise further.

3. Discuss with your partner what you have found out about thesis statements and topic sentences.

SPECIAL WRITING PROJECT

- ☐ Look back over the thesis statements and topic sentences you drafted. Choose one set, and jot down the points you would include in each paragraph if you were to draft a long piece of exposition.
- ☐ Exchange your work with your writing partner, and comment on each other's efforts.
- ☐ Hold onto your exploration notes. You may want to use them to develop a piece of expository writing.

24

Beginnings and Endings

"I've learned that the most important thing about a book is to have a great first chapter to grab your readers ... I've been sitting here for three hours and nothing's happened. So I'm going to make this my second chapter."

George Burns, **How to Live to Be 100 – or More**

Most writers find that beginning and ending a piece of writing are their most difficult tasks. The advice of the King of Hearts in *Alice in Wonderland* – "Begin at the beginning, go on until you come to the end, and then stop" – is much harder to follow than most people think. Even though there is no one way to begin or end your work, the following suggestions offer you several possibilities.

1. Beginnings

From your own experience, you know the importance of first impressions. Discuss with your writing partner some of the following.
- What attracted you to one of your friends?
- If you saw a recording by a band you did not know or had not heard before, what would cause you to buy the recording?
- What makes you pick up a magazine from a magazine rack?
- What kinds of opening sentences attract you to a story, article, essay, or some other work?

Consider also the people, clothes, music, and books that you have rejected because of your first impression of them.

Every writer works to compose a sentence or two that will grab the attention of the audience. Many writers, finding themselves unable to write an attention-getting opening, will complete their draft before they work on their beginning. They may not even begin to brainstorm titles until they complete their work. The following are some of the many types of beginnings that can be developed for the topic "Racquetball."

1. The statement, the most commonly used opening, does not exactly serve as an attention-getter, but it does indicate the subject of a piece.
• Racquetball has become very popular throughout North America.

2. The generalization, another common introduction, simply introduces the work with a broad statement.
• Everyone should have some way to stay physically fit.

3. You can use an attention-getting tactic such as an exaggeration, but be cautious about using it.
• Racquetball can save your life.

4. The question, another frequently used method of introduction, involves the audience immediately.
• Who says exercise can't be fun?

5. The summary, a useful introduction, presents an overview and then identifies the particular approach of the piece.
• All racquetball players have their reasons for taking up the game. One good reason for playing racquetball is a desire to find a sport in which both sexes can compete on equal terms.

6. The quotation, if it is appropriate, can give authority to your writing.
• A leading physical fitness expert says, "Racquetball provides one of the best ways to achieve all-round fitness."

7. The analogy, a comparison that can be sustained throughout the piece, can result in an effective piece of writing.
• For many people today, the war against flab is waged on a rectangular whitewashed battlefield – the racquetball court.

Choose a topic that you and your writing partner both know something about. Independently, draft beginnings for your topic in each of the seven ways outlined above. When you have both completed your seven beginnings, discuss the effectiveness of each. Together, revise your work.

The next time you are revising, check the beginning of your draft. If you have begun with an opening such as "I feel …," "I think …," or "In this essay I am going to …," think about how you can make your opening stronger.

2.   Endings

Life is filled with beginnings and endings. With your partner discuss some of the endings you have experienced. You might use the following suggestions as the basis for your discussion.

- How does one of your favorite songs end?
- What happened during the last moments of saying farewell to a friend or acquaintance?
- Which movie ending do you remember most vividly? Why?
- What do you look for in the ending of a novel? Why?
- How do your favorite stories end?

Ending a piece of writing can sometimes be difficult. How can you bring a fresh perspective to your subject? How can you leave your audience thinking about what you've written?

The best ending satisfies the expectations created in your audience by the rest of your piece. Imagine your surprise, perhaps even disappointment, on your birthday morning when you open a gift from a special person. Through suggestions and hints prior to your birthday, you are convinced that you will receive the very thing you desire – a digital wristwatch with a built-in calculator. But when you open your gift, you find an alarm clock! In the same way, if you have led your audience to expect a conclusion that presents the dangers of using hard drugs and you end with the statement, "Drinking coffee can also be habit-forming," you let your audience down. A poor conclusion may ruin even the most brilliant piece of writing.

As you move toward your conclusion, keep thinking about your topic and your attitude toward it. Then your conclusion should satisfy you, your purpose, and your audience.

1. Working with your partner, match these endings with the seven sample beginnings on the previous page.
a) Tennis is out; I have become a racquetball maniac.
b) That a sport can be so much fun and at the same time so healthful makes it a natural choice for almost anyone.
c) Why not try it?
d) Fight flab; take up racquetball.
e) If fitness is important to you, consider starting a racquetball program.

f) Any time my court and my opponent are ready, so am I.

g) No wonder I enjoy racquetball!

2. Look over the beginnings that you drafted as you worked through this chapter. Select one, think of three different ways that a piece of writing could develop from the beginning, and then write three possible endings. Avoid an ending that merely sums up and adds nothing of interest, such as "And these are the many things that describe a racquetball player." With your writing partner, discuss the strengths and weaknesses of each of your endings. Which is the strongest? Why?

3.   Titles

Many writers think of a title before they begin to write. Others use a working title, which they may or may not use for their finished piece. Still others do not even think about the title until they have completed their writing. No matter when you think of it, a good title is important.

In composing a title, try to stay away from simply putting down the name of your limited topic. A title should catch the attention of your audience and let them know what to expect from the work.

1. Draw on your own experience and discuss the importance of titles with your partner. You might use the following as a basis for discussion.

a) Flip through a newspaper or magazine, jot down five or six headlines (titles) that catch your attention, and discuss with your partner why the headlines were effective. Then skim the accompanying articles and decide whether the headlines accurately reflect the content. How could the headlines be improved?

b) Which bands have the most suitable names (titles)? Why? Which ones do you think do not suit their names? Why?

c) Think of several products that you use regularly, such as soap, deodorant, shampoo, and toothpaste. What first drew you to these products? How important are their names (titles)? Try to think of new ideal names for the products.

d) What kind of title would make you pick up a book? Why?

2. Look over some of the writing in this book, and discuss with your writing partner the effectiveness and suitability of the titles. Then select one piece that you feel has a weak title, and draft two or three new ones for it. You might exchange and discuss your work with another pair of students.

4.   Narration and Description

Yes! You can enliven the beginnings and endings of your narrative and descriptive writing. Here's how.

1. Assume that you and your partner are going to write a narrative about one of the following topics:
• a car accident;
• a political election or debate;
• a rock concert;
• a murder trial;
• an exam you didn't study for;
• a job interview.

a) Independently, write two different beginnings (so that you'll be able to talk about *four* beginnings).
b) Compare your work. Decide which would likely be the most effective opening, and why.
c) Then, independently, write two different endings.
d) Compare your work. Decide which would probably provide the most satisfying conclusion, and why.
e) Then, independently, write two different titles.
f) Compare your work. Decide which title would most likely grab the attention of an audience, and why.

2. Repeat the project, but write a description of, for example, your favorite food, the main character in a story you like, your doctor's office, one of your relatives or friends, or an animal.

SPECIAL WRITING PROJECT

> □ Read "Writing is Easy" (on the next page) and then, in your journal, write a similar piece on "Endings."
> □ Share your work with your partner. On another occasion, you might want to develop your piece for publication. Think about how you might enliven your work by quoting some famous endings.

Writing is Easy
from *The Globe and Mail*, April 1, 1989
Dennis McCloskey

"Writing is easy," says author Gene Fowler. All you do is sit staring at a blank sheet of paper until the drops of blood form on your forehead."

Most authors will agree that the most difficult stage in writing a novel, short story or poem is getting started. Writing that opening sentence of chapter one can sometimes be murder. Not that there aren't a lot of available counsellors who are more than willing to provide advice. Bernard Malamud says, "The idea is to get the pencil moving quickly." Others, such as Irving Thalberg, ask: "What's this big deal about being a writer? It's just putting one word after another."

Sure! No sweat! That's fine if you're writing the Bible. Obviously you're going to start out: "In the beginning God created the heavens and the earth." But for most of us lesser mortals who write all day every day and, like Senator Davey, don't have a "regular job," the task of coming up with a great beginning to our work can be hell.

Lord Edward George Earle Bulwer-Lytton, author of *Paul Clifford*, would certainly vouch for that. He's the author who began his book with the now-infamous line "It was a dark and stormy night." That uninspired beginning has been lampooned by just about everyone, from Snoopy (via Peanuts creator Charles Schulz) to creative writing teachers everywhere who have decreed that it is the worst opening sentence in any book in the history of the written word.

In their book *Technique in Fiction*, authors Robie Macauley and George Lanning say a good opening sentence should give the first pleasure and the first shock of anticipation. "There are openings that sound out like a bell simply because the words are so memorable and so evocative," they write. The most famous of all beginnings, they suggest, is that of Tolstoy's *Anna Karenina* because it is such an elegant example of oblique prophecy; it has very little to do with the book's plot and everything to do with the book's thematic meaning. It begins: "Happy families are all alike; every unhappy family is unhappy in its own way."

Whenever I browse in a bookstore, I judge a book in many ways: by its cover, author, title and very often by the opening sentence. Years ago before I had heard of Canadian author Aritha van Herk, I bought her book *Judith* on the basis of the opening sentence. Since then, I have purchased scores of books based on their great beginnings.

"The point of good writing is knowing when to stop."

L.M. Montgomery

25 Unity

"All must work together or the Body will go to pieces."

Aesop, ***The Belly and the Members***

When you draft a piece of writing, you have to organize (or unify) and link all the information you include. For example, in an expository piece, everything should deal with the same limited topic and support your thesis statement and the point of view you want to express. In a piece of narrative or descriptive writing, everything should advance the writing in some way – the plot, the character development, or the establishment of the mood or setting of the piece. In this chapter you'll find suggestions to help you organize your information. The next chapter offers suggestions for linking your information within your text.

As you explore and prewrite, you assemble information and supporting details for your writing. You may even begin to organize your material while you collect it. Try to get into the habit of frequently referring to your exploration notes to make sure you are developing your draft in the best possible way. Be sure to take a fresh look at material you linked in your exploration notes. Does it still work as you've linked it? How could it work better? Think about your material as you draft.

Decide on the types of supporting details you need to develop in your piece. Which details will best serve your purpose? For example, in writing about the view from a window, you will need to use **descriptive details** (the maple tree in the front yard, the peeling paint on the window frame, the shimmering clouds and the sky). If, however, you are writing an argumentative essay about the dangers of nuclear power, you will have to collect **reasons** that nuclear power might be dangerous (risk of serious accidents at power plants, problems with the storage of spent fuel, contamination of air and water). Other types of supporting details include examples, facts, results, incidents, illustrations, questions, lists, and quoted material. You will find examples of these in this chapter.

1.   An Oral Middle

Form a group of four or five, and get into a circle. Select one of the following openings (or make up a new one) for a short story.
- There was nothing special you'd notice about Howard upon meeting him, but when …
- Although I had always thought of my Aunt Beatrice as a stereotypical prude, it shocked me when I found …
- Right up until I was eighteen, I thought the only real benefits of growing up were not having to wear knee socks or eat cereal, but then …
- Ruined. Definitely ruined. And for what? …
- "You're making this up," Rajid's mother said. "There's no way …"
- Seeing Lionel after the accident gave me kind of a sick and confused feeling – I didn't know whether …

Begin by reading the opening aloud. Then each group member in turn can continue the story for a minute or so, taking the story in any direction he or she wishes. At a part of the story where one of the characters must make a decision, the storyteller should stop before providing the answer or solution. The next person can then continue the story.

After about ten minutes, bring the story to a conclusion. Then, as a group, discuss the effectiveness of the middle part of the story. You might consider the following.
- Was it interesting? Satisfying? Believable? Or just plain silly? Why?
- Did everything in the middle have a direct relation to the beginning? In other words, was the story unified? Did any of the storytellers ignore all or part of the beginning?
- Who do you think would have enjoyed listening to the story? Why?

2.   Visual Organization

If you find that you have trouble unifying a first draft, experiment with organizing your information using one of the following exploration techniques from Chapter 22:
- Pro/Con Ladders
- Comparison/Contrast Ladders
- Flowcharts

Keep in mind that these graphics are writing tools. The more you use and work with them, the more confident you will feel in adapting them to an individual purpose. You may even develop your own graphics.

1. With your partner, study several of the graphics in Chapter 22. Discuss the kinds of supporting evidence presented in each (details, examples, reasons, and so on). Then arrange some of your own exploring notes in a graphic. Identify the main kind of supporting evidence you are listing. How are you organizing it?

In other words, does your supporting evidence consist of details, narrative illustrations, quotations, facts, reasons, examples, and so on? Are you using comparison/contrast, cause and effect, sequential order, climactic order, etc.? (Later in this chapter, you'll find more information about other methods of organization.)

2. Use one of the following ideas (or one of your own choice) and, independently of your partner, construct a graphic containing it. Then fill in the graphic with supporting evidence. You should both use the same idea so that you can compare your completed graphics.
- Everyone should learn to swim.
- Lake Louise offers magnificent, exciting underwater scenery for swimmers.
- Swimming is a great sport for humans and otters.
- My swimming holiday at Camp Fantasy involved one disaster after another.
- An unfortunate pool incident when I was five led to my fear of the water.

3. Compare your graphic with your partner's. Should you add or delete anything in either graphic to further unify the information?

4. You might want to try organizing a piece of writing by drawing cartoons or pictures, by gathering pictures and making a collage, by preparing storyboards, or by drawing a line or bar graph. While you create your visual display, decide on the order of your cartoons or pictures. From your completed visual display, you should be able to write your first draft.

SPECIAL WRITING PROJECT

☐ Assume that you must write a paragraph on all the topics mentioned below. With your partner, discuss how you would organize your information: in clusters, ladders, flowcharts, cartoons, pictures, storyboards, or a collage, or on a graph.

☐ Independently, choose one of the topics and explore it using a graphic. Then draft a paragraph based on your graphic.

☐ Exchange your paragraphs, and discuss the completeness and effectiveness of each.

Here are the topics to explore in this Special Writing Project:
- the history of the dinner plate
- types of dogs
- the duties of a vice-principal
- a contrast of Canadian and American football
- what modern authors have written about the future
- the food of the poor and wealthy
- everyone should learn to type
- television sitcoms of the 1980s

3.   Comparison/Contrast

One way to organize a piece of writing is to point out similarities (comparisons) and differences (contrasts) in two topics. For example:

Oldies but Goldies
from Maclean's, July 6, 1987

[In late June 1987, two] men died whose careers seem certain to remain etched indelibly in the history of entertainment: Fred Astaire and Jackie Gleason. Each was quite unlike anyone who had come before. And at the same time, it is hard to imagine two men so wholly different from each other. The cultured Astaire, master dancer, was the epitome of gentility and sophistication. The rough-hewn Gleason, master comedian, was the incarnation of lovable vulgarity. Of their breed, they were the best. A tip of the top hat and the bus-driver's cap to them both.

List the two performers' similarities and differences.

To practise using comparison/contrast to organize a piece of writing, assume that you have to write a paper for social studies in which you compare and contrast Sir Wilfrid Laurier and Pierre Elliott Trudeau. Here is some information to get you started.

Sir Wilfrid Laurier: 1841–1919; Prime Minister of Canada 1896–1911. Born in the small town of St. Lin, Quebec; father a land surveyor; family not well off; parents spoke French, but Laurier learned English while attending school in a nearby town and became fluently bilingual; studied law at McGill University; was elected to the House of Commons in 1874; became Prime Minister in 1896; knighted in 1897; was defeated in 1911 but continued as Leader of the Opposition in the House of Commons until his death; disputed with Henri Bourassa, leader of the Quebec Nationalist party; helped to change Canada from a colony to nation. Married Zoë Lafontaine; no children.

Pierre Elliott Trudeau, 1919– ; Prime Minister of Canada 1968–79, 1980–84. Born in Montreal; father French Canadian, a wealthy entrepreneur; mother of Scots descent; fluently bilingual; studied classics at Collège Jean de Brébeuf and law at the University of Montreal; studied at Harvard and in London and Paris; was professor of law at University of Montreal; co-founder of magazine *Cité Libre* in 1950s; elected to House of Commons 1968 and became Prime Minister the same year; defeated 1979; re-elected 1980; resigned 1984; fought with René Lévesque and the Parti Québécois on the issue of Quebec nationalism; campaigned for federalism over separatism before 1980 Quebec referendum; brought Constitution from Britain; initiated Charter of Rights and Freedoms; champion of third-world countries. Married Margaret Sinclair; divorced 1984; three sons.

1. To begin, you might draw up a set of writing variables. For example:

Limited Topic: prime ministers Wilfrid Laurier and Pierre Elliott Trudeau
Audience: fellow social studies students
Purpose: to compare and contrast the lives of Laurier and Trudeau
Format: a long paragraph (to be read aloud)
Focus: I've heard Trudeau being compared to Laurier, and I want to find out how they are alike and how they are different.
Topic Sentence: Sir Wilfrid Laurier and Pierre Elliott Trudeau were Canada's two best-known francophone prime ministers, but their careers differed in many ways.

(Keep in mind that you can change any or all of these writing variables as you draft, revise, and edit.)

2. Use Comparison/Contrast Ladders (Chapter 22) to organize the material about the two prime ministers. Record similarities and differences in the appropriate spaces on each ladder; thus, you will be not only gathering supporting evidence for your paper, but also organizing how you will develop it.

3. a) Then decide how to present the facts. How will you compare or contrast? You can, for example, use the AAA/BBB method to compare Laurier and Trudeau. With this method, you begin by setting out all your information about Laurier; then you compare all similar information about Trudeau. You then use the same AAA/BBB method to contrast the two leaders.

The following draft uses the AAA/BBB method.

Sir Wilfrid Laurier and Pierre Elliott Trudeau are Canada's two greatest French Canadian prime ministers, but their backgrounds were very different. Laurier was born in 1841 in the small town of St. Lin, Quebec. His father was a land surveyor, and his family was not well off. His parents were French-speaking, but Laurier learned English by attending school for a year in a nearby English-speaking town. The year Laurier died, Trudeau was born in Quebec's largest city, Montreal. His father was a wealthy businessman. Trudeau's mother, of Scots descent, spoke English to him while his father spoke French, so he grew up fluently bilingual.

For practice, write a new paragraph focusing on how both prime ministers dealt with Quebec nationalism. Using the AAA/BBB method, organize the material from your ladders and any additional knowledge you have of the two men (you might need to do some research to continue the comparison/contrast). Refer to Chapter 26 for a list of suitable transitional words to keep your audience on track.

b) In a different form of organization, the ABABAB method, you might mention one fact about Laurier, and, at the same time, compare or contrast one fact about Trudeau. The following draft uses the ABABAB method.

Sir Wilfrid Laurier and Pierre Elliott Trudeau are Canada's two greatest French-speaking prime ministers. Their backgrounds, however, were very different. While Laurier was born in a small Quebec town, Trudeau was born in cosmopolitan Montreal. Laurier was the son of lower-middle-class parents (his father was a land surveyor); Trudeau, on the other hand, was the son of a wealthy businessman who sent him to school in a chauffeured limousine. Both grew up fluently bilingual, Trudeau because his mother spoke English to him at home and Laurier because his father sent him to school for a year in a nearby English-speaking town.

Use the ABABAB method of organization to write a new paragraph focusing on what Laurier and Trudeau did for Canada. Refer to Chapter 26 for a list of suitable transitional words to keep your audience on track.

4. When you and your writing partner have completed your paragraphs, exchange and discuss your work. What are the advantages and disadvantages of each method of organization to both the writer and the audience? If you were writing the paragraph on Laurier and Trudeau, which method would you use? Why?

SPECIAL WRITING PROJECT

☐ Choose two characters in a piece of literature that both you and your partner know well, and compare and contrast them in a paragraph. To begin, you might collect and organize your information in Comparison/Contrast Ladders.

☐ Exchange your completed paragraph and your brainstorming notes with your partner. Discuss the effectiveness of your paragraphs. How have you organized your paragraph: AAA/BBB or ABABAB? Why?

4.   Sequential Order

Use sequential order to give instructions for putting something together, for making something, or for finding something. For example:

Perfect Milk Partners
Kim Darling, student

One of my favorite cookie recipes, mainly because it's so simple to make, is for peanut butter cookies. In a medium-sized bowl, cream together 125 mL each of margarine and peanut butter. Then add 125 mL each of white and brown sugar, and mix until smooth. Next, add 2 mL each of salt, baking soda, and vanilla (if you measure the dry ingredients first, you won't have to scrape salt off a wet spoon), one egg, and 300 mL of all-purpose flour. Blend until the dough is smooth. Drop by 5 mL balls onto an ungreased cookie sheet and bake at 180°C for ten to fifteen minutes, or until the tops of the cookies are golden brown. You will end up with 20 to 24 delicious cookies; with a glass of milk, they're a real treat!

You can also use sequential order when you analyse a product to see how it has been made, or when you write a literary or scientific analysis.

To arrange supporting evidence in sequential order, list items in the order in which they should be (or have been) carried out.
1. Choose one of the following topics, or make up one of your own:
• how to cook an omelette
• how to change a typewriter ribbon
• how to find a book in your school or local library
• how to serve a tennis ball

Make up a list of instructions, writing each instruction on a separate piece of paper. Give all the pieces of paper to your partner, who can organize them in sequential order. Then reverse roles with a new set of instructions.

2. Choose one of the following topics, or make up one of your own:
- how I write an essay
- how I won a particular game
- how I study for an exam
- how the author achieves tension, suspense, or a successful climax in a story that you know well

Make up a list of processes, writing each item on a separate piece of paper. Then have your partner organize the pieces of paper in sequential order, as if he or she were developing a process analysis. Then reverse roles with a new process analysis.

SPECIAL WRITING PROJECT

☐ Using one of the sequences you have just explored, write a paragraph for your partner. (Refer to the list of transitional words in Chapter 26 to keep your reader on track.)

☐ Give your piece to your partner. Compare and discuss the kinds of supporting evidence in your paragraphs: examples, details, facts, reasons, and so on. Keep your sequential list handy so that you can revise it, if you choose to.

5.   Spatial Order

To arrange information in spatial order, present your details as you want your audience to see them: near to far, far to near, right to left, up to down, or in some other order you think appropriate. For example:

Backyard Wonderland
Margaret Staley, student

One of the great joys of my childhood was staying at my grandmother's cottage during the summer holidays. Every morning I would rush to the window and look down into the yard, through the branches of the huge oak that grew up past the roof, to see what animals I could see. Sometimes I would see two or three squirrels scrambling among the branches in what seemed like an endless game of tag. Occasionally mother raccoon and several fat babies would cross the lawn in single file. And if I was very quiet and very lucky, I might see, at the edge of the yard, a beautiful white-tailed deer quietly cropping the grass. These animals, especially the deer, never stayed long, but disappeared into unfenced woodland at the back of the property.

How has this writer organized her paragraph?

1. Describe to your partner a room that you are familiar with. As you speak, your partner can draw a map of the room. (Don't look at your partner's map while you describe.) Begin with the dimensions of the room, giving the location, number, and size of the doors and windows. Next, give the exact position of the largest piece of furniture so that your partner can position everything else in relation to it. Then try to mention at least twenty things to include on the map. (To help you to make your oral description clear, use transitional words such as *next to, above, opposite to*, and *behind*. Consult Chapter 26 for other spatial transitional words.)

2. When your partner finishes the map, judge how accurately you have described the room. Discuss why any glaring mistakes occurred.

3. After discussion, reverse roles. You can map while your partner describes.

SPECIAL WRITING PROJECT

- Using spatial order, write a paragraph describing a place with which you are familiar. Imagine that you are looking at this place through a window. In what order would you describe what you see – near to far, top to bottom, left to right, centre to edges?
- Give your descriptive paragraph to your partner. Discuss how you have used spatial order.

6. Chronological Order

In following chronological order, you arrange events in the order in which they occur. If you introduce events out of order (flashbacks or flash forwards), you should prepare your reader for the shift in time.

How I Spent My Winter Vacation
Eddie Andrews

Several years ago I had the opportunity of doing something I'd only dreamed of: visiting New Zealand and Australia. I decided to go during January and February; that way, I not only escaped the Canadian winter but also enjoyed summer "down under." I arrived in Auckland, New Zealand's largest city, and later visited Rotorua, the home of some of New Zealand's most famous hot springs. Afterwards, I went on to Wellington, New Zealand's capital. Before returning to Auckland to fly on to Sydney,

I drove through the beautiful city of Christchurch. Once in Australia, I explored Sydney's famous harbour, opera house, and zoo, then boarded the "Indian-Pacific" train for the three-day trip to Perth. I later took another famous train, the *Ghan*, to Alice Springs, where the temperature was close to 40°C; now *that* was summer weather! Needless to say, I truly enjoyed my winter vacation.

1. Tell your partner a story from the first-person viewpoint (*I*) or the third-person viewpoint (*he* or *she*). Use chronological order. Your partner should jot down and number each new event that happens in your story. To keep your narrative coherent, you can use transitional devices, such as *although, as, in order that, then*, and *since*. See Chapter 26 for other transitional words that help to express chronology.

2. Discuss with your partner the order of your events. Did your story have a beginning, middle, and end? Were the events in the best order? In what other order could you have told the story? For example, could you have begun *in medias res* (in the middle) or started at the end and told your story through flashbacks?

3. Now your partner should tell his or her story while you number the events. Then you can discuss your partner's story.

SPECIAL WRITING PROJECT

□ Using chronological order, write a short narration about a recent holiday (or a subject of your choice). You might find it useful to list all events in proper order, but decide to start near the end of your story and use flashbacks. To tighten the story and emphasize an important event, you might also decide to leave out some events altogether.

□ Give your narration to your partner, along with any brainstorming notes you have made, and discuss the effectiveness of the time order. Does your partner think you left out information you should have included – or included information you should have left out?

7. Climactic Order

In following climactic order, you arrange events, details, facts, or reasons in the order of their importance, with the most important one coming last. For example:

Championship Season
Mary Povah

Only four players in tennis history have won the four "Grand Slam" tournaments – the French and Australian opens, the Wimbledon championship, and the U.S. Open. When two young European players, Mats Wilander of Sweden and Steffi Graf of West Germany, both won the singles titles at the 1988 Australian Open in Melbourne and then at the French Open in Paris, tennis fans hoped to see two Grand Slam champions in the same year. Mats Wilander's chances faded when he lost in the quarter-finals at Wimbledon; Steffi Graf, however, won the women's title after a strenuous match with defending champion Martina Navratilova. She then went on to defeat Argentina's Gabriela Sabatini in the U.S. Open to become the fifth and youngest player to win the Grand Slam.

1. Working with your partner, choose one of the following statements (or make up your own):
*   Some of the rules at our school could be eliminated.
*   Many kitchen gadgets are useless.
*   Teenage clothing is conformist.
*   The environment should be everybody's concern.

Individually, get ready to take a strong stand for or against the statement you have chosen. Jot down six or seven reasons, facts, and examples to support your position. Then present your argument to your partner. Open with a *general* statement and then have *particular* examples to support the statement. (Transition words such as *furthermore, similarly, moreover, in addition*, and *finally* will help organize each idea according to its importance. Other suitable transitional words appear in Chapter 26.)

2. Discuss your items and how you have ordered them. If you start with the least important item and end with the most important, you are building to a climactic ending. Do the ideas move from least to most important? Should you move any item? Why?

SPECIAL WRITING PROJECT

□ Using one of the above topics or another of your choice, write a short persuasive piece presenting a particular point of view. Make a list of the facts, reasons, or examples you will use and then decide which is most important. This will be the climax of your piece.

□ Give your piece to your partner, and discuss your use of climactic order. Have you built to the most important piece of information?

26 Coherence

> *"Transitional words ... are part of the glue that keeps paragraphs together."*
>
> W. Ross Winterowd, **The Contemporary Writer**

When your writing is coherent, your audience does not get lost in it. Coherence ties sentences together clearly and logically. To keep your writing flowing and to help your audience follow your ideas, concentrate on the following four points when you draft.

- □ Use a logical method of organization (Chapter 25).
- □ Structure your sentences so that their sequence links them to each other (Chapter 25).
- □ Use transitional devices to connect sentences and paragraphs (this chapter).
- □ Repeat key words or phrases to remind your audience of the important points in your piece of writing (this chapter).

1. Transitions

Transitions show relationships among thoughts and give a sense of direction and continuity to your writing. They assist your audience in moving not only from detail to detail within a single sentence, but also from sentence to sentence and paragraph to paragraph. Like signposts, transitions inform your audience that one part or stage of the discussion has ended. As well, transitions also suggest to your audience how your next phase of thought connects to your just-completed phase. Effective transitions will help you to keep your audience on track.

The following list contains some useful transitional expressions and conjunctions. As you and your partner read the list, notice the specific reasons for introducing certain words into your sentences. Keep this list handy whenever you draft.

addition: in addition, besides, moreover, further, furthermore, equally important, in fact, likewise, next, too, then, and, both ... and, not only ... but also, first, second, third (or in the first place, in the second place, and so on). (Do not use firstly, secondly, thirdly.)

comparison: similarly, likewise, in like manner, by comparison, compared to, just as surely, in the same way, not only ... but also, both ... and, either ... or

contrast: but, however, yet, still, nevertheless, on the one hand, on the other hand, for all of that, on the contrary, notwithstanding, in contrast, in contrast to, rather, neither ... nor, although, though, in spite of, whereas

emphasis: in fact, indeed, in truth, certainly, definitely, emphatically, unquestionably, undoubtedly, without a doubt, undeniably, without reservation, naturally, obviously

example: for example, for instance, in this case, in another case, on this occasion, in this situation, as proof, as evidence, take the case of ..., the proof of this, the evidence of this, thus

exception: yet, still, however, nevertheless, in spite of, despite, nonetheless, though, although

place: near, beyond, opposite to, adjacent to, at the same place, here, there, from over, in the middle, around, in front of, in the distance, farther (physical distance), further (abstract distance), here and there, above, below, at the right (or left), between, in the foreground, on this side, beside

purpose: for this purpose, in order that, in this way, since, so that, on that account, in case, with a view to, for the same reason

repetition: in other words, that is to say, as I have said, again, once again

result: accordingly, thus, consequently, hence, therefore, inevitably, under these conditions, as a result, as a consequence, consequently, because, because of, so that

sequence: first, second, third, next, then, at the outset, following this, at this time, now, at this point, after, afterward, after this, subsequently, lastly, finally, consequently, before this, previously, preceding this, simultaneously

summary: in brief, on the whole, in sum, to sum up, to conclude, hence, for this reason, in short, in summary, in conclusion time: at once, immediately, in the meantime, meanwhile, at the same time, in the end, in the interim, then, soon, not long after, at length, at last, finally, some time ago, later, afterward, from this time on, from time to time, after, before, until, at present, all of a sudden, instantly, at this instant, suddenly, now, without delay, at this point, a few minutes later, formerly, yesterday, later in the day, since then, when, whenever, next, henceforth, thereupon, sometimes, in a moment, shortly, previously, in the past, in the future

2.   Experimenting with Transitions

Examine the following sentences with your partner.

No Transition
Much of Canada is still undeveloped. The country boasts of many species of wildlife.

Transition Added
Much of Canada is still undeveloped; *as a result*, the country boasts of many species of wildlife.

Weak Transition
The beaver is Canada's national animal, but it was almost wiped out by overhunting.

Stronger Transition
The beaver is Canada's national animal; *in the past*, it was almost wiped out by overhunting.

Weak Transition
Musk-oxen can survive the severe arctic winters, for they grow a dense coat of underhair in the fall.

Stronger Transition
Musk-oxen grow a dense coat of underhair in the fall; *thus*, they can survive the severe arctic winters.

No Transition
Moose live in some of the most attractive country in Canada; caribou live in a much more hostile environment.

Transition of Contrast Added
Moose live in some of the most attractive country in Canada; caribou, *on the other hand*, live in a much more hostile environment.

Transition of Emphasis Added
Moose live in some of the most attractive country in Canada; *unquestionably*, caribou live in a much more hostile environment.

No Transition

The remote ancestors of whales once walked on land. They started to live in the sea. Their hind limbs disappeared altogether. Their forelimbs evolved into flippers.

Transition of Time and Addition Added

The remote ancestors of whales once walked on land; *later*, they started to live in the sea. *During this time*, their hind limbs disappeared altogether, *and* their forelimbs evolved into flippers.

No Transition

The mink's luxurious fur keeps it warm on land. Its fur helps it survive in cold water.

Correlative Conjunctions Added for Transition

The mink's luxurious fur *not only* keeps it warm on land *but also* helps it survive in cold water.

No Transition

Sea lions can live on land for long periods. They cannot feed except in water.

Co-ordinate Conjunction Added for Transition

Sea lions can live on land for long periods, *but* they cannot feed except in water.

Subordinate Conjunction Added for Transition

Though sea lions can live on land for long periods, they cannot feed except in water.

3.   Working with Transitions in Sentences

1.   Independently of your partner, give a reason for joining each of the following sets of sentences. Then use an appropriate transition to join them. Compare your use of transitions with your partner's.

a)   The whooping crane remains Canada's most famous bird. Hunting drove the bird nearly to extinction. Its numbers are slowly increasing.

b)   The red-tailed hawk has adapted to life in cities. It perches on telephone poles as readily as on treetops.

c)   The calliope hummingbird is the smallest North American hummingbird. It is the tiniest bird in Canada.

d)   Bobolinks used to live only in eastern Canada. They can now be found as far west as Alberta.

e)   The arctic tern migrates farther than any other bird. It flies from the Arctic to the Antarctic and back each year.

2.   Read the following, and then do the Special Writing Project for your partner.

Topic Sentence
- We must preserve some areas in their natural state, so that future generations can enjoy Canada's abundant wildlife.

Supporting Evidence
- Most large animals such as wolves and bears need open undisturbed space.
- Canada is a huge country.
- It contains a remarkable number of species of birds and animals.
- Some species are disappearing.
- Human beings have developed the ability to live almost anywhere on earth.
- Large animals cannot live near human settlements.
- Small animals such as raccoons and squirrels have become city-dwellers.
- An entire animal or bird species can disappear if human activity destroys its habitat.
- People have destroyed animal habitats.

SPECIAL WRITING PROJECT

> ☐ Rearrange the supporting evidence in a logical order in a paragraph, making sure every sentence is relevant. Change some key words to pronouns and use some of the transitional devices from this chapter.
>
> ☐ Compare your draft with your partner's. Have you both produced coherent paragraphs?

4.   Key Words

One method of achieving coherence is to repeat your subject throughout your writing, but repetition for its own sake can be dull. Try to find good replacement nouns or pronouns instead. For example, in an essay discussing the Prime Minister, you might refer to him as "The Right Honorable gentleman" or "the leader of the governing party," as well as using his name and pronouns such as "he," "his," or "himself." So long as you do not overuse these nouns and pronouns, your audience should remain interested in what you have to say.

SPECIAL WRITING PROJECT

☐ Prepare a one-minute talk for your partner on a topic of your choice (such as a relative, friend, famous person, or your favorite city). As you talk, your partner should record your use of key words. Afterward, you might like to prepare a short piece of writing on your topic, making sure that you use key words as a transitional device.

☐ Discuss with your partner what you learned from presenting your talk (and from your writing).

Self-Editing, Peer-Editing, and Teacher-Editing

27

"Rewriting isn't virtuous. It isn't something that ought to be done. It is simply something that most writers find they have to do to discover what they have to say and how to say it. It is a condition of the writer's life."

Donald Murray

Writers revise their writing all the time. Most of their pieces are read by a number of editors and go through several rewrites.

Every section of this book has been rewritten several times, and revised, reformed, refined, and reshaped, as the author listened to the opinions of fellow teachers, editors, consultants, and students who worked to make every point as clear as possible. The manuscript was then tested in classrooms by teachers and students. And *The Writer's Workshop* is the result.

In this chapter you will find suggestions, guidelines, and checklists for revising and editing your own writing and that of your peers. Before you start, however, you should realize that there is no single list of questions that you can apply to everything you work on. As editor, you have to keep the writer's own style but at the same time make sure that the audience will understand the message.

You are also probably aware of editing packages for the computer. These often include spelling, thesaurus, and grammatical and punctuation correction aids. Use these as a writing tool if they are available to you, but don't substitute their capabilities for actually reading and thinking about a piece of writing.

In general, every draft of everything you write will benefit from being looked at by someone else before you present it to your intended audience. An editor makes a draft easier to read by paring down, building up, moving things around, quickening the pace, clarifying confusion, improving grammar, and questioning errors and inconsistencies. This job doesn't have to be difficult. You might simply say to a writer, "I love this because ..." or "I don't understand this point. Let's discuss it."

1.   Revising Your Own Work

Before you give a piece of writing to an editor or to your intended audience, examine it yourself. Accompanying all of the writing projects in this book are guidelines to help you revise your work. As well, if you have written a piece of exposition, consult the following checklists on content, organization, style, and usage and mechanics, and decide whether your writing is good, average, or needs work. If, after doing this, you are not satisfied with your work, prepare another draft. (Many of the suggestions apply to all kinds of writing, but they really will help you revise your expository writing: your informative and argumentative essays, research essays, feature articles, instructions, reviews, biographies, letters to the editor, and so on.)

Content Checklist

For most nonfiction, and some fiction as well, content involves the limited topic (subject, main idea, thesis) and its development.

Good
- ☐ The central idea is fresh, true, specific, and clear. It is expressed accurately and interestingly in a thesis statement or topic sentence.
- ☐ The idea is suitable for the length of the work and is well developed.
- ☐ The central idea is supported with high-quality facts, reasons, examples, or other concrete details.

Average
- ☐ The thesis statement or topic sentence is clear but not interesting or original.
- ☐ The development relies on predictable details.
- ☐ The development is incomplete or repetitious and includes unimportant, obvious, or occasional unrelated facts.
- ☐ The limited topic may not be logically developed.

Needs Work
- ☐ Either there is no central idea, or the central idea is not clearly expressed in a thesis statement or topic sentence. If it is clearly expressed, it may be dull or unimportant.
- ☐ If there is a good idea, it is not supported by appropriate details.
- ☐ The development of the main idea is confused.
- ☐ The thesis statement and its development are not appropriate for the length of the project, so that the idea is either underdeveloped or repeated.

How would you judge the content of your piece of writing: good, average, or needs work? Why?

Organization Checklist

Organization involves how a piece of writing is developed, how the sentences within a paragraph are linked, and how the writing moves from one sentence or paragraph to the next. (See Chapters 25 and 26.)

Good

- □ The central idea is developed clearly and logically, and the writing variables have been taken into account. The audience moves effortlessly from one section of the work to the next.
- □ The writing is specifically organized; for example, it uses comparison, shows cause and effect, or uses spatial, chronological, or climactic order. Each supporting detail has just the right emphasis. The supporting details are also in exactly the right places in the work.
- □ There is nothing in the work that does not belong there.

Average

- □ The writing seems to have an organizational plan, but at times it loses its focus.
- □ There is something wrong with the emphasis or order of some of the points. They are either stressed too much or not enough, or they are in the wrong places.
- □ The writing is sometimes hard to follow because there are not sufficient transitional devices to move the audience from one point to the next.
- □ There may be too many transitional words, so that the writing does not seem to treat the audience with respect.

Needs Work

- □ There is no clear organization.
- □ The supporting details are either incomplete or repetitive.
- □ The paragraphs are not unified or coherent; either there are not sufficient transitional words or the ones that are used are confusing.
- □ A new idea may be introduced in a paragraph before a previous idea is fully developed.

How would you judge the organization of your piece of writing: good, average, or needs work? Why?

Style Checklist

Style involves not only the choice of particular words and sentences but also the effectiveness, arrangement, and appropriateness of these words and sentences in a particular piece of writing. (For a discussion of style, see Chapter 29.)

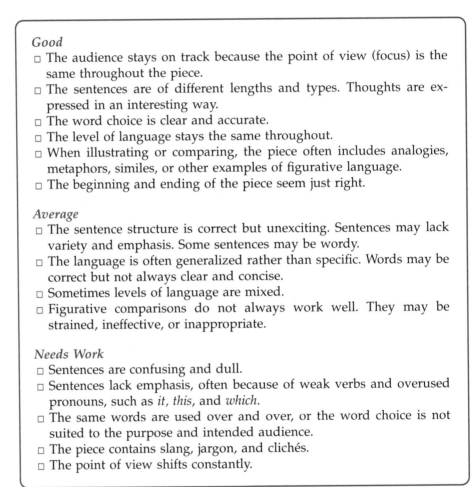

Good
- ☐ The audience stays on track because the point of view (focus) is the same throughout the piece.
- ☐ The sentences are of different lengths and types. Thoughts are expressed in an interesting way.
- ☐ The word choice is clear and accurate.
- ☐ The level of language stays the same throughout.
- ☐ When illustrating or comparing, the piece often includes analogies, metaphors, similes, or other examples of figurative language.
- ☐ The beginning and ending of the piece seem just right.

Average
- ☐ The sentence structure is correct but unexciting. Sentences may lack variety and emphasis. Some sentences may be wordy.
- ☐ The language is often generalized rather than specific. Words may be correct but not always clear and concise.
- ☐ Sometimes levels of language are mixed.
- ☐ Figurative comparisons do not always work well. They may be strained, ineffective, or inappropriate.

Needs Work
- ☐ Sentences are confusing and dull.
- ☐ Sentences lack emphasis, often because of weak verbs and overused pronouns, such as *it, this,* and *which.*
- ☐ The same words are used over and over, or the word choice is not suited to the purpose and intended audience.
- ☐ The piece contains slang, jargon, and clichés.
- ☐ The point of view shifts constantly.

How would you judge the style of your piece of writing: good, average, or needs work? Why?

Usage and Mechanics Checklist

Usage and mechanics deal with the nitty-gritty of writing: spelling, punctuation, grammar, and so on.

Good

- ☐ Grammar usage, punctuation, and spelling are generally accurate.
- ☐ The writing is almost free of small mechanical errors, such as misuse of apostrophes and hyphens, errors in citing numbers or in using capital letters, and so on.
- ☐ The writing is correctly punctuated and makes use of more complex punctuation marks such as semicolons, parentheses, and dashes, as well as double and single quotation marks.
- ☐ The writing contains no serious sentence errors, such as unintentional fragment faults, dangling modifiers, run-on sentences, lack of subject/verb agreement, and so on.

Average

- ☐ Occasional mechanical errors creep into the writing.
- ☐ The writing is often correct and careful but uses only commas and periods when punctuation marks such as semicolons, colons, and dashes might be more appropriate.

Needs Work

- ☐ Because of mechanical errors, the audience often cannot make sense of the writing. Tense or voice shifts in mid-sentence. Sentences run together. Unintentional sentence fragments stand as complete thoughts.
- ☐ Punctuation marks are absent or incorrectly used.
- ☐ There are frequent spelling errors.
- ☐ Many pronoun referents are wrong.
- ☐ Incorrect or inappropriate word choices flood the writing.
- ☐ Idioms are fractured.

How would you judge the usage and mechanics in your piece of writing: good, average, or needs work? Why?

2.   Revising the Writing of Your Peers

An editor is an important part of the writing process of most professional writers. Try to get in the habit of asking for – and offering – assistance on each writing project. Once you become comfortable with editing the work of your classmates, you will probably find yourself asking a fellow student for comments as you draft, as well as after. Taking your writing through peer-editing sessions will mean your writing will be that much better when you pass it to your teacher-editor or your intended audience.

The more familiar you become with the workshop sections of this book, the more suggestions for revision you will be able to share during peer-editing sessions. In essence, a good peer-editing session should give you an idea of the effect that your writing will have on your intended audience and provide ideas and suggestions on how to make that effect better.

SPECIAL WRITING PROJECT

Keep a record of your attitude toward peer-editing. Right now, take a few minutes to write a journal entry on your feelings about peer-editing. You might also comment on what you know and what you expect to learn. After each peer-editing session, make an entry describing what happened, how you felt, and what you learned.

3.   One Way to Edit

1. To begin with, find out what help the writer feels he or she needs to make the writing better. You might also consult the "Ask Your Peer-Editor" questions found in each writing project.

2. Before you read the piece of writing, discuss with the writer his or her writing variables: Who is the intended audience? What is the purpose for writing? What is the format? What voice is the writer using? What is the limited topic? Then read the piece as if you were the intended audience so that you can respond honestly from that audience's point of view.

3. Read the whole piece of writing at once to get a sense of it as a whole. Do not put any comments on it, but make a mental or actual note of your first impression of the piece.

4. Read the piece again, but this time more slowly. Write comments, suggestions, and questions in pencil directly on the piece of writing. Use the checklists in this chapter as well as the "Guidelines for Revising" in each writing project. Whenever possible, use the proofreaders' symbols on pages 443–445.

5. If you feel that you are not going to help the writer enough, take more time to prepare. You might even ask a friend or relative for help. Remember

that the more you have to share with the writer, the more help the writer will have when he or she begins to revise the piece of writing.

6. Meet with the writer either in or out of class. Make sure you have at least half an hour for a short piece and an hour for a longer piece. Go over all your comments with the writer. Encourage the writer to ask questions. If you cannot answer a question, be honest and say so. Talk through any problem so that together, you can arrive at a possible solution.

7. If you edit the revised draft, repeat the above six steps.

8. When you finish editing, take a few minutes to write in your journal about what you thought worked well and whether and how you would change your process the next time you edit.

9. If your teacher-editor has a writing conference with your writer, try to sit in on the session. It will probably interest you to hear any new questions your teacher asks, and the next time you edit a piece by one of your fellow students, you may raise similar questions.

10. If the writer presents the piece of writing to its intended audience, ask the writer to share the audience's reactions with you. Was the audience satisfied with the piece? If not, why not? How can your knowledge of the audience's reaction improve your future editing sessions?

4.   Publishing

Like professional writers who work to see their writing published, you should publish your final product, too. As this book uses the term, **to publish** simply means to present your writing to its intended audience. After you have spent so much time exploring your subject and drafting, revising, and editing your work, you should sometimes try to share your writing instead of putting it into your writing folder.

In most cases, you will publish by giving or sending your work to your audience. For example, you will give your piece of writing to your family, fellow students, or teachers, or send it to newspapers, officials, or people who live far from you. You might produce class collections of writing projects in anthologies and present them to hospitals, doctors' and dentists' waiting rooms, other classrooms, or places where unknown readers might enjoy your work. If you think your work might be published in a print medium, consult a word processing program that shows a variety of ways to present a printed text. Using different type styles and sizes can add to the effectiveness of good writing. And don't ignore the possibilities of reading your work aloud or, with a few of your classmates, presenting it in some other visual or dramatic medium.

28

Summarizing – Paraphrase, Précis, and Outline

"Popular news magazines … have a large readership because of their ability to condense seven days of news into short, readable articles highlighting key personalities, events, and issues."

Philip C. Kolin, **Successful Writing at Work**

As a student, you have likely had to take notes during your classes, condense essays, boil down chapters of textbooks, or rewrite complicated passages. In most cases you were the audience, and the purpose of condensing was to make reviewing the material faster and easier. Rather than beginning with writing your own ideas, you started with reading or listening to someone else's work and then wrote a summary of it. In this chapter you will examine three forms of summarizing: paraphrase, précis, and outline. As well, you will learn how to pick out thesis statements or topic sentences.

This chapter on summarizing, however, has another important purpose. It comes after the chapter on revising and editing to show you how to use summarizing as an editing tool. If you are having difficulty self-editing or editing someone else's writing, you might try to summarize all or a portion of the work in the form of a paraphrase, précis, outline, or statement of the main idea. The summary might point out something that is missing in the original piece of writing: a step in a set of directions, a cause of an effect, or an important point in an argument. The process of summarizing can show a writer something that should be included in a final draft.

1. Getting Familiar with Summarizing

1. Tell your partner a story, anecdote, joke, personal experience, or anything else that you can think of. Your partner should listen to and enjoy your story without interrupting.

2. When you have finished, your partner should retell in his or her own words what you have said. This story, repeated in your partner's words, is a **paraphrase** of your original words. The paraphrase can be either shorter or longer than the original piece.

3. Now, ask your partner to retell the story, condensing it to half its original length. He or she must decide what to include and what to leave out. The main point and only the most important parts of the development should remain. This summary is a **précis** of the original. A précis is a shortened version of either the original piece or the paraphrase.

4. Next, your partner should write an **outline** of your story following these steps.
a) List about three to five important points in the order they occurred, leaving at least three lines between each point. Put a Roman numeral and a period (for example, II.) before each point.
b) Underneath each important point, list at least two details that tell more about that particular point. Put a capital letter and a period (for example, B.) before each detail.
   The following example shows how Roman numerals and capital letters might appear in an outline:

        I.
          A.
          B.
       II.
          A.
          B.
          C.
      III.
          A.
          B.
          C.
          D.
(For an example of a completed outline, see Chapter 13.)

5. Finally, your partner should write a single sentence that both sums up your story and includes its main idea or theme.

6. Then switch roles. Your partner can tell a story, and you can do the summarizing.

2.   Paraphrasing an Essay

1.   Find a piece of nonfiction writing about 300 words long from the editorial pages of a newspaper or magazine.

2.   Read the article aloud to your partner. Your partner may make notes but may not interrupt you or look at what you are reading.

3.   When you finish, ask your partner to tell you about the article. Your partner will be paraphrasing. Remember, whether the paraphrase is shorter or longer than the original, your partner should show that he or she understands the content of the original.

4.   When your partner finishes the paraphrase, discuss whether your partner left out or didn't clarify any important points.

5.   Then, together, produce an outline.

6.   Switch roles. Have your partner read an article to you so that you can paraphrase it.

3.   Writing a Précis

In many colleges, students take a test to determine whether they will be admitted into the regular first-year English course. Often, as part of the test, they must write a précis. The original material is usually about 600 words long; the students are required to write a précis of approximately 300 words.

1.   Write a précis of "The Biodegradable Myth!" (in Chapter 33) or "Notes on Punctuation" (in the appendix), reducing the piece to its main point and only the most important parts of its development. Imagine that you are writing for a college entrance test. Keep in mind that the college wants to find out how well you can read and write.

2.   When both you and your partner have completed a précis, compare the effectiveness of the two pieces. Do both find the main point of the article? Do both include the same important parts of its development? Does either précis include irrelevant material?

4.   Using All the Kinds of Summarizing

1.   Write a paraphrase, précis, outline, and thesis statement for this excerpt from Owen Phillips's *The Last Chance Energy Book*.

In the search for new energy sources, the sun is an obvious candidate. It is generally believed that solar energy is surely the long term answer, and this belief is almost certainly justified. In the United States, we have been somewhat behind other countries in developing solar power. Even a casual visitor to Western Australia would notice that many of the new houses there have solar panels built into their roofs. It is quite routine, not at all exceptional. That part of the world has always been energy poor – there is no oil, not much coal (the deposits that do exist being of indifferent quality), and little hydroelectric power. On the other hand, the climate is generally sunny with a month of cloudy weather per year so that solar panels, together with a small back-up system, provide plenty of hot water for heating and for household use. Why cannot we do the same thing in this country on a larger scale?

No doubt we shall; this is one of the personal options open to us. It takes no great foresight to anticipate that domestic solar panels will become increasingly more economical over the long run as the technology for their manufacture improves and as the prices of alternative fuels rise. They will make a great difference to our personal budgets and will help to reduce the national demand for oil and natural gas. But solar panels are not for everyone. What about all the people who live in apartment houses, hotels, and condominiums? Or in areas of the country where the sun shines only intermittently in winter, precisely the time when the heat is needed most? It is probably an overstatement of the case, but not an outrageous one, to assert that domestic solar collectors will provide for the energy problem the same kind of contribution that backyard vegetable plots provide for our food supply – sufficient for a relatively few fortunate people and a valuable supplement for others, but that's all.

Solar energy may indeed be the long-term answer, but the use of domestic collectors is not the only way to capture it. Another option could be to cover the deserts with solar collectors, using the heat to generate electric power. But there are problems. Do we really want to cover the deserts with solar collectors? New Englanders may not mind, but the people who live in Arizona may be less than enthusiastic. The ecology of the desert is a fragile thing, and the impact of large farms of solar collectors may be difficult to assess. Are we prepared for the enormous capital costs? Solar collectors work very well when the sun is shining, but they are not very useful at night. Energy would need to be stored in very large amounts to carry us through for nighttime use or during extended cloudy periods; either this or a back-up system of large capacity that is used only intermittently and is consequently expensive. Solar power from the deserts may well be part of the solution, but we should not assume that it is the whole solution.

Compare and contrast your summaries with those your writing partner has done. If you do not agree on the essentials, have another look at the instructions in this chapter for writing these summaries.

5.   Revising by Summarizing

You can summarize to help you revise one of your completed drafts.
1. Choose a partner who is unfamiliar with your writing.

2. Ask your partner to read your draft.

3. After reading, your partner should paraphrase your draft.

4. By listening to your partner, you will hear what your intended audience will get from your writing. Are you satisfied with your partner's paraphrase? If not, what is the problem? Is it that your writing does not include what you thought was in it? Or did your partner not completely understand what you wrote? Why might that have been?

5. Discuss with your partner what you should revise in your writing.

6. You can vary this procedure by asking your partner to present a précis or an outline of your writing instead of a paraphrase. From your partner's work, you should be able to note any problems in your draft and, as a result, revise it with confidence.

6.   Summarizing and Graphics

A **graphic** shows relationships in visual form.
1. As a variation on the previous procedure, have your partner read your draft and then draw a graphic of its organization and content. (See Chapter 22 for some examples of graphics.) By arraying the essentials of your draft on ladders or in a cluster or flowchart, your partner will help you to see whether you need to include more supporting details, whether there are problems with your organization, or whether any of your items are out of order.

2. By completing the graphic that your partner has drawn, you will be able to revise your work more easily.

7.   The Twenty-Five-Word Summary

When you summarize a piece of writing in twenty-five words, you give only the overall idea of it.
   The benefits of writing a twenty-five-word summary are many:
* you practise summarizing;
* you ensure that you understand the meaning of a selection;
* you choose exact, powerful words;
* you improve your vocabulary;
* you use precise punctuation.

**SPECIAL
WRITING
PROJECT**

☐ In twenty-five words, summarize a piece of writing that your partner gives you. Whether a word has one letter or twenty, consider it as one word; however, don't count the author's name and the title of the selection in the twenty-five words.

☐ Eliminate extra words from your draft. There is no room for repetition, passive voice, weak verbs, or ineffective adjectives and adverbs. Although you may use more than one sentence, try to write only one – especially one that demonstrates clear sentence structure.

Before you write your twenty-five-word summary, you might read the following example, which summarizes the excerpt from *The Last Chance Energy Book* in this chapter.

[Owen Phillips] in [*The Last Chance Energy Book*] states that even though solar power might supplement other energy sources in sunny areas, it can only partially meet America's long term energy needs.

"In composing, as a general rule, run your pen through every other word you have written; you have no idea what vigor it will give your style."

Sydney Smith

Second Workshop: Style

About the
Second Workshop

This section will help you improve particular aspects of your writing. At times you may need to refer to a dictionary, thesaurus, or handbook. Perhaps your teacher will recommend specific reference books so that you and your classmates will be using the same authorities when you work on a writing project.

You can apply each chapter to any writing project you are doing. If you are writing an exposition, for example, and are worrying about your word choice, look at Chapter 33. If you are writing a letter and want to include a figurative comparison, look at Chapter 32. If you are working on a research paper and want to make sure your bibliography is correct, look at Chapter 35.

If you take some time to discover what this workshop section contains, you can then turn to a particular chapter (or part of a chapter) and use it when you need to. If you cannot decide which chapter to begin with, do the first few. One of your editors may suggest that you work on a particular chapter so that you can sharpen an aspect of your writing. And be sure to check the index.

As you tackle chapters or parts of chapters, work with one other person – a classmate at school, a friend, or a relative at home. Although you can get some benefit from working alone, you really need someone to talk to, to check with, and to ask and answer questions. Whenever possible, talk through whatever you are working on with your partner; then, and only if you need to, do it in writing. This way, you'll be able to familiarize yourself with a lot more of the material.

With the help of your teacher-editor or peer-editor, decide which aspect of your style you should work on. Sometimes you can work through an entire chapter; sometimes only a part. Sometimes you may start at the beginning of a chapter; sometimes in the middle. If only one partner needs to do a chapter, the other should act as an adviser and helper. (By teaching your partner, you will learn new things yourself.) The important thing to remember in using the Second Workshop chapters is that they should fulfil your writing needs.

Each chapter contains one or more special writing projects that you can do for your partner. It is possible for you to do a special writing project for your teacher-editor as well.

29 Style

"Style! I have no style. I merely wait till the mud settles."

Stephen Leacock

Every day you encounter things with style: clothes, music, telephones, stores, and so on. Writing also has style – qualities that distinguish the work of one writer from that of another.

Some beginning writers consider a personal writing style difficult to define and impossible to achieve. They believe that only the professionals such as William Shakespeare, Margaret Atwood, or Robertson Davies have a writing style that is all their own. Nothing could be further from the truth! This chapter will show you how to identify and develop your personal writing style.

1. Style in Comics

1. Bring newpaper comics (preferably the color comic section from your week-end newspaper) to class.

2. With your partner, determine which is the most formal comic strip – that is, the one that is most sophisticated or that uses above-average dialogue and cartooning techniques. Be sure to consider the following: the cartooning technique, the subject, the story line, the uses of color, and the dialogue of the characters.

Example
"Prince Valiant" is the most formal. The artist draws realistic pictures instead of cartoons; the use of color makes each panel seem like an oil painting; the story line is about the high deeds of knights in King Arthur's

time; and the dialogue – not placed in balloons – communicates the serious thoughts of the characters.

3. When you have discussed all the specific things about each comic strip, choose an overall word to describe the style of each strip. This word should cover all the comments you made about the strip.

Example
The style of "Prince Valiant" is dignified.

2.   Dialogue for Comics

1. Find a comic strip from a newspaper that is a few weeks old (so that your partner will not remember it). Cut the words from all the speech balloons, and bring the comic strip to class.

2. Exchange blank comic strips with your partner. Supply each balloon in the cartoon your partner gives you with dialogue that seems to fit the characters and the situation. When you're finished, discuss the appropriateness of the dialogue for the comic strip. (If the cartooning style is informal, for example, the dialogue should not be formal.)

3. Next, supply each balloon with the dialogue that you think the creator of the comic strip wrote. When you're finished, compare yours with the original. How close were you? Were yours and the creator's style close? What word would you use to describe the overall style of the original comic strip?

4. Provide appropriate dialogue for this cartoon:

3. Newspaper Styles

1. Bring a newspaper and a pair of scissors to class.

2. Cut out the photos that you think are the most serious, the most comic, and the most sensational.

3. Exchange photos with your partner. Label each of your partner's photos *serious*, *comic*, or *sensational*. Jot down several reasons for each of your choices.

4. Discuss your reasons with your partner.

5. Then cut out ads that you think are the most dignified, the most comic, and the most sensational. Exchange ads, and follow points 3 and 4 once again.

6. Cut out two headlines from different newspapers: one headline that you think is sensationally misleading and one that is completely factual. Exchange headlines with your partner; give your partner the accompanying articles as well. After reading each article, rewrite its headline, changing its style.

> *Example*
> You can change the sensationally misleading **MILLIONS WILL STARVE** to the completely factual **WHEAT SHORTAGE FEARED**.

7. Cut out several letters to the editor, and arrange them in order from the most cautiously written to the most aggressively written. When you're finished, discuss your arrangement (and your reasons for your arrangement) with your partner.

8. Cut out articles that have the following styles: serious, comic, sensational, matter-of-fact, dull, exciting. Exchange articles with your partner, and discuss your reasons for your choices.

4. Topic vs. Style

1. Bring to class at least three different articles that deal with exactly the same topic. (One could be from your daily newspaper; one from a weekly newspaper; and one from a news magazine such as *Time* or *Maclean's*.)

2. Exchange articles with your partner.

3. Read the articles. As you do so, jot down their similarities and differences so that you can determine the style of each. You might take into account the following.
a) Vocabulary contributes to style. Words can be classified as formal, colloquial, or slang.
b) Attitude contributes to style. A writer can take a positive or negative approach to a topic. A sincere, direct piece is quite different from a comically satiric piece.

c) The length of sentences can contribute to style. A writer may compose a selection with short, direct sentences (under ten words); with long, involved sentences (more than thirty words); or with a combination of short-, long-, and medium-length sentences.

d) A writer can develop the thesis in specific, concrete ways or in more general, abstract ways.

e) If a writer uses too many rhetorical devices too often, the style may seem contrived rather than natural.

f) Sometimes a writer may use many figurative comparisons (even lengthy analogies); other times a writer may use no figures of speech at all.

g) Point of view affects style. Sometimes a writer uses a persona rather than his or her own voice.

h) Tone contributes to style. Writers use an objective tone when they provide facts and details without much emotion and a subjective tone when they share their feelings about the facts and details.

4. In determining style, try to place each piece you read on a scale between very aggressive and very cautious. Use details from the piece to help you decide.

5. With your partner, discuss the stylistic differences in your articles. (You might want to use the following questions to help you guide your discussion.)

- Which article is easiest to read? Why?
- Do any of the articles mix levels of vocabulary? In what ways?
- Which article contains the longest sentences?
- Which article develops in the most specific, concrete way? What makes you say so?
- Which article develops in the most subtle, abstract way? What makes you say so?
- Do any of the articles contain figurative language? (See Chapter 32.) Of what sort?
- Which writer is closest to the reader? How does he or she do that?
- Which article is the most personal? The most impersonal? What makes it that way?
- Which article is the most aggressive? The most cautious? What makes it that way?
- What word would you use to describe the overall style of each article? (You might use the list of words in the following section to help you decide.)

5.   Your Style

Being able to recognize style in something you read is useful, but it is even more important to recognize and develop your own writing style. Many things influence your writing style: your age, education, experiences, travel, interests, opportunities, and so on – and the amount and kind of reading and writing that you do. You should not think of your writing style as better or worse than someone else's style – just different. Perhaps you've never thought of naming your writing style. Now is your opportunity to do so.

1. Take a look at a writing project you have recently completed, and, with your partner, apply the questions in the previous section. Use specific details from your writing as you discuss your answers to each question. Finally, decide which of the following terms most accurately describes your style:

cautious	ironic
distinguished	impressive
moving	down-to-earth
breezy	uneven
serious	concrete
subjective	personal
aggressive	straightforward
technical	familiar
stiff	slangy
didactic	confusing
sincere	impersonal
informal	ambiguous
mixed	colloquial
vigorous	dignified
eloquent	journalistic
formal	comic
direct	humorous
consistent	abstract
rambling	*or some other term*

2. Do the same for a recent writing project of your partner's.

3. Discuss with your partner how you might change or further develop your style.

6.   Persona

Most of your writing will probably be from your personal point of view. Throughout this book, however, there are opportunities for you to put yourself in the place of another person and use that **persona** as you write. You might use a persona to fulfil a special purpose for a particular piece of writing. Have you ever imitated another person's way of talking to give an impression of that person? If so, you have already used a persona.

1. With your partner, read these three pieces by Mark Twain.

from *A Connecticut Yankee in King Arthur's Court*

A proud moment for me? I should think so. Yonder was Arthur, King of Britain; yonder was Guinevere; yes, and whole tribes of little provincial kings and kinglets; and in the tented camp yonder, renowned knights from many lands; and likewise the selectest body known to chivalry, the Knights of the Table Round, the most illustrious in Christendom; and biggest fact of all, the very sun of their shining system was yonder couching his lance, the focal point of forty thousand adoring eyes; and all by myself, here was I laying for him. Across my mind flitted the dear image of a certain hello-girl of West Hartford, and I wished she could see me now. In that moment, down came the Invincible, the rush of a whirlwind – the courtly world rose to its feet and bent forward – the fateful coils went circling through the air, and before you could wink I was towing Sir Launcelot across the field on his back, and kissing my hand to the storm of waving kerchiefs and the thundercrash of applause that greeted me!

from *The Adventures of Huckleberry Finn*

It was a real bully circus. It was the splendidest sight that ever was when they all come riding in, two and two, and gentlemen and lady, side by side, the men just in their drawers and undershirts, and no shoes nor stirrups, and resting their hands on their thighs easy and comfortable – there must'a' been twenty of them – and every lady with a lovely complexion, and perfectly beautiful, and looking just like a gang of real sure-enough queens, and dressed in clothes that cost millions of dollars, and just littered with diamonds. It was a powerful fine sight; I never see anything so lovely. And then one by one they got up and stood, and went a-weaving around the ring so gentle and wavy and graceful, the men looking ever so tall and airy and straight, with their heads bobbing and skimming along, away up there under the tent-roof, and every lady's rose-leafy dress flapping soft and silky around her hips, and she looking like the most loveliest parasol.

from *The Great French Duel*

First, we drew up my principal's will. I insisted upon this, and stuck to my point. I said I had never heard of a man in his right mind going out to fight a duel without first making his will. He said he had never heard of a man in his right mind doing anything of the kind. When he had finished the will, he wished to proceed to a choice of his "last words." He wanted to know how the following words, as a dying exclamation, struck me:

> "I die for my God, for my country, for freedom of speech, for progress, and the universal brotherhood of man!"

I objected that this would require too lingering a death; it was a good speech for a consumptive, but not suited to the exigencies of the field of honor. We wrangled over a good many ante-mortem outbursts, but finally I got him to cut his obituary down to this, which he copied into his memorandum-book, purposing to get it by heart:

"I DIE THAT FRANCE MAY LIVE."

I said that this remark seemed to lack relevancy; but he said relevancy was a matter of no consequence in last words, what you wanted was thrill.

2. Discuss the following with your partner.
a) What can you deduce about the identity of each persona (the *I* in each piece)? What sort of person is each? What makes you say so?
b) For what purpose has Twain assumed each persona? How do you know?
c) How do the differences in sentence structure and word choice reflect the purpose of each piece?
d) If you had a chance to read one of the entire selections from which these excerpts were taken, which would it be? Why?

3. In *Gulliver's Travels*, Jonathan Swift assumes the persona of an adventurous young doctor. Harper Lee assumes the persona of Scout, a young girl, to narrate *To Kill a Mockingbird*. Can you think of other writers who have assumed a persona?

4. Tell your partner how you felt after watching a recent movie, TV show, or sports event.

5. Now assume the persona of someone whose reaction was opposite to yours, and tell your partner how you feel.

6. Assume the persona of a visitor from another planet who is bewildered by the antics of human beings. Role-play your character.

**SPECIAL
WRITING
PROJECT**

☐ Write three short pieces about a topic from three different points of view.
☐ Give your three pieces to your partner. If you've used one or more personae, invite your partner to identify them. Then discuss their effectiveness.

7. **Detecting Style**

With your partner, comment on five specific aspects of the style of each of the following selections. Use the items in **Topic vs. Style** (section 4) to get you thinking. Then choose one word to describe the overall style of each selection.

from *Caesars of the Wilderness*
Peter C. Newman

Pemmican was eaten either raw, sliced, coated with flour and fried or cut up into a thick soup called *rababoo*. It required no preservatives and seemed to last forever. There was considerable dispute about exactly how palatable the stuff really was. Those who ate it staunchly declared there wasn't anything else quite like it, claiming it tasted like nothing but pemmican. The liveliest description of that unmatched flavour is in H.M. Robinson's *The Great Fur Land*: "Take the scrapings from the driest outside corner of a very stale piece of cold roast beef, add to it lumps of rancid fat, then garnish all with long human hairs and short hairs of dogs and oxen and you have a fair imitation of common Pemmican."

Dialing It In
from *Road and Track*, February 1989
Ted West

We got Top Secret clearance at the best road-racing team in America and here's what we saw....

The car rolls into the pits. The engine switches off. Immediately, team engineer and crew close in around the driver, muttering in furtive tones. Their mouths are concealed behind clipboards, preventing lip reading. Their eyes scan the area for spies....

Secrets. How they tantalize.

The trouble is, most racing secrets you're never going to learn. The Real Gold, the hidden stuff that spells victory or humiliation – it's as secret as the next generation of stealth interceptors.

Until now, that is. See, we've just unearthed some of the darkest secrets ever. What's more, we're going to blow them all.

We had to get some cooperation, of course. And who else would have the sturdy self-confidence to talk candidly but the blokes from the IMSA GTP series who race the unbeatable Electramotive Nissan GTP ZX Turbo? To our vast pleasure, they welcomed us into their councils of war at IMSA's Watkins Glen weekend. They even promised to walk us through the most top-secret process of all, the "dialing-in" of the car.

At last, we'd find out what all the infernal muttering was about.

The Nissan GTP ZX Turbo, to set history straight, came by its invincibility the old-fashioned way – it *earned* it. Three years ago, it was a darting, dangerous shambles.

But painstaking ground-up reengineering raised the car to competence. Tub, bodywork, wings, engine block, fuel-management system, transmission, front and rear suspensions – all were redesigned. What began as a very troubled

Lola T810 now became a superbly American racer. It had a made-in-El Segundo aluminum racing block, Don Devendorf's state-of-the-art Electramotive fuel-management system, an underwing and dual-element rear wing developed in the team's own moving-ground wind tunnel. Probably no race car in history has ever generated more gross aerodynamic downforce than this one.

Indeed, the Nissan GTP is so biased toward downforce, despite its concomitant aerodynamic drag, that the team is quite happy to sacrifice as much as 15-20 mph of top speed. Ironically, on the straights this car is among the very slowest of GTPs. But at most tracks, cornering comprises the vast majority of a lap – at Road Atlanta, for instance, the straight-away accounts for 14 seconds out of a total lap time of 1:10. In modern high-downforce cars, top speed is all but secondary to competitive lap speeds.

But that doesn't get us any closer to the secrets we promised – or does it?

Yes, it does.

For this is a team that technologically has made its own way and is deservedly proud. As Trevor Harris, team engineer, chief designer and our guru for the week, put it, the chassis sorting process he's about to show us isn't so much a matter of "secrets" as of finesse and execution. Electramotive, he means, can tell all the world – and still execute better.

And the record, we might add, proves him right.

Celebratory Leap: Toronto Dance Theatre is 20 and Thriving
from *Maclean's*, January 30, 1989

At its 20th birthday party, members of Canada's most enduring modern-dance company were clearly in an exuberant mood. Performing in the converted inner-city church that is its home, Toronto Dance Theatre capped the evening's program last month with the finale from *Baroque Suite*, a 1983 piece chor-eographed by TDT cofounder David Earle. The work recalls the stately joy-ousness of court dancing, but, instead of wearing the usual pastel leotards and flowing skirts, the dancers appeared onstage in outfits ranging from Wonder Woman costume to an elephant suit. Over the years and through financial crises, TDT has retained a fervent commitment to modern dance. But evi-dently, the company – once described by a critic as "serious to the point of glumness" – has also learned to laugh a little along the way.

Lately, the troupe has had ample cause to celebrate. Last year, its found-ers – Patricia Beatty, 52, David Earle, 50, and Peter Randazzo, 46 – won a Toronto Arts Award. Jurors noted that the trio had "changed the face of dance in Canada." And, in 1988 TDT was the only North American modern-dance company to be invited to the Olympic Arts Festival in Seoul. Later this month, the company's 14 dancers will embark on a tour of the United States and Central and Western Canada and in the spring they will perform in Europe. Holding fast to the principle that art should be challenging as well as enter-taining, the company is at last gaining the kind of recognition it has sought. Said Randazzo: "We're finally getting the audience we should have; not people looking for novelty, but people who think and aren't afraid to get involved."

Currently, there are more than 30 professional modern-dance companies across Canada, but, when TDT was created, the art form had yet to take root in the country. The alternative – classical ballet – did not interest the three founders. Said Earle: "Classical dance can be very moving and powerful but generally isn't. All three studied with Martha Graham and other leaders of modern dance. By 1968, they were living in Toronto and decided to join forces, creating TDT and its school. At present, the school, which offers a three-year professional program, has 60 students.

Despite their common grounding, the three have always had distinct chor-eographic styles: Beatty inclines toward symbolic impassioned action, Earle to flowing lyricism, and Randazzo to clean, incisive movement. The combined strength of their work has attracted some of the rising stars of the modern-dance world. By the late 1970's, the company employed such artists as Danny Grossman and Robert Desrosiers, now internationally known choreographers with their own companies. In 1978, dancer Christopher House came to TDT, becoming a resident choreographer three years later. Now 33, he has injected the company with the innovative, bracing athleticism of his own dancing and his award-winning creations.

While the late 1970's were a period of artistic excitement at TDT, the company was struggling under a mounting debt. In 1980, the financial situation forced the company to cancel its season at the St. Lawrence Centre. Half of the company's dancers left. By 1982, it appeared that the company might have to fold. Said Beatty: "From Day 1, we choreographed, we taught, we balanced the books, we cleaned. And we just got tired." In order to recharge themselves, the founders handed TDT's artistic leadership to Kenny Pearl in 1982. During Pearl's tenure, which lasted until Earle took over as artistic director in 1987, the company began to struggle back from the brink. Partly as a result of improved management and marketing, the organization's deficit, which stood at more than $300,000 three years ago, is now down to $139,000.

Meanwhile, TDT has flourished in other ways. National Ballet principal dancer Veronica Tennant, who has appeared as a guest artist several times in TDT's Christmas show, singles out the company's school as a source of growth. Said Tennant: "I've never seen the company stronger in terms of the quality of its dancers than I did this season." But TDT's founders are too intent upon the future to revel in the present. Said Randazzo: "I don't think we'll ever feel we've arrived." The artists of Toronto Dance Theatre clearly have never forgotten that without movement, there is no dance at all.

On The Meaning of the Word "It"
Jonathan Willcocks, student

Is it not amazing, perhaps even ludicrous, that certain very ordinary little words that we use dozens of times a day so stubbornly elude any exact definition? Is there not any one of us who is not brought to a sudden halt when confronted with the demand to define the word "if"; or how about "as"; or would you believe "a"? These are words that even the smallest child uses without difficulty and yet to define their meaning requires a scholar's knowledge of language, often of logic, and even of philosophy.

Such a word is – "it." Surely there are few words in the English language that are more often used and in such a variety of situations as this little word, but how do we define it? In my *Encyclopaedia Britannica Dictionary* "it" takes up more space than any other single word on the page and the definition is full of four-syllable words of the most complex, difficult, and obscure meaning. For instance: "the personal pronoun of the third person, singular number, and neuter gender: used as a substitute for a noun or clause mentioned or understood, as anticipative subject of a verb whose logical subject follows, as nominative of verbs that are impersonal; and then as pointing out the leader in a children's game or a player that takes some special part; as, I'll be it; etc., etc."

Or what about the logical and philosophical implications in a statement such as "It is raining"? What in blazes does the "it" in this sentence refer to?

Is it clouds, weather, God, or perhaps the weather forecaster? The only thing that is apparent in a statement like this is that our language is so constructed that we must always have a subject and an object, whether it corresponds to reality or not. In that our prime tool of thinking is language itself which, in certain instances, does not correspond to reality, how indeed can we ever then apprehend reality? Before we know it, by starting out with an intent to define this little word, we are confronted with the largest eternal questions that people have ever asked themselves.

If this word can create so much trouble without even trying, perhaps we should avoid its usage, at least in its more ambiguous forms. But what a nightmare! I have used the word no fewer than eleven times already in this short essay … Help! It is a mystery – whoops! There I go again.

from "Raindance"
Kathryn A. Sinclair

It was around midday, if one could judge such things in the perpetual grey-ness, when the man reached the top of a ridge and saw the town. The cluster of buildings on the far side of the plain held no special interest for him beyond the fact that it was inhabited and therefore must be approached with caution. But he had not slept under shelter for several nights, and even under his heavy rubber poncho his clothes clung to his body with a dampness composed of sweat and the rain which worked its way down his neck no matter what he did to stop it. His shoulders and knees ached, his eyes were blurred with fatigue and he needed to be dry and warm.

The Lighthouse
Michael McMillen, student

It stands proud and tall,
sending its shimmering light across
the water.
From inside you can hear the
pounding surf against the rocks,
its strong walls making you feel
warm and secure.

The smell of the wet cobblestones
seeps through the cracks.
The touch of the water makes
you shiver with cold.

from "Just Wind and Horses: A Memoir"
Sinclair Ross

Yes, as I said in the beginning she was a difficult woman, as difficult to describe as to live with. Domineering, unreasonable, with a sharp and sometimes reckless tongue, foolish in her way of drawing the long bow, outrageous in her way of telling all-out whoppers with a straight face, insultingly taking for granted you were too stupid to see through her – but I cut short my list remembering that, redemptively, she worked. And remembering, I suddenly see her working – over there, right over there –

Up to her eyes in extra harvest hands ... harried and irritable, face flushed and sagging with near-desperation weariness, untidy wisps of hair whipped across her forehead ... killing and plucking chickens along with churning and scrubbing and cleaning just as usual – feet and ankles swollen twice their normal size ... swearing at the dog to get the cows out of the garden – the half-acre vegetable garden that was her responsibility, spring to freeze-up – onions and peas, beets and carrots, a few bachelor's buttons and nasturtiums squeezed in, no time to look at them or smell them ... the same as the two-acre potato patch – planting, hoeing, digging – people ate a lot of potatoes in those days – her responsibility too. Yelling at me if I had finished my chores to get on with my homework, never mind what's going on in the stable or what the hired men are saying ... afraid I'd be Pete Ross all over again, determined never to let it happen.

Life as a Runner
Marty Park, student

A running shoe, can you believe it, not a hiking boot or a dress shoe, but a running shoe.

It all started in the factory. I was manufactured with 5000 other Colt runners, and I must say I was the cutest of the 5000.

Now I live in Calgary with a rotten owner. Why, he's got the smelliest feet, and when he sticks them in me I have trouble standing up. Then there are the hockey schools and school teams. Those practices are awfully hard on my insoles.

The dreaded moments of my life come when I'm stuffed in that deep dark and dirty closet. Many times I am trapped with all those reject shoes. You know the ones ... the ones that could use a good washing and have built-in air conditioning.

Let me tell you, life as a running shoe is no fun.

Musée des Beaux Arts
W. H. Auden

About suffering they were never wrong,
The Old Masters: how well they understood
Its human position; how it takes place
While someone else is eating or opening a window or just walking dully along;
How, when the aged are reverently, passionately waiting
For the miraculous birth, there always must be
Children who did not specially want it to happen, skating
On a pond at the edge of the wood:

They never forgot
That even the dreadful martyrdom must run its course
Anyhow in a corner, some untidy spot
Where the dogs go on with their doggy life and the torturer's horse
Scratches its innocent behind on a tree.

In Brueghel's *Icarus*, for instance: how everything turns away
Quite leisurely from the disaster; the ploughman may
Have heard the splash, the forsaken cry,
But for him it was not an important failure; the sun shone
As it had to on the white legs disappearing into the green
Water; and the expensive delicate ship that must have seen
Something amazing, a boy falling out of the sky,
Had somewhere to get to and sailed calmly on.

Aerial Bombardment
after "Musée des Beaux Arts"
Jane Lang, student

About aerial bombardment they never thought,
The old soldiers. How well they understood
Conventional butchery: how fighting starts
When someone steps toward a regal coach
And goes on for years in muddy trenches.
With guns and gas and bayonets
They killed in fear and blood.
They saw whom they massacred,
Shot them in their knowledge: life for them
Was no more certain
Than light from a falling flare.

In Picasso's *Guernica*, though, how everything
Misses the personal touch; faces turn
Upward in horror, cattle roar and stare
At the disaster, not of their making:
With outstretched arms, men and women appeal upward.
Those in machines, however,
Do not see the dismembered limbs or anguished faces,
The world broken on the rack of their bombs.
The city smokes, the horse screams, the arm
Lies limp, clutching its broken sword.

SPECIAL WRITING PROJECT

- Write a short selection. Concentrate on unifying the content, tone, word choice, and sentence structure so that you achieve a distinctive style. For this project, you might experiment with using a persona. If you decide to do so, put yourself entirely into your persona's position. Write firmly, using the style of the persona.
- Invite your partner to edit your draft to improve your style by adding, subtracting, or substituting.

30 Sentence Variety

> *"The unit of speech is neither the individual sound nor the individual word but the sentence, conveying a complete concept."*
>
> *Mario Pei*

In this chapter, you and your partner can begin to examine some of the infinite variety of sentence structures and ask questions, test emphasis, and clear up problems.

1. Simple to Complex

Every sentence contains one basic idea, but some sentences add to the basic idea, making the sentence's idea more complex.

Simple Idea

Bobby Jones set a record.

Complex Idea

In 1930 the great golfer Bobby Jones set a record, which still stands, by winning the U.S. Open, the U.S. Amateur, the British Open, and the British Amateur tournaments.

1. Do you see the simple idea, *Bobby Jones set a record*, within the complex idea?

2. Now work separately from your partner to convert the following simple ideas into more complex ones.

a) My grandfather played golf.
b) The golfer won money.
c) The golfer attracts fans.
d) The golfer made a hole in one.
e) The young golfer won a university scholarship.

3. Compare your sentences. Chances are that no sentence is identical to another. Are you already noticing the possibilities of sentence variety?

2.   Complex to Simple

The reverse process is just as easy to apply. It's useful to be able to isolate the parts of a complex idea when you are combining sentences.

Complex Idea

The gymnast earned a perfect score of 10 points while performing flawlessly in the floor exercises.

By taking every important word, you can put the parts into simple sentences.

Parts

There is a gymnast.
The gymnast earned a score.
The score was perfect.
The score was 10 points.
The gymnast performed.
The performance was flawless.
The gymnast performed in the floor exercises.

1. Working separately from your partner, break the following sentences into their parts.
a) The People's Republic of China sent an impressive gymnastics team to the Seoul Olympics.
b) Brian Orser and Elizabeth Manley both earned medals in figure skating at the 1988 Winter Olympics, which were held in Calgary.
c) Jeff Tiessen won a silver medal for his performance in track and field, amputee division, at the 1984 Paralympics.
d) Olga Korbut and Nadia Comaneci inspired thousands of young people throughout the world to start gymnastics training.

2. With your partner, compare and discuss your simple sentences.

3.   Sentence Combinations

Notice how you might break down the following sentence into seven parts, each with a simple idea.

The talented young skater executed a perfect triple axel and won a gold medal.

There is a skater.
The skater is young.
The skater is talented.
The skater executed a perfect jump.
The jump was a triple axel.
The skater won a medal.
It was a gold medal.

Read over some of the different ways of combining these sentences with simple ideas.

a) After executing a perfect triple axel, the talented young skater won a gold medal.
b) The talented young skater who executed a perfect triple axel won a gold medal.
c) By executing a perfect triple axel, the talented young skater won a gold medal.
d) The talented young skater who had executed a perfect triple axel won a gold medal.
e) A gold medal was won by the talented young skater who executed a perfect triple axel.
f) The talented young skater, the one who executed a perfect triple axel, won the gold medal.
g) A perfect triple axel was executed by the talented young skater who won the gold medal.
h) Executing a perfect triple axel, the talented young skater won a gold medal.
i) With a perfectly executed triple axel, the talented young skater won a gold medal.

See how many ways you and your partner can combine the following sentences.

1. *Sentence with Two Ideas*

Alain Prost won the 1989 Formula One driving championship.
He was driving a McLaren.

2. *Sentence with Three Ideas*

Ayrton Senna won the Formula One driving championship in 1988.
He was Alain Prost's teammate.
He is a fearless driver.

3. *Sentence with Four Ideas*

The 1988 Formula One race in Montreal was cancelled.
There were problems over sponsorship of the event.
Race fans were disappointed.
So were the drivers.

4. Rearranging

Because there are so many ways to combine sentences, you need to determine which combination best serves your purpose. If you are dissatisfied with the way you have written one of your sentences, rearrange the most important words to achieve the greatest impact for your specific purpose and audience. Often, the best places for key words are at the beginning and end of sentences.

Example

In the 1981 Wimbledon tennis finals, five-time champion Bjorn Borg lost to American John McEnroe on a hot July day before a packed Centre Court.
a) Five-time champion Bjorn Borg lost to John McEnroe in the 1981 Wimbledon tennis finals on a hot July day before a packed Centre Court.
b) In the 1981 Wimbledon tennis finals on a hot July day before a packed Centre Court, five-time champion Bjorn Borg lost to American John McEnroe.

1. Discuss with your partner which of the preceding sentences creates the most impact. How does it do that? Which sentence has the least impact? Why?

2. Working separately from your partner, rearrange the parts of the following sentences to create the greatest impact for an imagined audience and purpose. To begin, pick out the idea you want to stress, and place it in a position of importance.
a) Over the past ten years, because of the extensive television coverage, tennis has become a very popular sport in North America and around the world.
b) Tennis has become such a popular and profitable sport that many parents send their talented children to tennis camps to receive professional training.
c) The Davis Cup, open to both amateur and professional players, is a world championship in which there are frequent upsets.
d) Coveted by every player is the "Grand Slam" of tennis, for which in one year a player must win the Australian Open, Wimbledon, the French Open, and the United States Open.

3. Meet with your partner to compare and discuss the impact of your sentences.

5.   Emphasizing

1. Working separately from your partner, combine each group of ideas into the best possible single sentence. Concentrate on making each sentence emphatic.

a) Richard Petty is probably the most famous stock car racer of all time.
His father, Lee Petty, was a champion driver.
His son, Kyle, is also a driver.
He holds a number of NASCAR records.

b) She was the first woman licensed to run Top Fuel dragsters in the United States.
Her story was told in the film *Heart Like a Wheel*.
She is from Michigan.
Her name is Shirley Muldowney.

c) Many motor races take place on special tracks.
"The Brickyard" at Indianapolis is the most famous motor racing track in North America.
Indy car races also take place on city streets.
An Indy car race is held every year in Toronto.

d) A.J. Foyt has won 67 championship races.
He has won the Indianapolis 500 four times.
He has finished second at Indianapolis twice.
He also won at LeMans in 1967.

e) Many people consider motor racing a dangerous sport.
Talented drivers have been killed during races.
Two of these drivers were Jim Clark and Gilles Villeneuve.
Motor racing is still a very popular spectator sport.

2. With your partner, compare and discuss your sentences. Which are most emphatic? What makes them that way?

6.   Subtracting

Subtracting certain unnecessary words can add emphasis and variety to your sentences.

Example

From
The team of male basketball players that represented the United States of America in the Olympic Games held in Los Angeles in the summer of 1984 won first place and was awarded a gold medal.

To
The U.S. men's Olympic basketball team won a gold medal at the 1984 Summer Olympics in Los Angeles.

Working with your partner, subtract the unnecessary words from these sentences.

a) Players whose height is greater than 2.13 m now appear on a regular basis in basketball as played by both professional and college teams.

b) Wilt Chamberlain, who bore the nickname of "The Stilt" because he was so tall, played professional basketball and also played professional volleyball.

c) If a professional basketball player commits more than five infractions that are considered personal fouls, the player is disqualified and forbidden to play any more in that game.

d) Bill Russell played in the position of centre for the Boston Celtics basketball team, and he was also the first black person to coach a major professional team because he coached the Boston Celtics from 1965 through to 1969.

e) The University of California at Los Angeles, which has a basketball team that is called the Bruins, has had more players from its team join the National Basketball Association than has any other college or university.

7.   Expanding

Keep your audience in mind as you write, and create the best possible impact by combining, rearranging, and subtracting ideas. If there is a possibility that your audience may be confused, be prepared to expand your ideas to make them clearer. Pose the questions *who, what, where, when, why*, and *how* as you write to help you discover the effectiveness of adding to a sentence.

Needs expanding for clarity:

Tom Dempsey kicked a field goal to set a record.

Key Idea: kicking a field goal
Who: Tom Dempsey of New Orleans
When: November 8, 1970
Where: in a game against Detroit
Why: to set a record
How: it travelled 63 yards (58 m)
What: (already indicated)

In the following, notice the processes of combining, rearranging, and expanding.

a) On November 8, 1970, in a game against Detroit, Tom Dempsey of New Orleans kicked a field goal that travelled 63 yards to set a record.

b) Tom Dempsey of New Orleans set a record on November 8, 1970, in a game against Detroit, when he kicked a field goal that travelled 63 yards.

c) During a game against Detroit on November 8, 1970, Tom Dempsey of New Orleans set a record when he kicked a 63-yard field goal.

1. With your partner, discuss: Does any one sentence show the most emphasis through combining, rearranging, and expanding, or are they equally emphatic?

2. Working independently of your partner, expand each of the following key ideas into a full sentence. Then present to each other the one sentence that you consider the most emphatic. Discuss the effectiveness of your choices.

playing high-school hockey
playing in the school band
seeing a Stanley Cup game
becoming a sports fan

8.   Reforming

1. Working separately from your partner, use rearrangement and subtraction to combine the following sentences into one well-formed paragraph. Make sure your sentences are varied; use some short sentences, some long. Put key words first in some, last in others. Make sure that your whole paragraph flows logically and smoothly.

Soccer is a popular game. It is played all over the world. Few North Americans watch it. Even fewer play it. Outside North America, soccer is called "football." More people watch soccer than any other sport. A soccer team consists of eleven players. One player is the goalkeeper. Only the goalkeeper can pick up the ball. The other players move the ball around the field. They can kick the ball. They can bounce the ball off their heads. The players try to score goals. The team with more goals wins the game. Soccer is not a complicated game. It is exciting and challenging.

2. When you both finish, compare the variety of your sentences and the emphasis of your paragraphs.

9.   Kinds of Sentences

To this point, all of the sentences in this chapter have made statements or declarations. **Declarative sentences** are the most common in English. There are three other types of sentences, however, that can add variety to your writing: **questions**, **exclamations**, and **commands**. Notice what you can achieve without using a declaration.

Who was the greatest baseball player of all time? Stop and think a minute. Was it the fabulous Babe Ruth, probably one of the most popular sports figures of all time? "Hammerin' Hank" Aaron, who broke the Babe's home-run record? Ty Cobb, "the Georgia Peach," whose career hit record has stood for more than fifty years? Or was it perhaps a pitcher, such as Walter Johnson, who pitched an astounding 113 shutouts during his career? Don't forget more recent players such as Nolan Ryan! Hard to decide, isn't it?

Notice the punctuation of each of the sentences. Which are questions? Exclamations? Commands?

SPECIAL WRITING PROJECT

> □ Although you should not overuse these three kinds of sentences in your writing, try to write a paragraph without using a single declaration.
>
> □ Ask your partner to check that you have not used any declarative sentences and that your paragraph holds together. Discuss the effectiveness of your paragraph.

10. Minor Sentences

The usual definition of a sentence is that it is a group of words with a subject and a verb. According to some old composition texts, a sentence is incomplete without a subject or verb. It becomes a **sentence fragment**, said to be taboo in good writing. So throughout their schooling, many students have been encouraged to avoid anything resembling a fragment; instead, they've spent their years perfecting whole sentences. Complete thoughts.

But writers do use fragments in order to communicate. (Which sentence in the preceding paragraph is a fragment? Did you understand it? Also, take a look at the fragments in the paragraph in section 9. From the context, you can easily supply the missing parts of these minor sentences, so you will not misunderstand them.)

Perhaps the following paragraph uses the rhetorical fragment excessively. But how does the style of the writing relate to its topic? Do the minor sentences communicate complete thoughts?

> Sunday afternoon. Crisp fall weather. Time for football! Off to the stadium. Pep rallies. Thousands of fans. Bands. Cheerleaders. Go team! Touchdown! We won! What greater thrill can there be than a well-played game and victory?

Here's another example of a paragraph that contains minor sentences. Read and discuss it with your partner.

> Has this workshop whetted your appetite? If so, you should plan to spend time learning the finer details of sentence variety. You can work alone. At your own pace. In school. At home. Anywhere. Any time. Start right away! By experimenting with sentence variety, you will have acquired one habit of good writing. And once acquired, the habit will be yours for life.

SPECIAL WRITING PROJECT

☐ Independently of your partner, write a short piece in which you use at least one minor sentence.

☐ Exchange your pieces of writing and discuss whether you have written a rhetorical fragment (that works) or a fragment fault (that needs revision).

☐ Write a paragraph in which you use various kinds of sentences, including minor sentences. With your partner, discuss the effectiveness of your sentence variety.

31 Rhetorical Devices

"Rhetoric will determine whether a stylistic choice is effective – that is, whether a particular locution conveys the intended meaning with the clarity, economy, emphasis, and tone appropriate to the subject matter, occasion, audience, and desired effect."

Edward P. J. Corbett

Rhetorical devices are techniques that you can use to create a certain effect on an audience. When used with discretion, rhetorical devices can enliven your prose and help you to achieve your purpose – to emphasize, to shock, to add humor, to draw attention to word choice, to create suspense, and so on. You'll find rhetorical devices throughout this book; this chapter will discuss in detail only those you won't find elsewhere.

Consider working one or two of these tricks of the writer's trade into your writing, but use them carefully; overuse of rhetorical devices can result in an unnatural, or even unintentionally humorous, effect.

1. Examples of Rhetorical Devices

With your partner, read each of the following rhetorical devices, and discuss the purpose it serves. Then think up a new example for it and discuss its effectiveness with your partner.

1. Use a **rhetorical question** when you want to ask a question whose answer is already known or implied.

   Are you denying that videotape has revolutionized the film industry?

2. Use **abnormal word order** – a variation on the usual subject-verb sentence pattern – to give variety and emphasis to your writing.

Normal Word Order (Subject-Verb)
The actor's worst nightmare stood laughing at him from the shadows.

Abnormal Word Order (Verb-Subject)
Laughing at him from the shadows stood the actor's worst nightmare.

3. Use a **minor sentence** or **rhetorical fragment** when a full sentence is not necessary for sense.

Trained dogs. Big black-and-tan dogs. Snarling. Attacked the movie star.

4. Use **repetition** for emphasis and rhythm.

It was a strange night, a hushed night, a moonless night, and all you could do was go to a movie.

5. Use a **pun** when you want to play with words.

The axe-murderer in that B-movie hacked and bludgeoned thirty-five people. Now that's overkill!

6. Use **exaggeration (hyperbole)** when you want to emphasize a fact.

Bela Lugosi became so famous as Dracula that blood banks locked their doors when they saw him coming.

7. Use **understatement (litotes)** when you want to create the reverse effect (and add a touch of irony) by making the fact seem less significant.

Harrison Ford's most famous character, Indiana Jones, has occasionally found himself in a bit of a jam.

8. Use **climactic parallelism** – going from least to most important – when you wish to present several facts in order of importance.

The young actress's career rise was meteoric: after beginning as a bit player she shifted into seasonal parts, and three short years later she became a star of several movies.

9. Use a **balanced sentence** when you wish to express two or more equal and parallel ideas.

Many TV actors work hard all through the season; they play in films all through the hiatus.

10. Use **opposites** when you want to contrast two opposing ideas.

Gina Lollobrigida, a star in front of the camera, has also had a successful career behind the camera as a photographer.

11. Use **reversals (chiasmus)** when you want to make a balanced sentence even more memorable.

Many of the characters James Woods has portrayed would agree with the saying: "When the going gets tough, the tough get going."

12. Use a **periodic sentence** when you wish to withhold an important part of the sentence until the end. The sentence should not make complete sense until you have read the last word.

From his beginnings in film, in a supporting role in *The Woman of Dolwyn*, through Shakespeare and Edward Albee, to his last role, with his daughter Kate in the miniseries *Ellis Island*, strode one of Britain's greatest gifts to American film, Richard Burton.

13. Use a **figurative comparison** when you wish to present your audience with a strong image. (Figurative comparisons are discussed more fully in Chapter 32.)

Sylvester Stallone shines like a diamond in the rough in the *Rocky* films, but he only twinkles like a *Rhinestone* next to Dolly Parton.

14. Use an **allusion** when you want to save yourself a great number of words and you think your audience will appreciate the reference. (Allusions are discussed more fully in Chapter 32.)

Her roles in films such as *E.T.* and *Irreconcilable Differences* made Drew Barrymore the Shirley Temple of the 1980s.

15. Use **alliteration** – repetition of the initial sounds of words – to draw attention to a string of words.

As Frankenstein, Boris Karloff rambled, raged, and roared.

16. Use **rhyme** to make two or more words memorable.

In 1984 Bill Murray was both frightened (in *Ghostbusters*) and enlightened (in *The Razor's Edge*).

17. Use **onomatopoeia** – words that imitate or suggest sounds – when you want to draw attention to the sound of a word.

Today's films are as likely to feature the beeps and buzzes of computers as the chirps of birds. Cascading waterfalls have been replaced by humming machines and whirring laser swords.

18. Use **underlining (italics)** to emphasize certain words.

Many Americans would be amazed to know that Mary Pickford, known as "America's Sweetheart," was born <u>Canadian</u> Gladys Smith.

2.   Publicity and Rhetorical Devices

With your partner, look for these rhetorical devices in "The Shape of Things to Come": alliteration, climactic parallelism, exaggeration, rhetorical fragment, pun, rhyming words, rhetorical question, and opposites. Then discuss whether the author has effectively used these devices.

The Shape of Things to Come

Patricia Davies, student

Hey, guys and gals! If you've been dreaming about a slim, strong, sleek physique, now is the time to do something about it.

If you're pining for a willowy figure and want to whittle the excess "waste" off your trunk, there's no need to be stumped for a solution. We have numerous branches in the city ready to help you.

In our centres, there are as many different kinds of equipment as there are clients. We have facilities to suit every taste: an indoor track, a dance studio, an exercise room, a swimming pool, a sauna, a whirlpool, and even a licensed restaurant.

Some people visit "The Shape of Things to Come" to enlarge their bodies; others come here to shrink them. We design programs to suit each person's individual needs.

Come and have a personal talk with one of our helpful representatives, who will be pleased to provide full details on all our equipment and programs.

Who doesn't want to look great? A dynamic physical appearance can be a great confidence-builder when you're looking for employment or meeting new people.

Use your head! Think ahead! The time to start doing something is now. Satisfaction guaranteed or money refunded.

SPECIAL WRITING PROJECT

- ☐ Write an advertisement in which you include at least five rhetorical devices. Try to attract your partner's attention so that he or she will come, go, buy, sell, or do whatever you want.
- ☐ List the rhetorical devices you used. With your partner, evaluate your use of them.

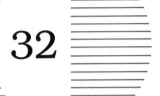

32 Figurative Language and Allusions

"Though analogy is often misleading, it is the least misleading thing we have."

Samuel Butler

Have you ever used expressions like the following? "She was really flying!" "He's as sly as a fox." "She breezed through the exam." Or "He runs like the wind." Most people use **figurative language** – that is, language that relies on a comparison for its effect. When you use figurative language naturally in your writing, you can add freshness and interest to it.

To become comfortable with using figurative language in your writing and to avoid artificiality, you and your partner might play a verbal game that begins:

> If my *friend (sister/brother/favorite rock star, etc.)* were a car *(flower/dress, etc.)* he/she would be a ... because ...

Example
If Enrico were a household appliance, he'd be a garbage disposal unit because he's always eating junk food.

Have fun with figurative language and use it only in moderation, and it can give a fresh lift to your writing.

1. Literal and Figurative Comparisons

A comparison can be either literal or figurative. She *runs like an Olympic champion* is a literal, or factual, comparison. She *runs like the wind* is a figurative comparison. If taken literally, the latter expression does not make much sense.

1. Independently of your writing partner, develop three literal (factual) comparisons for the appearance of a friend. You could use someone or something who actually looks like your friend. For example:

> Estelle looks like Amanda.
> Estelle looks like her mother did at the same age.
> Estelle looks a little like Lisa Bonet.

2. Now develop three figurative comparisons. (In choosing your comparisons, you should think of at least one aspect of your friend's appearance to compare with a similar aspect of something or someone else.)

> Doug looks like a young prince.
> Doug looks like a Greek god.
> Doug looks like death warmed over.

3. With your partner, evaluate your comparisons. Which type (literal or figurative) was more effective? Why?

2.   Original Figurative Comparisons

1. Working with your partner, try to complete some of the following with a humorous or serious figurative comparison.

> Going to school is like ...
> Falling in love is like ...
> Learning to drive is like ...
> Eating spaghetti is like ...
> Writing an exam is like ...
> Playing football (or another sport) is like ...
> Watching TV is like ...
> Going on a first date is like ...
> Getting up in the morning is like ...
> Apologizing is like ...

2. Discuss the effectiveness of each of your comparisons.

3.   Kinds of Figurative Comparisons

There are several different kinds of figurative comparisons. With your partner read over each type and example below; you'll probably recognize some of them. Then, make up sentences about one of your friends, using each type of figurative comparison.

1. A **simile** is a figurative comparison that uses a word of comparison such as *like* or *as*.

> Hugh fights like a pit bull.
> Nadine's temper is as hot as boiling tar.

2. A **metaphor** is a figurative comparison stating or implying that one thing is something else.

Hugh is a pit bull.
Nadine burns everyone with her temper.

3. **Personification** gives human characteristics to lifeless or inanimate objects.

The lily hung its head in despair.

4. An **allusion** makes a comparison by reference to a character from literature, film, mythology, history, or legend.

Wendy thinks she is Olive Oyl, but she is actually more like Princess Leia.

5. An **analogy** is an extended figurative comparison. It may sometimes be a paragraph long, sometimes an entire essay, or sometimes even an entire book.

Auntie Muriel is both the spider and the fly, the sucker-out of life juice and the empty husk. Once she was just the spider and Uncle Teddy was the fly, but ever since Uncle Teddy's death Auntie Muriel has taken over both roles. Elizabeth isn't even all that sure Uncle Teddy is really dead. Auntie Muriel probably has him in a trunk somewhere in the attic, webbed in old ecru lace tablecloths, paralyzed but still alive … Auntie Muriel, so palpably not an auntie. Nothing diminutive about Auntie Muriel.

Margaret Atwood, **Life Before Man**

6. Discuss with your partner which of these figurative comparisons you might like to experiment with in your writing.

4.   Guidelines for Figurative Comparisons

There are benefits to using figurative comparisons, but there are a few pitfalls to avoid when you do so.

Read the following guidelines, and study the examples. Then, with your partner, follow the suggestions (after each guideline) to write sentences with figurative comparisons.

1. *Guideline One:* In a figurative comparison, the two things being compared are usually not alike in every respect. For the comparison to work, however, they must have at least one thing in common. For example:

My aunt's sapphire eyes frightened me more than all her harsh words.
(The aunt's eyes are being compared to sapphires. Both sapphires and her eyes are blue and hard.)

Subject: a person's eating habits
Comparison: the way a bird eats

2. *Guideline Two:* In a figurative comparison, the object you compare your subject to should be able to do in reality what you want it to do figuratively. If your comparison does not make complete sense, your metaphor will be strained. Why does this metaphor not work?

> Jim's fists stabbed his opponent like rocks.
> (Generally, rocks *smash*; they do not *stab*.)

Subject: your report card
Comparison: a battlefield (Make sure that whatever happens in, on, or to your report card also happens on a battlefield.)

3. *Guideline Three:* In a figurative comparison, you should not begin with one comparison and end with another. Why would a mixed metaphor such as the following be confusing?

> After Susan's campaign caught fire, she snowballed her way into the presidency of the student council.
> (A snowball cannot catch fire any more than a fire can snowball.)

Subject: the weather
Comparison: an animal (Do not mention anything that is inconsistent with either the animal or the weather.)

5.   Dead Metaphors

1. When using figurative comparisons, try to avoid **dead metaphors** – metaphors that have been used too often and are now clichés (sometimes called stale expressions). Read the following examples:

> When he won the scholarship, Svend was *happy as a lark.*
> After *working like a dog* for months, Melissa had saved enough money to buy a surfboard.
> Paolo was *pounding the pavement* for weeks trying to find a summer job.
> Despite the commotion, Chandra remained as *cool as a cucumber.*
> My sister *hit the roof* when she discovered I'd eaten the whole cake she baked.

2. Now, working separately from your partner, substitute new figurative comparisons for the italicized clichés. As you do so, try testing each one according to the Guidelines for Figurative Comparisons in section 4.

You would not use *happy as an elephant, working like a skunk, pounding the ocean, cool as a turnip,* or *hit the chair* because these substitutes do not provide logical comparisons (Guideline One). You would not change *happy as a lark* to *happy as a moose* because in reality a moose is not known for its cheerfulness

(Guideline Two). If you were to change *hit the roof* to *hit the bucket*, you would be mixing metaphors (Guideline Three).

3. Meet with your partner to compare and discuss your figurative comparisons. Are your comparisons both original and logical?

4. Now, independently of your partner, write three sentences containing dead metaphors. Exchange your sentences, and substitute three original figurative comparisons for the clichés your partner has written. Share and discuss your completed work. Do your new comparisons work? Why – or why not?

6. Analogy

An analogy is an extended comparison of two things that have one or more features in common. Using an effective analogy in your writing will not only catch the interest of your audience but also clarify a particular idea. (The purpose for including an analogy is to illustrate or make something clear. If you use an analogy to try to prove a point logically, you may produce a shaky argument or a false analogy.)

Poets and fiction writers are not the only ones who use analogies; scientists often use them to make their technical information easier to understand.

1. Work with your partner to develop an analogy. You might assume that the subject is a friend and that you are going to compare her or him to a whirlwind. Bring your subject to life by using the figurative comparison in your description. To begin, jot down at least ten words or phrases that you would use to describe a whirlwind. For example:

My Friend	Whirlwind
	powerful uncontrollable made up of air carries all before it can't be stopped must run its course *and so on*

In writing your analogy, choose words from the right-hand column to describe your subject. Because not all of the words will apply to your subject, you will not be able to use all of them. For example, a person is not made entirely of air. Also, remember when you write an analogy that you should not use any descriptive terms that describe only your subject. For example, you cannot mention a person's long, unruly hair because a whirlwind does not have hair.

You might begin your piece of writing with "My friend is like _____," and use details of similarity to sustain your analogy. When you finish, test your writing to see that you have brought your subject to life. For example, compare the following pieces.

Effective Analogy

My friend is like a whirlwind. She is a powerful force who, once she has decided to do something, carries everyone along with her.

False Analogy

My friend is a whirlwind. She moves at 150 km/h, smashing windows and tearing the leaves from trees as she goes.

2. When you have completed your analogy, discuss with your partner what you learned from writing it.

SPECIAL WRITING PROJECT

☐ Write an analogy developing one of the following epigrams or on a topic of your choice. Continue the analogy until you can no longer sustain it.
- All the world's a stage. (William Shakespeare)
- Illusions are like umbrellas; you no sooner get them than you lose them. (Oscar Wilde)
- Memory is the diary that we all carry about with us. (Oscar Wilde)
- I am a camera with its shutter open, quite passive, not thinking. (Christopher Isherwood)

☐ Share your analogy with your partner. You might both evaluate it, keeping in mind the Guidelines for Figurative Comparisons.

7. Allusions

An **allusion** is a reference (often to a work of literature) that a writer expects the audience to recognize. Writers who use allusions can save themselves dozens of words. When their subject is similar to something else they know well and their audience is likely to understand, they will unhesitatingly link the two.

An audience will not fully appreciate an allusion unless they are familiar with the specific reference; they will be like Saint Paul on the road to Damascus, blind and uncomprehending. (Do you understand this allusion?)

1. Look in recent newspapers and magazines and find five titles containing allusions. Share them with your partner. Does he or she recognize each reference? (For example, an article called *"The Night Stuff"* would refer to Tom Wolfe's *The Right Stuff.*)

2. Explain the following allusions:
   "Moby Duck"
   "The Merchant of Venom"
   "Bored in the U.S.A."
   "The Quarterback of Notre Dame"
   "The Sound of Muzak"

3. Find five allusions in newspaper or magazine articles. Share them with your partner. Does he or she recognize each reference?

4. Examine each of the following, noting the allusion (in italics) as you do so. Make a record of those you definitely understand, those you could make a reasonable guess at, and those that elude you. Discuss with your partner the significance of each allusion that you recognize.
   a) Like *Sisyphus*, cancer researchers are pushing uphill.
   b) The outcome would be uncertain, but even a victory would not be much sweeter than it was for the defenders of *Masada*.
   c) The industry-government coalition that supported free trade is now shedding *crocodile tears* over the laid-off workers.
   d) We'd rather be accused of *crying wolf* than not doing the proper thing at the proper time.
   e) It's a great paper, but its editors are *Luddites* when it comes to television.

8.   Figurative Language in Cartoons

1. Find five cartoons with figurative comparisons in your local newspaper or in magazines. (Many cartoonists use figurative comparisons, especially allusions.)

2. Share and discuss them with your partner.

SPECIAL WRITING PROJECT

□ Look for figurative comparisons in your reading. Share them with your partner, and experiment with them in your writing.
□ Read the following. Test the figurative comparisons, and discuss their effectiveness with your partner.

Rainy Nights
Chuck Kahn, student

At midnight it starts to rain.
The pavements get black and shiny,
Reflecting the colored lights
Of the Chinese restaurant across the street.

In a little while I'll slip on my
Trenchcoat and fedora and go out.
The rain will have stopped by then,
I'll stand under the golden light of a street lamp.

Then I'll hunch my shoulders, turn up
The collar of my slightly battered trenchcoat,
And walk slowly out of sight
Down the dark and dangerous street.
That's all they want of me really,
It's an easy job – dead easy,
All I have to do is be Bogey
In a million people's dreams.
I like my work –
I work by night.

The Child of Deceit
Viki Young, student

Hard and glazed,
Indestructible –
A shell sees the world.
He has many surfaces,
Smooth veneer.
Different is each
And different tales are told.
The mask does not come off,
For there is none
To appreciate the core.
This, the child of
Deceit.

Sea Battle

Margaret O'Connell, student

The waves attack the shore like soldiers in battle – charging the beach in frenzy, dying in foamy agony. And as each wave slowly falls, then retreats into the sea, the next one comes in its place. It, too, seems eager to make its hopeless assault; it, too, is doomed, as sure of defeat as its predecessor. On and on the battle goes, an incessant and futile struggle against the impregnable defenses of the shore.

SPECIAL WRITING PROJECT

- Write a short piece in which you create a figurative comparison of your choice: simile, metaphor, allusion, analogy, or whatever.
- With your partner, evaluate your completed work according to the Guidelines for Figurative Comparisons.

33 Slant

> *"To be conscious of language is to be proud of the magnificent and subtle instrument in your hands; to be self-conscious about the possibility of error, or fearful of the derision of your listener at your experiments with the instrument, is to be a nerd, a schnook, and a wimp."*
>
> *William Safire*

The term **slant** is used to describe the way in which a writer may, consciously or unconsciously, convey attitudes or feelings to the audience. As a result of the writer's purpose or attitude, the writing may have a **positive slant** or **negative slant**.

Before you use slant in what you write, ask yourself: Do I want a positive or negative slant in my writing? Or do I want a mixture of positive and negative slant because I want to support one thing and reject another? Always consider your audience when you are making these decisions.

1. A Talk

1. Recall the last time you were out with a friend. Think about the kind of time you had. Write down several key words that honestly describe your experience – for example, *great, stupid, terrific, lousy*, etc. These words are for your eyes only.

2. Now, imagine reporting to the person you were out with about the time you had. Write down the words you would use. Compare your original list to the new list. Which of the original words would you not use? What words would you use instead? (For example, if you had used *terrible* to describe the

occasion, you might not want to use that word to your companion. You might use *not bad* instead.) What words from your first list might you leave unsaid?

3. Next, imagine reporting to one of your parents (new audience) about the time you had. Which words in the previous lists would you not use? Which words would you use instead? Which details about the experience would you leave out of your account? Why?

4. Now, in the classroom, tell your partner (new audience) about the time you had. How many of the original key words did you not use? Why?

2. Description

Your presentation is also affected by your attitude toward your subject.
1. With your partner, choose a subject (for example, a famous person, a city, or a sport) that one of you likes and one of you dislikes.

2. Independently of your partner, write a description of your subject. Do not state how you feel about your subject, but merely describe it.

3. Compare your descriptions. Discuss the differences in word choices, facts, and so on.

3. Ways to Slant

There are several ways that writing may be slanted in either a positive or negative manner. Here are three.

Words. Words with positive connotations will cause your audience to feel good about your subject and possibly about you; words with negative connotations will cause your reader to react against your subject and possibly against you as well. Which of the following sentences use words with positive connotations? With negative connotations? Which sentences merely state the facts?

* The team members ran into position on the court.
* The so-called team members stumbled to their spots.
* The team members quickly took their positions on the gym floor.

* The man laughs a lot with his friends.
* The fool giggles his head off with his buddies.
* The fellow chuckles a great deal with his pals.

Comparisons. If you compare your subject with something pleasant, your audience will know you approve of your subject; if you use unpleasant comparisons, your audience will know you disapprove of it. With your partner, discuss which of the following common comparisons are positive and which are negative.

- Mei Lin eats like a bird.
- Warren eats like a pig.

- Joe looks like Mel Gibson.
- Bram looks like Daffy Duck.

- Ingrid has a voice like a nightingale.
- Kristine has a voice like a crow.

Now, make up three positive comparisons and three negative comparisons.

Details. You can influence your audience by the specific details that you choose to report about your subject. If you choose only favorable details and ignore unfavorable ones, you are slanting your material in a positive manner. If you choose only unfavorable details, you are slanting negatively. Read the following statements and decide whether each has a positive or a negative slant.

- Wars give an economy a much-needed boost.
- Cars are a menace; they kill people all the time.
- Joggers can suffer shin damage and shin splints.
- The benefits of jogging include improved cardiovascular fitness.
- You can learn a great deal about life from watching soap operas.
- Making a lot of money means having to pay a lot of income tax.

4.   Degrees of Slant

Words can have a positive slant, no slant, or negative slant. For example:

Positive	No Slant	Negative
physician	doctor	pill pusher
satiate	consume	gobble up
overhear	listen	eavesdrop

1. Draw a chart similar to the one above. Working independently of your partner, choose five of the words from the list below (or five words of your own), and write them in the *No Slant* column; then write words for the positive and negative columns that mean almost the same thing as your original word.

   police officer, child, muscular, sleeps, eats, small, large, round, money, prison, party, angry, language

Remember that within the positive and negative categories there will be degrees of slant. For each term, you could have several words, each a little more positive or negative than another. This could make your search for the right word even more challenging.

2. If you have a word-processing package, check your thesaurus software to see how many choices you have for your five words.

3. When you're finished, go over your chart with your partner. You might find it interesting if you both select a word, work on it separately, and then compare your responses.

5.   Slant in Advertising

Advertising overwhelms us with examples of slant – television and radio commercials, newspaper and magazine ads, direct-mail circulars, and billboards.

1. Choose ten advertisements from the print media that illustrate either positive or negative slant. Consider the names of the products. Also discuss words that are used to describe the product. (Most advertisements will have positive slant. In what ways might they use negative slant?)

2. Exchange advertisements with your partner to see whether you can find the examples of negative and positive slant in each other's collection. Discuss your findings.

3. Choose one of the advertising pieces and write an ad based on it that uses a different slant.

6. Propaganda

Propaganda also provides examples of slant. Notice the use of negative and positive slant in the following sentences:

> Visionaries are carving the future out of the tropical rainforest with up-to-the-minute land management techniques that optimize the available agricultural and grazing land but that have the least possible impact on the people of the Amazon basin.

> Slashers and burners in the Amazon are destroying the traditional way of life of the Amazon peoples, wasting irreplaceable virgin rainforest, drying and ruining the soil, and contributing to the general global warming known as the "greenhouse effect."

Can you pick out examples of each kind of slant? The writers have carefully chosen language that appeals to the audience's emotions. A careful and critical audience soon realizes that propaganda arouses the emotions.

SPECIAL WRITING PROJECT

> □ Write a short piece of propaganda on the subject of your choice (or telling why one political party is better or worse than another).
> □ With your partner, discuss your use of slant.

7. Slant in Writing

Read the following selection; then, using the questions that follow the selection, discuss it with your partner.

The Biodegradable Myth!
from *Probe Post*, Fall 1988
Colin Isaacs

Biodegradable has been rediscovered by the retail marketing sector as the latest gimmick with which to con the consumer and befuddle the politician. The word has been used on detergents and household cleaning products since the mid-1970s, but now biodegradable is also being used to describe plastic shopping bags, diapers and magazine wrappers. The public's desire to do something good for the environment has finally caught the attention of the advertisers, but, as seems common in advertising, neither the real meaning of the word biodegradable nor the products advertised as being biodegradable have anything to do with protection of the environment.

Dictionaries rarely keep up with current language use, and I found this to be true with the word biodegradable. I expected to find that biodegradable meant having the ability to break down under the action of natural organisms into basic substances like water and carbon dioxide. Indeed, I opened the dictionary expecting to find an environment-friendly definition with which I could lay a complaint of misleading advertising against a biodegradable bag promoter. Unfortunately, a hunt through many dictionaries came up with the definition "capable of decaying through the action of natural organisms." Decay is further defined as "a gradual falling into an inferior condition." In other words, biodegradable means very little!

Surely, people say to me, even if biodegradable only means "capable of falling apart," making disposable products biodegradable will at least help to alleviate our landfill problems. After all, landfills destroy neighbourhoods, waste prime agricultural or development land, and, because of the uncontrolled mess of material dumped into them, threaten both air quality and water quality. Unfortunately, switching to biodegradable plastics and such products as biodegradable diapers will not help solve any of these problems.

Biodegradable plastic is a mixture of starch and plastic blended together. The starch may be broken down by bacteria in the soil causing the plastic to fall apart. Unfortunately, small pieces of plastic are no better for the environment than "plastic sheet." Biodegradable hucksters claim that small pieces of plastic biodegrade more quickly than plastic sheet, but no less an authority than Dr. David Wiles, director of the National Research Council of Canada's division of chemistry, asserts plastics never break down, no matter what form they come in. In fact, Dr. Wiles goes on to say that it is just as well that plastic does not biodegrade, because breakdown would add to the already serious problem of gas and leachate production, possibly adding toxic chemicals much more damaging to the environment than the plastic wastes themselves.

Diapers are another contentious product. Both biodegradable and disposable diapers are made of a cellulose fibre or paper-like material and a plastic cover. In biodegradable diapers, the plastic is mixed with starch. Paper is one product that really does break down into basic materials under the action of naturally occurring bacteria: after all, that's how trees decay to maintain the viability of the forest. However, the breakdown does nothing to help our landfill situation, because the breakdown products of any throw-away diaper, disposable or biodegradable, take up just as much room in the landfill as the original, so we don't get to put more waste into the landfill, even if we wanted to. Worse still, the problem with diapers in landfills is the human waste. We don't allow medical waste and infectious waste into our landfills for obvious sanitary reasons, yet, each year, millions of tonnes of soiled diapers, possibly disease infected, are dumped into landfills not equipped to handle them. The environment is put at risk simply by the act of discarding them, even if they are biodegradable!

Biodegradable detergents are another marketing gimmick. Almost all detergent ingredients break down under the action of living organisms in water. Phosphates, often regarded as the environmentally damaging ingredient in detergents after they helped "kill" Lake Erie in the 1970s, are themselves biodegradable, and are actually consumed by living organisms so quickly as to cause runaway algal growth. This "algal bloom" can continue until all oxygen in the water has been used up, leading to the death through suffocation of most higher species such as fish. Phosphates are *too* biodegradable!

Wastes from some biodegradable products can cause problems because their breakdown products are toxic to higher species or because they contain additives or heavy metal salts which are released during the biological breakdown process. Concern of this kind exists for some types of printing ink and cleaning compounds, and for some of the additives included in plastics.

By giving a false sense of security, biodegradable products may remove part of the incentive for the environmentally sound 3Rs approach to waste management – reduce, reuse, and recycle. It is clearly better not to produce waste in the first place, or to reuse it, or to recyle it into new products than it is to continue dumping it into landfill sites. Further, biodegradable wastes, especially biodegradable plastic, may pose an even greater threat than just removing the incentive for recycling. Recyclers are being told that plastic waste containing even a fraction of starch will not be accepted for recycling, because the starch interferes with the recycling process and damages the quality and consistency of the recycled product. Plastics are difficult enough to recycle without this added problem! Unlike metal and glass containers, which can be recycled into brand-new containers, recycled plastics are generally used only for secondary products like fence posts or car bumpers where biodegradability is not wanted. Mixing biodegradable plastics into the waste stream will make it even more difficult to find recycling opportunities for waste plastics.

The word biodegradable is rapidly turning into the marketing manager's dream, once again to the detriment of the environment. When the plastic components on your next car fall apart, it might just be due to society's gullibility for the word.

Your Writing

1. Jot down at least three examples of slant in the piece. Then, with your partner, identify the author's point of view.

2. Which members of the community does the author present in an unfavorable light? How does he do so?

3. If you were the magazine editor writing the headline for this opinion piece, what would be your understanding of the word "myth"? Why would you use it here? How is the use of the word a kind of slanting?

4. With your partner, brainstorm a list of other "myths" around you. Consider saving some of these topics in your journal or in an idea file for future writing projects.

**SPECIAL
WRITING
PROJECT**

- ☐ Find a piece you have already written and rewrite it to give it a stronger slant, either positive or negative.
- ☐ Ask your partner to discuss the effectiveness of your use of slant. Does it help to achieve your purpose, or does it leave him or her unconvinced or mistrustful?

34 Satire

"Satire is a sort of glass wherein beholders do generally discover everybody's face but their own."

Jonathan Swift

To satirize is to ridicule a social ill, condition, or tradition; an aspect of the human condition; or even a specific person. Of all the types of writing, you will perhaps find satire the most difficult to write, although it is usually easy to see in other people's writing. Before you use satire in any format (from a serious expository essay to a humorous personal letter), you should decide whether the purpose and topic warrant a satiric treatment and whether your audience would appreciate it.

1. Selecting Topics

Satire blends facts and commentary, both of which must be present in a piece of satiric writing, so it's wise to begin thinking of satirical topics in areas that warrant commentary. For example, you and your partner can make a list of ten things that are wrong with politics, education, social behavior, or any other aspect of modern society.

Example of Fact
There are too many regulations to follow and forms to fill out.

Which item from your list would you find easiest to satirize? How would you satirize it?

Example of Satiric Treatment
In the future there will be so many forms to fill out that people will have to fill out an application simply to get permission to fill out an application.

With your partner, jot down a list of ten aspects of the human condition. Try to think of some of those silly, human things you do that seem serious at the time but that you laugh about afterward.

Example
When you discover a blemish on your face, you think everyone notices.

Which item from your list would you find easiest to satirize? How would you satirize it?

Example of Satiric Treatment
When I noticed my first … oh, I can't say the word … but when I noticed It, I knew I would have to go into hiding until my face cleared up.

2.   Satire in Cartoons

You can see satire at work in newspapers. Almost every editorial page has a political cartoon depicting the latest actions of civic, provincial, federal, or world leaders. No one is immune to the mockery of a cartoonist. To appreciate satiric cartoons you need to have background knowledge. For example, in the following cartoon, what do you have to know about the Four Horsemen? Where would you find out? Could you guess and still get some appreciation of the cartoon?

1. Bring two satiric cartoons to class. Exchange them with your partner. Discuss what is being satirized. Study each cartoon carefully to see the overall effect as well as the details. What is being held up to ridicule?

2. With your partner, select an event or a person to satirize. Sketch a cartoon that would accomplish your satiric message. Write a caption, too.

3.   Sardonic Satire

Many columnists satirize society's ills. Of the many specific kinds of satire they could use, they seem to delight in airing their insults in sardonic (biting, contemptuous, usually witty) ways.

1. Find a column that uses sardonic satire, and discuss it with your partner. Try to come to a conclusion on the following:
a) What exactly does the columnist want changed?
b) In what ways is the satire sardonic?

> *Example*
> The television, surely the most misused invention in the history of humanity, dispenses violence as regularly as deodorant commercials. Slayings are fed to us as we eat our TV dinners. We have gotten to the point where we can tune out the violence in our society as easily as we tune out the sponsor's message.
>
> *Analysis*
> a) The writer does not want violence on TV because viewers become accustomed to violence.
> b) By comparing the regular appearance of violence to the constant advertising of deodorants, he shows sardonic satire.

2. With a partner read "Griefkit" at the end of this chapter. Comment on the tone of this performance piece. Is the tone an element of the satire? What other elements make the piece satiric?

3. With your partner choose a topic that angers you. Use sardonic satire to write about your subject.

4.   Invective

Reviewers and critics are sometimes unkind. They will often pour out satirical **invective** (a verbal attack often using insults) as they write a critique of a book, play, movie, or event.

1. Find an example of a critic's invective satire, and exchange it with your partner.
a) What has displeased the critic?

b) Is invective the most effective means of commenting? Would another type of satire or a straightforward review have worked as well? Why do you say so?

Example

"The orchestra ... was, of course, out of sight in the pit, but the curious sounds that wafted forth from the bunker-like refuge gave the impression that much of the score was being played on jugs and bottles, combs and toilet tissue, and, possibly, kazoos."

Christopher Dafoe

Analysis

a) Dafoe was displeased with the quality of the music.
b) Simply saying "The orchestra did not play well" would not create the impact of this review. Neither would it suggest how badly the orchestra played, in the critic's view. If the music was truly bad and people wasted their money by buying tickets, the invective may be justified.

2. With your partner, write an example of invective about a movie, book, television show, concert, or recording that disappointed you. You might exchange your completed work with another pair of students and discuss the effectiveness of the piece you receive.

3. Discuss with your partner Michael Darling's use of satire, rhetorical devices, and figurative language and allusions. (See section 7 of this chapter.) You might experiment with writing a similar review of a collection of literature you are familiar with.

5.   Parody

On television and stage you often see an impressionist who satirizes well-known celebrities, politicians, or movie stars. The impressionist obviously has studied the subjects very well in order to **parody** them (make fun of them through exaggeration).

1. Talk about parodists with your partner. Do you have a favorite? Weird Al Yankovic writes and sings parodies of popular songs, and André-Philippe Gagnon has his own parody of "We Are the World." SCTV, Saturday Night Live, and Monty Python frequently use parody in their skits. Some of Mel Brooks's movies are parodies of other movies, and Ogden Nash wrote parodies of famous poems. Make a list of all the personal things that are parodied by a successful parodist. Think of a parody you have seen or read recently. Describe for your partner how you identified the object of the parody.

2. If you imitate another writer to poke fun, you are parodying. You can do this by imitating the writer's style and tone or by using words from the original piece (as Stefan Gerber has done in "Tomorrow's Technology." See section 7 of this chapter).

Many school songs are parodies. You and your partner might experiment with writing a new song for your school. Choose a popular song, and use many of its original words as well as its rhythm and melody. You might begin by writing out the original to see which words you need to change to fit your school. Although a parody can contain invective, you might try to keep yours good-natured.

3. Here are three famous and often-parodied quotations from Shakespeare. Working separately from your partner, write a parody of each (or choose one or more that you'd prefer to work with).

a) from *Hamlet*

To be, or not to be that is the question:
Whether 'tis nobler in the mind to suffer
The slings and arrows of outrageous fortune,
Or to take arms against a sea of troubles,
And by opposing, end them.

Sample first line of parody: To pass, or not to pass, that is my problem.

b) from *Romeo and Juliet*

O Romeo, Romeo, wherefore art thou Romeo?
Deny thy father and refuse thy name;
Or, if thou wilt not, be but sworn my love,
And I'll no longer be a Capulet.

c) from *Macbeth*

Tomorrow, and tomorrow, and tomorrow,
Creeps in this petty pace from day to day,
To the last syllable of recorded time;
And all our yesterdays have lighted fools
The way to dusty death.

6. Irony

Irony may be used to achieve satire. Irony is a figure of speech in which the words express a meaning that is often the direct opposite of the intended meaning. For example, if someone says to you, "Lovely weather, eh?" when there is a sub-zero blizzard, that person would be either grossly out of touch with reality or ironically satirizing the weather.

Although you can often use irony effectively, avoid using **sarcasm**, a form of irony used to wound a hearer or reader. Sarcasm is usually found in speech, where tone of voice can make a biting taunt even more biting.

1. Working separately from your partner, write a piece of irony satirizing a social problem or an aspect of the human condition.

Many writers of irony adopt a persona, making sure that readers will know that what the persona thinks is not what the writer really thinks. In Jonathan Swift's *Gulliver's Travels*, for example, Lemuel Gulliver praises people's ability to wage war. But the reader knows that Swift really condemns the bloodthirsty practices his persona praises.

Some writers adopt a persona – perhaps a philosopher, scientist, professor, or politician – who spouts pretentious and absurd ideas. Other writers use a persona who pleads ignorance and in an innocent but shrewd way exposes the silliness of commonly accepted practices or attitudes. If you use a persona as a vehicle for irony, the kind that you use is up to you.

2. Share and discuss your ironic piece with your partner.

3. Read "Sports or Music?" (in section 7 of this chapter), an ironic story about a sibling relationship. With your partner discuss the ironic reversal upon which the story hinges and how the author emphasizes the ironic reversal.

7.   Recognizing Satire

Read the following examples of satire. With your partner, discuss what each writer is satirizing and the devices of satire that the writers use.

Griefkit
Kate Lushington

Good evening. My name is Veronica Mandel, and I've come to talk to you tonight about the psychiatric effects of nuclear war, or what can be done for mental health after the Bomb has dropped.

American psychiatrist Robert Jay Lifton has identified one of the major problem areas as "psychic numbing": a profound blandness, insensitivity, and inability to experience grief – or indeed to feel anything at all. This will be detrimental to our continued development as whole human beings inside the bomb shelter, and may seriously limit our capacity to form co-operating groups in the new world outside.

The natural mourning process, which could alleviate the severe symptoms of "psychic numbing," will be inhibited in many cases, or made very difficult, by the absence of bodies to bury – through vaporization, incineration, or other forms of corporeal annihilation. It is hard to bury a shadow on the wall. Another problem with nuclear devastation is its scale. Try to imagine one hundred million dead. Try it. And of those of us left, how many will be therapists? On a more individual level, it is unlikely that we will survive together with anyone close to us, or even be anywhere near our loved ones at the moment of impact. In the aftermath, the process of grieving and saying goodbye to those we have lost may assume supreme importance.

It is vital – and I use the word in its original sense of "essential to life" – that we are all prepared, in the event of nuclear attack, to be our own therapists. There are self-help books now available: *Good Life, Good Death*, by Dr. Christian Barnard; *Positive Thinking at a Time Like This*, by Norman Vincent Peale; *How To Be Awake and Alive*, by Mildred Newman and Bernard Berkowitz. These are no longer enough. Researching into more appropriate ways to meet an imminent need, psychologists have devised a "griefkit," to keep always by you in a safe, accessible place. It is very simple, consisting of ordinary household items:

- a box, with a well-fitting lid – clearly marked with your name
- a cushion or pillow
- photographs of the people you love
- a safety pin
- some kitty litter.

In the coming emergency, we believe that grief and mourning must have their place: the dead, as well as the living, need space. To this end there will be racks made available for griefboxes in every government shelter, but it is up to the individual to be responsible for his or her own kit. So, when the warning sounds, be sure to bring yours with you. Your future sanity could depend upon it.

Now, how to use your griefkit:

Place the pillow directly in front of you. Take the photographs one by one and name them, give them a name, their name:

- Grandad
- Suzy and Michelle
- Bill
- Jimmy
- Anita.

Visualize them. See them smile. Hear them breathe. Now, take a safety pin and pin your loved ones to the griefpillow. Say to yourself: "This is me. I am here and I am alive. These are the people I love. They had their own individual existence, and now they are dead." Take the pillow and hold it to you for a moment. (*Pause.*) Now, bury them: place the pillow in the griefbox, take some kitty litter, a handful should be enough, and sprinkle it over the ones you love, repeating:

"Death is random, death is not fair,
death is random, death is not fair,
death is random ..."

When you are ready to say goodbye, close the lid firmly and put your box away alongside the others, making sure you can find it again handily should the need arise.

Remember, when the nuclear warning is given, if you bring nothing else, bring this. It may mean the difference to your emotional well-being, after the Bomb has dropped.

Thank you.

from "Canadian Writing 1987: A Review"
Michael Darling

Let us begin with an appropriate example of the Canadian book in the post-literate age: *The Solitary Outlaw*, by B. W. Powe. This is a work that has been called "dazzling," whose pages are said to "crackle with anger, brilliance, energy, authority, and a sweeping range of vision," and which is confidently proclaimed "the most important [book] of the year." Of course, all this puffery did appear in *Books in Canada*, but it is disturbing none the less to find a book as egregiously bad as this one being praised in such hyperbolic terms. Only in Canada, you say? Pity.

Powe's book consists of five essays on twentieth-century intellectuals who might also be considered "solitary outlaws": Wyndham Lewis, Marshall McLuhan, Pierre Elliott Trudeau, Glenn Gould, and Elias Canetti. The idea of Trudeau as an intellectual is, as his ex-wife might put it, beyond reason, but let that pass for the moment. The main problem with the book is that its form and content are irrevocably opposed. Powe deplores post-literature culture but reflects it in every paragraph of his writing. His style is a bizarre mixture of the ponderous and the elliptical, and can best be described as "*Chatelaine* edited by Margaret Atwood." One-word paragraphs shout "Significant Word Here!" Sentence fragments replace independent clauses in order to show emphasis. The colon is used interminably. It says: I am now going to say something important. There is much use of blank space, different typefaces, bold type, quotation, epigraphs, and so on. The long shadow of McLuhan falls heavily across the page. Indeed, the whole book might more accurately be titled *A McLuhanite Discovers His Master's Voice in Unexpected Places*. But I must not digress. Here is a random sampling of the sins of Powe:

> Or: if you are conscious and intelligent, you are outside the mainstream.
> Picture: a World War I battlefield
> We add: the origin of the tragic may be in a person trying to become a machine.
> The effect: of a mind thinking, not a unified theory.
> The reaction: bewildered.

Particularly offensive is his repeated use of "Note" followed by a colon, as in "Note: the word 'zero' is repeated with ominous regularity in his last books." Powe has evidently learned the use of the colon from high school mathematics textbooks.

When he is not being self-consciously clever (Powe has all the right qualities to review books for *The Journal*), he descends into the flatlands of cliché: "go with the flow," "Lest we forget," "the media's darling," "Caveat lector," "political chameleon." But the banal journalist-Powe is a great deal easier to take than the social philosopher-Powe who is capable of producing nonsense like the following:

The average novelist-poet-critic (each vocation distinct from the other; you must accept your box in the Great White North) stumbling in from the nineteenth-century bush, taught to detest North American society, having received the blessings of the Two Essential Grants (George and the Canada Council), after ripping out in record time (ten years) yet another work on the True Themes (bestiality and the Small Town) – well, you wouldn't expect those who claim that they don't do research to see that electric politics determine most of our social-cultural environment.

Does this make any sense at all? Is this supposed to pass for wit, for insight, for informed reflection on the state of Canadian writing? Of course, this is only one paragraph, and as Powe succinctly reminds us, "with certain writers you have to read a lot of their work before you can approach what they say."

The book is replete with quotations set off by their own bold-type headlines. Alas, few of these quotations are even vaguely related to the subject under discussion. They intrude into the text with all the pertinence of a sanitary-napkin commercial during the broadcast of a football game. What follows, though regrettably unaccented by the three different typefaces of the original version, is vintage Powe:

> Concentration is constantly shattered; the word is processed; and ours may already be the anti-book world that Lewis anticipated.
> SOLITARY OUTWIT
> You can't expect people to pay you for enjoying yourself! Pound to Lewis. Yet when I return to Lewis's writings, I find pleasure in his outmoded demand for truth …

Powe evidently subscribes to the Maidenform-bras theory of quotation, hoping that other people's words will lift and separate his own flaccid prose into something shapely and aesthetically pleasing. Unfortunately, the attempt sags noticeably.

I give *The Solitary Outlaw* pride of place in this review because it is the very best example of that "sadly undistinguished" prose that B.W. Powe has discovered in Canada. I warn of its baneful existence because Norman Snider, writing in the *Globe and Mail*, calls it "endlessly provocative, mandatory reading for anybody in this country who still cares about reading, writing or ideas." I lament – in bold type – its publication because it panders to the debased literary values of the Norman Sniders who form the tastes of Canadian readers. I predict that *The Solitary Outlaw* will win the Governor General's Award for Non-Fiction. It is that bad.

Tomorrow's Technology
Stefan Gerber, student

O, say can you see
By the nuclear light
What so loudly we ruin
By the victim's last glowing
With their eyes bulging out
Radiation about
We see no day after
'Cause there's no one left living
And the rocket's red glare
The bombs bursting in air
Gave proof through the night
That mankind doesn't care
O, say do these mortals continue to rave
Of the land of the free and the home of the grave?

Sports or Music?
Billy T.P. Chan, student

When I was about twelve years old, my brother, with a songbook in his hand, came to me saying, "Come on, Billy, Let's sing this song together." Cesar, my dear brother, was at that time a real music lover. He had a children's songbook with him wherever he went. Cesar had a very pretty voice; everybody liked it; and he happily sang the songs from his songbook to my parents and to every visiting friend or relative who would listen to him. When my brother asked me to sing with him, I always refused. I would rather watch soccer and baseball games on TV, and my brother felt frustrated.

Sports were my passion. I never missed any soccer, baseball, or other game on TV. I was familiar with every player of every team of every game of every kind of sport. I especially tried to convince Cesar that sports were better than music; I even said once, "Music will not help you in anything; it won't give you health or money. Sport, however, is a good exercise for your mind and body, and you can also make money if you are a sports star." I still remember these words, and now I regret having said them.

A couple of years later, I started to learn the guitar – because of my parents' pressure. After playing several classical and modern songs, I learned about the greatest melodies, singers and musicians in the world. My parents and friends said I was splendid when I played the guitar, and this motivated me to improve my talent as a musician. "It would be wonderful if Cesar sings as I play the guitar," I thought. "We could make money if we started a musical career." By this time, I was not interested in sports anymore. I was totally devoted to music. I knew so much about music. My passion was music.

The trouble was that when I changed my interest, my brother was changing his, too! Gradually, he had become a sports fan; I still cannot understand how. He knew everything I knew (and more) about sports, so today, he is totally familiar with every player of every team of every game of every kind of sport. One day, I asked him to sing a song as I played the guitar. He refused. He would rather watch baseball and hockey games on TV, and I felt frustrated.

SPECIAL WRITING PROJECT

- □ Investigate your present surroundings for something you can satirize for your partner. Keep in mind that you cannot suddenly drop a single example of irony, parody, and so on, into your straightforward, logical prose. Your entire piece of writing should have a satiric tone.
- □ Share your satiric piece, and discuss the methods of satire you used.

35 Research Skills and Documentation

"Knowledge is of two kinds. We know a subject ourselves, or we know where we can find information upon it."

Samuel Johnson

Much of this chapter deals with the second kind of knowledge: knowledge of how and where to find information. This kind, essential if you are preparing to write a research paper, is also very useful for other kinds of informative writing.

The rest of the chapter deals with documentation: the currently accepted forms for showing where you got your information.

1. A Library Tour

Before you and your partner work with specific references such as the card catalogue, take a library tour to find out what your school or local library has to offer and where different kinds of material are located. In particular, make note of the following.

The card catalogue. Some catalogues are on cards classified by subjects, titles, and authors; some are wholly or partly on microfilm or microfiche (microfilm on plastic sheets); and some are on computers. No matter what system your library uses, take some time to learn how to find the **call numbers** of the books in the library's collection. The call number allows you to locate the section of the library where a book is shelved. Call numbers are based on either the Library of Congress system or the Dewey decimal system. (You'll learn more about these systems in this chapter.)

The reference area. This area contains important research books, as well as dictionaries, encyclopedias, indexes, atlases, and almanacs. These reference books are not usually allowed out of the library. If you use the reference area a good deal, you will soon get to know where specific reference works are kept.

The periodical area. Most well-stocked libraries subscribe to current magazines and newspapers. Back issues are often bound in hardcover, year by year, or kept on microfilm. To find out how to get back issues, ask the reference librarian.

The media area. Many libraries contain collections of tapes, records, slides, films, microfilm, and microfiche. To familiarize yourself with this area, plan to spend some time there. You may find, for instance, that you are able to borrow a film or set of slides to help you with a special presentation you have to make.

The vertical file. Many libraries maintain files that contain pamphlets and clippings on various subjects.

The stacks. The stacks, often the largest part of a library, contain the library's books. Books are usually divided into fiction and nonfiction, with fiction arranged alphabeticallly according to author and nonfiction arranged according to either the Dewey decimal system or the Library of Congress system.

1. After you and your partner tour your school or community library, chart or map the location of the following kinds of material: (a) fiction books; (b) nonfiction books; (c) an unabridged dictionary; (d) the card catalogue; (e) encyclopedias; (f) magazines; (g) newspapers; (h) the media area; and (i) the vertical file. As well, indicate any special features of your library.

2. Try to find answers to the following. If you are not sure about an answer, consult the librarian, unquestionably a library's most important resource. Most librarians have a knowledge of and love for their collections and are only too glad to encourage you to get to know their library. So if you have not already done so, make yourself known to your local librarian.
a) Are the nonfiction books in the library organized according to the Dewey decimal or Library of Congress system?
b) What is the smallest dictionary in the library? The largest?
c) Does the library have any special-purpose encyclopedias, such as scientific or biographical encyclopedias?
d) Give the title of one world atlas in the library.
e) Which almanacs does the library's reference section contain? What information does an almanac provide?
f) Name two current magazines and one newspaper available in the library.
g) Which index(es) to periodical literature does the library have?
h) If the library has a media area, what does it offer?

i) If the library does not have a book you want, can it help you get that book through interlibrary loan?

2. The Card Catalogue

If you want to find a book about a particular subject, you can use the slow way – browsing among the shelves – or the fast way – consulting the card catalogue, microfiche, or computer.

Almost all libraries keep a record of their books on a catalogue system, arranged alphabetically either in a set of cabinets with small drawers or on microfiche or a computer. There are at least two entries for a fiction book: one under the name of the author, the other under the title. There are at least three entries for a nonfiction book: author, title, and subject. Some books can be classified under more than one subject, and so there is more than one subject entry for them. Notice the following example:

```
971.034              Canada-History-War of 1812
BER


    971.034              War of 1812
    BER

            Berton, Pierre
                Flames across the border
                Toronto, McClelland and Stewart, 1981
                    492 p.: maps
                Includes index.
                Ports on lining papers.
                Bibliography: p. 465-479
```

In addition to author, title, and subject, a catalogue system provides other information.

The call number. The book's call number, appearing in the upper-left corner of the catalogue card, is based on either the Dewey decimal system (which uses number codes) or the Library of Congress system (which places letter codes for subjects first, followed by number codes). These codes help you locate the books on the shelves. For example, in the illustration of the card for Pierre Berton's book, you'll notice the call letters 971.034 in the upper-left corner. Underneath are the first three letters of the author's name. You would go to the 971 shelf and look for 971.034 on the spine of the books, facing you. Then you would look alphabetically for the Bs until you came to BER. Most Canadian school and public libraries are using this Dewey decimal system, while Canadian colleges and universities prefer the Library of Congress system.

Other useful information. The card catalogue indicates the publisher of the book, the year it was published, how many pages it has, and its special features, if any. The publication date suggests how up-to-date the information is. Sometimes you may want the very latest information. If you wanted the most recent book about the war of 1812, would you consult *Flames Across the Border*?

The publisher's name is sometimes useful. Certain publishers have a reputation for publishing especially fine books in such fields as medicine, engineering, or art history. Who published *Flames Across the Border*?

The special features can help you, for example, if you need maps tracing explorers' routes in the New World. From the catalogue card, you can quickly and easily find out whether a book contains maps. The special features will also tell you if a book has a bibliography to direct you to other sources of information. If a book is illustrated or has portraits, the special features will show this. Does *Flames Across the Border* provide illustrations or have other special features?

Some catalogue cards also indicate other categories under which a book can be found. If you are trying to think of a related subject to look up, this information can be useful. Under what category other than the author card of "Pierre Berton" could you find *Flames Across the Border*? Where is this information given on the author card?

1. With your partner, research the following subjects in the catalogue system. List the author, title, call number, publication date, publisher, and special features of a book about each subject.

nuclear energy	African folklore
scientists	famous suffragists
Canadian poets	motor racing
the plays of Shakespeare	ancient Mayan civilization
nutrition	the pyramids

2. With your partner, discuss your research and what you discovered about the card catalogue.

SPECIAL WRITING PROJECT

□ Write a short set of instructions on how to locate a specific nonfiction book in your library. Assume you are writing to someone who does not know the library.

□ Invite your partner to follow your instructions.

3. How Libraries Organize Books: The Dewey Decimal and Library of Congress Systems

Libraries organize their nonfiction books according to the Library of Congress or Dewey decimal systems. Many college and university libraries and large research libraries (and, of course, the Library of Congress) use the Library of Congress system, which classifies books by letter and number codes. The letter *A*, for example, indicates general works; *J* indicates books about political science; *N*, books about the fine arts; and *P*, books about language and literature. Most other libraries – including school and local libraries – use the Dewey decimal system.

Melvil Dewey was a student library assistant at Amherst College when, in 1872, he began to develop this system for organizing a library's books. Since then, many libraries have adopted his system, which uses the numbers 0 to 999 to classify books.

Major Categories of the Dewey Decimal System

000–099: General works, including encyclopedias, yearbooks, guides, almanacs, and books about journalism and library science

100–199: Philosophy, including logic, ethics, and ancient, medieval, and modern philosophy

200–299: Religion, including the Bible, the history of religions, and devotional and practical religion

300–399: Social sciences, including political science, economics, public administration, and education

400–499: Language, including the study of language and dictionaries and grammars of various languages

500–599: Pure science, including mathematics, astronomy, physics, chemistry, earth sciences, and biology

600–699: Technology, including medicine, engineering, agriculture, and chemical technology

700–799: The arts, including architecture, sculpture, painting, photography, music, theatre, films, recreation, and sports

800–899: Literature, including fiction, poetry, drama, and the literature of nations

900–999: History and related subjects, including geography, travel, biography, Canadian history, and the histories of other nations

---

Just like decimal numbers, Dewey decimal categories can be divided and subdivided. For example, the category 900–999 (History) subdivides into the following categories:

Major Categories of the Dewey Decimal System: History

900–909: General Geography and History
910–919: Geography and Travel
920–929: Biography and Genealogy
930–939: History of the Ancient World
940–949: History of Europe
950–959: History of Asia
960–969: History of Africa
970–979: History of North America
980–989: History of South America
990–999: History of Other Areas

These categories can, in turn, divide into even more specific categories. For example, 970–979 includes 971 (Canadian history), 972 (Central American and Caribbean history), and 973–979 (U.S. history), and each of these has further subdivisions. Pierre Berton's book *Flames Across the Border* carries the Dewey number 971.034 (the category for the War of 1812).

Even though you will probably be relying more on the call numbers from the catalogue to find books about a particular subject, a general knowledge of the Dewey decimal categories can be useful when you research. When you know the Dewey number of a subject you want to research, you can simply walk to a shelf to see what books your library has.

1. Working independently of your partner, find the general categories under which you will likely find the following books. (A history of British drama, for example, would be found under the general category 800–899 – Literature.)
a) a Spanish dictionary
b) a book about raising cattle
c) a book about the Super Bowl
d) a book about French Impressionist painting
e) a book about recent discoveries in physics
f) a book about the early Christian Church
g) a history of French settlements in North America
h) a book about the economics of running a small business
i) a book about encyclopedias
j) a collection of modern British poetry

2. Compare your findings with your partner's.

4.   Information about Information: *The Readers' Guide to Periodical Literature* and Other Indexes

Indexes are guides to publications in which information can be found: magazines, newspapers, books, and other sources. Probably the most widely used index, and the one you will use most, is *The Readers' Guide to Periodical Literature*, a guide to information in magazines.

The Readers' Guide lists all the articles published within a certain period of time in a variety of magazines. This guide comes in several forms: as a paperbound booklet published twenty-two times a year; as a thicker booklet covering three months of publication; and as a hardbound book, serving as a guide to articles published in a year.

When using *The Readers' Guide*, be sure to check the period it covers. If you want the very latest information, consult the most recent *Readers' Guide* you can find. If you are looking for information about an event that took place during a certain year, look first in *The Readers' Guide* for that year.

Like a card catalogue, *The Readers' Guide* organizes its information alphabetically under both author's name and subject. Information is presented in a compact form, almost in a kind of code. But you can crack the code with very little effort.

Suppose you wanted to find articles about Michael J. Fox, and you looked in *The Readers' Guide* for November 1987. You would find:

Fox, Michael J.

about
Little big guy: Michael J. Fox. il pors *McCalls* 114:70 Ag '87
Michael J. Fox [excerpt from The Michael J. Fox scrapbook]
M. Kasbah. il pors *Good Housekeeping* 205: 50+ Ag '87

This entry indicates that an article called "Little big guy: Michael J. Fox" appears on page 70 of the August 1987 issue of *McCall's* magazine. (The notation "114:70" indicates first the volume number of the magazine and, after the colon, the page number of the article.) This article contains both illustrations ("il") and portraits ("pors") of Fox. The second article appears in the August 1987 issue of *Good Housekeeping* and also contains illustrations and portraits.

As you can see, *The Readers' Guide* makes extensive use of abbreviations. If you are puzzled by an abbreviation, consult the key to abbreviations at the front of the *Guide*.

You can use *The Readers' Guide* as you would a card catalogue. If you are looking for articles by a particular writer, look for entries under that writer's name. If you are looking for articles about a particular subject, look for that subject heading. Like many card catalogues, *The Readers' Guide* indicates other related headings under which articles can be found. For example:

Canadian helicopters *See* Helicopters
Canadian literature
    See also
    Children's literature – Canada
Canadian Medical Association
    Ethical issues of AIDS. A. Steacy. *Macleans* 100:46 S 7 '87
Canadian nuclear submarines *See* Nuclear submarines, Canadian
Canadian Odeon Theatres Ltd.
    See also
    Cineplex Odeon Corporation
Canadian Radio-Television and Telecommunications Commission
    The contest for cable. P. Young. il *Macleans* 100:46 Ag 24 '87
    The fight to rule the airwaves. M. Janigan. il *Macleans* 100:49-50 Jl 20 '87
Canadian rock groups *See* Rock groups

With your partner read the above excerpt from *The Readers' Guide*. Make sure you can indicate titles of articles, magazine titles, volumes, page numbers, dates, and so on.

SPECIAL WRITING PROJECT

☐ Copy an entry from *The Readers' Guide to Periodical Literature* as it appears in the *Guide*. Then, in a sentence or two, restate its information.
☐ Compare your restatement with your partner's and discuss which best sums up the information given in *The Readers' Guide*.

For example, the entry for the second article about Michael J. Fox on the previous page can be restated as follows.

An article about Michael J. Fox comes from an excerpt from his scrapbook. It begins on page 50 and goes on for several pages of the August 1987 (Volume 205) issue of *Good Housekeeping* magazine. The article is accompanied by illustrations and portraits.

Other useful indexes include:

Biography Index
Book Review Digest (guide to reviews of books published in a particular year; also includes excerpts from reviews)
Canadian Periodical Index
Essay and General Literature Index
Facts on File
Granger's Index to Poetry
Humanities Index

New York Times Index (guide to all articles published in the *New York Times*; especially useful for information on current events and events occurring in a particular year)
Short Story Index
Social Sciences Index

5.   Encyclopedias and Other Useful Reference Works

In addition to indexes, libraries have many other reference works, including encyclopedias, atlases, almanacs, and biographical works. You'll likely find these books useful when you are doing research, so take some time to familiarize yourself with the information they contain.

Encyclopedias. Encyclopedias are essentially collections of articles about a wealth of subjects. Most encyclopedias consist of many volumes and organize their articles alphabetically. The latest edition of the *Encyclopaedia Britannica*, the most comprehensive general-use encyclopedia, is an exception to this rule.

If you wish to consult the *Britannica*, you should know that it is organized into a one-volume *Propaedia*, which provides an outline of all the information in the encyclopedia and also functions as a topical guide to the *Macropaedia*, which contains more than 4,000 long, comprehensive articles on a great variety of subjects. The *Micropaedia* contains more than 100,000 much shorter articles.

(Many libraries have an earlier, as well as the latest, edition of the *Encyclopaedia Britannica*. Earlier editions of this work do, like other encyclopedias, organize their articles alphabetically.)

Other useful encyclopedias include:

The Canadian Encyclopedia
Collier's Encyclopedia
Encyclopedia Americana
World Book Encyclopedia

In addition, the following one- and two-volume encyclopedias provide useful introductions to many subjects:

Columbia Encyclopedia
Random House Encyclopedia

Almanacs. Almanacs are collections of facts and statistics, many of them in the form of lists. If you look in an almanac, you might find the following:

a perpetual calendar
noted personalities and entertainers
Pulitzer Prize winners
Nobel prize winners
a table showing some endangered North American wildlife species

Useful almanacs include:

Canadian Almanac and Directory
Information Please Almanac
New York Times Encyclopedic Almanac
The World Almanac and Book of Facts

Atlases and Gazetteers. An atlas is a collection of maps. Many atlases also provide statistics and information about such things as climate or population distribution in a country. A gazetteer is a geographical dictionary that organizes its information alphabetically under the names of places.

Useful atlases and gazetteers include:

Columbia-Lippincott Gazetteer of the World
Historical Atlas of Canada
Macmillan Atlas of Canada
National Geographic Atlas of the World
Rand McNally Cosmopolitan World Atlas
Times Family Atlas of the World
Webster's New Geographical Dictionary

Biographical reference works. In addition to individual biographies, libraries have books that provide information about many noted persons.

Useful biographical reference works include:

Current Biography (articles about newsworthy persons)
Dictionary of Canadian Biography
Dictionary of National Biography
Who's Who (various volumes: British, Canadian, and U.S.)

The following works may be useful for literary research:

American Authors 1600–1900
Benét's Reader's Encyclopedia
British Authors Before 1900
The Oxford Companion to Canadian History and Literature
The Oxford Companion to English Literature
Something About the Author
Twentieth Century Authors and *Twentieth Century Authors: First Supplement*
World Authors: 1950–1970

6. Researching

When you are preparing to write a research paper, you will likely need to spend a few hours in the library, gathering facts. The following suggestions should make your research easier.

1. Use an index card or individual sheet of paper for each piece of information you gather. Write one note per card or sheet so that you can organize your notes as you wish.

2. If you plan to quote directly or indirectly from a book, make up a bibliographic entry for it. The card should look something like this:

Call number	971.034 BER
Author's name	Berton, Pierre
Title	<u>Flames Across the Border</u>
Facts of publication	Toronto: McClelland and Stewart, 1981

3. At the top of the next card or sheet of paper, write a subject heading to help you organize and find your information quickly. Identify the source of your quotation by listing the author's last name and the page number on which you found the quotation. When you quote an author's exact words, use quotation marks around them; in this way you will help yourself avoid unintentional plagiarism. Your entry should look like this:

Berton, p. 424   Who won the War?

"Having won the last battle, the Americans were convinced that they won the War of 1812. Having stemmed the tide of invasion and kept the Americans out of their country, Canadians believed that they won the war. Having ceded nothing they considered important, the British were serene in the conviction that they won it."

4. Wherever possible, summarize what you read. This way, you can select and extract what is important to your purpose. Too many quotations in a research essay or report may give your audience the feeling that you have not written it but have merely strung together statements made by others. When you summarize long portions in your research notes, you should still identify the source and provide a subject heading.

Berton, pp. 96-99   The burning of York

On July 31, 1813, 250 American troops under the command of Commodore Isaac Chauncey landed in York, now Toronto. The Americans seized all the supplies they could, evacuated the town, burned all the buildings, and sailed away the next day.

5. For practice, have your partner make up a research topic for you, or use one of the following: foreign aid, cross-country skiing, medieval mystery plays, Wayne Gretzky, the lumber industry, amnesia. Then go to the library.

a) Write on an index card or individual sheet of paper one direct quote that you would use if you were to write an essay on the topic.

b) On another index card or sheet of paper write out the bibliographical information on the book you used.

c) Find another book or magazine on your topic and write a summary of the information you would use if you were to write the essay. If your summary takes up more than one card or page, indicate at the top of each card: 1st of 2 and 2nd of 2. This will help you to keep your information organized.

d) On a fourth index card or sheet of paper write out the bibliographical information on the book or magazine you used for (c).

e) Invite your partner to check your notes for completeness.

7.   Parenthetical Citations: Documenting Your Sources Within a Research Paper

Documenting means backing up all the quotations and information you use by showing where you found them. You document a research paper in two ways:

you include a bibliography listing all your sources at the end of the paper (bibliographies are discussed in the following section), and you acknowledge a source each time you present someone else's information or opinion or a quotation within the paper.

1. The traditional way of indicating sources in a research paper is through footnotes. In 1984, however, the Modern Language Association (MLA), an organization of scholars, recommended a new method now used in most colleges and universities. The new method is easier to use and makes your research paper easier to read.

2. As recommended by the MLA, a writer shows a source by using a **parenthetical citation**, a brief reference in parentheses. Such a reference is enclosed *within* the sentence presenting the information, quotation, or idea. The most common parenthetical citation includes both the name of the author of the book or article from which the information came and the page number on which the information can be found. For example, a paper about the War of 1812 might contain the following citation that refers to a direct quotation:

> Who won the War of 1812? After the war, all the combatants claimed victory: "Having won the last battle, the Americans were convinced that they won the War of 1812. Having stemmed the tide of invasion and kept the Americans out of their country, Canadians believed that they won the war. Having ceded nothing they considered important, the British were serene in the conviction that they won it" (Berton 424).

Notice that no mark of punctuation separates the author's last name from the page reference and that the period ending the sentence appears *after* the parenthetical citation.

3. In another paragraph, the writer presents information from the same book without quoting it directly. Nevertheless, she does cite the source of her information.

> According to Pierre Berton, two hundred fifty American troops landed at York, now Toronto, on July 31, 1813. After seizing all the supplies they could find, they burned the town and left (96–99).

Because the student mentions Berton's name in her own prose, she does not have to put his name in parentheses.

4. If you are using two books or articles by the same author, then include a shortened form of the title (the first word or two). In this case, a comma should separate the author and title, but no punctuation should separate the title and page number. For example, assume you included the following two books by Desmond Morton: *A Military History of Canada* and *A Short History of Canada*. Notice how one writer included parenthetical citations from these books in her essay:

An examination of the results of the war shows why no one could truly claim victory. "The war changed no boundaries, brought no reparations, avenged no wrongs" (Morton, <u>Short</u> 34). However, "The war had been good to most British North Americans, … [and] traces of destruction were hard to find within months of the peace" (Morton, <u>Military</u> 70).

The writer has used ellipses (…) in the quotation to indicate that she left out part of it. She has also used square brackets within one of the quotations to indicate that she added "and" to the original quotation.

5. If you quote or give information from a book or article by two authors, use both their last names in the parenthetical citation. If no author is mentioned, use a shortened version of the title. You may have to do this when you cite from magazines, newspapers, dictionaries, encyclopedias, and handbooks. In the following example, the writer has enclosed the short version of an article's title in quotation marks ("War").

Twenty-eight American soldiers who died during the attack on Fort Erie were saluted by representatives of Canada and the U.S. "The victims ranged in age from mid-teens to 40…. Archaeologists were able to determine that the skeletons were American but were unable to make individual identifications" ("War"). The soldiers' bones were re-buried at Arlington National Cemetery, near Washington, D.C.

The following full citation will then appear in the bibliography.

"War of 1812 victims honored." <u>Vancouver Sun</u>, June 30, 1988: B8.

If the shortened title were a book's title, you would underline it or put it in italics.

6. Often in research papers, you might use several dictionaries or encyclopedias. So that the reader knows exactly which one you are referring to, set up your parenthetical citations this way:

Troops on both sides of the War of 1812 probably subsisted on a native North American food known as pemmican. "Originally prepared by North American Indians" ("Pemmican," <u>Random</u>), pemmican's main ingredients were "dried lean meat pounded into a paste with melted fat" ("Pemmican," <u>Senior</u>). They sometimes added "dried fruit or berries" ("Pemmican," <u>Random</u>). During the fur-trading era, "a rawhide bag containing 90 pounds [about 41 kilos] of pemmican" ("Pemmican," <u>Concise</u>) also came to be known as "pemmican"; one or two pemmicans full of concentrated protein and fat could sustain a traveller or soldier for weeks.

The abbreviated title of a dictionary or an encyclopedia lets you know specifically where the writer found the quotation. You can then go to the bibliography for full details. The bibliography for the above three dictionary citations would be:

"Pemmican." <u>A Concise Dictionary of Canadianisms</u>. 1973 ed.
"Pemmican." <u>The Senior Dictionary</u>. 1973 ed.
"Pemmican." <u>The Random House Dictionary of the English Language</u>.
   1987 ed.

7. Although this book suggests that you use parenthetical citations to document sources, remember that a research paper is written for a specific audience, usually the teacher who has assigned the paper. If your teacher prefers that you use footnotes rather than citations, refer to a handbook published before 1984 as a guide to proper footnote forms. Check with your teacher about the form he or she prefers.

8.   Bibliography

Most readers expect a research paper to include a **bibliography** or alphabetical list of all its sources of information. If you use parenthetical citations within your paper, it is especially important to present a bibliography at the end, since the bibliography makes clear what works you cited within parentheses.

According to the MLA guidelines, a bibliography, titled "Works Cited," should include all the sources of your facts, quotations, opinions, and ideas (if they are borrowed from someone else). The list should be alphabetical, according to the author's last name. If no author is given for the book or article, then it should be alphabetized according to the first word of the title, other than *a*, *an*, or *the*.

A Typical Entry for a Book

Author's last name, first name. <u>Underlined Title</u>. City of publication:
   Abbreviated publisher's name, Year of publication.

Notice how the entry is punctuated. A comma separates the author's last and first names. Periods follow the author's first name, the title, and the year of publication. A colon follows the city of publication, and a comma follows the publisher's name. The second line is indented or set in five spaces from the first line.

A Typical Entry for a Magazine Article

Author's last name, first name. "Title of Article in Quotation Marks."
   <u>Underlined Title of Periodical</u>. Date of publication: page number(s).

Again, notice the punctuation. Periods follow the author's name, the title of the article, the name of the magazine, and the page number. A colon follows the date of publication.

The best way to understand how to record the various bibliographic entries is to look at a few examples. When you and your partner examine each of the following, note the information given, the order in which it is given, and the use of capitalization and punctuation. In addition, the MLA suggests that you shorten the publisher's name – for example, "AW" for Addison-Wesley or "Harper" for "Harper & Row."

One author

Kluger, Richard. Simple Justice. New York: Knopf, 1975.

Two authors

Millet, Nancy C. and Helen J. Throckmorton. How to Read a Short Story. Boston: Ginn, 1969.

Three authors

Young, Richard E., Alton L. Becker, and Kenneth L. Pike. Rhetoric: Discovery and Change. New York: Harcourt, 1970.

More than three authors

Chester, Lewis, et al. An American Melodrama. New York: Viking, 1969.

(*Et al.* means "and others.")

Two works by the same author

Kaplan, Justin. Mark Twain and His World. New York: Crown, 1983.
———————— . Mr. Clemens and Mark Twain: a Biography. New York: Simon and Schuster, 1966.

(A line that is approximately the same length as the author's name, followed by a period, is substituted for the author's name.)

Editor as author

De Bell, Garret, ed. The Environmental Handbook. New York: Ballantine, 1970.

Another edition

Voeks, Virginia. On Becoming an Educated Person. 3rd ed. Philadelphia: Saunders, 1970.

Book with no author

A Manual of Style. 13th ed. Chicago: University of Chicago, 1984.

A work in more than one volume

Sandburg, Carl. Abraham Lincoln. 3 vols. New York: Harcourt, 1969.

Article in a book edited by someone else

Trilling, Diana. "The Image of Women in Contemporary Literature." <u>The Woman in America</u>. Ed. Robert J. Lifton. Boston: Houghton, 1965.

A translation

Dostoevsky, Feodor. <u>Crime and Punishment</u>. Trans. Jessie Coulson. Ed. George Gibian. New York: Norton, 1964.

Corporate author or public document

American Red Cross. <u>Standard First Aid and Personal Safety</u>. 2nd ed. Garden City: Doubleday, 1979.

Signed magazine article

Goldman, Francisco. "Daniel, Dona Violeta, Democracy: On the campaign trail in Nicaragua." <u>Harper's</u>. Feb. 1990: 70–78.

Unsigned magazine article

"What's the Word For...?" <u>Harper's</u>. Feb. 1990: 45–51.

Signed newspaper article

Feldmann, Linda. "Soviet Hot Spots." <u>The Christian Science Monitor</u>. 2 Feb. 1990: 11.

Unsigned newspaper article

"High winds blamed for skid of politicians' plane." <u>Globe and Mail</u>. 24 Feb. 1990: A9.

Signed encyclopedia article

Ryther, John H. "Marine Biology." <u>World Book Encyclopedia</u>. 1976 ed.

Unsigned encyclopedia article or dictionary entry

"Country Music." <u>Encyclopedia Americana</u>. 1974 ed.

Motion pictures

<u>Indiana Jones and the Temple of Doom</u>. Dir. Steven Spielberg. Paramount. 1984.

Television or radio programs

"Nancy Aster" part 7. <u>Masterpiece Theatre</u>. PBS. WNET, New York. 27 May 1984.
White, Jim. <u>At Your Service</u>. KMOX. St. Louis. 13 Mar. 1981.

Stage play

<u>Cats</u>. By Andrew Lloyd Webber. Based on T.S. Eliot's <u>Old Possum's Book of Practical Cats</u>. Dir. Trevor Nunn. New London Theatre, London. 11 May 1981.

Recording

Newhart, Bob. "Merchandising the Wright Brothers." <u>The Button-Down Mind of Bob Newhart</u>. Warner Bros. WS 137, 1960.

Computer software

Oogle, Boris. <u>Fun with Numbers</u>. Computer software. Krell Software, 1985.

Personal Interview

Atwell, Nancie. Personal Interview. 24 Feb. 1990.

SPECIAL WRITING PROJECT

☐ Ask your partner for a question to which he or she does not know the answer. Research and then answer the question in no more than 100 words. Include at least one direct quotation and one paraphrase, each from a different source, in your answer. Make sure that your parenthetical citations and your bibliography are accurate and written correctly.

☐ As your partner edits your short research report, he or she should consider the following:

- Is the research thorough? Is the question fully answered?
- Are all sources properly acknowledged, or are there signs of plagiarism?
- Does the quoted material blend smoothly with the writer's own words?
- Are the quotations punctuated correctly? Are the parenthetical citations and the bibliography presented correctly?

"If we understand our own minds, and the things that are striving to utter themselves through our minds, we move others, not because we have thought about those others, but because all life has the same root."
William Butler Yeats

Appendix

Literature

Inside His Mind

Barbara Coad, student

There was a mountain. It was just a huge mountain thrusting into the sky, its cracked rim cloaked in a ragged grey shawl of cloud that the wind teased into a fine mist to settle in the forested valley below.

There was a silence as there is in nature, only the sound of trees moving in the wind, rushing through the air. An occasional piercing shriek of an eagle would tear through the silence, the echoes creating a symphony off the mountain's sides.

You could smell and taste the winter in the air. It was a tangible feeling that encompassed the whole valley in an icy blanket of chill air that would hide throughout the summer months in lofty crevasses until now, when it could come rolling down into the valley. It was free of pollution, and free of people.

It was free … free.

"Come on guys, rise and shine! Breakfast in ten minutes!" The guard's black booted feet clicked down the corridor, his loud, cheery voice invading the cells where the sleepy inmates gingerly placed bare feet on cold floors. Conversation gradually welled up as though someone had turned a faucet to let it come streaming out, filling the building to almost overflowing.

Like an automaton the convict dragged himself from the pleasant retreat of his dream and rose, saying little to his cellmate as he dressed. Silently he wished it was as still inside as he knew it would be outside. The institution was so far away from anywhere else, it was said you could hear a shout from a mile away.

"I wish there was a window, so that I could see it," he mumbled. "Just a small one. They could put bars on it if they liked."

"What was that, buddy?" His fat cellmate grinned, his face folding into rolls that almost hid his eyes.

"Nothing," the convict said.

That afternoon the prisoners had recreational activities. The convict could have played basketball with the other guys on the court, but going to the court depressed him most of the time.

"No," he decided, "I don't want to go. Better to stay and daydream. Better to drift."

Over a crystalline lake, a mirror for the sky, the still water reflected grey-white. It was snowing here now, huge feathery flakes piling high in drifts that looked like waves frozen in time. So silent; so peaceful. Green looked black on the white canvas nature provided.

"I wouldn't be cold," he thought. "The trees would protect me from the snow while I watch it fall. I would have a coat that keeps out all cold and chill. A coat like the coat I had so long ago as a child. A coat ..."

"Why aren't you outside?" The guard walked up and asked, his cheery face pushed in front of the convict's. "You might like it."

The convict shook his head. By outside, the guard meant the court, which was a large covered area with painted walls to give the illusion of being outside. That's what depressed him. How could the rest be so happy? he wondered. Always smiling, encouraging him to be happy too.

"Listen," the guard said conspiratorily, as if reading his thoughts. "I've got it from an inside source that they might take you guys out. I mean really out, outside."

"Really?" For the first time, the convict looked interested.

"Really. But don't tell no one, okay? I might get into trouble for telling you." With that, the guard left.

Outside. The thought consumed his mind every waking moment. When he fell asleep he would dream of walking through the doors and breathing the fresh air.

It would be so good to go out again, he thought. For him it had been many years since he was first stuck in the institution, but all those years didn't matter anymore. He was going out!

One evening when the guard came to check on him he asked, "What's it like? I mean, out there?"

"Greatest thing you ever saw," the guard replied. "Nothing for miles and miles. No people, no cities, no pollution, just nothin'. I'm sure you'd like it."

"I'm sure I would," said the convict. Nothing, he thought. Nothing but wilderness. Huge, jagged mountains and rolling hills smothered in trees. Little mountain streams, icy water that gurgled by.

Time passed, and it was spring now. The land would be emerging from the freezing grip of winter, breaking loose to run rampant into spring.

The convict could imagine how the snow sparkled like diamonds in the sun as it melted. The air would be fresh and new, smelling of living things. Birds and animals enjoying the relief from the cold in the beautiful wilderness.

"Soon?" he asked the guard one day.

"Soon," the guard assured.

It was not to be until summer, but the spring flew by as he waited in anticipation.

Summer will be a perfect time, he thought. Summer, when all the colors are so vibrant and alive. There would be an azure blue sky with clusters of snowy, billowing thunderheads floating overhead, waiting for a stray breeze to mold them.

He could remember warm summer nights that began with spectacular sunsets, streaking the sky with lavender, red, and orange as the sun was slowly dragged behind a mountain's peak. Then the night was filled with the music made by the buzz or chirp of insects and nocturnal animals, lulling him to sleep.

"Yes," he sighed, "summer will be perfect."

One morning when he was roused from a sleep cluttered with dreams spawned by excitement, the corridor was filled with the buzz of excited conversation. The announcement had come: tomorrow they would go out.

As he listened, he could hear some talk of the chance of escape, while others said it was a plot to spring one of the prisoners. Over all loomed the thought that it was all a trick, but nobody knew what to expect.

All of the prisoners had been in an enclosed cell flown in by a helicopter that would land on a pad next to the buildings of the institution. They would always come at night, and the pad itself was surrounded by high cement walls so they couldn't see their surroundings before they were quickly hustled into the building.

As all had heard, there was a vast wilderness surrounding the institution. Many brought up the question of, if they did escape, how would they survive?

The convict always smiled at the question. He could survive. He could live out there for the rest of his life without any civilization whatsoever and still survive. All his life the wilderness in the mountains had been his home. They were his place; he belonged there.

For everyone, the whole day dragged its heels as though stuck in clay. Fights broke out from nervous energy on the court, and guards were constantly pacing the corridors to penalize anyone openly discussing running away.

When night fell at last, the convict could not sleep. Sweat covered his body as he trembled with anticipation. Wild thoughts of escape churned through the pistons of his mind, and intermittently he would doze off, but never for long.

Before long, morning dawned and for once the prisoners did not talk, dressing in silence, the occasional words said unnaturally loud.

After a rushed breakfast, all of the prisoners were taken to the court and assembled into four single file lines. The director stood before them and issued dire warnings of what would befall those who dared to try and escape. Nervous shuffling filled the rows as the director talked, and when he finished, a sigh of relief was breathed by all.

Still silent, the prisoners were marched through countless iron gates and barriers down endless halls towards the outdoors. Some of the newer inmates remembered taking this trip when they first arrived, but none knew their way.

Finally they reached what looked like just another ordinary door, but when they passed through it they found themselves on the helicopter pad.

Bright, hot sun beat down on them from above, and looking up curiously, the convict saw only a wide expanse of bright blue.

Something's wrong, he thought. It's not right, its too warm. This early in the morning it should be cooler.

Pushing to the front of the line, he found himself standing before a large door that led to the outside.

"Open it!" the director told one of the guards that accompanied them. The door swung back with a creak and a groan, hitting the wall with a loud thump! A rush of hot, heavy air rushed through and caressed the convict's face.

This is it, he thought. He closed his eyes and stepped through the doorway. Even through his eyelids he could see the awesome brightness of his surroundings.

Now, he thought. Now.

He opened his eyes.

Before him stretched miles and miles of empty desert, burning hot under the summer sun. Swirled peaks of all sized sand dunes formed a brown ocean where nothing grew. It was a wasted land worse than any he had ever seen.

Frozen, his feet planted in the shifting sand as if anchored there, he stared at the desert. All joy and hope inside of him crumbled and blew away like the sand in a single moment.

"Sand," he whispered. "All sand...."

Late one night ...
Lou Cornacchia, student

Late one night, an absent-minded professor
Placed the first round rubber ball into a metal
Cylinder
The rest is History.
From coast to coast,
Family room to family room,
To millions of people,
It began:
Set-shots, lay-ups, 3-man weaves,
From Bill Russell to Jerry West,
About, Wilt "The Stilt" Chamberlain
It continued and became:
Soaring, high wire, mid-air, slam-dunking hysteria,
From as high as the top of the key
To as low as the baseline,
A cup dunk, a gorilla dunk
Like the Chrysler DeSoto to Hyundai Pony
Innovation continues

The Kill
Dirk Derstine, student

Swiftly, silently, hungrily, murderously
the lioness stalked her prey
Daintily, unexpectedly, uncaringly, innocently
a small buck came to drink
Silently, unerringly, cruelly she approached
Quickly, wonderingly, unsurely he looked up
Swiftly, intelligently she sprang
Fearfully, panicfully he screamed and fell
Satisfied, she ate.

Thank You, Uncle Ben, for the Nicest Whatever-It-Is That Ever Ruined a House

Maggie Grant

I usually manage to finish writing my Christmas thank-you notes by Jan. 31 at worst, but this year I've bogged down on Uncle Ben. That's my rich uncle, the one who's going to leave me a nice legacy if I survive him. Which seems doubtful at the moment.

There is also this about Uncle Ben: he's the type who would cut a person out of his will if that person failed to thank him for a Christmas present, or even failed to be adequately enthusiastic about it. My problem this year is that – well, just glance at these unfinished notes and perhaps you'll understand.

December 28

Dear Uncle Ben,

We had a lovely Christmas with all sorts of exciting presents, particularly yours. At first we were puzzled about its use, since no instruction sheet was enclosed, but suddenly light dawned – an electric bean pot, what a marvelous idea! To be able to plug in and bake old-fashioned beans right at the table is such an innovation we've invited a few friends in to participate in your gift's debut. At this very moment the feast is hissing away in the dining room and...

January 3

Dear Uncle Ben,

I know you'll be amused to learn that when we opened your lovely present we jumped to the conclusion it was a bean pot. We realized the error of our ways when some beans we were cooking exploded all over the dining room. The pattern they made on the ceiling looked exactly like Santa Claus and his eight tiny reindeer! Fortunately our insurance covers the cost of repainting the room and repairing the chandelier.

Now our neighbor has told us your present is actually a bed-warmer and we're pleased as punch because John and I suffer from cold feet these winter nights and as a matter of fact he is now snoring peacefully abed with the warmer toasting his ...

January 5

Dear Uncle Ben,

Excuse the scribble, but I'm writing this in my lap so I can stay close to John's bed in case he needs anything. He's under sedation after burning his feet (I won't bother you with the details of how it happened) but will soon be able to get about on crutches. Luckily a personal injury clause in our insurance policy will pay his salary while he's off work.

I must delay no longer in thanking you for the lovely humidifier, it was so generous of you. About an hour ago I set it going in the living room and already ...

January 20

Dear Uncle Ben,

At last a peaceful moment to write you! We've been higgledy-piggledy lately due to the living room broadloom having to be torn up and taken away to be dyed. It got badly stained in a foolish little mishap we had with steam and boiling water and my Sheraton table had to be refinished. But it's an ill wind, etc., because I love the rug's new color and insurance paid for everything.

Now to business! We are simply delighted with your Christmas present though I'm going to confess that at first we were unsure about its function. Then John's office manager dropped in and told us it's an outdoor barbecue. How silly of us not to realize it at once! To celebrate the new look in the living room we're going to prepare dinner there tonight, with John acting as chef. As I write he is fussing around with steaks and things ...

January 31

Dear Uncle Ben,

As you can see by this letterhead, we are staying at a hotel. We had a fire at the house, but don't be alarmed, it wasn't too bad, mostly smoke damage. A marvelous cleaning crew is at work busily washing walls, shampooing furniture and so forth. I understand this is a frightfully costly operation so thank goodness we were covered by insurance. In connection with this, I am expecting the company's adjuster to call at any moment, but meanwhile am dashing this off to thank you for ...

February 1

Dear Uncle Ben,

If a Mr. Smither, an insurance adjuster, should try to get in touch with you in any way, I do beg you to disregard him – I'm afraid he's mentally ill. He called in to see me about some claims we've had recently and suddenly started screaming and shouting dreadful things about the lovely Christmas present you sent us. Well, really! No man in his right mind would act that way about an inanimate object! The only thing to do is ignore him. And now, my darling uncle, I hope you are going to forgive the long delay in writing to thank you for the ... for the ...

Charles
Shirley Jackson

The day my son Laurie started kindergarten he renounced corduroy overalls with bibs and began wearing blue jeans with a belt. I watched him go off the first morning with the older girl next door, seeing clearly that an era of my life was ended, my sweet-voiced nursery school tot replaced by a long-trousered, swaggering character who forgot to stop at the corner and wave good-bye to me.

He came home the same way, the front door slamming open, his hat on the floor, and the voice suddenly become raucous shouting, "Isn't anybody here?"

At lunch he spoke insolently to his father, spilled his baby sister's milk, and remarked that his teacher said we were not to take the name of the Lord in vain.

"How was school today?" I asked, elaborately casual.

"All right," he said.

"Did you learn anything?" his father asked.

Laurie regarded his father coldly. "I didn't learn nothing," he said.

"Anything," I said. "Didn't learn anything."

"The teacher spanked a boy, though," Laurie said, addressing his bread and butter. "For being fresh," he added, with his mouth full.

"What did he do?" I asked. "Who was it?"

Laurie thought. "It was Charles," he said. "He was fresh. The teacher spanked him and made him stand in a corner. He was awfully fresh."

"What did he do?" I asked again, but Laurie slid off his chair, took a cookie, and left, while his father was still saying, "See here, young man."

The next day Laurie remarked at lunch, as soon as he sat down, "Well, Charles was bad again today." He grinned enormously and said, "Today Charles hit the teacher."

"Good heavens," I said, mindful of the Lord's name. "I suppose he got spanked again?"

He sure did," Laurie said. "Look up," he said to his father.

"What?" his father said, looking up.

"Look down," Laurie said. "Look at my thumb. Gee, you're dumb." He began to laugh insanely.

"Why did Charles hit the teacher?" I asked quickly.

"Because she tried to make him color with red crayons," Laurie said. "Charles wanted to color with green crayons so he hit the teacher and she spanked him and said nobody play with Charles but everybody did."

The third day – it was Wednesday of the first week – Charles bounced a see-saw on the head of a little girl and made her bleed, and the teacher made him stay inside all during recess. Thursday Charles had to stand in a corner during story-time because he kept pounding his feet on the floor. Friday Charles was deprived of blackboard privileges because he threw chalk.

On Saturday I remarked to my husband, "Do you think kindergarten is too unsettling for Laurie? All this toughness and bad grammar, and this Charles boy sounds like such a bad influence."

"It'll be all right," my husband said reassuringly. "Bound to be people like Charles in the world. Might as well meet them now as later."

On Monday Laurie came home late, full of news. "Charles," he shouted as he came up the hill; I was waiting anxiously on the front steps. "Charles," Laurie yelled all the way up the hill, "Charles was bad again."

"Come right in," I said as soon as he came close enough. "Lunch is waiting."

"You know what Charles did?" he demanded, following me through the door. "Charles yelled so in school they sent a boy in from first grade to tell the teacher she had to make Charles keep quiet, and so Charles had to stay after school. And so all the children stayed to watch him."

"What did he do?" I asked.

"He just sat there," Laurie said, climbing into his chair at the table. "Hi, Pop, y'old dust mop."

"Charles had to stay after school today," I told my husband. "Everyone stayed with him."

"What does this Charles look like?" my husband asked Laurie. "What's his other name?"

"He's bigger than me," Laurie said. "And he doesn't have any rubbers and he doesn't ever wear a jacket."

Monday night was the first Parent-Teachers meeting, and only the fact that the baby had a cold kept me from going; I wanted passionately to meet Charles's mother. On Tuesday Laurie remarked suddenly, "Our teacher had a friend come to see her in school today."

"Charles's mother?" my husband and I asked simultaneously.

"Naaah," Laurie said scornfully. "It was a man who came and made us do exercises; we had to touch our toes. Look." He climbed down from his chair and squatted down and touched his toes. "Like this," he said. He got solemnly back into his chair and said, picking up his fork, "Charles didn't even do exercises."

"That's fine," I said heartily. "Didn't Charles want to do the exercises?"

"Naaah," Laurie said. "Charles was so fresh to the teacher's friend he wasn't let do exercises."

"Fresh again," I said.

"He kicked the teacher's friend," Laurie said. "The teacher's friend told Charles to touch his toes like I just did and Charles kicked him."

"What are they going to do about Charles, do you suppose?" Laurie's father asked him.

Laurie shrugged elaborately. "Throw him out of school, I guess," he said.

Wednesday and Thursday were routine; Charles yelled during story hour and hit a boy in the stomach and made him cry. On Friday Charles stayed after school again and so did all the other children.

With the third week of kindergarten Charles was an institution in our family; the baby was being a Charles when he filled his wagon full of mud and pulled it through the kitchen; even my husband, when he caught his elbow in the telephone cord and pulled telephone, ashtray, and a bowl of flowers off the table, said, after the first minute, "Looks like Charles."

During the third and fourth weeks it looked like a reformation in Charles; Laurie reported grimly at lunch on Thursday of the third week. "Charles was so good today the teacher gave him an apple."

"What?" I said, and my husband added warily, "You mean Charles?"

"Charles," Laurie said. "He gave the crayons around and he picked up the books afterward and the teacher said he was her helper."

"What happened?" I asked incredulously.

"He was her helper, that's all," Laurie said, and shrugged.

"Can this be true, about Charles?" I asked my husband that night. "Can something like this happen?"

"Wait and see," my husband said cynically. "When you've got a Charles to deal with, this may mean he's only plotting."

He seemed to be wrong. For over a week Charles was the teacher's helper; each day he handed things out and he picked things up; no one had to stay after school.

"The PTA meeting's next week again," I told my husband one evening. "I'm going to find Charles's mother there."

"Ask her what happened to Charles," my husband said. "I'd like to know."

"I'd like to know myself," I said.

On Friday of that week things were back to normal. "You know what Charles did today?" Laurie demanded at the lunch table, in a voice slightly awed. "He told a little girl to say a word and she said it and the teacher washed her mouth out with soap and Charles laughed."

"What word?" his father asked unwisely, and Laurie said, "I'll have to whisper it to you, it's so bad." He got down off his chair and went around to his father. His father bent his head down and Laurie whispered joyfully. His father's eyes widened.

"Did Charles tell the little girl to say *that*?" he asked respectfully.

"She said it *twice*," Laurie said. "Charles told her to say it *twice*."

"What happened to Charles?" my husband asked.

"Nothing," Laurie said. "He was passing out the crayons."

Monday morning Charles abandoned the little girl and said the evil word himself three or four times, getting his mouth washed out with soap each time. He also threw chalk.

My husband came to the door with me that evening as I set out for the PTA meeting. "Invite her over for a cup of tea after the meeting," he said. "I want to get a look at her."

"If only she's there," I said prayerfully.

"She'll be there," my husband said. "I don't see how they could hold a PTA meeting without Charles's mother."

At the meeting I sat restlessly, scanning each comfortable matronly face, trying to determine which one hid the secret of Charles. None of them looked to me haggard enough. No one stood up in the meeting and apologized for the way her son had been acting. No one mentioned Charles.

After the meeting I identified and sought out Laurie's kindergarten teacher. She had a plate with a cup of tea and a piece of chocolate cake; I had a plate with a cup of tea and a piece of marshmallow cake. We maneuvered up to one another cautiously, and smiled.

"I've been so anxious to meet you," I said. "I'm Laurie's mother."

"We're all so interested in Laurie," she said.

"Well, he certainly likes kindergarten," I said. "He talks about it all the time."

"We had a little trouble adjusting, the first week or so," she said primly, "but now he's a fine little helper. With occasional lapses, of course."

"Laurie usually adjusts very quickly," I said. "I suppose this time it's Charles's influence."

"Charles?"

"Yes," I said laughing, "you must have your hands full in that kindergarten with Charles."

"Charles?" she said. "We don't have any Charles in kindergarten."

The Well-Wrought Urn
Irving Layton

"What would you do
if I suddenly died?"

"Write a poem to you."

"Would you mourn for me?"

"Certainly," I sighed.

"For a long time?"

"That depends."

"On what?"

"The poem's excellence," I replied.

Without Benefit of Tape

Dorothy Livesay

The real poems are being written in outports
on backwoods farms
in passageways where pantries still exist
or where geraniums
nail light to the window
while out of the window boy in the flying field
is pulled to heaven on the keel of a kite.

Stories breed in the north:
men with snow in their mouths
trample and shake at the bit
kneading the woman down under blankets of snow
icing her breath, her eyes.

The living speech is shouted out
by men and women leaving railway lines
to trundle home, pack-sacked
just company for deer or bear –

    Hallooed
across the counter, in a corner store
it booms upon the river's shore:
on midnight roads where hikers flag you down
speech echoes from the canyon's wall
    resonant
    indubitable.

Falling Song
Daniel David Moses

There was the sweet but reedy
honking of geese coming down
this morning with rain over
rush hour streets, coming
through like bells that celebrate.

I got right up, pushing up
close to the sooty window
pane. I peered out and up through
the weather, imagining
that that line of winged dots would
be shifting as if waves moved
easily through them, as if
waves floated them south. I wanted
to catch them riding, spots on
the wake of the wind, marking

the certain direction of
their migration. But I got
no satisfaction. Mist kept
them mysterious, quickly
dampening their call. Leaning

over the sill, I gaped at
a window shade dull sky, at
a hollow city, and felt
like I'd missed a parade I
would have wanted to follow.

Leaving Home
Haike Rodenstein, student

I won't leave
It doesn't make sense
I'm not crazy enough to exchange all the
    sweet comforts of home for
    the hardships of T.V. dinners, laundromats,
    and making my own bed:
I'm staying and that's final
I'm happy here
They can't make me leave.

    Can they?

Dentist and Patient

William Saroyan

(NOTE: "Dentist and Patient" is a segment from William Saroyan's *Anybody and Anybody Else*, an evening of theatre made up of thirty-one separate episodes.)

Characters
ANYBODY
ANYBODY ELSE

ANYBODY: I'm this dentist in this little cubbyhole of an office, and you're in the chair. Open wider, please.

ANYBODY ELSE: Why are you a dentist?

A: Everybody's got to be something. I always liked teeth.

AE: That's strange; why should anybody like teeth?

A: Just a little wider, please. Teeth have form, and no two teeth are alike. A new customer comes here and opens his mouth, and I get a new surprise. This variety makes me stop and think.

AE: Stop and think about what?

A: This won't hurt, but it may put your nerves on end. It will take only a moment or two. I have seen some amazing mouths.

AE: What can possibly be amazing about a mouth? Isn't a mouth a mouth?

A: Yes, of course, but there are mouths and mouths, and each is unique. The alignment of the teeth, the size of the whole mouth, the coloration of the gums and cheek walls, the size and shape of the tongue, the tonsils – it is all fascinating.

AE: I wouldn't be a dentist for all the money in the world.

A: I am not a dentist for money. I thought I was making that clear. It is more a matter of art, or even philosophy. What are you?

AE: Well, what do you think?

A: Judging from your mouth, I'd say you are a professional man, perhaps a lawyer.

AE: Wrong. Guess again.

A: Doctor?

AE: Try again.

A: The whole mouth suggests a man of intelligence, is it possible you are in trade? A grocer, perhaps?

AE: No, try again.

A: Just a little more of this drilling, and then the annoying part will be over. Annoying to you, to me it could never be annoying, it is always fascinating. Are you a tailor?

AE: No, perhaps you had better not try any more.

A: Your mouth definitely suggests you enjoy food, the molars are quite worn from heavy chewing. Do you own a restaurant?

AE: No, you're not even warm. Give up?

A: Perhaps I'd better.

AE: I'm a millionaire, retired.

A: The mouth doesn't suggest that at all.

AE: Perhaps not, but I would never imagine the mouth could suggest anything more than itself.

A: Gold or silver?

AE: My money? It's in gold, silver, paper, stocks, bonds, and in all of the other forms it takes.

A: Shall the filling be gold or silver?

AE: Gold of course, I'm a millionaire.

A: I have heard they are thrifty. The price of gold filling has gone up; the price for this filling will be ten dollars.

AE: The best quality gold?

A: The very best. How did you ever become a millionaire? I have always wanted to ask a millionaire that question. How in the world did you ever manage such a difficult thing?

AE: Cheating.

A: That's not easy to believe. Your mouth is not the mouth of a cheater. The cheater tends to have a small tight mouth which he very much dislikes opening wide. Just a little wider, please, so I can pack the gold properly. Yours is a large, open, easy, and comfortable mouth, not the narrow, tight, small mouth of a cheater.

AE: Every millionaire I know is a cheater, most of them bigger cheaters than I am, even. I try to cheat only the rich who can afford it, but some millionaires cheat widows and orphans, and fathers and mothers who have many children, and ignorant old people.

A: Why do millionaires cheat poor people?

AE: I don't believe they know why. I don't believe they even know they cheat; I believe they believe they are doing business, that's all.

A: Do they perhaps deceive themselves?

AE: They don't seem to know the difference between cheating and not cheating, so of course it isn't necessary to deceive themselves. They just go right on cheating and getting more and more money.

A: For what?

AE: To have.

A: And then what do they do, when they are old, when they are very old and know they must soon die? What do they do?

AE: They have already taught their children how to cheat, and so they leave their money to their children.

A: Clench your teeth, please.

AE: Are you finished?

A: Almost. And it's perfect.

AE: I expect the best.

A: Rinse your mouth, please.

AE: Tastes good; what is that red stuff?

A: Lavoris, dentists have been using it for fifty years.

AE: I thought I had tasted it before.

A: You may step down, now.

AE: Thank you.

A: Why – please don't misunderstand my asking – how did it happen that you came here?

AE: I was told I could get a gold filling for ten dollars here. Other dentists charge twenty, some thirty, and a few millionaire dentists charge fifty.

A: Millionaire dentists? Is such a thing possible?

AE: There are many millionaire dentists.

A: How do they do it?

AE: By overcharging, by not keeping books, and by not paying taxes.

A: Amazing.

AE: Please accept your payment, and thank you very much. Good day. (*He goes.*)

A: Good day, come back again. Fifty dollars for a gold filling. Imagine the audacity of the rascals. Ten is the most I have ever charged. And he paid in crisp new one-dollar bills – one, two, three, four, five, six, seven, eight, nine. I guess two were stuck together. One, two, three, four, five, six, seven, eight, nine. Ah, well, new currency does stick together. It could happen to anybody.

THE LIGHTS FADE

The Late Man

Andreas Schroeder

On the morning after the storm, the fishermen got up earlier than usual to survey the damage and repair what could be saved. Unusually strong winds and rain had scattered the nets and flattened gardens, bushes, even trees. Fishing boats lay strewn about the beach like broken teeth. Everywhere an exhausted silence hung limply; even the occasional seagull screech seemed blunted and uncertain. Across the mud-flats the faint rush of breakers seemed to fade, though the tide was coming in, slowly and without apparent conviction.

At this time in the morning the fishermen rarely spoke. They arranged their lines, oiled pulleys, checked over their engines and wordlessly pushed out to sea. To break the fragile silence of the first few hours would have been like bursting a delicate membrane without preparation; it was tacitly understood that a man needed more time to clear away in his mind the rubble and destruction of the preceding night than was available to him between his getting up and the launching of his boat. Even after they had cleared the beach and set their course for the large fishing-grounds farther north, the fishermen rarely raised their voices – as if in instinctive respect for the precariousness of the human mind launched before sunrise on an uncertain sea.

But someone broke the silence that morning; as the last remaining boats poled into deeper water to lower their engines, a young bearded fisherman pointed to a single unattended boat lying on its side on the beach and asked in a low voice: "Where's he?"

The man being addressed looked startled, puzzled, then shrugged his shoulders.

The bearded fisherman risked a further offence. "Could he be sick, d'you think?"

There was no response. The other man slid his oar into the water and pushed them off.

A man opens his cabin door and steps into view. He is the late man, the man whose boat still lies untouched on the beach below his cabin. There is nothing particularly unusual about this man except perhaps a certain slight hesitation in his manner; the hesitation of a man for whom the world became at some point intensely suspect, for whom, at that point, a glass on a table became less and less a glass on a table and more and more a thing too strange and amazing to grasp by name. As he stands in his doorway, his hand rests gingerly on the frame, as if constantly ready in case of attack.

About fifteen minutes have passed since the last boat was launched and the late man stepped from his cabin. Now, his boat ready and his outboard spluttering half-submerged, he pushes off and follows the fleet toward the fishing-grounds.

A few hours later the fishing village begins to yawn, stretch and get up; children and fishwives clutter the streets and tangle the air with punctuation marks.

When they return in the early evening and pull their boats out of the water above the high-tide markers, the late man is not with them. During the interval of time between the last fisherman's ascent from his stranded boat to his waiting dinner and the late man's arrival at the launching site fifteen minutes later, silence holds the beach like an indrawn breath. The sound of his prow on the pebbles, therefore, grates in an unusually harsh way on the nerves of the woman waiting for him above the high-tide markers. He has caught fewer fish than the other fishermen.

The next morning the late man appears at his cabin door half an hour after the fishermen have left the beach. Their boats are already vague in the distance when he finally manages to haul his boat to the water-line, which has by this time fallen far below his landing place with the receding tide. He seems somehow weakened, older, leaning wearily against the wheel of his boat. When the fishermen return that night he is an uncertain speck on the horizon, half an hour behind the last of the fishing fleet, and when the catch is scored, he has caught fewer fish than the day before.

Around noon the following day the boats were anchored in clusters to share both lunch and small-talk on the fishing-grounds, and the conversation turned to the late man. "Can't figure 'im out," one fisherman mused, pulling thoughtfully at his beard. "Won't tell nobody what's wrong." "Ain't sayin' a thing," another agreed. "Asked him yesterday what the problem was, but I'll be damned if he didn't seem like he wasn't even listening." There was a pause as if to let the spoken words disperse. Then: "Sea can do that to a man. Catches up with him, it does." The speaker slowly shook his head, threw an orange peel overboard, then absently ignored a deck-hand who had asked him what he meant. The deck-hand finally turned away, assuming his question was naïve; he was new in the fleet and often found himself being unanswered. As it was, he was already on the other side of the boat when the old man muttered his answer to no-one in particular: "I don't know what happens; I just know it does. Ain't no man can whirl the world by hand."

The next morning the late man launched his boat some forty-five minutes after the fleet had left the beach.

Little is known of the late man's history, though this isn't realized until he first begins to attract attention by his mystifying dislocation of schedule; suddenly everyone rummages about in their memory for initial impressions, former opinions, latent suspicions, old predictions. Little in the way of substantial information is collected. It is generally agreed that he is a relatively young man, hard-working and "well-disciplined." Some feel him to be a little too much given to reflection, but one suspects this is said chiefly in reaction to his if not exactly anti-social, at least fairly reticent manner. He cares little for other people, though he has been known to go to the aid of a complete stranger for no reason. A slightly more observant villager notes his peculiar tendency to touch (with a curiously disbelieving air) whatever happens to be around him; the remark is received in uncertain silence. Many frankly admit they have no idea what to make of the whole business, and that the man is probably simply under the attack of some unsettling virus. This fails to explain, however (as someone quickly points out), his consistent, almost plan-like deceleration of pace in relation to the normal fishing schedule of the village – by this time he is reported leaving the beach a full three hours after the last of the other boats has been launched.

By the time the late man pulls his boat from the water, the sun is little more than an almost-submerged leer on a mindless horizon and the waves have jelled to heavy, slowly swirling jibes. Night winds begin to cover the eastern part of the sky with a thick, cumulus ceiling of ridicule. Sardonic chuckles ripple along the waterline where the undertow pursues an endless foreplay with beach gravel. The late man stands motionless, looking strangely as if he belongs neither to the water nor the land; his face is a ploughed field but his eyes dart about the beach like frightened piranhas. His boat is a crazily tilted sneer lying on its side in the pebbles, with rope dangling from the prow like corded spittle. Wave upon wave of curling laughter lampoons the beach. Everywhere, everything grins. The late man no longer defends himself. He has committed the blunder of allowing himself and the universe to discover his detective activities, his secret investigations into the nature and composition of himself and whatever he finds it possible to apprehend. But he has allowed this discovery prematurely, before he has had time to properly anaesthetize his specimens, and now, suddenly aware of a spy in the midst, they have disintegrated into countless labyrinthine possibilities and traps and the late man is cut off without the possibility of retreat. He has long since given up trying to sledge-hammer his brain to sleep.

But a violated universe will not be satisfied with the simple deflection of an inquisitive mind, and as if to make certain that such a trespassing will never again be possible, it has turned glaring spotlights against the late man's brain, blinding and overwhelming it with confusion and derision. Stiffly aligned principles and corollaries suddenly go limp and begin to collapse; endless qualifications overrun simple premises and leave behind a shambles of tattered and useless shreds of belief. Above all, the horror is set creeping up the back stairs of the late man's mind that all this is beyond his control, and that like a retaining pin pulled from a spring-loaded wheel, this destruction will continue relentlessly until it has unrolled the tension from the spring.

There appears to be little he can do but to hold on until all is done, and to hope that he doesn't become so weakened in the process as to fall prey to a useless madness.

In a matter of months the departures and arrivals of the late man and the fishing fleet have diverged to such an extent that the returning fishermen see the late man's boat heading toward them at dusk, on its way north toward open water. He stands huddled over his wheel, eyes staring unseeing at the darkening horizon as if in purposeful blindness. The fishing fleet parts to let him pass; though no one appears to understand, everyone sees the desperate undertow in his eyes and says nothing. When all the boats are secured and the gear locked away, the late man is a dissolving blotch against black evening. A few moments later he is gone.

The late man had returned the previous morning with no fish at all. As he sat down to dinner, the young fisherman who had asked about the late man early one morning suddenly spoke of him to his wife. "Nobody knows anything, or they won't say anything. Everybody pretends to ignore him. I've got to find out."

His wife said nothing. He looked at her curiously, then threw down his knife. "Well damn it, here's a man digging his own grave in plain view of a whole village, and nobody has the guts to look into the matter." His wife remained silent but a worried look began to unsettle her face. The young fisherman stood up abruptly. "I'm going to find out," he said, reaching for his squall-jacket and opening the door. "Even if for no other reason than a simple matter of self-defence!" he added as the door slammed shut. Footsteps receded from the cabin. Within minutes the sound of his outboard began to move across the bay toward the fishing grounds and the open sea.

For a time the young fisherman directs his boat through thick total darkness; a bulging cloud-cover muffles the moon and the night sways and sidesteps in ponderous movements that are blind but everywhere. The occasional clear splash falls short among the sluggish gurgle and sagging cough of deep-water waves beneath the keel. The young fisherman peers at the bleakness but steers his boat by instinct.

As he moves farther and farther into deeper water the night begins to thin out; his eyes detect edges, outlines, occasional glimpses of phosphoric glitter – eventually the moon disentangles from the clouds and trudges higher into the sky, spraying a fine shower of thin light over the fishing grounds. By this time the young fisherman can make out the dark shape of the late man's boat, lying at anchor on his starboard side. The young fisherman shuts off his engine and drifts closer. The booms on the boat before him are out, trailing thin glistening lines into the water. The late man is fishing.

The young fisherman sits unmoving at his wheel, uncertain as to what should follow. Possibilities dart in and out of his mind, unwilling to bite. He waits, his brain idling slowly, his thoughts loose.

A creak from a rusty tackle interrupts the silence. A glass float dips and scrambles; the late man comes alive and begins to reel it in. A strike.

The young fisherman straightens up and strains to see. The glass float tugs and splashes at the end of a stiff line; the late man's figure curves against the mast, his arms taut like two rigid claws shaking with exertion. The young fisherman feels an instinctive excitement thrill through his body as if the strike were his own. Something huge is on the end of that line.

The glass float is almost at boat's-edge, momentarily calmer. The late man reaches for his fish-net and plunges it over the side, scooping carefully. His back is turned to the young fisherman, obscuring the float as he brings it to the boat's side. The fish-net rises from the water, then stops.

Surprised, the young fisherman leans forward but sees only the hunched back of the late man leaning over his net. A fierce rippling movement shakes the arm holding the handle as something twists and writhes in the meshes, but the late man makes no move to pull it into the boat. Ten minutes pass; the late man still stands bent over his net, gazing at his catch. The young fisherman is unable to see his face.

Finally, in a slow but deliberate movement, the late man empties his net into the sea and straightens up.

The young fisherman watches, still dumbfounded, as the late man repeats the same procedure moments later when another line snaps alive. This time his demeanour seems to indicate recognition or less interest; a short look suffices to make him empty the net again. After a short pause a third float begins to bob and the late man reels it in. Half an hour later he is still engrossed in the net's contents ignoring all the other lines which are jerking at the boom. Bent over the gunwale, his hair blowing about his head like spray in the wind, the late man stares at his catch in silence, then throws it back into the sea.

As a faint paleness begins to tinge the outermost edges of the dark, the young fisherman stands up stiffly, a nervous flutter in his stomach, strangely excited yet uncertain why. He detects traces of the intoxication of discovery in his feelings, though he has no idea what he has discovered or realized.

Carefully pulling out his oars, he mounts them in the oarlocks and prepares to slip away. By the time the sun appears he will be back in the bay and his cabin. Then there will be time to think.

A small sound from the other boat stops his raised oars short. The late man has emptied his net and stepped back toward the mast. As he half-turns to re-apply bait to one of the lines the young fisherman catches a glimpse of the late man's face. He almost drops his oars.

The late man's face is totally disfigured. Crumbled skin, twitching lips and bleached white hair, he is suddenly old – an uncertain fool barely able to hold his balance in the rocking boat. The young fisherman is stunned. The late man was of the same generation as the others in the fishing fleet – chronologically about thirty years old. Now he looks three times that age.

But there is no time to lose; the horizon is becoming a thin pencil-line of light across the dark and he will be discovered. Stealthily moving his oars, the young fisherman pulls away toward the south and the fishing village.

As his boat moves into the bay, he sees the first cabin doors opening and fishermen walking down the beach toward their boats. Several of them look up, surprised to see his incoming boat at such an odd time. Obviously his wife has said nothing. He steers toward an unused part of the beach and runs his boat aground.

There, his boat bouncing slightly to the rhythm of his fading wash, he sat on the bow and twisted a piece of rope between his fingers; uncertain, almost nervous, uncertain again. The spreading sun warmed his back as he sat, but his stomach remained cold and unsettled; he felt the desperate urge to run, to commit a violence, tear something to shreds, but somehow he was numbed or simply unable to move. For no apparent reason something seemed to have snapped; his senses coiled and bunched up in twisting knots, thoughts whirled in ever-tightening circles about his head and a steadily mounting pressure threatened to explode inside him like a surfacing deep-water fish.

Then the faint growl from a distant engine punctured the silence and the tension drained away with an almost audible hiss. The young fisherman looked over his shoulder and watched the late man's boat increase toward the bay. Several of the other fishermen paused and shaded their eyes. For a short while everything hung in suspension....

Suddenly the late man's boat is in the bay, its engine silent, drifting toward the beach. As its prow gouges into the sand the late man struggles feebly to climb off the deck onto the gravel, half-falling several times in the process.

Then, hoisting the bow rope over his shoulder, he attempts to pull his boat higher up onto the beach.

Later, after the late man had been buried and the fishermen had returned to their boats, the young fisherman was heard to say that in a totally paralyzed landscape, the only moving thing had been the late man trying to beach his boat. They had watched him for an incredibly long time, trying to raise the bow above the gravel, and when he finally collapsed, still no-one had moved. When they eventually began to climb down toward the fallen figure, the landscape seemed to stretch and expand in every direction and they walked for hours before reaching him. They found him lying on his back, his face contorted with a mixture of agony and amazement; it was the oldest face they had ever seen. So they had buried him, quietly and without looking at each other, and the young fisherman had beached the boat. The next morning, due possibly to the tiring events of the preceding night and day, the young fisherman slept a little longer, and eventually launched his boat some fifteen minutes after the last of the fishing boats had cleared the bay.

Fiend
Rod Smylie, student

There's a man under my bed.

I can hear him, late, late at night, when everything is still and dark. So dark.

I lie awake, sweat rolling down my chest, one drop after another, each one following the path of the one before, like pioneers venturing into unmapped territory. My ears are wide, so that I do not miss a single murmur of sound. Night after night.

He's been there for three months now, off and on, and I still do not know why, or how. Some nights he is not there, and for that I am grateful. But the others ... I turn out the light and, after a while, he begins. Moving, rustling. At first I turned on the light and peered beneath my bed, thinking I had some form of rodent for an unwelcome guest, but there was nothing there. No man, no animal, nothing.

I dismissed it the first few times, assuming that the rat or whatever scurried to some other area whenever I suddenly lit the room. During the daytime I moved my bed away from the wall and looked for holes, droppings, anything that would shed light on the mystery, but without success. I considered laying traps, buying poison. I gave up these ideas when the man started to whisper to me at night.

The first time it happened, I spent the rest of the night locked in my bathroom, doubting my sanity. When daylight came, it seemed like a nightmare, but I knew it was not. It was horrible, rock-solid reality.

What could I do? I couldn't move. This place is the pits, but it is the cheapest apartment available, and I can hardly afford *it*. Sleep in the park? Perhaps he would be beneath my bench, chuckling away merrily. I could sleep on the floor perhaps; at least then he wouldn't be under me. But for some unclear reason that terrifies me more than sleeping on top of him. At least then there is a bed between us, and I don't think that he can get at me while I'm there. Wouldn't he have done so already?

I can't tell the police; one more crazy to be locked away. I have no friends or relatives, none that I care to know anyway. I cannot stay out all the time; I have to sleep. But in that period just before blessed unconsciousness arrives, the man can say a lot of things. He suggests that I go and commit twisted deeds, and then he laughs when I shudder with horror and revulsion. Is he in my mind? Can I be so unstable that I hallucinate like this?

But tonight, this night, we will see. After months of terror, I am going to find out who he is once and for all. I bought a flashlight with what money I had saved, on this basis: I believe that the evil, warped man disappears between the time I reach up to turn on my lamp and when I get my eyes below my bed. But I will fool him, finally, and know who he is, what he is.

I am lying with my new ally in bed, the sweat coming down my body even more profusely than usual. I stare blindly into the darkness, waiting for him to begin. I ready myself. Will my plan work? What will I see? Do I *want* to see?

With a roar I thrust my head over the side and turn on the flashlight, fully illuminating the scene beneath me.

There is nothing there. I pant and stare, dumbfounded. Then, slowly, I lower myself to the floor. I take one last look around, then I crawl beneath my bed, and turn off the light.

Naaholooyah

Mary TallMountain

Nobody's hands were quite like Mamma's. They were narrow with long thin fingers, and thumbs that bent out at the ends. The nails were scarred with nicks from the cutting of Salmon. In fish time they had rims of black, which had faded by winter till they were their usual pink-brown color. The hands acted as if they knew just what they were doing. When Mamma rested they folded, one on top of the other, and it seemed as if they were sleeping, but they were always ready to jump up. When they did, the turned-out thumbs gave them a busy air. The skin of her hands was both soft and rough. She thought about Mamma's hands coming toward her and Michael, usually holding things. It made her drowsy and comfortable.

At fish camp she had spent hours watching those hands work.

The right hand sailed clear up over the mother Salmon's big grey and pink body to her head, where it made two short strong chops with the sharp *toeeaa-maas* that made Salmon's head slide away on the slippery table. From then on, how fast it moved! Every move was important. First, the two upper fins were flipped away and the lower one was sheared off low on the pearly breast over the sweeping fan of the tail. Next, Mamma's hand lifted and *toeeaamaas* drew a long red stroke that opened Salmon's belly. There in her silver lining were the perfect little jelly-red eggs. Ever so slowly, the right hand pried out the clump of eggs. Not much else was there, because Salmon ate hardly anything when she was going home with her eggs, which Mamma said were baby Salmon. Now the right hand ran *toeeaamaas* in another quick red line along the ivory-colored backbone. Both hands pressed the two halves out flat. They picked up *toeeaamaas* again and made slanting slices out from the thick inner body almost to the thin outer edges. These cuts were so fine that the skin was still all whole and was one skin, and its inside was red velvet. There was the smell of new fish, the smell that Lidwynne thought she had always remembered from some dark place inside. It was a good smell and made her saliva bubble up. She thought she would like to taste a piece of that beautiful red velvet, right now.

When Mamma cut Salmon, the hands acted more careful than they ever did. It took both of them to dip Salmon into the tub of water and hoist the two halves up to hang over the drying rack. Lidwynne kept thinking now about the full racks of red king salmon, and the taste buds puckered more strongly. She could almost taste the sweet, smoky fish, the oil that was being heated out by the sun. How heavy *toeeaamaas* was, how Salmon's body pushed back at the sharp blade, but always gave and divided under it. Someday, she intended to cut Salmon herself. By the time she got to be ten, maybe even nine, Mamma would let her do it. Her hands would be big enough then, but now they were too small. Most Salmon were as big as she was. Much bigger than Michael, she thought.

He was grinning at her, with one tooth missing. It made him look wild and cockeyed. A blue sweater peeked out under his wadded and patched overalls that had once belonged to Lidwynne. "Where *eenaa*?" he asked. The wind gently rumpled his curls.

"In the house, Michael." She looked up at the window. Nobody was there. She had been upset, these days. Mamma and Daddy Clem had talked a lot, secretly. She was sleepy and lazy now because she'd lain awake so long trying to hear what they said. Mamma was very tired, too. Scary things had happened yesterday: first the soldiers fighting here in the yard, then Sister coming to see Mamma, her heavy black veil over her face that frowned. It seemed that all over the village, people were mad.

Mamma came outdoors. It was the first time since lunch that she had been out to see what was going on. Lidwynne was kneeling by *naaholooyah* now. There was a row of three, each with its little skin roof. The clay dirt had got dry, and the flaked mounds of the walls were pale brown, the color of pancakes. She pointed. "Look at *naaholooyah*!"

"*Snaa'*, you make dandy winter houses." Mamma sat down with her on the hard-packed ground.

"Maybe we go to Kaiyuh this winter and live in *naaholooyah*," Lidwynne said, excited inside at the thought. She had never been to Kaiyuh to winter camp. Sometimes Mamma and Grandpa and uncle and aunt and their children went out there to old hunting grounds. It was supposed to be a wonderful place.

"Mmm–hmm." Mamma's face had gotten serious.

"But you said we could!" Lidwynne cried.

"I said maybe, you little dickens!" Mamma grabbed her and carried her over to the boardwalk. Michael was rolling around on it, giggling. Suddenly he tumbled off into the soft grass. Mamma gave a big laugh and picked him up so he wouldn't get scared, but he squirmed and squealed, unusually cross.

Lidwynne complained, "Why didn't you come see *naaholooyah*? I called but you didn't listen."

Mamma's lips moved against her cheek. "There's no time. Too much visiting." She yawned.

"Why do they all come here and visit?" Lidwynne frowned.

"It's just one of those times." Mamma carried them into the cabin and put them down. When she poured milk into a pan to heat, Michael wrinkled up to cry. She laid him slanty on her lap and pried open his mouth. "There's a new tooth coming," she said. Lidwynne craned her neck. "*Baghoo'*," Mamma said, showing her the new tooth poking up.

"*Baghoo'*," Lidwynne repeated. "When I was four did I have those growing too?"

"Sure, and you were cranky too, like he is right now."

"I was?"

"Oh, you're a cranky little girl." Mamma grinned into her eyes. "You're just like Grandpa. Look here."

Lidwynne stared at herself in the looking glass. She didn't think she looked at all like Grandpa. She was so short and he was so tall.

"See? Short and wide, like him. And you sure have got his temper." Mamma's dimple showed.

Michael sucked loudly at his bottle. "He's not mad any more. Look at that. He was plenty mad today, though. He bawled a lot." Lidwynne patted his warm little forehead. Now that he's four, she thought, he ought to eat regular food like I do. Not just that milk. Doctor Harry got mad when she wouldn't drink milk. She didn't like it at all. Maybe if she ever went Outside, she would get to drink real cow's milk. Now they just drank canned Carnation milk, mixed with water. Mamma and Nellie had to talk real hard to get her to drink it at all, but Michael never got tired of it. His face smoothed out now, and his eyelids kept shutting. His arms dropped back and his mouth slipped off the bottle. Mamma laid him in *ts'ibi*. "You can cover him up," she said.

Ts'ibi was a shallow pouch of heavy, well-worn canvas a yard square, hung from the ceiling by four solidly braided ropes passed through a fat gray coil spring and made into a ball-shaped knot, from which they splayed out to the corners of the frame and looped under the hard wide lip of wood over the edge of which the canvas curved up tightly; precisely spaced, the ropes wrapped around and under the lip and were nailed with the edge of the canvas to the smooth bottom. It was a sturdy smooth bowl deep enough to hold Michael safely. A nudge of the hand set the spring dancing lightly to put him to sleep; a harder one set it bouncing fast enough to awaken him without frightening him. Uncle Obal had made it. Lidwynne was going to have one too, when she had babies herself. She never missed a chance to watch Michael sleeping. Then she gently rocked him in *ts'ibi*. But she was too excited to sit still today. She pulled up the marten fur blanket and tucked it solidly around him.

Mamma sat down in her rocking chair by the window. "Hand me my thimble," she said. It was a regular thing they did, and Lidwynne gave her the thimble, which was a piece of caribou horn, shaved thin and curled to fit Mamma's thumb. Mamma threaded a needle with the papery thin *tl'aah* made of reindeer sinew she used for sewing hides. The *tl'aah* was tough, all right. Those hides were strong. Lidwynne watched her mother intently. Piles of *yoo'yoo'*, pink, silver, and blood-colored, gleamed in the fat sunbeam that dangled across the room. Those long fingers picked up a pink bead on the very end of the needle and stitched it to the piece of moosehide in her lap.

"Some day Lidwynne's going to do that." She leaned on the arm of the rocker. "That's going to be mittens," she announced. "Mittens for Lidwynne this winter."

"Yes," Mamma sighed. That thinking look was in her face again. "For Lidwynne this winter."

"What's the matter?" Lidwynne looked into Mamma's face that was bent over the beads, so bright in her brown hands.

Mamma looked at her. "*Snaa'*," she said, lingering over the word. There was something different in the tone of her voice today. "I have to take you and Michael to stay with Doctor and Nellie."

"What for?" Lidwynne thought: Again? it must be a joke.

"I'm going to be too busy to keep you this week."

"What do you have to do?"

"I have to be ready if Grandpa calls me to council meeting."

Lidwynne's face brightened. She wasn't going away this time.

"Council meetings are about you and Michael."

"Why? What did we do?"

"Nellie and Doctor asked me if they could adopt you. You know that."

Oh, that crazy adoption stuff, again. "That what Grandpa was so mad about yesterday?"

"Mm-hmm."

"You mean you want to give Michael and me to them?"

Mamma looked out the window. The wind had started to blow in the grass, and the river was all rough. "Yes," she said.

Lidwynne's eyes got hot and trembly. "Why do you want to do that, Mamma?"

"Oh, *snaa'*, I don't want to." The last two words sounded heavy through her nose. But she went on talking in that funny sounding voice. "It's because I'm sick. That's the reason I have to let them keep you kids so much. They can take care of you better."

It wasn't a joke at all, then. Suddenly Lidwynne remembered Mamma coughing this summer, even when it was hot weather. And how when she laid her cheek on Mamma's chest she heard little whispers in there. She had thought before that it was just the way she breathed. Was that part of this sickness she was talking about? "They want to keep us all the time? At night and everything?"

"Yes, that's right." Mamma kept her face down looking at *yoo'yoo'*. Why won't she look at me? Lidwynne thought, putting her hands on Mamma's face. She turned around then to look out of the windows, and it felt like she'd gone a long way off.

Real fast, Lidwynne hugged her. "You love me?"

Mamma made a deep chest sound and began to cough. Lidwynne got one of her big white handkerchiefs and Mamma blew her nose. She stared into Lidwynne's eyes, and now she was back from wherever she'd gone. "Of course I love you, foolish little one. I don't want you to go away. But if you do, I know you'll have a nice life, the way Doctor and Nellie do."

"Grandpa won't let them have us."

"He hasn't got anything to say about it. He just makes sure council does everything right. They have to decide. He stays with them till they do." Mamma snipped off a little thread close to the knot she'd made in back of the mitten. She put the skins away and closed the box. Everything in the room got clear and sharp like Lidwynne's reflection in the mirror. She would never forget *yoo'yoo'* burning like fire in the sunbeam.

She flung her arms around Mamma. She wanted to hold her so hard that she couldn't get away from her, ever. "I don't want to go any place, not even with Michael. I want to stay here."

"Ah," Mamma said to herself. She nuzzled her face into Lidwynne's neck. Her breath was warm on Lidwynne's skin, and her words made puffs of damp air, tight against the little wrinkles of fat under her chin. "I want you to stay, too."

"But why do we have to leave you? Can't we just visit them like we visit Auntie Madeline?" Lidwynne moved away and stared into Mamma's huge eyes, the color of shining blackberries.

"Now, I told you I'm sick. We can't help that. It's just lucky the Merricks are here. You've already told me you like them. If you don't, why do you want to go there visiting all the time?" Mamma's words sounded like echoes of themselves in a big dark cave.

Lidwynne knew her lower lip was beginning to stick out. It was getting colder in here. It must be the wind. She kept silent.

"They're good to you. They love you, Lidwynne. Don't you see, after a while I'll get sicker." Her rough hands came up and held Lidwynne's cheeks tight, and she saw her own reflections like dark still twins in Mamma's eyes.

"You're never going to get well?" Tears jumped out of her own eyes. Mamma wiped them. Then her face was buried in Mamma's apron and the hands were on her hair, patting, patting.

"Lidwynne, remember this word. Consumption. Your mamma has consumption, and she can't get well."

"It's terrible, to hurt you," Lidwynne sobbed, throwing her arms around Mamma's legs, hugging. The hands kept patting. Mamma rocked gently, and it was quiet in the room except for the little squeak of the rocker.

"Hey, *snaa'*, remember how mad Grandpa was yesterday, jumping all around?" Mamma was shaking a little. She must be laughing. Lidwynne peeked. Mamma was all dimpled up and her eyes were squeezed shut. She hollered, "Hoh, hoh! that funny Grandpa!" Lidwynne started to think of Grandpa and how he had looked. His face was red, his eyebrows were squeezed down into a white fringe so you couldn't see his pupils, and oh how mad he was, just yelling and yelling. Pretty soon she was laughing too, and they laughed till they were so tired they couldn't laugh anymore, and they were hugging and kissing, and Mamma wiped their faces and rocked her for a while. Squeak, squeak, that's all that you could hear, and the two of them there warm and cozy in the quiet place.

Suddenly Lidwynne sat straight up. "Why can't we live at the barracks with Daddy?"

"He works for Uncle Sam, and he's got to go to Fort Gibbon pretty soon because Uncle Sam needs him there."

"Oh, that Uncle Sam!" Lidwynne filled the granite dipper at the water pail. She gulped the fresh river water, trying to swallow something that seemed to have gotten stuck in her throat.

She stared out the window. The wind had grown so strong it roared around the trees, stirring them up as if it had a spoon as big as a cloud. It whined over the roof and down the stovepipe and teased the fire so it flickered fast as red devils back of the little flower-shaped vents in the firebox of the stove. Its voice was like lots of people singing, far away.

It had blown *naaholooyah* away. There were only three small brown circles left on the ground.

Notes on Punctuation

Lewis Thomas

There are no precise rules about punctuation (Fowler lays out some general advice (as best he can under the complex circumstances of English prose (he points out, for example, that we possess only four stops (the comma, the semicolon, the colon and the period (the question mark and exclamation point are not, strictly speaking, stops; they are indicators of tone (oddly enough, the Greeks employed the semicolon for their question mark (it produces a strange sensation to read a Greek sentence which is a straightforward question: Why weepest thou; (instead of Why weepest thou? (and, of course, there are parentheses (which are surely a kind of punctuation making this whole matter much more complicated by having to count up the left-handed parentheses in order to be sure of closing with the right number (but if the parentheses were left out, with nothing to work with but the stops, we would have considerably more flexibility in the deploying of layers of meaning than if we tried to separate all the clauses by physical barriers (and in the latter case, while we might have more precision and exactitude for our meaning, we would lose the essential flavor of the language, which is its wonderful ambiguity)))))))))))).

The commas are the most useful and usable of all the stops. It is highly important to put them in place as you go along. If you try to come back after doing a paragraph and stick them in the various stops that tempt you you will discover that they tend to swarm like minnows into all sorts of crevices whose existence you hadn't realized and before you know it the whole long sentence becomes immobilized and lashed up squirming in commas. Better to use them sparingly, and with affection, precisely when the need for each one arises, nicely, by itself.

I have grown fond of semicolons in recent years. The semicolon tells you that there is still some question about the preceding full sentence; something needs to be added; it reminds you sometimes of the Greek usage. It is almost always a greater pleasure to come across a semicolon than a period. The period tells you that that is that; if you didn't get all the meaning you wanted or expected, anyway you got all the writer intended to parcel out and now you have to move along. But with a semicolon there you get a pleasant little feeling of expectancy; there is more to come; read on; it will get clearer.

Colons are a lot less attractive, for several reasons: firstly, they give you the feeling of being rather ordered around, or at least having your nose pointed in a direction you might not be inclined to take if left to yourself, and secondly, you suspect you're in for one of those sentences that will be labelling the points to be made: firstly, secondly and so forth, with the implication that you haven't sense enough to keep track of a sequence of notions without having them numbered. Also many writers use this system loosely and incompletely, starting out with number one and number two as though counting off on their fingers but then going on and on without the succession of labels you've been led to expect, leaving you floundering about searching for the ninethly or seventeenthly that ought to be there but isn't.

Exclamation points are the most irritating of all. Look! they say, look at what I just said! How amazing is my thought! It is like being forced to watch someone else's small child jumping up and down crazily in the center of the living room shouting to attract attention. If a sentence really has something of importance to say, something quite remarkable, it doesn't need a mark to point it out. And if it is really, after all, a banal sentence needing more zing, the exclamation point simply emphasizes its banality!

Quotation marks should be used honestly and sparingly, when there is a genuine quotation at hand, and it is necessary to be very rigorous about the words enclosed by the marks. If something is to be quoted, the *exact* words must be used. If part of it must be left out because of space limitations, it is good manners to insert three dots to indicate the omission, but it is unethical to do this if it means connecting two thoughts which the original author did not intend to have tied together. Above all, quotation marks should not be used for ideas that you'd like to disown, things in the air so to speak. Nor should they be put in place around clichés; if you want to use a cliché you must take full responsibility for it and not try to fob it off on anon., or on society. The most objectionable misuse of quotation marks, but one which illustrates the dangers of misuse in ordinary prose, is seen in advertising, especially in advertisements for small restaurants, for example "just around the corner," or "a good place to eat." No single, identifiable, citable person ever really said, for the record, "just around the corner," much less "a good place to eat," least likely of all for restaurants of the type that use this type of prose.

The dash is a handy device, informal and essentially playful, telling you that you're about to take off on a different tack but still in some way connected with the present course – only you have to remember that the dash is there, and either put a second dash at the end of the notation to let the reader know that he's back on course, or else end the sentence, as here, with a period.

The greatest danger in punctuation is for poetry. Here it is necessary to be as economical and parsimonious with commas and periods as with the words themselves, and any marks that seem to carry their own subtle meanings, like dashes and little rows of periods, even semicolons and question marks, should be left out altogether rather than inserted to clog up the thing with ambiguity. A single exclamation point in a poem, no matter what else the poem has to say, is enough to destroy the whole work.

The things I like best in T.S. Eliot's poetry, especially in the *Four Quartets*, are the semicolons. You cannot hear them, but they are there, laying out the connections between the images and the ideas. Sometimes you get a glimpse of a semicolon coming, a few lines farther on, and it is like climbing a steep path through woods and seeing a wooden bench just at a bend in the road ahead, a place where you can expect to sit for a moment, catching your breath.

Commas can't do this sort of thing; they can only tell you how the different parts of a complicated thought are to be fitted together, but you can't sit, not even take a breath, just because of a comma,

Poets are Still Writing Poems About Spring and Here is Mine: Spring

Miriam Waddington

You're an ice-thing
a landslide, a whale,
a huge continental
cold nose-ring
dragging the world
by the tail into
a universal grandstand
before it ever thought
of being born.

Maybe not: maybe
you're more like
a fern all curled up
in a juicy green bud
that any minute now
is going to burst out
of the loamy seams
of this workaday lazy
earth into a fresh
fernfan.

You'll be festive
with lacey little
pinked edges cut
out with God's own
zigzag scissors and
his million laughs,
you'll be cagey
and cunning and
you'll brush your
fingery fronds fond
as whiskers against

everyone's bare
legs, and you'll touch
us all with little
barbs of hot prickly
light, and we'll be
dyed green by the
crowds of wildly
cheering fernfans
sitting in the packed
high galleries of summer.

Proofreaders' Marks and Other Symbols for Editing

After you are satisfied with the overall content and organization of a piece of writing, you and your editors should take the time to polish it for its intended audience. You should be able to answer "yes" to questions such as these:

- Are my sentences clear?
- Are they grammatically correct?
- Did I use the right words?
- Is my punctuation correct?
- Is my spelling correct?

Following are some proofreaders' marks and other symbols that you and your editors can use when you edit a piece of writing.

Symbol	Meaning	Example	Edited Version
℮	delete a word	Take it ~~out.℮~~	Take it.
⌣	delete a space	He is out͜spoken.	He is outspoken.
∧	insert a word	This is my ^best^ writing.	This is my best writing.
#∧	insert a space	picture#frame	picture frame
⊙	insert a period	He finally left ⊙	He finally left.
ŷ	insert a comma	A polished publishable piece ŷ	A polished, publishable piece

Symbol	Meaning	Example	Edited Version
˯˯	insert an apostrophe	teachers guide	teacher's guide
˯˯	insert a quotation mark	"Out! he shouted.	"Out!" he shouted.
(tr) ∿	transpose a letter or or word	(tr) Transpose word this	Transpose this word.
CAP ≡	use a capital letter	CAP newfoundland	Newfoundland
(lc) /	use a lowercase letter	(lc) Northern Canada	northern Canada
⊄	begin a new paragraph	⊄ Even though I...	Even though I...
⌒	do not begin a new paragraph	...often. Once we started...	...often. Once we...
]	move to the right	] Quick, march!	Quick, march!
[	move to the left	[We were playing.	We were playing.
(stet) ⌇⌇	stet (let it stand)	(stet) Eat your dinner.	Eat your dinner.
(sp) ○	write out in full	(sp) ...and only ②rats.	...and only two rats.
(ital) ___	put in italic	(ital) Don't do that.	Don't *do* that.
(rom)	put in roman (ordinary) type	(rom) *Surely* you jest.	Surely you jest.
	spelling error	mistake ~~misteak~~	mistake
(t)	tense	(t) I have went.	I have gone.
(u)	usage	(u) I did good.	I did well.
(ro)	run-on sentence	(ro) It was my first day even I was happy.	It was my first day; even I was happy.
(cs)	comma splice	(cs) It was my last day, I was sad.	It was my last day; I was sad.

Symbol	Meaning	Example	Edited Version
(f)	fragment	(f) Because I wanted to go to the concert.	I went because I wanted to go to the concert.
(mm)	misplaced modifier	(mm) She had only swum two laps.	She had swum only two laps.
(dm)	dangling modifier	(dm) Running down the street, the burning house came into view.	Running down the street, I saw the burning house.
(agr)	agreement of subject and verb	(agr) Everyone in the stands are dressed warmly.	Everyone in the stands is dressed warmly.
(p)	pronoun referent	(p) Henry and Bill gave me his drinks.	Henry and Bill gave me their drinks.
(?)	unclear	(?) This is a problem.	The mess is a problem.
(ss)	subject shift	(ss) One should do his best.	One should do one's best.
(ts)	tense shift	(ts) He gives while I took.	He gives while I take.
(vs)	voice shift (active to passive or passive to active)	(vs) I gave it to him and suddenly it was eaten.	I gave it to him and suddenly he ate it.
(r)	repetitive (redundant)	(r) They linked together.	They linked.
(T)	transition needed	(T) He refused to come out for practice. The coach dropped him from the team.	He refused to come out for practice. Consequently, the coach dropped him from the team.
||	lacks parallelism	|| He was strong and of a tall stature.	He was strong and tall.

Glossary

allusion: a **figurative comparison** that refers to something (often a work of literature) that the writer expects the audience to recognize.

analogy: an extended **figurative comparison**.

archetypal character: in a literary work of art, a character representing a general, universal type.

archetypal conflict: in a literary work of art, a conflict that occurs frequently in literature and that is common in human experience.

audience: a **writing variable**; the intended recipient of a piece of writing.

balanced sentence: a **rhetorical device**; a sentence in which each half has a main clause or similar pattern.

bibliography: in a research paper, a list of the sources of information.

brainstorming: a term used to name a group of methods for generating ideas and supporting details, either by oneself or in a group.

chronological order: organization of events in a piece of writing according to the order in which they occur.

cliché: a figurative expression or other phrase that has become stale and lost its effect through overuse.

climactic order: organization of details in a piece of writing according to their order of importance.

climax: the decisive moment or turning point in a narrative.

conflict: a physical or mental struggle against someone or something or within oneself.

connotation: the ideas or impressions connected to a word, in addition to its dictionary meaning.

dead metaphor: a **metaphor** which, through overuse, is no longer thought of as an acceptable or effective **figurative comparison**.

demand essay: a piece of writing that must be completed within a specific period of time; often an answer to a question on an essay test.

denotation: the exact, literal meaning of a word; see also **connotation**.

description: a picture in words; a piece of writing that depicts a person, place, or object.

dialogue: the words that characters speak in narrative or dramatic writing.

documenting: backing up all the information and quotations in a research paper by listing their sources.

drafting: when a writer pulls together preliminary exploration notes and ideas and begins to write.

exaggeration (hyperbole): a **rhetorical device** using overstatement for effect.

exploring and prewriting: when a writer generates ideas and details for a writing project.

exposition: a piece of writing that presents ideas, information, opinions, or arguments.

familiar-to-unfamiliar order: when a piece of writing introduces an unfamiliar item, explains it in terms of something familiar, and then concludes with the unfamiliar item.

figurative comparison: one in which two objects or concepts not usually considered alike are compared.

figurative language: language that relies on comparison, either stated or implied.

focus: an idea or statement that leads to a **thesis statement**.

formal response to literature: often a **literary essay**, which interprets a work of art.

format: a **writing variable**, the form in which a piece of writing will be presented to its audience; for example, an essay or poem.

freewriting: continuous writing, for a prescribed period of time, of whatever comes to mind as a writer thinks about a word or topic; a potential source of ideas.

graphic: a structure (such as a flowchart) that shows relationships in visual form.

imagery: word pictures that appeal to the senses.

informal response to literature: a brief interpretation of a work of art that can take a written, oral, or dramatic form.

instant writing: writing on a specific topic at a specific time for a specific number of minutes.

invective: harsh, abusive, insulting speech or writing.

irony: the use of words in a way that expresses their opposite meaning.

journal: a book in which a writer can jot down feelings, thoughts, and experiences; an excellent source of topics for writing.

literary essay: an essay that interprets a work of art, or a part of it.

metaphor: a **figurative comparison** stating or implying that one thing is something else.

minor sentence: a **sentence fragment** that is understood as containing a complete thought.

narration: a piece of writing that tells a story; an account of one or more events.

narrative illustration: a brief story that serves as an example of a **thesis statement**.

opposites: a **rhetorical device** used to contrast two opposing ideas.

organization: the arrangement of a piece of writing; it depends on how the writer orders the details, how the sentences in a paragraph link, and how the writing progresses from one paragraph to the next.

outline: a plan indicating the arrangement of ideas which are or will be contained in a written work.

overall impression: the final effect that all the details in a piece of writing combine to create.

paraphrase: a restatement of a piece of writing in one's own words.

parenthetical citation: a method of documenting information in a research or scholarly paper by citing the last name of the source's author and the number of the page on which a fact or quotation appears.

parody: a form of speaking or writing that makes fun of its subject through imitation and exaggeration.

peer-editing: revising and editing suggestions made by a classmate.

periodic sentence: a **rhetorical device**; withholding an important part of a sentence until the end.

persona: a fictitious **voice** a writer adopts.

personification: a **figurative comparison** giving an inanimate object human characteristics.

plagiarism: trying to pass off another writer's words or ideas as your own; a serious offence for a writer.

point of view: in a narrative work of art, the perspective from which the author chooses to tell the story; first (*I*), second (*you*), or third (*he, she* or *it*) person.

précis: the condensation of a piece of writing to about half its original length.

publishing: as this book uses the term, presenting a piece of writing to its intended audience.

purpose: a **writing variable**; the reason for writing.

repetition: a **rhetorical device**; restating key words or phrases for emphasis and rhythm.

research paper: an expository piece that presents information that is documented through parenthetical citations (or footnotes) and a bibliography.

résumé: a summary of a job applicant's work experience, education, and other qualifications.

reversal: a **rhetorical device**; reversing the order of a phrase or clause to make a **balanced sentence** even more memorable.

review: a kind of argumentative essay presenting an opinion, with reasons to back it up, about a particular work of art.

revising and editing: the stages of writing in which a writer rethinks the content of a piece and then polishes it for its final audience.

rhetorical devices: techniques used to create a certain effect upon the audience of a piece of writing.

rhetorical question: a **rhetorical device**; asking a question whose answer is already known or implied.

rhyme: the similarity of sounds at the ends of words such as *take* and *make*.

rhythm: the regular beat or pulse of poetry or music.

satire: a form of writing in which persons or institutions are ridiculed in order to convey to an audience the necessity for change.

sentence combining: various techniques of achieving a better style by combining short jerky sentences into smoother long ones.

sentence fragment: a group of words that is punctuated as a complete sentence but that does not contain both a complete subject and a complete predicate.

sequential order: organization of details in a piece of writing according to the order in which they should be or have been carried out.

simile: a **figurative comparison** that uses a word of comparison, such as *like*.

slant: a choice of words made by a writer to achieve a favorable (positive) or unfavorable (negative) reaction to an idea from an audience.

spatial order: organization of descriptive details in a piece of writing according to the order in which the writer wants the audience to see them, such as from near to far.

style: the choice of words and sentences as well as the effectiveness, arrangement, and appropriateness of the words and sentences; also the choice and arrangement of words as they reflect the personality of the writer.

summarizing: reducing a piece of writing to its main points as a guide to revising it.

symbol: in a literary work of art, a person or object representing both itself and a larger idea.

textual evidence: evidence from a literary work of art – such as quotations, details from the plot, or the recurrent use of symbols – to support the interpretation of that work in a formal literary response.

theme: a major idea behind the characters and events in a literary work.

thesis statement: a sentence that controls the content of an entire piece of writing.

tone: in a literary work, the author's attitude toward the plot and characters as revealed through word choice.

topic: a **writing variable**; the subject of a piece of writing.

topic sentence: a sentence that controls the content of a paragraph.

transitional device: a word or phrase that links one part of a piece of writing to another.

understatement (litotes): a **rhetorical device** that makes a fact seem less significant; often used for **irony**.

unity: the final impression to which all the details in a piece of writing contribute.

visual organization: methods of organizing details in a composition by using a visual form, such as ladders.

voice: how the writer talks to the audience; a **writing variable** that reveals the writer. See also **persona**.

writing process: the stages (**exploring and prewriting, drafting, revising and editing, publishing**) in which a writer composes and polishes a piece of writing and then presents it to its final audience.

writing variables: the circumstances that may influence the composition of a piece of writing. The writing variables include **topic, audience, purpose, format,** and **voice**.

Index

Index of Selections by Genre

Non-Fiction

Drama

Acknowledgments

Permission to reprint copyrighted material is gratefully acknowledged. Information that will enable the publisher to rectify any error or omission will be welcomed.

Chapter 1

Excerpt from **Lady Oracle** by Margaret Atwood. Copyright © 1976 by Margaret Atwood. Used by permission of the Canadian Publishers, McClelland and Stewart, Toronto.

Excerpt from **And No Birds Sang** by Farley Mowat. Copyright © 1979 by Farley Mowat. Reprinted by permission of Farley Mowat Limited.

"The Nervous Man" by Jennifer Bauld from **Mysterious Special Sauce – Poems by Canadian Students**. Copyright © 1982 The Pandora Charitable Trust of the Canadian Council of Teachers of English. Reprinted by permission of the Canadian Council of Teachers of English.

Excerpt from **The Accidental Tourist** by Anne Tyler. Copyright © 1985 by Anne Tyler. Reprinted by permission of Alfred A. Knopf, Inc.

Chapter 2

"The Flamingo" by Tamara Neufeld. Copyright © 1986 by Tamara Neufeld. Reprinted from **BCETA Journal '86**, a publication of the British Columbia English Teachers' Association.

Excerpt from **Obasan** by Joy Kogawa, © 1981. Reprinted by permission of Lester & Orpen Dennys Publishers Ltd., Canada.

"A Memory of Grandmother" by Laura Moorhead. Copyright © 1987 by Laura Moorhead. Reprinted by permission of the author from **Chestnut Road 87**, a publication of the London Board of Education.

"The Construction Worker" by Ross Eckroth from **Mysterious Special Sauce – Poems by Canadian Students**. Copyright © 1982 The Pandora Charitable Trust of the Canadian Council of Teachers of English. Reprinted by permission of the Canadian Council of Teachers of English.

"Just Like You" by Chrystos. Copyright © 1986 by Chrystos. Reprinted from **Fireweed**, Winter 1986, Issue 22.

"Saturday Afternoon at Kensington Market" is reprinted from **Collected Poems of Raymond Souster** by permission of Oberon Press. Copyright © 1984 by Raymond Souster.

Chapter 3

"Poem After Months" by Margaret Sparling Mills. First published in **Woman, Be Honest**, Herring Cove Press, Halifax, Nova Scotia, 76 pp., 1974. Copyright © 1974 by Margaret Sparling Mills.

"Why Levi's Changed the 501" from **Everybody's Business: An Almanac** edited by Milton Moskowitz, by Michael Katz and by Robert Levering. Copyright © 1980 by Milton Moskowitz, Michael Katz, and Robert Levering. Reprinted by permission of Harper & Row, Publishers, Inc.

Chapter 4

"The Burrowing Owl" by Dale Hjertaas. Copyright © 1988. Reprinted from **Probe Post**, Volume 11, No. 3, Fall 1988.

Chapter 5

Excerpt from **The Power of Myth** by Joseph Campbell and Bill Moyers. Copyright © 1988 by Apostrophe S Productions, Inc. and Alfred van der Marck Editions Inc. for itself and the estate of Joseph Campbell. Reprinted by permission of Doubleday, a division of Bantam Doubleday Dell Publishing Group, Inc.

Chapter 32

Excerpt from **Life Before Man** by Margaret Atwood. Copyright © 1983 by Margaret Atwood. Used by permission of the Canadian Publishers, McClelland and Stewart, Toronto.

"Rainy Nights" by Chuck Kahn. Copyright © 1986 by Chuck Kahn. Reprinted by permission from **Cornucopia '86**, a publication of the East York Board of Education.

Chapter 33

"The Biodegradable Myth!" by Colin Isaacs from **Probe Post**, Fall 1988. Reprinted by permission of **Probe Post**.

Chapter 34

"Griefkit" by Kate Lushington. Copyright © by Kate Lushington. Reprinted by permission.

Excerpt from "Canadian Writing 1987: A Review" by Michael Darling from **The Macmillan Anthology 1**. Reprinted by permission of the author.

"Tomorrow's Technology" by Stefan Gerber. Copyright © 1986 by Stefan Gerber. Reprinted by permission from **Cornucopia '86**, a publication of the East York Board of Education.

"Sports or Music?" by Billy T. P. Chan. Copyright © 1989 Billy T. P. Chan. Reprinted by permission.

Appendix

"Late one night …" by Lou Cornacchia. Copyright © 1986 by Lou Cornacchia. Reprinted by permission from **Cornucopia '86**, a publication of the East York Board of Education.

"Inside His Mind" by Barbara Coad. Copyright © 1986 by Barbara Coad. First published in **BCETA Journal '86**, a publication of the British Columbia English Teachers' Association. Reprinted by permission of the author.

"The Kill" by Dirk Derstine from **Mysterious Special Sauce – Poems by Canadian Students**. Copyright © 1982 The Pandora Charitable Trust of the Canadian Council of Teachers of English. Reprinted by permission of the Canadian Council of Teachers of English.

"Charles" from **The Lottery** by Shirley Jackson. Copyright © 1948, 1949 by Shirley Jackson. Renewal copyright © 1976, 1977 by Laurence Hyman, Barry Hyman, Mrs. Sarah Webster, and Mrs. Joanne Schnurer. Reprinted by permission of Farrar, Straus and Giroux, Inc.

"The Well-Wrought Urn" from **Balls for a One-Armed Juggler** by Irving Layton. Copyright © by Irving Layton. Used by permission of the Canadian Publishers, McClelland and Stewart, Toronto.

"Without Benefit of Tape" from **Dorothy Livesay: Selected Poems**. Copyright © 1986 by Dorothy Livesay. Reprinted by permission of the author and Press Porcepic Ltd.

"Falling Song" from **First People, First Voices** by Daniel David Moses. Copyright © 1983 by Daniel David Moses. Reprinted by permission.

"Leaving Home" by Haike Rodenstein. Copyright © 1986 by Haike Rodenstein. First published in **BCETA Journal '86**, a publication of the British Columbia English Teachers' Association. Reprinted by permission of the author.

"The Late Man" by Andreas Schroeder is reprinted from **Fourteen Stories High** by permission of Oberon Press.

"Fiend" by Rod Smylie. Copyright © 1986 by Rod Smylie. Reprinted by permission from **Cornucopia '86**, a publication of the East York Board of Education.

"Naaholooyah" by Mary TallMountain from Rayna Green, ed., **That's What She Said**. Reprinted by permission of the Indiana University Press.

"Notes on Punctuation" from **The Medusa and the Snail** by Lewis Thomas. Copyright © 1979 by Lewis Thomas. All rights reserved. Reprinted by permission of Viking Penguin, a division of Penguin Books USA, Inc.

"Poets are Still Writing Poems about Spring and Here is Mine: Spring" from **Collected Poems** by Miriam Waddington. Copyright © Miriam Waddington, 1986; reprinted by permission of Oxford University Press Canada.

Photo Credits

Canapress: 26, 60, 86 (left), 305 (both), 315

Miller Services: 332

World Wildlife Fund: 71